The Bible
FOR
DUMMIES®

**by Jeffrey Geoghegan, PhD and
Michael Homan, PhD**

WILEY

Wiley Publishing, Inc.

The Bible For Dummies®

Published by
Wiley Publishing, Inc.
111 River Street
Hoboken, NJ 07030
www.wiley.com

Copyright © 2003 by Wiley Publishing, Inc., Indianapolis, Indiana

Published simultaneously in Canada

For general information on our other products and services or to obtain technical support, please contact our Customer Care Department within the U.S. at 877-762-2974, outside the U.S. at 317-572-3993, or fax 317-572-4002.

Wiley also publishes its books in a variety of electronic formats. Some content that appears in print may not be available in electronic books.

Library of Congress Control Number: 00-112065

ISBN: 978-0-7645-5296-0

Manufactured in the United States of America

15 14

1B/RS/QU/QU/IN

About the Authors

Dr. Jeffrey Geoghegan is Assistant Professor of Biblical Theology at Boston College. He received his doctorate from the University of California, San Diego, where he also taught courses covering everything from Socrates to Shakespeare. A lover of history and literature, he has made the study of the Bible and the ancient Near East his professional preoccupation. Jeff has traveled throughout the "land of the Bible" and has authored or coauthored a number of books and articles on the Bible, including two recent collaborations with Michael Homan: *The Nine Commandments: Uncovering the Hidden Pattern of Crime and Punishment in the Hebrew Bible* (also with David Noel Freedman) and a forthcoming *Bible Atlas* to be published by Eerdmans.

Dr. Michael Homan is Assistant Professor of Biblical Studies at Xavier University of Louisiana, where he teaches courses on the Bible, ancient religions, and archaeology. He earned his doctorate in ancient Near Eastern History from the University of California, San Diego, has over 12 years of archaeological experience, and is an expert on the material culture and geography of ancient Israel. He has traveled extensively in the Middle East, living in both Israel and Jordan for several years. In addition to his collaborations with Jeff Geoghegan, Mike has published widely on subjects relating to the Bible and the ancient Near East, and is currently working on a book about alcohol in the ancient world (which includes a chapter on how the ancients brewed a pretty mean beer — complete with do-it-yourself recipes!).

Dedication

This book is lovingly dedicated to our families, and especially our wives, Jannetta and Therese, without whose help and support this book, and so much else in life, would not be possible or worthwhile.

Authors' Acknowledgments

We would like to acknowledge our teachers at the University of California, San Diego, whose insights on the Bible, its history, and life in general fill the pages of this book. These include: David Noel Freedman, Richard Elliott Friedman, William Propp, Thomas Levy, and David Goodblatt.

Special thanks are also due to the people at Wiley Publishing who made this project possible, especially Alissa Schwipps, whose encouragement and feedback kept us on track and helped make this a better work, and Pam Mourouzis, whose capable leadership was instrumental at all stages of this project. We would also like to thank Kevin Thornton and Andrew Corbin for helping to get this project in motion.

The contributions of our colleagues and students at Boston College, Xavier University of Louisiana, the Albright Institute of Archaeological Research, and the University of California, San Diego, are also much appreciated.

Publisher's Acknowledgments

We're proud of this book; please send us your comments through our Dummies online registration form located at www.dummies.com/register/.

Some of the people who helped bring this book to market include the following:

Acquisitions, Editorial, and Media Development

Project Editor: Alissa D. Schwipps

Acquisitions Editor: Pam Mourouzis

Copy Editors: Elizabeth Netedu Kuball, Patricia Yuu Pan

Technical Editor: Dr. Bernard F. Batto

Senior Permissions Editor: Carmen Krikorian

Editorial Manager: Jennifer Ehrlich

Editorial Assistant: Nívea C. Strickland

Cover Photo: ©CORBIS/Carl and Ann Purcell

Cartoons: Rich Tennant, www.the5thwave.com

Composition Services

Project Coordinator: Nancee Reeves

Layout and Graphics: Amanda Carter, Sean Decker, Melanie DesJardins, Carrie Foster, Joyce Haughey, LeAndra Johnson, Tiffany Muth, Jackie Nicholas, Barry Offringa, Julie Trippetti

Special Art: British Museum Winged Lion image from the Antiquity Archives of Preserving Bible Times, Inc., P.O. Box 83357, Gaithersburg, MD, 20883-3357, www.preservingbibletimes.org.

Proofreaders: John Bitter, Andy Hollandbeck, Angel Perez, Aptara

Indexer: Aptara

Special Help:
Chrissy Guthrie, Melissa Bennett, Michelle Hacker, Mary Yeary

---

Publishing and Editorial for Consumer Dummies

Diane Graves Steele, Vice President and Publisher, Consumer Dummies

Joyce Pepple, Acquisitions Director, Consumer Dummies

Kristin Ferguson-Wagstaffe, Product Development Director, Consumer Dummies

Ensley Eikenburg, Associate and Publisher, Travel

Kelly Regan, Editorial Director, Travel

Publishing for Technology Dummies

Andy Cummings, Vice President and Publisher, Dummies Technology/General User

Composition Services

Debbie Stailey, Director of Composition Services

Contents at a Glance

Table of Contents

Introduction

• •

*T*he Bible has the distinction of being the best known, least understood book in the world. Although it's been translated into more languages, sold more copies, and been read by more people than any other book in history, its message and meaning are matters of ongoing, and often heated, debate. The Bible has been used to justify wars and to found relief organizations, to support slavery and to condemn it, to fuel hatred and to promote love and understanding. So what exactly is the Bible all about?

As university professors, we have a lot of experience in making the Bible accessible and relevant. The Bible can be an intimidating book, but with the right guide, your journey through its pages can be exciting and rewarding.

As authors, we've written a number of books and articles on the Bible, making us sensitive to the variety of ways people approach the biblical text. The Bible isn't just a religious text; it's a work of history and a literary masterpiece. Throughout this book, we point out these various facets.

We've traveled extensively throughout the lands of the Bible, and have participated in archaeological digs at biblical sites. This experience allows us to give you that Indiana Jones edge to a book full of mystery and adventure. (We even discuss where the Ark of the Covenant *really* is.)

Finally, we're balanced, not just psychologically (not a trivial point when discussing religious texts) but in our presentation of the Bible and the faiths it represents. We've written *The Bible For Dummies* so that no matter what your faith, or even if you have no faith at all, you can benefit from this book.

The *For Dummies* series is a name that you've come to trust for giving you the straight scoop on everything from cooking to computers, so what better resource to help you understand the Bible than *The Bible For Dummies*?

About This Book

People come to the Bible for a variety of reasons. You may be coming to the Bible to find inspiration and faith. You may be reading the Bible to understand a text that plays such an influential role in our world. You may simply want to know more about what is undeniably a great work of literature. Or you may just want to improve your score on *Jeopardy!*.

Whatever your reasons for wanting to know more about the Good Book, *The Bible For Dummies* is for you.

Here's what you can expect from this book:

- ✔ Quick overviews of what's in the Bible
- ✔ Answers to the "Who wrote the Bible?" and "What does it all mean?" questions
- ✔ Easy-to-use maps, charts, and pictures to help make sense of the Bible
- ✔ Simple summaries of the differences between Jewish and Christian Bibles
- ✔ Fascinating historical and cultural insights that bring the Bible to life
- ✔ Clear explanations of how the Bible's traditions have given rise to three of the world's major religions: Judaism, Christianity, and Islam
- ✔ Informative commentaries on the Bible's influence on art, literature, and movies

In short, *The Bible For Dummies* is your one-stop reference for understanding the Bible and its continuing impact on the political, religious, and artistic landscapes of our world.

How to Use This Book

Although the Bible is a story, and therefore best experienced as a narrative, *The Bible For Dummies* has been written so that you can drop in and out of the tour at any time. You can linger at a site as long as you like, or visit your favorite places again and again — without ever feeling lost or left behind!

The Table of Contents is a good place to find the parts of *The Bible For Dummies* that most interest you. We also provide a complete overview of the Bible in Chapter 2, which points you to other places in the book where you can find more details about a particular topic or story. In addition, you'll find a very thorough index at the back of the book, with entries on just about everything having to do with the Bible.

Conventions Used in This Book

Before you begin reading *The Bible For Dummies*, you should be aware of some of the special abbreviations, definitions, and ideas you find in this book.

When mentioning dates, we use the designations B.C.E. (before the common era) and C.E. (common era), since these terms are more inclusive than the traditional B.C. (before Christ) and A.D. (from the Latin *anno domini,* or "year of our Lord," *not* "after [Jesus'] death"). If you're used to the traditional designations, don't worry, because the years are reckoned the same (30 C.E. = A.D. 30).

The term Old Testament refers to those sacred texts that Christianity shares with Judaism, while Jews call this same corpus the Hebrew Bible or the Tanak. We follow the Jewish practice (Hebrew Bible) unless talking about the Christian Scriptures, in which case we use both the Hebrew Bible and the Old Testament (because the early Christians were both Jews and non-Jews). For Jews and Protestants, the Hebrew Bible and Old Testament contain the same books, though in a slightly different order. For Catholics, the Old Testament has additional books, called the Apocrypha, which we discuss in Part III.

God goes by many names in the Bible, but most often God is called "God" or "the LORD." The latter term is the usual English translation of God's personal name in Hebrew, Yahweh, which to many devout Jews (and some Christians) is unspeakable. Therefore, we use this name sparingly in this book. Yet, using the word LORD for God sounds too preachy. So when referring to God we use the word — get ready for this — "God," unless we're making a special point about one of God's other names.

Although the Bible portrays God as transcending our ideas about gender (see, for example, Genesis 1:27, where being created in God's image includes both male and female), the biblical authors almost always use masculine pronouns and imagery to describe God. We follow the biblical convention, and always with capital letters for clarity (that is, He or Him).

And speaking of Genesis 1:27, this is the standard way to cite passages from the Bible. The name (Genesis) refers to the book of the Bible where a particular passage can be found, the number left of the colon (1) is the chapter number, and the number right of the colon (27) is the verse number. Because we give you the place in the Bible where you can look up what we're talking about, you want to keep this information in mind.

If you're wondering what translation of the Bible we're using in this book, wonder no longer: it's our own. It's not the Revised Dummies Version, mind you, because such a version doesn't exist (at least, not yet). We translate straight from the original languages of the Bible, which are Hebrew, Aramaic, and Greek. When we translate the Bible, we try to be as true to the original language as possible, while still making sense in English. No two translations of the Bible are the same, so you'll notice that our translations don't exactly match other translations. We recommend that when reading the Bible you refer to several different translations, especially when trying to interpret difficult or controversial passages.

How This Book Is Organized

This book is divided into six parts. Here's what you find in each part.

Part 1: What the Bible Is All About

Part I provides the overall picture of what the Bible is, where we got it, and what it's all about. Here, you find nifty summaries and outlines of how the Bible is put together, why it's put together the way it is, the differences between Jewish and Christian Bibles, and what you can expect along your journey through the Bible. We even give you a synopsis of the entire Bible in Chapter 2.

Part 11: Exploring the Hebrew Bible — The Old Testament

Part II examines the Hebrew Bible (or Old Testament). We begin by looking at what is arguably the most influential work of world literature — the Book of Genesis. Because of its importance, and because it sets the stage for what happens in the rest of the Bible, we devote four chapters to exploring this rich and diverse book. We then examine the rest of the Hebrew Bible, reliving its history, understanding its laws, interpreting its prophecies, contemplating its wisdom, and singing its psalms.

Part 111: Revealing the Bible's Hidden Treasures in the Apocrypha

In this part, we explore the Apocrypha. The books making up the Apocrypha are some of the Bible's most intriguing, yet seldom read, books. One reason for this neglect is that the Apocrypha is not part of Jewish or Protestant Bibles, but only of Catholic and Eastern Orthodox Bibles. We discuss why these books are absent from some Bibles and not others, where they came from, and what they're all about. The Apocrypha is a diverse body of literature, and includes history, poetry, philosophy, and prophecy. Becoming familiar with the Apocrypha helps you to understand the differences between Protestantism, Catholicism, and Eastern Orthodox Christianity.

Part IV: Discovering What's New About the New Testament

Part IV covers the books making up the New Testament. We begin by examining the four gospels — Matthew, Mark, Luke, and John — as they describe, each from its own perspective, the life and teachings of Jesus. We then chart the growth of early Christianity as recounted in the Book of Acts. After getting the big picture of Christianity's birth and growth, we focus our attention on the New Testament letters or *epistles*, beginning with the letters of Paul, which have formed the basis of many of Christianity's central doctrines. Next, we turn to the General epistles, works written by other early leaders of Christianity, including (according to tradition) some of Jesus' closest followers. Finally, we decipher the Book of Revelation, which describes the end times, when evil will be unleashed on the earth, but good will win out in the end.

Part V: That Was Then, This Is Now: Discovering the Bible's Enduring Influence

This part looks at the impact of the Bible through the ages. The Bible's traditions have given rise to three of the world's religions — Judaism, Christianity, and Islam — and have inspired some of the greatest works of art and literature ever produced. We chart its influence over the centuries and consider how its message still impacts us today. We even look at one of the most disturbing misuses of the Bible — Hollywood movies! Actually, there have been both good and bad Bible movies, and we give you a handy guide to the most notable.

Part VI: The Part of Tens

The final section, "The Part of Tens," is a *For Dummies* distinctive. Here, you find short biographies of ten (or so) of the most important people in the Bible, as well as ten holidays you can take thanks to the Bible. (Whether your boss will actually let you have the day off is another matter.)

Icons Used in This Book

Throughout this book, you find icons that highlight worthwhile bits of information or direct you to important points of interest.

The Bible is a vast book, containing lots of interesting ideas and profound insights. This icon signals those things worth remembering, either to guide you through the Bible or to guide you through life.

The Bible has many hidden dangers. When you see this icon, approach with caution, because you are about to encounter a passage or idea that has been commonly misinterpreted or has proven to be a pitfall to unsuspecting readers of the Bible (such as the dreaded *who-begat-whom* lists).

The Bible provides the active mind with much to think about, such as "Why are we here?", "Where did evil come from?", "Why do bad things happen to good people?", and "Why are there weeds in my garden?" This icon highlights questions or concepts worth thinking about.

Although Indiana Jones is a fictional character, many real-life archaeologists are continually making amazing discoveries. Also, some of the most amazing discoveries, in the form of literary insights, have come from "excavating" the Bible. When you see this icon, you know you've happened upon a great discovery.

We all love trivia, and the Bible is a treasure trove of names, places, and events. Items marked with this icon are guaranteed to wow your friends.

Theologians and Bible scholars love to make up words both to impress people and, sometimes, to keep "non-experts" out of the conversation. Items marked with this icon get you back into the discussion.

Where to Go from Here

Reading the Bible is like going on an adventure — an adventure where you travel to distant lands, encounter fascinating people, and experience a whole new world. Such a journey shouldn't be undertaken without the proper gear. Think of this book as your travel book and of us as your tour guides. You can jump into the adventure wherever you like. If you're still not sure where you want to go, we recommend starting at the very beginning. Part I will give you a bird's-eye view of the entire Bible.

Now, prepare yourself to be transported back in time to experience the Bible as you've never experienced it before (especially if you haven't experienced it before!). You're about to go on the adventure of a lifetime — actually, of many lifetimes — as you relive the events and meet the people who have literally changed our world (for better or for worse — we let you decide). Fasten your seat belts. Put your lid on your latte. Here we go!

Part I
What the Bible Is All About

The 5th Wave   By Rich Tennant

"This is our family Bible. It's truly a lamp to my feet, a light for my path, and a balance unto our bookshelf."

In this part . . .

You find out what the Bible is, how we got it, why it's so important, and what it's doing in your hotel room nightstand (actually, we don't cover that last point). Plus, you discover the difference between Jewish, Catholic, and Protestant Bibles. Lastly, you take the journey of a lifetime (actually many lifetimes) by traveling through the entire Bible "in a nutshell."

Chapter 1

From Moses to Modernity: Introducing the Good Book

· ·

In This Chapter

▶ Discovering what the Bible is, where it came from, and how we got it

▶ Understanding the importance of the Dead Sea Scrolls

▶ Appreciating the Bible's enduring influence

▶ Choosing a translation that's right for you

· ·

The Bible is the ultimate publishing phenomenon. It's been atop the best-seller list ever since Johannes Gutenberg, the inventor of the printing press, ran the first copies some 500 years ago. Since then, it's been translated into more languages and sold more copies than any other book in history. Recent statistics indicate that well over 150,000 new Bibles are sold or given away *each day!*

So what is the Bible, who wrote it, and how did we come to possess it? In this chapter, you discover the answers to these and other important questions. In addition, you get some helpful tips for finding the Bible that's right for you.

Tracing the Bible from Old Scrolls to the Bestseller of All Time

In the movie *The Gods Must Be Crazy,* a man from a remote village discovers a soda bottle that was dropped from a passing airplane. He's convinced that this mysterious object is from the gods, and much of the rest of the movie chronicles his quest to find its owner (don't worry, we won't give away the ending). Many people have a similar view of how we got the Bible. One day, Moses or Jesus was walking along when all of a sudden — "thud!" — there it was: the Bible, air express from heaven. These holy men then gave it to their followers, who, in turn, passed it on to their followers, who eventually passed it on to us. And we've been on a quest to find its Owner ever since.

That's not exactly how it happened (except, perhaps, for that last part). Nor is it really correct to think of the Bible as a single entity.

What is the Bible?

The word *Bible* comes from a Greek word, *ton biblion,* which means "the scroll" or "the book." This word derives from the ancient city of Byblos, located in what is today modern Lebanon. Byblos was the official supplier of paper products to the ancient world, and as a result, the city became so intimately associated with the production of paper goods that its name became synonymous with the word "book" or "scroll." This is similar to today, where a word like Kleenex has come to mean "tissue," no matter what brand.

Yet, the Greek word for the Bible is actually plural — *ta biblia,* which means "the scrolls" or "the books." Although we tend to think of the Bible as a single work, those bringing these books together understood it for what it really is — a collection of works by a variety of authors. And it's quite a diverse collection at that!

The Bible includes legal texts, history, poetry, philosophy, music, personal correspondence, and prophecies. Those who wrote the Bible were also a diverse bunch, and include shepherds, kings, farmers, priests, poets, scribes, prophets, and fishermen (to name a few). There is also quite a moral diversity among the biblical authors, from morally upstanding citizens, to, let's say, morally challenged individuals. For example, among those contributing to the Bible, you find traitors, embezzlers, adulterers, murderers, and — brace yourself — ancient IRS workers (yes, we were shocked, too). We discuss how this motley crew found common cause in the Bible throughout this book

Only much later were the books making up the Bible brought together into a single volume, and in Judaism and Christianity, different books were included in their respective libraries.

Where did the Bible come from?

In order to better understand the Jewish and Christian Bibles, it's important to know a little something about the history of their development, as well as what you can expect to find in each library.

The Hebrew Bible (or Old Testament)

The books making up the Jewish Scriptures are often called the *Hebrew Bible*, because, with few exceptions, this material was originally written in Hebrew. In Christian tradition, these same books are referred to as the *Old Testament*.

According to Jewish tradition, Moses wrote the first five books of the Hebrew Bible (also known as the *Torah,* from a Hebrew word meaning "instruction" or "law," or the *Pentateuch,* from a Greek word meaning "the five scrolls"). The Five Books of Moses, as this material is also called, covers everything from the creation of the world (see Chapter 3) and humankind's early history (see Chapter 4), to the emergence of ancient Israel's ancestors (see Chapters 5 and 6) and their formation as a nation under Moses (see Chapter 7).

Following Moses, Jewish tradition maintains that the history of ancient Israel was preserved by various authors, most of whom were near contemporaries to the events they describe. For example, Joshua himself penned the account of Israel's conquest of its Promised Land under his leadership (see Chapter 8). The era following Joshua, known as the Period of the Judges, was recorded by Israel's last judge, Samuel, who also composed half the Book of Samuel (until his own death). The remaining material in Samuel was composed by Samuel's contemporaries, including two prophets, Gad and Nathan, as well as Israel's great king, David (see Chapter 9). The history of Israel's kings after David (see Chapter 10) was preserved by royal scribes, who recorded matters of state; priests, who wrote mostly about Israel's religion; and prophets, who, besides recording their own prophecies, also recorded their interactions (read: "confrontations") with Israel's kings. (Prophets and kings rarely got along, as Chapter 13 explains.)

But then tragedy struck. In 586 B.C.E., the Babylonians destroyed Jerusalem, including its royal palace and temple. There's no telling how much of Israel's library was lost, but many scrolls survived and were taken to Babylonia by Jerusalem's exiles. (For the stories of those living in exile, see Chapter 11.)

In Babylon, these documents were edited and compiled. Although this process involved many people, the person credited with heading up the project was the scribe and priest Ezra (see Chapter 12). Not long afterwards, Ezra brought these scrolls back to the now rebuilt Jerusalem, where he instigated a religious reform based on these Scriptures (around 450 B.C.E.). During this period, additional works were penned and included in this library, eventually resulting in a relatively complete edition of the Jewish Bible. Beyond Jerusalem, copies of these scrolls could be found in the other great centers of Jewish learning — in particular, Egypt and Babylonia.

Here are the books that ultimately made it into the anthology of the Hebrew Bible. (***Note:*** Because these books are ordered differently in Jewish and Christian Bibles, we give you both lists for ease of reference and comparison.)

The Hebrew Bible	*The Christian Old Testament*
The Law (or Torah)	**The Pentateuch**
Genesis	Genesis
Exodus	Exodus
Leviticus	Leviticus
Numbers	Numbers
Deuteronomy	Deuteronomy

The Hebrew Bible	*The Christian Old Testament*
The Prophets	**History**
The Former Prophets	Joshua
Joshua	Judges
Judges	Ruth
Samuel (1 scroll in Hebrew)	1 and 2 Samuel
Kings (1 scroll in Hebrew)	1 and 2 Kings
	1 and 2 Chronicles
The Latter Prophets	Ezra
<u>Major Prophets</u>	Nehemiah
Isaiah	Esther
Jeremiah	
Ezekiel	**Poetry and Wisdom Literature**
	Job
<u>The Twelve (1 scroll in Hebrew)</u>	Psalms
Hosea	Proverbs
Joel	Ecclesiastes
Amos	Song of Songs
Obadiah	
Jonah	**The Prophets**
Micah	*Major Prophets*
Nahum	Isaiah
Habakkuk	Jeremiah
Zephaniah	Lamentations
Haggai	Ezekiel
Zechariah	Daniel
Malachi	
	Minor Prophets
The Writings	Hosea
Psalms	Joel
Proverbs	Amos
Job	Obadiah
Song of Songs	Jonah
Ruth	Micah
Lamentations	Nahum
Ecclesiastes	Habakkuk
Esther	Zephaniah
Daniel	Haggai
Ezra-Nehemiah (1 scroll in Hebrew)	Zechariah
Chronicles (1 scroll in Hebrew)	Malachi

The three-part structure of the Hebrew Bible — Law, Prophets, and Writings — has given rise to another name for this work: the *Tanak* (sometimes spelled Tanakh), which derives from the first letter of the Hebrew words for these sections: *Torah* (Law), *Nevi'im* (Prophets), and *Ketuvim* (Writings).

The Apocrypha

With the spread of Greek culture throughout the ancient Near East in the wake of Alexander the Great's conquests (around 330 B.C.E.), fewer and fewer Jews could read or understand Hebrew, the primary language of their scriptures. (For an account of this period, see Chapter 16.) This circumstance, along with a request by a Greek king of Egypt, resulted in the translation of the Hebrew Bible into Greek beginning around 250 B.C.E. This work came to be called the *Septuagint*, a Greek word meaning "70" and reflecting the tradition that 70 (or, in some traditions, 72) scribes, although working independently, produced the exact same translation of the Torah. This "coincidence" confirmed that the Greek translation was reliable, and even divinely inspired. Eventually, however, the Septuagint came to include a number of Jewish historical and religious writings that were not part of Ezra's Bible. Although most Jews held these works in high esteem (some even considering them a part of the Bible), these works were ultimately rejected as not being divinely inspired — a decision that, according to tradition, was given official expression by a group of Jewish scholars at Yavneh, a city about 25 miles west of Jerusalem (around 90 C.E.).

Meanwhile, between the translation of the Septuagint (around 250 to 100 B.C.E.) and the decision at Yavneh, a little thing known today as Christianity happened. Because the early Christians used the Greek Septuagint, many Christian communities embraced these additional works as part of the Bible. However, when the Church father Jerome (fourth to fifth centuries C.E.) eventually translated the Bible into Latin, the absence of these additional books in the Jewish Bible earned them the designation "Hidden," which in Greek is *Apocrypha* (although some scholars think Apocrypha might refer to the hidden or esoteric teachings of these works). Although Jerome, following Jewish tradition, believed that these books were valuable, he also believed that they shouldn't be considered part of the Bible. (To find out more about these "hidden" books, and the history behind them, see Chapters 16 and 17.) Yet many Christian leaders disagreed — a view that eventually won out. It wasn't until the Protestant Reformation in the sixteenth century that these additional books were removed from the Old Testament, and then only in Protestant Bibles (and even this wasn't done universally). Today, Catholic and Eastern Orthodox churches still consider the majority of these "hidden" books or the Apocrypha to be part of the Bible.

Here's a list of the material making up the Apocrypha:

The Apocrypha

Tobit	Prayer of Azariah and the Song of the Three Jews
Judith	Susanna
Additions to Esther	Bel and the Dragon
Wisdom of Solomon	1 and 2 Maccabees
Ecclesiasticus	1 and 2 Esdras
Baruch	Prayer of Manasseh
Letter of Jeremiah	

Eastern Orthodox additions to the Apocrypha

3 and 4 Maccabees

Psalm 151

The New Testament

The history of the New Testament's composition is much briefer, it being written within a period of about 50 to 75 years (as compared to about 1,000 years for the Hebrew Bible). Yet the process of deciding which books should be included in the New Testament is no less interesting.

The writings of the New Testament, written in common, or *Koine,* Greek, consist of histories of the life of Jesus (called *gospels,* from a word meaning "good news"; see Chapters 18 and 19), a history of the early church (called the Acts of the Apostles; see Chapter 20), and letters written by leaders of the early church (the apostle Paul and various other first-century-C.E. Christians; see Chapters 21 and 22). The final book of the New Testament, Revelation, falls into its own category, called apocalyptic literature, from a Greek word meaning "to reveal" and referring to end-time prophecies (see Chapter 23).

By tradition, these works were written under divine inspiration by Jesus' close followers (called *disciples*) and other leaders of the early church (called *apostles*, though this designation can refer to disciples as well). Yet, by the second century C.E., questions arose about whether all the books claiming to be written by these early church leaders actually were. These questions required that the church determine which writings were authentic and which were not — a process known as *canonization* (from a Greek word, *canon,* meaning "rule" or "measure"). By the end of the second century C.E., most of the books that now make up the New Testament were determined to be authentic. However, it wasn't until the fourth century C.E. that St. Athanasius, bishop of Alexandria, Egypt, made an authoritative pronouncement fixing the number of New Testament books at the present 27.

Here are the books that make up the library of the New Testament:

The New Testament

History

Gospels (Life of Jesus)
Matthew
Mark
Luke
John

Life of Early Church
Acts of the Apostles

Letters

Paul's Letters
Romans
1 and 2 Corinthians
Galatians
Ephesians
Philippians
Colossians
1 and 2 Thessalonians
1 and 2 Timothy
Titus
Philemon

General Letters
Hebrews
James
1 and 2 Peter
1, 2 and 3 John
Jude

Apocalypse (future events)
Revelation

This overview is based largely on Jewish and Christian traditions. Today, scholars question many parts of these traditions, and we discuss the more important questions scholars are raising throughout this book.

How did we get the Bible?

It's important to point out that we don't possess any of the original writings of the biblical texts — Jewish or Christian. No first printings, no limited editions, and certainly no autographed copies. We lack these original writings because the material upon which the biblical books were written (usually *papyrus,* made from the tall water plant of the same name) deteriorated over time. Because photocopiers were in short supply 2,000 years ago, the books making up the Jewish and Christian Bibles had to be copied and recopied by hand to preserve them. Yet, the popular notion that this continual copying means that the books we now possess are hopelessly corrupted is inaccurate.

In the case of the New Testament, for example, we possess thousands of hand-written manuscripts of the books making up this collection, allowing scholars to determine with a fairly high degree of certainty what the earliest manuscripts said. In addition, early Christian writers quoted the New Testament extensively in their writings, giving us more data to determine whether the manuscripts we have are accurate. Finally, from a very early period, the New Testament manuscripts were translated into a number of different languages, giving us still another external check on their reliability.

The case of the Hebrew Bible is a bit more complicated given the antiquity of the texts involved. For example, much of the Hebrew Bible was written anywhere from 500 to 1,000 years before the New Testament. Another complication is that, in contrast to early Christian communities, Jewish communities kept tighter control over who could possess or handle biblical manuscripts. Part of the reason for this tight control was the sacred nature of the text itself. Jewish communities wanted to make sure that those copying the text did so accurately. Yet, herein lies one of the main checks on the accuracy of the Hebrew Bible's manuscripts: quality control. According to Jewish sources, manuscripts were copied with the utmost care, and even the most minor errors had to be fixed or a manuscript was discarded. Another check on the reliability of the Hebrew manuscripts is by comparing them with the Greek translation of the Hebrew Bible (the Septuagint), which was produced between 250–100 B.C.E.

Yet, even with these various checks, most scholars found it a little unnerving that the oldest copies of the Hebrew Bible (called the *Masoretic text,* after the

Jewish scribes responsible for its production) dated to around the tenth century C.E. — well over 1,500 years from the time many of the books of this library were written!

But then, a little over 50 years ago, the most amazing discovery took place: the Dead Sea Scrolls.

Discovering the Dead Sea Scrolls

The story of the Dead Sea Scrolls is straight out of Hollywood, only it didn't take place under the lights and cameras of Tinseltown, but in the arid desert of Israel. In 1947, as the story goes, a young shepherd boy was watching his flock when he threw a rock in an attempt to corral his straying sheep. His rock flew into a cave and landed with a crash. Entering the cave, the shepherd saw something that would change the study of the Bible forever. His errant throw had uncovered a cache of 2,000-year-old scrolls of the Bible and other ancient writings stored in ceramic pots.

Eventually, 11 caves were discovered containing numerous biblical and non-biblical scrolls, as well as thousands of fragments of the Hebrew Bible. These manuscripts dated to before the time of Jesus, providing scholars with Hebrew manuscripts of the Bible more than 1,000 years older than any previously possessed. In many cases, these manuscripts demonstrated just how carefully scribes copied the biblical text over the centuries. Yet, there were also some interesting differences, giving biblical scholars plenty to investigate.

Who wrote the Dead Sea Scrolls?

Scholars still debate who wrote the 2,000-year-old scrolls found in caves near the Dead Sea. However, most agree that the scrolls belonged to the community living adjacent to the caves. Although the exact origin of this group is unknown, they seem to have belonged to a Jewish separatist group known as the Essenes. Their own documents say that they were founded in the mid-second century B.C.E. by someone called the "Teacher of Righteousness." The movement he established was largely monastic in character, with those being initiated vowing to give up worldly pursuits and possessions. The Essenes believed that they alone followed God's law, and they awaited the day when God would overthrow the corrupt priesthood in Jerusalem, as well as the political powers of their day. This overthrow would be accomplished by a divinely appointed deliverer or *Messiah* (from a Hebrew word meaning "anointed one"). Until then, the community dedicated itself to studying the Bible and living a life of ritual and moral purity. The Dead Sea Scroll community was eventually destroyed by the Romans during a Jewish uprising known as the Jewish Revolt (66–72 C.E.). It's thought that the community hid its writings in these caves for protection. And protected they were, lying undetected for nearly 2,000 years!

If you ever find yourself at the Dead Sea, we highly recommend visiting the caves and the remains of the community at what is today called Qumran. You can even enter several of the caves (we know what you're thinking — we've looked, and we didn't find anything). The Dead Sea itself is a fascinating place. It's the lowest body of water on earth, with a salt content around 30 percent. As a result, nothing can live in its waters (hence the name). Today, the Dead Sea, far from being "dead," is a very lively place. Resorts dot its shores, because the mineral deposits in this unique body of water are believed to rejuvenate the body and soul. The salt content is so high, in fact, that you can float on the water without effort — though we strongly recommend that you don't shave before going in.

Fathoming the Importance of the Bible

It's remarkable that a library containing books written over a 1,500 year period, by countless authors and editors, who lived on three different continents, and who wrote in three different languages, still affects you on a daily basis. But it does! Whether it's debates about the ethics of human cloning, abortion rights, the constitutionality of saying prayers or the pledge of allegiance in public schools, or posting the Ten Commandments in public places, the Bible is front-page news. (And this is to say nothing of the "battle of the bumper stickers," where fish alternately represent Jesus and Darwin!)

Moreover, understanding the times in which we live is difficult without some knowledge of the Bible. The Bible informs the traditions of three of the world's major religions — Judaism, Christianity, and Islam — and a familiarity with its message and meaning can help you understand the similarities and differences between these religions, as well as the prospects for peace (see Chapter 24).

Finally, you can't fully appreciate many works of art and literature without some basic Bible literacy. Whether it's the great paintings of Michelangelo or Leonardo da Vinci or the literary masterpieces of Shakespeare and Milton, biblical themes and imagery fill our world. Even movies borrow extensively from the Bible. (We discuss Bible movies, as well as other influential works of art and literature in Chapter 25.)

Finding a Translation You Like

Reading the Bible in translation has been compared to kissing through a veil: It's not as good as the real thing, but it's better than nothing at all. Yet, few people have the time or inclination to learn several ancient languages to facilitate their reading of the Bible. So how do you find a translation that's right for you?

BIBLE TRIVIA

The history of the English Bible

With the increased intellectual freedom brought on by the Renaissance, as well as a growing discontent among many Europeans with the established Church, there existed an increased desire to translate the Bible from Latin, which only the highly educated could read, into the common language of the people. However, there was also considerable opposition to this enterprise for fear that the untrained might distort or misinterpret the Bible's message. Unfortunately, this opposition sometimes had violent manifestations, and many involved in translation were imprisoned or even executed. Eventually, however, the Bible was translated into the common languages of Europe. Although each story is worth telling, here's a brief history of the Bible's translation into English.

✔ **Around 700–1350:** English church clerics translate portions of the Latin Vulgate (mostly the psalms and the gospels) into Anglo Saxon and Middle English.

✔ **1380–1397:** John Wyclif and his associates produce the first translation of the entire Bible into English, using the Latin Vulgate. Although Wyclif was not executed, it was not for a lack of desire on the part of those opposed to his work. In fact, not long after his death, his bones were exhumed and burned as punishment for his translation work and "heresies."

✔ **1526:** William Tyndale produces the first New Testament translation from the original Greek language, which also becomes the first printed edition of the New Testament in English.

✔ **1530–1531:** Tyndale produces the first English translation of the Torah and the book of Jonah from the original Hebrew.

✔ **1535:** Miles Coverdale translates the entire Bible into English using two Latin versions, Tyndale's English work, and Luther's and Zwingli's German translations. This translation becomes the first entire Bible to be printed in English.

✔ **1536:** Tyndale is burned at the stake for his translation work.

✔ **1537:** The Thomas Matthew Bible, containing the entire Bible in English, is published. "Thomas Matthew" was actually a pseudonym for Tyndale's friend, John Rogers, who used Tyndale's and Coverdale's translations.

✔ **1539:** The Great Bible, which is Coverdale's revision of the Matthew's Bible, becomes the first *authorized* Bible printed in English. King Henry VIII orders that copies be placed in every church.

✔ **1560:** The Geneva Bible, a revision of the English Bible, is produced in Geneva by those finding refuge from Queen Mary's actions against Protestants. This becomes the first English Bible to use numbered verses and is the Bible used by Shakespeare. This Bible is also the one that the Pilgrims brought to America in 1620.

✔ **1568:** The bishops of the Church of England produce the Bishops' Bible, a revision of the English Bible, in response to Queen Elizabeth's injunction that Bibles again be placed in every church in England.

✔ **1611:** The King James Bible, begun in 1604 by command of King James I, is completed. This translation, still unrivaled for its combination of accuracy and literary beauty, involved 54 scholars working from Greek and Hebrew manuscripts and English editions of the Bible.

✔ **1782:** Robert Aitken's Bible (the King James Version without the Apocrypha) becomes the first English Bible printed in America.

And the rest, as they say, is history.

First, you need to determine what's most important to you when reading the Bible. Some people like to read the Bible to appreciate its literary genius. Some read the Bible for study or research. Still others read the Bible for its entertainment value. (And some, like us, read it for "all of the above.") So the first question you need to ask and answer when picking a Bible translation is, what do *you* want from your Bible reading? Different translations accomplish different things. The following sections offer some advice.

Literary versus literal translations

If you want to read the Bible for study, such as for a class or Bible study, you'll probably want a translation that's fairly literal. Literal translations try to convey the original language as closely as possible while still remaining readable. Some time-tested literal translations include: King James Version (KJV), New King James Version (NKJV), Revised Standard Version (RSV), New Revised Standard Version (NRSV), New American Bible (NAB), New American Standard Bible (NASB), New Jerusalem Bible (NJB), New English Bible (NEB), New International Version (NIV), and, although it contains just the Hebrew Bible, the Jewish Publication Society's *Tanakh*. (**Note:** Many publications refer to these translations only by their initials, so we provide these acronyms here.)

The downside of literal translations is that some people find them too wooden or stiff. As a rule, those Bibles with the word "New" in the title have tried to rectify this problem — some more successfully than others. In our opinion, if you want to appreciate the Bible's literary beauty, while still reading an accurate translation, there's no better Bible than the King James Version (KJV). Having said that, we realize that reading the King James Version, which is written in fairly antiquated English, can be even more difficult than reading Shakespeare (though no less satisfying when you get used to it). That is, for all the King James' literary beauty, you don't want your experience of reading the Bible in translation to be like kissing through a wall.

Contemporary versus paraphrase

If you've tried some of the literal translations we listed and found them difficult to understand, we recommend choosing a translation that tries to put the Bible into everyday language. The best known in this category is the *Good News Bible,* but others exist, and the best way to choose a favorite is to go to the bookstore or library and try some out.

The danger with contemporary language translations, however, is that some, in trying to be too modern, obscure what's really being said or remove the cultural distinctiveness of the Bible. For example, some translations place the biblical events in modern America, where Jesus comes across more like James Dean in *Rebel Without a Cause* than anyone found in the Bible. Others try to be too hip, having Moses say something like, "Yo, dudes, let's chill it on the sleeping around scene." (Can you identify the commandment?) Okay, we made that example up, but it's not too far from how some translations take liberties with the biblical text.

The easiest-to-read Bibles are called *paraphrases*. These can be very helpful, especially for young or first-time readers of the Bible. The best known of this type is *The Living Bible*.

However, we don't recommend paraphrases for those wanting to study the Bible, because they are, by definition, paraphrases or summaries of what the Bible says. Moreover, paraphrases usually summarize passages in units, so individual verse demarcations are lost. If you're reading a book that refers you to a particular verse in the Bible (such as *The Bible For Dummies*), you'll have a hard time finding it in a paraphrase.

Shakespeare and the "Bible Code"

It's a remarkable fact that Shakespeare, arguably the greatest playwright of all time, was in the employ of King James when the King James Bible, arguably the greatest Bible translation of all time, was being prepared. It's an even more remarkable fact that Shakespeare turned 46 the same year the King James Bible was completed (1611). Why is this remarkable, you ask? Well, if you go to Psalm 46 in the King James Bible (and this only works in the King James Bible) and count 46 words from the beginning of the psalm, you come to the word *shake*. Then, if you count 46 words from the end of the psalm, you come to the word *spear*. We're not making this up.

So did Shakespeare put a secret code in the King James Bible to let future generations know that he helped with its translation? Most likely not. Yet this raises a related question about the so-called "Bible Code," where some have argued that hidden in the Bible are prophecies of future events. You discover these hidden messages, people argue, by counting equally distanced letters in the Hebrew Bible (for example, every 12th letter). Among the things "predicted" by this method have been the assassination of Yitzhak Rabin and the AIDS epidemic. Many people have argued that these codes reveal the "fingerprint" of God upon the text. (Although some have even argued that space aliens wrote the code.)

So is there a Bible Code? Several considerations make this theory extremely unlikely. For example, the Hebrew manuscripts we possess have textual variations (words spelled differently, words arranged differently, different words altogether, and so on). By this theory, however, if you remove or add even one letter, the "prediction" is lost. Another consideration is that if you look long and hard enough at any book with thousands of words (the Hebrew Bible contains over 300,000 words), you're destined to begin seeing things — if not predictions of future events, then little dots in front of your eyes. Finally, many of these "predictions" were made after the fact. That is, a major event would happen, and then, after countless hours of computers crunching every possible scenario — *voilà!* — there, in clear black and white, is the prediction.

Whence cometh the chapter and verse divisions?

Although the Jewish scriptures had already been divided into sections for the purposes of study and liturgical use, the chapter divisions found in nearly all Bibles today, whether Jewish or Christian, were the work of Archbishop Stephen Langton from Canterbury, England, in the thirteenth century C.E. Archbishop Langton divided the text of the Latin Vulgate, which was then transferred to the Hebrew Bible. The present verse divisions, which, with few exceptions, are the same in both Jewish and Christian Bibles, were carried out in the sixteenth century C.E.

Commentary versus unembellished

Some Bibles provide commentary or "study notes" on the Bible. These can be very helpful if you're reading the Bible for study, especially as a quick reference guide or to shed light on the use of a particular word or phrase. Yet the danger with study notes or commentary is that those who write them sometimes allow their particular beliefs to dictate what they write. We all have opinions, especially when it comes to the Bible. But you want to find notes that, as Sergeant Friday used to say, "stick to the facts," not that embellish the Bible with the doctrines of a particular religion or church.

The best way to avoid buying an overly biased Bible is to see who sponsored the translation and notes. The sponsor is usually spelled out in the introduction. (If it's not, don't use it.) Study notes by *interdenominational* (representing many different denominations within a particular faith) or *ecumenical* (representing many different faiths) committees are usually safe. But study notes sponsored by, say, The Church of Elvis Sightings in the Greater Graceland Area should probably give you cause for concern.

Gender-specific versus gender-neutral

A final thing to consider when choosing a translation is your own sensibilities. For example, most older translations of the Bible use masculine pronouns, even in cases where the author intends to be inclusive. Thus, rather than say "the children of Israel" or even "the Israelites," most older translations say "the sons of Israel," because, as in many languages, a mixed group is rendered in the masculine. We prefer gender-neutral Bibles, because, in many cases they come closer to what the biblical authors intended.

Other translations extend gender-neutral language to the Bible's presentation of God. Rather than saying "He," the translators use the generic "God" or use masculine and feminine pronouns interchangeably. The good thing about such translations is that they remind you that many people's view of God — including the biblical authors' (see Chapter 3) — transcends our notions of gender. However, our main hesitation with such translations is that by changing the way the biblical authors present God (who is almost always referred to by using masculine pronouns and imagery, although some notable exceptions exist — see, for example, Isaiah 49:15), they may change what the authors are attempting to communicate about God.

The final step: "Playing the field" of Bible translations

With the above guidelines in mind, we recommend that you approach finding the right translation the same way you might look for Mr. or Mrs. Right. "Date" a number of different translations. Take them out for coffee, have lunch together, enjoy candlelit dinners together. As is the case with dating, you'll find that some translations will repel you, others will interest you, and still others will captivate you. And who knows? Perhaps someday you'll find that special "someone" — a translation that brings out the best in you, makes you feel more alive when you're together, a translation that you just can't be without . . . even if you're still kissing through a veil.

What's in a name? The dangers of translation

God has many names in the Hebrew Bible. He is often called "God," from the Hebrew *Elohim* (less commonly *El*). Another designation, though far less common, is *El Shaddai*, typically translated "God Almighty." God's personal name, however, is rendered with the Hebrew consonants *YHWH*, from the verbal root meaning "to be." Thus, God's name seems to mean "He who is" or "He who causes to be." Most translations of the Bible render YHWH as "the LORD" (all capital letters). Since Hebrew is written without vowels (or, more accurately, "very, very few vowels"), no one knows for sure how God's name was pronounced (though most scholars think it was

Yahweh). By the time vowels were inserted into the Hebrew Bible (by the Masoretes near the end of the 1st millennium CE), the divine name was no longer pronounced due to its sacred nature. To ensure that people didn't pronounce the divine name, the Masoretic scribes placed the vowels for the word "Lord," Hebrew *adonay* (a-o-a), between the consonants of YHWH, resulting in YaHoWaH. Those unaware of this tradition later mistook these vowels as the actual vowels of God's name, resulting in God's name becoming *Yehowah* or, in English, *Jehovah* – a name still found in many translations of the Bible.

Chapter 2

Lights, Camera, Action! Previewing the Bible's Stage and Storyline

- -

In This Chapter

▶ Becoming familiar with the biblical stage: Ancient Israel

▶ Understanding the central theme of the biblical drama: Covenants

▶ Watching a preview of the entire Bible

- -

The Bible is a big book. After all, it covers everything from the beginning of Creation to the end of time. But the Bible doesn't have to be intimidating. It was written to be read, and it contains some of the world's greatest literature.

Like many works of literature, the Bible is best experienced as a continuous narrative. However, we realize that different people have different interests. You may wish to take in the botanical wonders of the Garden of Eden and experience what it's like to live in Paradise with Adam and Eve. You may desire to journey to Egypt to see the pyramids and relive Israel's deliverance from slavery under the leadership of Moses. You may want to venture to the Sea of Galilee and interact with Jesus and his followers, witnessing firsthand Jesus' teaching and miracle working.

Whatever your interests, this chapter gives you the layout of the biblical stage and a preview of the entire biblical drama, allowing you to see the big picture and identify the people, places, and events you want to see first.

Getting a Glimpse of the Biblical Stage

The Bible, like most dramas, is easier to understand if you have an idea of the layout of the stage. Although the Bible's stage extends across three continents (Asia, Africa, and Europe), here's a map of center stage, where most of the biblical drama takes place (see Figure 2-1).

Figure 2-1:
The map or
"stage"
where much
of the
biblical
drama
unfolds.

This "stage" goes by many names during the nearly 2,000 year period covered by the Bible, including *Canaan* (after its early inhabitants, the Canaanites), *Israel* (after the ancestors of Jacob, also named Israel, who later lived here), and *Palestine* (after the Philistines, who once dominated its coastal region). In this book you find all three names, depending on where you are in the story.

With this map, and the short summary of the biblical drama that follows, you can dive into the Bible wherever you want . . . without getting lost!

Seeing a Preview of the Biblical Drama

The Bible, though a vast work, has a coherent plot and storyline that centers around its main character: God. That's right. The Bible, at its heart, is an account of the "life and times" of God. In fact, if we were to write a one-sentence summary of the biblical drama, it would read something like this:

> *The Bible tells the story of God and His relationship with His creation—most particularly, humankind—which He initiates through a series of covenants.*

Of course, there's a lot to this relationship and its development, which we explore throughout this book. For now, we should say a word about covenants, since they play such an important role in the biblical text.

Briefly, a *covenant* is an agreement or, as we might say in modern legalese, a contract, that obligates one or more parties to fulfill specific promises or duties. Now, if you're a lawyer, you may be thinking, "Wait a minute! Your definition is wrong — a contract obligates 'two or more parties,' not 'one or more.'" This is true in most cases, but not when it comes to God. In fact, the Bible presents God as making at least one "contract" where He obligates Himself without requiring *any* explicit obligation from the other party (the Abrahamic Covenant, which we discuss in more detail in Chapter 4).

If you're a lawyer, you're probably thinking, "God needs a good lawyer." And this may be true. But, in the end, it probably wouldn't help, because the Bible presents God as not only entering willfully into this "one-sided" agreement but *initiating* it. What's more, the Bible portrays God as maintaining His end of the bargain *no matter what the behavior of the other party.* This preferential treatment will raise your moral hackles at times, especially when God blesses complete scoundrels simply because He made a covenant with them or their ancestors. Yet, even in the face of these seeming injustices, the biblical authors are trying to make a point: God is faithful (He keeps His promises) and forgiving (He shows kindness even to total rogues).

Experiencing the saga of the Hebrew Bible

The Hebrew Bible (or Old Testament) begins "In the beginning," which, as Julie Andrews realized long ago, is "a very good place to start."

The primeval history (Genesis 1–11)

After describing the creation of the cosmos, the Bible focuses on the first humans, Adam and Eve, who, though starting out in "Paradise," end up "East of Eden" (literally, which is where the John Steinbeck book and subsequent James Dean movie got their title). The reason for this change of address is that a serpent convinces the first humans to disobey God's command not to eat the forbidden fruit (not an apple — we explain where this idea came from in Chapter 3). Soon things go from bad to worse — Adam and Eve's offspring, Cain and Abel (see Chapter 4), have the world's first sibling rivalry, which leaves Abel dead and Cain on the run. This downward spiral continues as the world becomes so filled with violence that God sends a flood to destroy it (see Chapter 4). The only survivors are a man named Noah and his family, along with the animals they bring on the cruise ship (called an ark) that Noah builds to ride out the flood. After the flood, God promises Noah never to destroy the earth again (called the Noahic Covenant).

Although given a fresh start, humans again begin down the wrong moral path by deciding to build a city and giant tower "whose top reaches into the heavens" rather than spreading throughout the earth, as God had commanded. Concerned that such unchecked power could lead to catastrophe, God disperses the inhabitants of this city by confusing their language. The unfinished tower and city are given the name Babel (from which we get the word *babble,* meaning to speak incomprehensibly).

Despite humankind's difficult beginning, God's plan is that humans experience the good life, which entails enjoying a relationship with Him and the riches of His creation. That's why Adam and Eve start out in Paradise, where they have an uninhibited relationship with God and one another, and where they enjoy the bounty of God's creation. Although humans are now living in *Paradise Lost*, God is determined to make the best of a bad situation.

The patriarchs (Genesis 12–50)

To carry out His plan of restoring humans to the good life, God chooses a man named Abram (meaning "exalted father"), whom He renames Abraham (meaning "father of many") in recognition of His intention to give Abraham and his barren wife, Sarah, numerous descendants (see Chapter 5). As further confirmation of this intention, God makes a covenant with Abraham (called the Abrahamic Covenant), promising him that his descendants will become a great nation, and that they will live in a land "flowing with milk and honey" (that's Bible-speak for bountiful flocks [milk] and fields [honey]). God's decision to bless Abraham, Sarah, and their descendants is not just for them, however. God intends that through Abraham and Sarah's offspring "all the nations of the earth will be blessed."

These promises are passed down to Abraham's son, Isaac, and then to Isaac's son, Jacob, whose 12 sons become the progenitors of the twelve tribes of Israel (see Chapter 6). Due to a severe famine in their homeland, Jacob and his sons and their families move to Egypt, where things go well for them largely due to the reputation and influence of Jacob's son, Joseph (of Technicolor Dreamcoat fame).

Moses and the exodus (Exodus, Leviticus, Numbers, and Deuteronomy)

Generations come and go, and a new Pharaoh (or king) arises in Egypt "who knew not Joseph." Feeling threatened by what is now a very large population of non-Egyptians in his borders, Pharaoh decides to enslave the Israelites (as they're now called, after their ancestor Israel/Jacob). For years, the Israelites "slave away" under their Egyptian taskmasters, until one day God chooses a man named Moses to deliver them from their bondage (see Chapter 7). At first, Pharaoh refuses to let the Israelites go, but God forces his hand by sending a series of plagues that leaves his country decimated. Now free at last, Moses and the Israelites depart from Egypt and arrive at Mount Sinai, where God gives this new nation conceived in liberty a constitution, known as the Mosaic Covenant. God tells the Israelites that their well-being as a nation will be a direct result of their continued obedience to the laws of this constitution, laws that are succinctly embodied in the Ten Commandments.

Joshua and the period of the judges (Joshua, Judges, and Ruth)

Moses' generation is prohibited from entering the Promised Land due to its continual rebellion against God, but the next generation enters and conquers it under the capable leadership of a man named Joshua (see Chapter 8). Soon after Joshua's death, however, the nation's moral resolve weakens, and the Israelites begin engaging in the forbidden practices of their neighbors, including worshiping other gods. As punishment, God raises up various nations from among Israel's neighbors, who harass and oppress them. When the Israelites repent and ask for help, God sends deliverers known as "judges" (see Chapter 8), who defeat Israel's enemies and initiate a period of peace. But this peace is short-lived, as Israel again turns away from God.

The united monarchy (1 and 2 Samuel, 1 Kings 1–11, 1 Chronicles, and 2 Chronicles 1–9)

Tired of the vagaries of life under the judges, the people ask the last judge, Samuel, for a king "to rule over us and protect us from our enemies." Although he feels that this is a rejection of God's "Kingship," God tells him to do as the people ask, and Israel gets its first king: a man named Saul. At first, God blesses Saul, giving him success after success over Israel's enemies. However, Saul soon falls out of favor with God, and He appoints a new king: a shepherd boy named David (see Chapter 9). David's rule, like Saul's, begins well, and David finds himself on top of the world. Unfortunately, from this vantage point David sees more than he ought to. One day, while walking on his palace roof, he spies a beautiful but married woman, named Bathsheba, with whom David commits adultery. To make matters worse, David has her husband killed so that he can marry her. Although God had promised David and his descendants an "eternal kingship" (known as the "Davidic Covenant")," David's reign, and the reigns of many of his descendants, will experience difficulty and disaster.

After David's death, his son, Solomon, takes the throne (see Chapter 10), and God gives him exceptional wisdom to rule his vast kingdom. Although his reign is marked by economic prosperity and international influence, Solomon's crowning achievement is the construction of Jerusalem's Temple. Despite these successes, Solomon's pork-barrel politics alienate a number of his constituents, and in his old age he turns toward other gods.

The divided monarchy (1 Kings 12–22, 2 Kings, and 2 Chronicles 10–36)

Shortly after Solomon's death (around 925 B.C.E.), the ten northern tribes of Israel secede from the union, forming their own kingdom called Israel (see Chapter 10). The southern kingdom remains under the sovereignty of David's descendants and takes the name Judah, from the name of David's tribe. The northern kingdom of Israel experiences a number of turbulent dynastic transitions, and only lasts until 721 B.C.E., when it's conquered by the Assyrians, a powerful nation from the Mesopotamian region. The Assyrians transplant many of Israel's inhabitants, resulting in the Ten Lost Tribes of Israel. The southern kingdom of Judah, which is ruled by a descendant of David throughout its history, lasts until 586 B.C.E., when it's conquered by the Babylonians, another powerful nation from the Mesopotamian region. When the Babylonians conquer Judah, they destroy Jerusalem, including Solomon's Temple, and send its most important inhabitants into exile, initiating what's known as the Exilic Period.

The Exilic and Postexilic Periods (Ezra, Nehemiah, Daniel, and Esther)

The Jews, so named from their status as former inhabitants of Judah, live in Babylonian exile until 539 B.C.E. (see Chapter 11), at which time the Persians conquer the Babylonians and give the Jews permission to return to their land. This begins the Postexilic Period.

Not everyone takes the Persians up on the offer to return home, however. In fact, many Jews choose to stay in their new "homeland." Yet enough people do return to reconstitute a Jewish community in the former territory of Judah. The Jews eventually rebuild Jerusalem and the Temple, initiating what's called the Second Temple Period (the First Temple being Solomon's). Under the leadership of Ezra, a priest, and Nehemiah, the governor of Judea, the Jews rededicate themselves to obey the Law of Moses (see Chapter 12).

Great expectations (The Prophets, Job, Psalms, Proverbs, Song of Songs, and Ecclesiastes)

The story of the Hebrew Bible ends with promises of future blessings for the Jews in their homeland under a king from the line of David who will come to deliver them from their enemies (see Chapter 13). Like David, their new king will rule over a reconstituted Israel and usher in a period of economic prosperity and international influence. Yet, unlike David, this new king will establish a kingdom of justice and peace that will be for all people and will never end. Until then, the Jews are to pursue wisdom and righteousness (see Chapter 14) and continue in their worship of God (see Chapter 15).

The history of the Hebrew Bible ends around the time of Ezra and Nehemiah. The Apocrypha and New Testament, although representing a continuation of Jewish history, do not constitute part of the Jewish Bible.

Appreciating the action of the Apocrypha

The Apocrypha, which is part of the Catholic and Eastern Orthodox Old Testament, is a collection of Jewish writings that, like the Hebrew Bible, is very rich and diverse. In the Apocrypha, you find history, poetry, philosophy, and theology, as well as stories about love and war, life and death, and all those other themes that produce best-selling books and hit movies. Yet, unlike the Hebrew Bible, we're not aware of any bestsellers or hit movies based on the Apocrypha. Moreover, the books making up the Apocrypha are not easily placed into a flowing narrative. Thus, the best way to give you an overview of this part of the Bible is to recount the history of the Jews during this period.

Alexander the Great and the Greeks (1 Maccabees 1)

About 200 years after the Persians conquer the Babylonians and give the Jews permission to return to their homeland, the Persians are themselves conquered by the Greeks, under the leadership of Alexander the Great (330 B.C.E). After Alexander's death in 323 B.C.E., his kingdom is divided among his four generals. Although the Greek kings ruling over the Jews are relatively benevolent toward them, one king in particular, Antiochus Epiphanes, takes a disliking toward them and attacks Jerusalem. In the process, Antiochus desecrates the Temple and prohibits the Jews from observing their sacred rites, including keeping the Sabbath and circumcising their infant boys.

The Maccabean Revolt (1 Maccabees 2 — 16 and 2 Maccabees)

These offenses prove too much for the Jews, and they eventually rise up in revolt, first under a man named Mattathias and then under his son, Judah. Judah's nickname, "the Maccabee" or "the Hammer," eventually gives the rebellion (the Maccabean Revolt) and the books recounting these events (1 and 2 Maccabees) their names (see Chapter 16). Judah and his forces soon free Jerusalem and cleanse the Temple — an event commemorated today as Hanukkah. Although Judah never lives to see the Jews obtain complete political and religious autonomy, later generations do. This state of affairs lasts for another 100 years, after which time a new power arises and conquers all the lands formerly held by the Greeks, and then some: Rome.

Watching the drama of the New Testament

When the curtain opens on the New Testament, Judea and the lands formerly known as Israel are under Roman rule. The Roman-appointed "King of the Jews" is Herod the Great, during whose reign Jesus is born.

The life of Jesus (Matthew, Mark, Luke, and John)

The gospels of Matthew, Mark, Luke, and John recount Jesus' humble beginnings as a baby born "in the little town of Bethlehem" (King David's hometown) and his upbringing in the even littler town of Nazareth in the north of Israel, near the Sea of Galilee (see Chapter 18). Once grown, Jesus attracts large crowds with his profound teachings and miraculous powers (see Chapter 19). Moreover, Jesus claims to be the promised Davidic king or *Messiah* — a Hebrew word meaning "anointed one" (Greek *christos,* from which the name Christ derives) — foretold by the Hebrew Bible. Jesus' growing popularity, however, does not sit well with certain Roman and Jewish authorities, who view this growing movement as a threat to their power and the well-being of the region. Thus, for reasons both political and personal, Jesus is tried, condemned, and crucified (see Chapter 19).

This is not the end of the story, though. According to Jesus' followers, he rose again from the dead. His death, they argue, was necessary as a sacrifice for humankind's wrongdoing as part of a "New Covenant" that God is making with all people, a covenant that marks the fulfillment of God's promise to Abraham long ago — that all the families on earth will be blessed through his "seed" (Jesus). Jesus' resurrection demonstrates that he has defeated sin and death, and that one day God's kingdom of righteousness and justice will be established on earth forever. In the meantime, Jesus' followers begin to spread his teachings "to the ends of the earth" with the purpose of seeing God's kingdom established in human hearts. A movement is born.

The early church (The Acts of the Apostles and the Epistles)

Soon thousands of people become followers of Jesus and his teachings (see Chapter 20). The spread of Christianity, as this movement comes to be called, is due in large part to a man named Paul, a onetime persecutor of Christians who has become one of its chief promoters. Through extensive traveling and letter writing, Paul founds churches throughout the Mediterranean basin (see Chapter 21). Others, too, contribute to the growth of Christianity, including Peter and John, two of Jesus' closest followers, and Jesus' brother, James (see Chapter 22). Soon this movement spreads throughout the Roman Empire.

The beginning of the end (Revelation)

Christianity's growth begins to be perceived as a threat to the Roman Empire because its followers give first allegiance to Jesus and not to Caesar. As a result of this "defiance," intense persecution breaks out against Christians, the character of which is described in the Book of Revelation (see Chapter 23). The author of this book, however, envisions a day when God will vindicate those who die as martyrs by overthrowing the kingdoms of this world and establishing the Kingdom of God. In the end, Paradise will be restored as Jesus defeats "the serpent of old" and the Tree of Life is again made available to all those who believe in him, symbolizing eternal life in heaven.

With this, the Christian Bible ends, but not before taking you on an unforgettable journey — a journey that has helped give rise to three major religions (see Chapter 24) and that continues to have an impact on the artistic and literary expression of our world (see Chapter 25).

Part II
Exploring the Hebrew Bible — The Old Testament

The 5th Wave   By Rich Tennant

"Okay, but this remains between the three of us, right?"

In this part . . .

You explore the Hebrew Bible (also known as the Old Testament) from the first "In the beginning" to the prophecies about the "end of days." You witness the creation of the cosmos with God, take in the botanical wonders of the Garden of Eden with Adam and Eve, ride out the Flood with Noah, traverse the Fertile Crescent with Abraham, and journey to Egypt with Joseph (of Technicolor Dreamcoat fame) and his family. (All these stories are in the book of Genesis alone! Because Genesis lays the foundation for the rest of the Bible, we treat you to four fun-filled chapters on the subject.) You also ride the roller coaster of Israel's national existence, including its emancipation from slavery with Moses, its amazing rise to international influence with David and Solomon, its calamitous fall with Jeremiah, and its miraculous rebirth with Ezra and Nehemiah. You also gain an appreciation for Israel's cultural legacy by contemplating the meaning of life with Proverbs and Ecclesiastes, understanding suffering with Job, singing the songs that make the whole world sing with Psalms, and experiencing love as you never have before with the Song of Songs (parental warning: sexually explicit lyrics).

Chapter 3

Creation, Paradise Lost, and Other Mysteries of Life (Genesis 1–3)

In the beginning, God created the heavens and the earth.

—Genesis 1:1

These are perhaps the best-known words of world literature, appearing in what is arguably the best-known *work* of literature — the Book of Genesis. Even if the Bible doesn't inform your own personal religious heritage or belief system, the narratives of Genesis have had a significant impact on you and the world around you.

Consider the following points:

- Three of the world's major religions — Judaism, Christianity, and Islam — trace their origins to the traditions found in Genesis.

- The belief that all humans are created "in the image of God," and are therefore equal, comes from Genesis.

- Many of the greatest works of art, architecture, and literature have been inspired by stories found in Genesis.

In this chapter, you explore the opening chapters of Genesis (1–3) — from the Creation of the cosmos to Adam and Eve's fateful choice to eat from the forbidden tree — in order to better understand the themes and plot tensions that direct the rest of the Bible, as well as to better appreciate the continuing impact of these narratives on our world.

Beginning "In the Beginning"

The name Genesis comes from a Greek word meaning origin or beginning. (You can see the Greek roots in the English word "genealogy," meaning, appropriately enough, the study of origins.) Originally, however, and still in Jewish tradition, the name for Genesis comes from its opening words "In the beginning," which in Hebrew is "Bereshith" (pronounced beh-reh-SHEET; be sure to pronounce this one right, or you may get yourself kicked out of synagogue or church).

As the "book of beginnings," Genesis seeks to answer some of the big questions of life, such as:

- ✔ Where did we come from?
- ✔ Why are we here?
- ✔ Is there a God?
- ✔ If so, how many?
- ✔ Why do we die?
- ✔ Why is there evil in the world?
- ✔ Why can't we all just get along?
- ✔ Why are there weeds in my garden? (Really, Genesis answers this question, but unfortunately with no immediate remedies.)

So get ready to begin your exploration of the "book of beginnings."

Who wrote Genesis?

Both Jews and Christians have traditionally ascribed Genesis, as well as the rest of the opening five books of the Bible (called the Torah or Pentateuch), to Moses. However, readers of the Bible have long observed that Genesis contains information that both pre-dates and post-dates Moses. For example, Moses wasn't there when God created the cosmos, and Genesis 36 provides a list of rulers who lived well beyond the time of Moses. Therefore, many scholars consider Genesis through Deuteronomy to be a collection of traditions passed down orally and in written form by a variety of people (including Moses) over a number of centuries. The most prevalent theory describing the origins of the Five Books of Moses is called the Documentary Hypothesis, which postulates a minimum of four literary sources behind these books.

What Are We Doing Here? Creation and the Meaning of Life (Genesis 1:1–2:3)

According to the opening verses of Genesis, when God began to create, the earth was "formless and void." The Hebrew words used to describe this state of affairs are *tohu wa-bohu* (TOE-hoo va-VOE-hoo). Beyond sounding like a brand of tofu (which, by the way, some theologians think is a fairly close description of what the biblical authors had in mind), these words rhyme, which gives this otherwise "chaotic" state a certain sense of order. Here, then, the biblical authors are already beginning to define their worldview and their view of God differently than how their neighbors perceived such things.

For example, according to the Mesopotamian creation myth, Enuma Elish, the cosmos was thought to be the end product of a war between the gods. The cosmos, in fact, *was* one of the defeated gods — the goddess Tiamat, who is a dragon-like creature embodying "watery chaos" (think of Ursula in Disney's *The Little Mermaid,* only on a much larger and more sinister scale — a scary thought indeed!). Therefore, when in Genesis 1 you encounter the rhythmic words "formless and void," and then see the "spirit of God hovering over the watery deep," you are being introduced to a God who, in contrast to His Mesopotamian counterparts, is in total control of the cosmos. In fact, the Hebrew name for "watery deep" (*tehom*) in Genesis 1 is linguistically related to the name Tiamat, making the comparison between the God of the Bible and the Mesopotamian gods all the more apparent.

Understanding the six days of Creation

Beyond providing a sense of order, the very words "formlessness and void" provide the outline or "agenda" for God's workweek. During the first three days, God *forms* the cosmos; during the next three days, He *fills* it.

The following table shows the pattern of the Creation account:

God Forms	*God Fills*
Day One: Light	Day Four: The sun, moon, and stars
Day Two: Sky and sea	Day Five: Birds and fish
Day Three: Dry land and plants	Day Six: Animals and humans

Therefore, in this opening Creation account, the Bible communicates not only that God created but that His creation has order and, by implication, purpose. This sense of order is further conveyed by the overall systematic unfolding of Creation ("It was evening, it was morning, the first day," "It was evening, it was morning, the second day," and so on).

The "days" of Creation: Literal or figurative days?

One question that inevitably arises when discussing the six days of Creation is, "Are these literal days (that is, 24-hour periods), or are they figurative for long periods of unspecified length (such as "in the *day* of the dinosaurs")? As early as the fourth century C.E., Saint Augustine, the "Father of the Church," asked this very question and then determined that the days of Creation were intended to be understood figuratively, and constituted *long epochs of time*. Now Augustine was no evolutionist. However, he did believe that the earth was much older than a literal understanding of these days would allow. In addition, Augustine (and others) noted that the sun, by which days are reckoned, isn't even created until the fourth day.

This isn't to say that everyone has understood the days of Creation to be figurative (or that they should be understood that way). For centuries, there have been attempts to calculate the exact date of Creation by taking the days of Creation literally and then adding to this the various generations enumerated in the Bible. Theologian and scholar James Ussher performed the most notable example of such "number crunching." In the seventeenth century C.E., he determined that Creation took place in the year 4004 B.C.E. Bishop Ussher's work became so influential that his dates were even printed in some editions of the King James Bible, giving them a kind of "divine (or at least "royal") stamp of approval."

Seeing the forest-maker through the trees

In addition to establishing that God created the cosmos and everything in it, in this opening Creation account the biblical author seeks to convey important information about God and His relationship with His creation.

Consider the following theological points deriving from Genesis 1:

✔ **God is powerful.** This point is clear from the very beginning "beginning." The Bible says that God merely "says the word" and, *voilà,* things come into existence. (Try this some time; it's not easy.)

Theologians describe God's method of speaking things into existence as *ex nihilo,* which is Latin for "from nothing." In truth, there is something there, namely the water-covered earth over which God's spirit hovers, but the point is well taken: God calls into being that which did not previously exist.

✔ **God is transcendent.** This is a fancy way of saying that God is distinct from His creation. This attribute may seem like a given to those coming from a biblical worldview, but when compared to the worldview of many ancient cultures — where gods were intimately identified with forces of nature, such as the sea, a storm, fertility, and so on — this idea was rather revolutionary.

✔ **God is good.** Finally, the biblical author presents God as the source of that which is "good" in this world. At every stage of Creation the Bible says "God saw that it was good." And at the end of His creating, the Bible reports:

And God saw everything He had made and, behold, it was very good.

—Genesis 1:31

The culmination of God's workweek: Humans

On day six, after God has made everything else, God makes humans. The biblical author isn't suggesting that humankind is an afterthought in God's mind. Rather, we are to understand that humankind is the pinnacle of God's creation. This idea is further emphasized by the notice that humans are made "in God's image." So what does it mean to be created in God's image? The Bible doesn't say, explicitly, but scholars usually propose two ideas:

✔ **Humans bear the physical image of God.** There are a number of biblical passages that describe God with human anatomical features. For example, God is said to have arms, eyes, hands . . . even a beard! So some think that being created in God's image means that humans look like God. Yet, God is also said to guard humans "under His wings," but few if any scholars think that the biblical authors imagine God with literal wings. So we need to be careful when interpreting passages that describe God's physical appearance, since the biblical authors are apt to use figurative language to describe God, who transcends human categories.

✔ **Humans bear the "spiritual" image (or character qualities) of God.** Others feel that when the Bible speaks of humans being created "in the image of God" it is referring to God's "inner" qualities, such as morality, creativity, compassion, intelligence, and so on. In short, the image of God refers to that which sets us apart from our fellow creatures. Certainly, animals may be said to have intelligence, compassion, and perhaps even creativity, but humans have a higher moral sense (whether we choose to exercise it or not is another question) and greater intellectual capabilities (ditto) than their animal counterparts.

One final observation needs to be made concerning the image of God. According to the Bible, both male and female are created "in the image of God." Note the wording:

And God created humankind in His image, in the image of God He created them; male and female He created them.

—Genesis 1:27

This point concerning the equality of all humankind is obvious, but important, because the Bible has been (mis)used to undermine the basic equality of just about everyone, including and especially the sexes.

Discovering the meaning of life

We discover part of the purpose for which humankind was created in the first command given to humans by God:

> *Be fruitful and multiply, and fill the earth and subdue it.*

—Genesis 1:28

According to the biblical text, then, humans have two main responsibilities: (1) to *multiply*, which is embodied in the words "be fruitful and multiply, and fill the earth," and (2) to *manage*, which is embodied in the word "subdue." That is, the purpose of human existence is precisely what we would hope our stockbroker would do on a more consistent basis: multiply and manage.

Other than multiplying and managing, human existence has at least one other "job description" or purpose: relationship. Although it isn't expressly stated in this first Creation account, humans were created to have relationship with God, with each other, and with the created order. And when things go wrong, the first thing that goes out the window is human intimacy with God (humans hide when they hear Him coming),with each other (humans become ashamed in each other's presence), and, eventually, with creation (animals are given the instinct to flee the dangers of humans).

Enjoying the first weekend

On the seventh day, the Bible tells us, "God rested from all the work He had done" (Genesis 2:3). In light of this statement, some have asked, "Did God really get tired?" To which we respond, "Wouldn't you?"

Although it's possible to understand descriptions of God resting or regretting or even remembering literally, later biblical passages assert that there is no diminishing of or deficiency in the divine being or essence. This is a fancy way of saying God doesn't really rest (as though He had lost energy), regret (as though He didn't know what was going to happen), or remember (as though He forgot something). Rather, God rests in the sense that He stops working, regrets in the sense that He is overwhelmingly saddened by human wrongdoing, and remembers in the sense that He is about to act on a promise. This style of writing uses *anthropomorphic language,* which simply means that the biblical writers describe God in human forms. In the particular case of God resting, the Bible tries to establish a pattern for humankind to emulate.

Thus, God rests, and the weekend is established. Therefore, next time you hear someone say, "Thank God it's Friday!" you'll appreciate this exclamation in a completely new light.

What it means to have "dominion" over the earth

The command to "be fruitful and multiply, and fill the earth" is straightforward enough, and is one that the human race is doing a more than adequate job at fulfilling. (Please consult your sixth grade "biology" textbook if you feel in the dark on this one.) But the commandments to "subdue" and "to have dominion over" the earth and its creatures are less straightforward, and have been misused to, well, *misuse* the earth and its creatures.

The Hebrew words for "to subdue" and "to have dominion over" are normally used to describe what a king is supposed to do with his kingdom. According to the Bible, good kings rule their kingdoms in a way that promotes the welfare of those under their dominion. Thus, the command to "have dominion over" creation is not an invitation to pollute the earth or hunt animals into extinction, but to take care of creation.

The Hebrew word used to describe God's "resting" from His work is *shabat*, which means "to stop" or "to cease." It's from this Hebrew word that we get the word "Sabbath," which is the name used for this "day of rest." In Jewish tradition the Sabbath is Saturday (more specifically, sundown on Friday to sundown on Saturday), while in Christian tradition the Sabbath was moved to Sunday to commemorate the day on which Jesus rose from the dead.

Living in Paradise (Genesis 2:4–25)

If you've read the Bible before, or if you're reading along in the Bible as you read this book, you may have noticed that in Genesis 2, and in particular beginning at Genesis 2:4, there is a second Creation account — with some notable differences.

Taking a second look at Creation

Perhaps the most obvious difference between the Creation accounts of Genesis 1 and 2 is the order in which God creates. Whereas, in Genesis 1, God creates plants before animals and humans, in Genesis 2, God creates a man (Adam), then plants, then animals, and, last, but not least, a woman (Eve). Perhaps you even noticed that the name used for God is different. Whereas, in Genesis 1, God is referred to as, well, "God," in Genesis 2, God is called "the LORD God." What's going on here?

✔ Some scholars have suggested that Genesis 1 and 2 represent two different Creation accounts that were only later brought together by the person compiling the biblical text. By this view, the differences in detail and divine name are the result of different traditions about how the world came to be and, perhaps, who created it (or at least, by which name the creator should be addressed).

✔ Still other interpreters have understood the seeming differences between these two Creation accounts as a literary technique: Genesis 1 provides the overview of Creation, while Genesis 2 provides the details. This shift is evidenced by the change in the word order from "heaven and earth" (Genesis 1:1) at the beginning of the first account to "earth and heaven" (Genesis 2:4b) at the beginning of the second account.

Regardless of one's conclusion on what interpretation is correct, these traditions have been read together for thousands of years, and it's the combination of these traditions that has informed many people's view of God.

Creating Adam and Eve

The earthly perspective provided in Genesis 2 expands on what you know from the heavenly perspective given in Genesis 1 — particularly when it comes to the creation of the first two humans: Adam and Eve.

✔ First, you discover that Adam was formed "out of the dirt of the ground" (confirming that boys are, indeed, made out of "slugs and snails and puppy dog tails"). In fact, the word for "man" in Hebrew is *adam,* and the word for ground is *adamah.* Thus, here we have a wordplay because the adam (man or "earthling") is taken from the adamah (earth).

✔ Second, you discover that humankind is animated (brought to life) by God's breath or spirit. This confirms that humankind's divine essence, or image, is primarily internal or spiritual in nature.

✔ Third, and as an example of humanity's participation in the divine image of "creativity," you discover that God gave to Adam (humans) the job of naming the animals. This responsibility emphasizes the difference between humans and animals. While animals have "language" (and some animals no doubt have "names" for humans), humankind names, classifies, categorizes and contemplates the world in a way that's different from our fellow creatures.

✔ Fourth, you discover that humans need each other. God expresses this need when He says, "It isn't good for man to be alone" (Genesis 2:18). God then performs what is the first surgery, even administering the first anesthetic. God causes a deep sleep to fall upon Adam, and while Adam is "under," God removes a part of his side and forms a woman.

That the woman came from the man's side has led some people to infer that the Bible teaches women are somehow "inferior" to men. The text expresses nothing of the sort. In fact, you can make the opposite argument: Woman is made of more refined stuff, coming not from the ground but from one who is already human. The biblical author isn't trying to make a point about the inferiority or superiority of one gender over the other, but rather is underscoring the close and intimate relationship between male and female (even if one is from Mars and the other from Venus).

Witnessing the first wedding

After God forms the woman, we witness the first wedding. When the man awakes, God escorts the bride down the aisle in the Garden of Eden (the ultimate garden wedding). God then presents the woman to the man, and performs the "ceremony."

Now, you may be thinking, "Does the Bible really mean for us to understand that God *literally* formed the man, breathed into him, opened his side, formed a woman, walked her down the aisle, and so on?" Probably. In fact, these descriptions highlight what is perhaps the most surprising discovery of this second Creation account: Although God is transcendent or separate from His creation (Genesis 1), He is also intimately involved with His creation. Both of these presentations of God are essential for understanding the Bible's view of God, and it took both Creation accounts to give us this full-bodied portrait.

Enjoying life in the Garden of Eden

The Garden of Eden was the place to be. In addition to being a botanical wonder, Eden had no death, no disease, no weeds, no crime, no violence, no injustice, no alienation between humans, God, or creation; it was, in a word, Paradise. Moreover, the Garden was a place to just relax and be yourself. In fact, Genesis 2 ends with the notice: "And the man and his wife were naked and unashamed" (Genesis 2:25). That's right, according to the Bible, humans were originally meant to walk around in their "birthday suits." What's more, they felt no shame in this. Yet, before you sign up for that nudist colony you've always wanted to join, hold on, because this idyllic condition of "naked and unashamed" is about to end.

Understanding the two trees

Amidst all the perfection of Eden, God plants "in the center of the Garden" two special trees: the Tree of Life (so far, so good), and the Tree of the Knowledge of Good and Evil (not so good). Regarding this latter tree, God tells Adam, "You shall not eat from it, for on the day that you eat of it, you will certainly die" (Genesis 2:17).

The presence of the forbidden tree raises several questions:

✔ **What's wrong with knowledge?** Actually, knowing things isn't really the issue, because Adam and Eve already know a lot, including language, the names of animals, how to manage the Garden, how to multiply (and all that entails), and so on. Moreover, this verse doesn't mean they don't know about good. Good is presumably all they know, because everything that God made is "good." Thus, the issue isn't knowing so much as it's knowing *evil* — and not just cognitive knowledge *about* evil, but experiential knowledge *of* evil. Adam and Eve will soon get both.

✔ **Why would God ruin a good thing by planting a bad tree?** The text doesn't say (explicitly), but some theologians have suggested that giving humans a choice between obedience and disobedience — good and bad — underscores a necessary part of being human: free will.

✔ **Why a tree?** The form probably doesn't matter, although part of what allures humans to this tree is that "it was good for food" and "a delight to the eyes." For Freud, however, the form was significant, because eating food is laden with sexual symbolism (of course, for Freud, everything was laden with sexual symbolism). Freud perceived the eating of this fruit as symbolizing sexual awareness, which is why Adam and Eve feel shame after eating. However, according to the Bible, humans already knew about the "s" word. Thus, contrary to Freud, sometimes, a piece of fruit is just a piece of fruit.

He Made Me Do It! The "Fall" and Its Fallout (Genesis 3)

All is well in the Garden of Eden — even with the presence of "the Tree" — until we're introduced to the arch villain of humankind: the snake.

Falling for a tempting proposition

No one really knows why the slithering, sinuous serpent was selected to be the bad guy. However, the biblical author does provide some light on the subject by saying that "the serpent was more crafty than any other wild animal that the LORD God had made" (Genesis 3:1). But still, why a snake?

Later reflection on this passage would understand this snake to be none other than the Devil himself. Although Genesis 3 doesn't make this equation, there are some indications that this serpent is more than just a serpent:

✔ **The snake tests humankind's moral fortitude and devotion to God.** Not the typical behavior of snakes.

✔ **The snake lies.** Snakes are sneaky, granted, but they seldom lie.

✔ **The serpent can talk.** This clue is perhaps the most telling because talking animals are unusual — even for the Bible. (A donkey will talk later in the Bible [see Chapter 7 of this book], but that's about it.)

With indications like these, later interpreters may be justified in seeing more behind this serpent than just a snake.

The Bible tells us that when the serpent approaches Eve, he poses a question:

> *Did God really say, 'You shall not eat from any tree in the garden?'*
>
> —Genesis 3:1

Before wondering why Eve doesn't act shocked at a talking snake, keep in mind that she's new to this whole creation thing herself, and that a talking snake would be no more unusual to her than a dancing rock.

Eve quickly corrects the serpent:

> *We may eat of the fruit of the trees of the Garden, but God said, 'You shall not eat from the fruit of the tree that is in the middle of the Garden, nor shall you touch it, or you will die.'*
>
> —Genesis 3:2–3

The serpent retorts by assuring Eve that she will not die. What God fears, the snake says, is that "your eyes will be opened and you will be like God, knowing good and evil" (Genesis 3:5).

What's interesting is that the humans were already like God, as they were created in His image. Yet the serpent holds out the extra incentive of knowing "good and evil," which, after all, is what the Tree promises. Therefore, the serpent isn't a total liar.

After a moment of contemplation, Eve takes a bite of the forbidden fruit and then gives it to her husband, who also eats it.

A malicious, delicious fruit

The Bible simply says that Adam and Eve ate the "fruit," not an "apple." The belief that the forbidden fruit was an apple seems to derive from the fact that the Latin words for apple and evil *(malum)* are identical, the only difference being the accenting of the word. Thus, apple growers the world over can breathe a corporate sigh of relief: The forbidden fruit is unknown.

Watching Adam and Eve's fateful choice

The effects of Adam and Eve's indiscretion are important to note, because for the author of this passage, their act of disobedience changed everything. For example, Adam and Eve immediately experience shame at their nakedness. In response, Adam and Eve sew fig leaves together to cover themselves, thus providing the explanation for why humans should wear clothes.

The biblical text then informs us that Adam and Eve hear the "sound of the LORD God as He was walking in the Garden." Quickly, Adam and Eve hide themselves. This would be the first game of hide and seek, only God had the distinct advantage of, well, being God. Yet, given this advantage, it should strike us as peculiar that God asks, "Where are you?" Does God not know?

As we discover elsewhere in the Bible (see, for example, Genesis 4 and Chapter 4 of this book), God doesn't ask questions to gain knowledge, but to give someone an opportunity to "come clean."

Adam does come clean . . . well, sort of. Adam admits that he ate of the forbidden fruit. But when God asks why, Adam says, "The woman, whom You gave me to be with me, she gave me of the fruit and I ate!" Adam's words are telling. He not only blames the woman, but in case that's not going to get him out of hot water, he says "whom *You* gave me." (Isn't it a relief to know humans have changed quite a bit since the days of Adam and Eve?)

Surprisingly, God actually turns toward Eve, and asks, "What is this you have done?" Eve, now realizing how this game is played, passes the buck once more. "The serpent tricked me, and I ate." This "blame game" can only go so far, and, beginning with the serpent, God declares His judgment against each of the guilty parties.

Suffering the grave consequences of sin

Although the Bible presents God as merciful, He is no pushover when it comes to handing out punishment. Therefore, in response to Adam and Eve's disobedience, God dispenses judgments or, as the Bible calls them in this particular case, curses.

Making the snake eat dirt

For the serpent, God says, "You will go about on your belly and eat the dirt of the ground." Some people suggest that this is the Bible's explanation for why snakes have no legs, and that prior to this, the serpent, and all his fellow snakes, could walk. Later medieval and Renaissance artists, in fact, often depicted this serpent with legs, or even as a serpent-like human. Other interpreters, however, have understood the serpent's judgment of eating dirt as a way to express God's ultimate humiliation and defeat of evil.

God also says to the serpent, "And I will put enmity between you and the woman, and your offspring and her offspring. He will strike your head, and you will strike his heel." Some have understood this to be an explanation for why humans have an inordinate fear of snakes, though later Christian interpreters understood the statement that "He will strike your (the snake's) head" as a reference to Jesus' ultimate defeat of Satan (see Chapter 23).

Making Eve labor

For the woman, God says, "with pain you will give birth to children." (You can say that again.) Moreover, God says to the woman, "Your desire will be for your husband, and he will rule over you." No one is quite sure what this means. Some have suggested that "your desire will be for your husband" means "you will have the hots for him." (Yeah, you wish, husbands!) Others have suggested that it means "you will desire to rule over him," thereby explaining the origins of the "battle of the sexes." Still others see in God's words the Bible's explanation for the distinction between gender roles. The woman will desire (that is, "have relations with") her husband in order to bear children, and the man will rule over (that is, "take care of") his wife. The reason Eve didn't need this kind of "care" before is because childbirth and obtaining food were easier. With the pain now present in obtaining both offspring and food, there is a need for the division of labor.

Making Adam labor

For the man, God curses him with "labor pains" of his own — increased pain when cultivating the land. (Humans already worked, but the idyllic conditions of Eden made work relatively painless.) In fact, the same Hebrew word for pain (*'itzavon*) is used to describe both Adam's and Eve's labor. God then says that the ground will cause the ultimate kind of pain, which is death. "By the sweat of your face you shall eat bread until you return to the ground, for out of it you were taken. For dust you are, and to dust you shall return" (Genesis 3:19). Yet, God's words raise a problem. God had earlier said, *on the very day* Adam ate of the fruit he would die. However, here God says he will *eventually* die. Did God lie? Well, it depends on what "dies" means. Several possibilities exist:

- ✔ Some have argued that when God said Adam and Eve would die "on the very day" they ate the fruit, He meant mortality or the death process would begin.

- ✔ Some have suggested that a spiritual death took place on the day Adam and Eve disobeyed God, which is evidenced in the damaged relationship between humankind and God (Adam and Eve hide) and humankind with each other (Adam and Eve feel shame toward one another).

- ✔ Still others have argued that God is mitigating an originally harsher sentence. That is, the fact that Adam and Eve didn't die immediately after eating the fruit may be an expression of God's compassion, even amidst His words of judgment.

Whatever the full explanation, death is now a part of life.

Losing the keys to Paradise

After speaking His judgments against Adam and Eve, God makes clothes for them from the skin of an animal. In so doing, some have suggested this marks the first "sacrifice for sin," as God kills an animal to atone for or, literally, cover Adam and Eve's sin, as well as their shame. God then escorts the humans out of the Garden of Eden to prevent them from eating from the Tree of Life and living forever.

To further ensure that humans don't return to eat from the Tree of Life, God places armed guards, called cherubs (Hebrew *cherubim*), at the entrance to Eden. Far from those cute little babies depicted in Renaissance art, biblical cherubim are ferocious, sword-wielding creatures whose job is to protect or guard sacred sites or individuals (see Figure 3-1).

Figure 3-1:
The cherubs of the Bible are probably like this human-headed lion with eagle's wings that guarded the throne room of an Assyrian king.

©Preserving Bible Times with permission of The British Museum

God's concern that humans might return to Eden raises a final question as we prepare to exit Paradise: According to the Bible, can someone, theoretically, ever return to the Garden of Eden in order to find and eat from the fruit of the Tree of Life? The answer is both yes and no. In the Hebrew Bible, the Tree of Life would later be associated with God's wisdom, which humans can pursue and achieve if they work at it and are so inclined. In the New Testament, the Tree of Life reappears in the eventual coming "Kingdom of God," where everything will be restored to perfection. Accessibility to the *first* tree, however, is out of the realm of possibility, according to the Bible.

Chapter 4

The Fallout from "The Fall" (Genesis 4–11)

In This Chapter

▶ Exploring the origins of sibling rivalry

▶ Surviving the genealogical lists in the Bible

▶ Understanding why God would destroy His own creation

▶ Explaining the reasons for cultural diversity in the world

*T*heologians have long debated the exact repercussions of Adam and Eve's choice to eat from the Tree of the Knowledge of Good and Evil (see Chapter 3). Did their disobedience set a bad example that the rest of humanity has followed ever since? Or did something irreparable happen to human nature that now makes us rebellious toward God (the ultimate authority figure) and alienated toward one another? Whatever the exact answer, things certainly go from bad to worse after Adam and Eve's fateful decision.

In this chapter, we trace the effects of "The Fall" (as theologians have called it) on the generations following Adam and Eve — from the rivalry between the first two siblings to humanity's corporate rebellion at the Tower of Babel.

The First Sibling Rivalry: Cain and Abel (Genesis 4)

Shortly after being cast out of the Garden, Adam and Eve have their first two children: Cain and Abel. Cain, the oldest, is "a tiller of the ground" (farmer) while Abel is "a keeper of flocks" (shepherd). Eventually, these two brothers bring an offering before God. For Cain, the natural choice is the produce from the ground, whereas for Abel, his offering comes from the flocks. All seems to be going fine, and then something goes terribly wrong.

Offering the first sacrifices

In a somewhat cryptic passage, the Bible says, "The LORD looked favorably upon Abel and his offering, but not on Cain and his offering" (Genesis 4:4–5). The reason for God's preference for Abel's offering from his flocks is unclear. Some scholars have suggested that God's favoritism reflects a preference for a migratory pastoral lifestyle over a settled agrarian existence. And, in seeming confirmation of this interpretation, Cain, who will soon be the first murderer, will go on to build the first city (Genesis 4:17). Yet, others have suggested that this "pastoral-agricultural" reading of the Cain and Abel story is too narrow to do justice to the Bible's universal themes of righteousness and justice. According to these interpreters, the key to understanding why Abel's sacrifice was preferred over Cain's is found in the language used to describe both offerings.

In the case of Cain, the Bible says that he "brought to the LORD *an* offering of the produce from the ground" (Genesis 4:3), without giving any specific description of the relative value of this produce. In Abel's case, however, the text goes out of its way to explain that he brought "the firstborn of his flock, including their fat portions." Now to the modern ear, firstborn and fat portions may not mean much. But to the ancient ear, the firstborn of one's flock meant both one's best and, as the word implies, one's firstborn — that is, the *only* one born at the time of the offering. This act of sacrificing a "firstling," as it is sometimes called, would demonstrate one's belief that God would provide more "where that came from." Fat portions, although perhaps offending the more fit-minded among us, also were thought to be among the choicest parts of an animal in the ancient world. (And, after all, fat doesn't have the same effect on God as it does on humans.)

That Cain's sacrifice may be a reflection of a deeper attitude problem seems confirmed by his response to the realization that God preferred Abel's sacrifice above his: "Cain became very angry, and his countenance fell" (Genesis 4:5). God, in demonstration of His care for humankind, personally approaches Cain and gives him a warning: "If you do what is right, will you not be accepted? But if you do not do what is right, sin is crouching at your door, and its desire is for you; but you must rule over it" (Genesis 4:7). Apparently, the introduction of the knowledge of good and evil into the world has made evil a clear and present danger to humanity, as it even "crouches at your door." Everyone is obligated, therefore, to be on guard and to struggle to overcome evil when it attacks. Cain fails in both regards.

Inviting Abel out into a field, Cain strikes his brother and kills him. Hence, the first sibling rivalry (of which there would be plenty more) ends in disaster and initiates the proceedings of the first murder trial.

Solving the first murder mystery

Shortly after Cain commits this act of murder, God shows up on the scene. Like any good detective, God begins by asking questions. And, as you may suspect, God prefers the straightforward approach: "Where is your brother Abel?" Readers of the Bible have long queried over God's question. First of all, does God not know where Abel is? And second of all, why does God say "your brother Abel"? God merely needed to say, "Where's your brother?" or "Where's Abel?" or even "Where's the other guy?"

Regarding God's question asking: As we observe with Cain's parents, Adam and Eve (see Chapter 3), God already knows the answers to the questions He asks. His questions seek to give humans an opportunity to come clean. Regarding God's redundancy: God often spells out the exact relationship of one person to another when addressing moral issues because, according to the biblical authors, distrust, alienation, and murder result when people forget their relationship to one another. In this case, God is trying to bring home the gravity of Cain's crime: Killing one's brother is a very personal and tragic act, impacting not only the dead but also the living.

Am I my brother's keeper?

Cain doesn't miss out on the gravity of God's question, as his response reveals: "I don't know, am I my brother's keeper?" (Genesis 4:9). This question, intended as an escape clause, is perhaps one of the most profound teachings in the Bible. The answer is yes! We are our "brother's keeper," and we must do all that we can to protect and assist our fellow human beings in their journey through this life.

Demonstrating that God already knew the answer to His own question, He confronts Cain in his lie: "What have you done? Listen, your brother's blood is crying out to me from the ground!" God gives a gripping description of murder. Although the person is gone, the effects of his death live on in this world, and, in the case of foul play, his murder cries out for justice.

Man on the run: Cain's curse

Similar to God's judgment on Adam and Eve, God curses Cain by telling him that he'll be alienated from the very ground that "opened its mouth to receive your brother's blood." That is, the soil will no longer yield its produce to Cain because he has polluted the ground with his brother's blood. (This pollution becomes important later; see the section, "Understanding why God would destroy His creation," later in this chapter.) Cain's plea is ironic: "My punishment is too great for me! Today, You have driven me away from the soil, and I will be hidden from Your face. I will be a fugitive and a wanderer on the earth, and anyone who finds me will kill me!" (Genesis 4:13–14).

Where did Cain get his wife?

Genesis 4:17 says that Cain "lay with his wife, and she conceived and gave birth to Enoch." But up until this point the only people mentioned as existing are Adam, Eve, and Cain (Cain's brother, Abel, is murdered just before this notice). So where did Cain get his wife? Although the Bible doesn't say explicitly, Genesis 5:3–4 says that Adam and Eve had a lot of other sons and daughters. Combined with the longevity of life during this time (see "Living long in the ancient world," later in this chapter), the earth's population would truly "explode." Thus, the biblical author seems to have in mind that Cain marries one of his relatives. (Incest, it seems, is not an issue at this point in the biblical text because the law forbidding incest has not yet been given.)

Cain is concerned that he'll be murdered. But he's a murderer! So we may expect God to say, "Tough luck! Eye for an eye, tooth for a tooth. You killed, and so you should be killed. It's only fair." But, notably, God expresses mercy, even in the face of judgment: "May it not be so! Whoever kills Cain will suffer seven-fold for their deed" (Genesis 4:15). God takes the added precaution of placing a mark on Cain so that anyone seeing him will leave him alone. What this mark is remains a mystery. Some have suggested that the mark is circumcision, although how anyone would know Cain is circumcised now that humans wear clothes is an even bigger mystery. ("Whoa! Okay, okay, I won't kill you.")

As an example of how the biblical text has been misused over the centuries, supporters of slavery suggested that Cain's "mark" was dark skin, and that his "curse" was the lot of all his descendants. This interpretation has significant problems, not the least of which is *absolutely nothing in the text even remotely supports it*. But beyond this minor interpretational barrier, Cain's "mark," whatever it may be, is a sign of protection, not oppression.

Tracing Your Family Tree: The First (of Many) Biblical Genealogies (Genesis 5)

In Genesis 5, you encounter what is perhaps one of the most vicious, merciless creatures in the entire Bible. We refer, of course, to the dreaded "who begat whom" lists. Actually, you come across these genealogical monsters not only in Genesis 5, but in many places throughout the Bible, leading people to ask, "Why would the biblical authors waste so much precious space on such trivialities?" And perhaps more importantly, "Should I read them?"

The reason the Bible preserves so many genealogies is because in ancient Israel (as in many cultures both then and now), family lineage or clan affiliation is essential for knowing one's place in the world. This concept is most obvious in the case of royalty, where one's connection to the royal family can produce significant benefits (or, in the case of certain royal families, significant detriments). In ancient Israel, the priesthood was also hereditary, as were inheritance rights and territorial claims. Therefore, careful preservation of one's family line was essential for securing rights and wealth for oneself and one's descendants.

Beyond their value for ancient Israel, the Bible's genealogies sometimes convey important information about the biblical authors' beliefs and values. For example, in Genesis 5, amidst all the "who begat whoms," we read:

> *When Enoch had lived 65 years, he became the father of Methuselah. Enoch walked with God after the birth of Methuselah for 300 years, and had other sons and daughters. Thus, all the days of Enoch were 365 years. Enoch walked with God, and then he was no more, because God took him.*
>
> —Genesis 5:21–24

Most interpreters understand the notice that "Enoch walked with God" to be a euphemism for "having a close relationship with" and "obeying" God. That is, the purpose of this particular genealogical notice is to make a theological point: God rewards those who seek to know Him and do what He commands. So what is Enoch's reward? Although some scholars have suggested that "God took him" simply means that Enoch died (hardly a reward for walking with God), most scholars agree that this phrase means that Enoch went to heaven. (In Trek-talk, God "beamed him up.")

Living long in the ancient world

Beyond Enoch's mysterious disappearance, the genealogies in Genesis 5 contain another peculiarity: Everyone is living sooo long. For example, look at the longevity of Enoch's son, Methuselah who lives 969 years! That's not bad. Methuselah is, in fact, the oldest person recorded in the Bible. Yet, this longevity may lead you to ask: "Are these human years or dog years or what?" Most likely, the biblical authors intend these years to be "normal" human years or, more precisely, lunisolar years, which are determined by counting both the sun and moon cycles. This leaves you anywhere from 5 to 11 days short for every solar year, but that's hardly anything when talking about such large numbers (actually, it's quite a bit when talking about such large numbers, but you know what we mean).

Now, we say that Methuselah is the oldest person *in the Bible* because, in ancient Mesopotamia, there existed legends of people who lived tens of thousands of years. These people, or "kings" as they're (justifiably) called, are said to have lived before the Flood, which is precisely when the Bible also says human life expectancy was unusually high.

Had you skipped the genealogical list in Genesis 5, you would've missed the hidden "theological treasure" of Enoch's life and mysterious disappearance. However, if you read every word of every genealogical list in the Bible, you'd soon feel yourself becoming overwhelmed by these monsters, or worse, bored by them. Our recommendation, then, is that you skim genealogical lists for any hidden treasures, but don't linger in them too long, or they may lure you into their lair!

Deluge-ional Ideas: Noah and the Flood (Genesis 6–9)

It's interesting that the most popular décor for a baby's room is one of the most disturbing events recorded in the Bible: the Flood. Admittedly, pictures of colorful zoo animals filing into a boat two-by-two with a rainbow-filled background makes for cute wallpaper and bed sheets, but the biblical description of the events surrounding the Flood is anything but "cute." For example, concerning human behavior before the Flood, the Bible says, "The wickedness of humankind was great on the earth, and every inclination of the thoughts of their hearts was on evil continually" (Genesis 6:5). That's not cute. But it gets worse. Because of this increase in evil, God decides to completely destroy all living creatures on earth. Now, that's really not cute. But the Flood narrative isn't all doom and gloom.

The first "survivors"

God makes some exceptions to His plan of complete destruction. There is someone on the earth who, like Enoch before him, walked with God: Noah. Because Noah is "righteous in his generation," God decides to spare him and his family, and, therefore, He instructs Noah to build a giant ark. Now most representations of Noah's ark show a medium-sized boat with animals milling about on top of the deck. However, Noah doesn't build a boat; he builds an *ark,* which is an antiquated English word for box or chest. And this is a good translation of the Hebrew word *'aron* because God commissions Noah to build a giant rectangular box in which to ride out the storm.

According to the biblical text, the ark was 300 cubits long, 50 cubits wide, and 30 cubits high. A *cubit* is an ancient measurement that, although later standardized, was originally determined by measuring the distance from the end of the elbow to the tip of the fingers (kind of like when a foot used to really mean a foot). The distance from elbow to fingertip is 18 inches on the "average" full-grown man. (Try it. You'll be amazed.) Therefore, the dimensions of the ark work out to about 450 feet long, 75 feet wide, and 45 feet high.

Who are the Nephilim?

According to Genesis 6, contributing to the wickedness leading up to the Flood is that "the sons of God" cohabitate with "the daughters of humans" and produce a race of "mighty heroes" called Nephilim. So who are the Nephilim? The answer to this question depends on who the "sons of God" are. Sometimes *sons of God* in the Bible denotes humans who have a special relationship with God. Therefore, some scholars believe the Nephilim are simply the offspring of some exceptional men, perhaps even the descendants of Seth, Adam and Eve's son who replaces the righteous Abel. Most often, however, *sons of God* means angels. Therefore, many scholars believe that the Nephilim are the offspring of angelic and human cohabitation (much like the Greek Titans). Whatever the exact meaning of *sons of God*, the result of this union is a race of humans that, according to a later report (Numbers 13), makes grown men look like insects. Although this comparison seems a purposeful exaggeration, the Nephilim were exceptionally big, which explains their status as "mighty heroes."

In addition, the ark has three levels, so this vessel has a lot of cubic storage space. And Noah and his family need that space because God asks them to bring "seven pairs of every kind of clean animal, and one pair of every kind of unclean animal." (You can check out Chapter 7 for all the details about "clean" and "unclean" animals. For now, we'll just say this isn't a reference to their bathing habits, but rather whether they're fit for human consumption and divine sacrifice.) The reason for needing more clean animals than unclean animals is quite simple: There's going to be a barbeque (read: sacrifice) after the Flood, and if you have only one pair of an animal, and you kill one, then . . . you get the idea.

Soon, the ark is finished, and Noah, his three sons (Shem, Ham, and Japheth), his wife, and his sons' wives climb aboard.

A three-hour tour . . . not!

Soon after Noah, his family, and the animals are aboard the ark, the storm begins. This rain is no spring shower, however. It's a deluge, where God opens the "floodgates of heaven" and the "springs of the deep." This represents an undoing of the created order God established "in the beginning" when He separated the "waters above from the waters below," creating a space called "sky." As evidence of the intensity of this deluge, it lasts *only* "forty days and forty nights," but the water doesn't recede to reveal dry land for over a year. During this time, we're to imagine Noah and his family taking care of the animals (don't worry, they packed food).

Searching for Noah's ark

Numerous expeditions have climbed Mount Ararat in search of Noah's ark, with some people even claiming to have seen it! Yet, whether this is actually the mountain and whether the ark could have survived to the present day are questions that perhaps only Indiana Jones could answer. However, you can be certain that if someone claims to have seen the ark and then goes on to describe what sounds a lot like a boat, he or she is either lying or was hallucinating at the nearly 17,000-foot elevation.

The waters subside, and the ark eventually comes to rest on Mount Ararat, which is identified today with a mountain on the border of eastern Turkey and Armenia. Having landed safely on dry ground, Noah sends out birds (first a raven, then a dove) to see if enough dry land has appeared to safely leave the ark. After a couple tries with the dove, it returns with a freshly plucked olive leaf in its beak. (The image of a dove with a leaf in its mouth has since become a universal symbol of peace.) On the third try, the dove doesn't return. Noah now knows it is safe to leave the ark, and, at God's command, he, his family, and the animals disembark. Noah worships God by offering a sacrifice.

Understanding why God would destroy His creation

Shortly after the Flood, God gives Noah some good news and some bad news. First, the good news: "I will never again curse the earth . . . nor will I destroy every living creature as I have done" (Genesis 8:21). Now the bad news: "for the inclination of the human heart is evil from its youth." In other words, the human condition hasn't changed as a result of the Flood. Just as every inclination of the human heart was evil before the Flood, so it is after the Flood. So if evil will still exist, why did God send the Flood?

The purpose of the Flood seems to be related to God's "good news" item. The earth was "cursed" before the Flood. Why? Just as when Cain killed his brother Abel and the "earth received his blood," the Bible says that after Cain's time, "violence increased on the earth," and, therefore, the earth took in a lot more blood. By sending the Flood, God not only judges humankind for its wrongdoings, He cleanses the soil of its pollution. In short, God is being presented as the great Cosmic Ecologist, who cleans up the earth from the damage caused by human sin. This motive for the Flood also explains the *commandment*, or mandate, God gives to Noah after the Flood:

> *Whoever sheds the blood of a human, by a human shall his blood be shed.*

—Genesis 9:6

Not only does the earth have a clean start, but humans do, too, and they're to deal more severely with murderers than God did with Cain. The ultimate reason for this commandment is tied to humankind's being created in the divine image: "For in His own image did God make humankind." Thus, to kill another human is to rob the world of a little bit of God's presence.

The Noahic Covenant

God's promise not to destroy the earth ever again is called a covenant. A *covenant* is a contract or agreement that obligates one or more parties to perform certain duties. In this particular covenant, called the Noahic Covenant, God's duty is not to destroy the earth again. As a sign of His promise, He places the rainbow in the sky. Humankind's responsibility is not to give God a reason to *want* to destroy the earth again. Fair enough.

God also enacts the following changes after the Flood:

- ✔ First, humankind's life expectancy will decrease until it levels off at about a maximum of 120 years. This shortening of human life is presented as an act of God's mercy in light of humankind's tendency toward evil. The shorter humans live, the less evil they can commit.

- ✔ Second, humans are now allowed to eat meat. Perhaps we're to see in this change a certain "nutritional" purpose because the natural order and the human constitution have undergone significant changes (embodied in human's decreasing life expectancy). Now, humans need more protein.

- ✔ Third, and corresponding to the previous change, animals are given a natural fear of humankind. Apparently, before now, animals and humans lived in relatively peaceful coexistence. Now, however, animals will have the instinct to flee the dangers of humankind (and for good reason).

Sign of things to come: Ham's curse

That humankind really hasn't changed after the Flood becomes evident even during Noah's life. Noah plants a vineyard, makes wine, becomes exceedingly drunk, takes off his clothes, and passes out on his bed. One of Noah's sons — Ham, by name — happens in upon his father and sees his father's nakedness. However, rather than cover his father, Ham goes out and tells his brothers, Shem and Japheth, about their father's condition. His brothers treat the situation with more delicacy by walking backward with a garment between them and covering their naked father. When Noah awakens and finds out what Ham did to him, he becomes angry and says, "Cursed be Canaan, lowest of slaves he shall be to his brothers" (Genesis 9:25).

The universality of universal flood stories

Stories of a catastrophic flood inundating the whole earth were common in the ancient world. The most notable comparison with the Bible's account is that found in the Mesopotamian tale of Atrahasis, and retold in part in the *Epic of Gilgamesh*. In the account given there, the gods decide to wipe out humankind because they made too much noise, making it difficult for the gods to sleep. (If you have noisy neighbors who play their stereo until "ungodly" hours in the morning, you can appreciate the gods' frustration.) The "Noah-figure" in these Mesopotamian accounts, whose name is given variously as Ziusudra, Atrahasis, and Utnapishtim, is warned by one of the gods of humankind's impending doom, and tells him to build a "box" (in this account, it is truly a cube-shaped box). Other similarities include sending out birds to see if there's dry land, landing on a mountain, and offering a sacrifice to the gods.

One difference, however, is that the Mesopotamian flood hero not only saves his family and the animals, but also some artisans and musicians, lest human culture should also perish in the flood. Another difference is that the gods, thinking they actually succeeded in killing all humankind, become frightened and angry, for now there is no one around to feed them. When they smell the flood hero's sacrifice, the text says that, having become so famished, they swarm around the meat like flies. Whew!

You may ask, "Canaan? Who's Canaan? And why is he cursed and not Ham?" Canaan is Ham's son, and one reason Canaan is cursed and not Ham is because, in the ancient world, one's blessedness or well-being was intimately connected to the well-being of one's descendants. The worst possible judgment one could imagine was that your bad behavior would affect your descendants. Of course, we hardly need to be convinced that one generation's sins affect future generations. However, the Bible gives concrete expression to this notion of "generational effects" through cursing one's descendants.

Yet, Noah's words also would have tremendous meaning to an ancient Israelite listening to this narrative centuries later. The Israelites lived in a land called "Canaan" — some of the inhabitants of which were their servants. As the Israelites thought themselves descendants of Shem, Noah's curse had come to fruition in their own time. This bad outcome isn't all because of Ham's actions, however. According to the Bible, the Canaanites will commit many more serious crimes than Ham, and it's for those sins that the Canaanites are ultimately judged. However, Ham gets the ball rolling.

Say What?! The Tower of Babel and the Birth of Nations (Genesis 10–11)

From Noah's sons and daughters-in-law the earth is again repopulated, in fulfillment of God's commandment to "be fruitful and multiply" (the one commandment God never rebukes humankind for not obeying). In Genesis 10, we see an account of where Noah's sons' descendants eventually end up:

- ✔ Shem's descendants settled mostly in the region of Mesopotamia.

- ✔ Ham's descendants settled largely in the areas of Canaan, Egypt, and northern Africa.

- ✔ Japheth's descendants were a bit more mobile, going west into Asia Minor (modern-day Turkey), Greece, and other parts of central Europe.

But Shem's, Ham's, and Japheth's descendants do not willingly "spread out over the face of the earth," as God had commanded them. This forces God to shake things up a bit.

Building the Tower of Babel

According to the Bible, Shem's, Ham's, and Japheth's descendants settle together in the region of Shinar (ancient Sumer) and begin building a city (eventually called Babel) and a tower (to be named the Tower of Babel) "with its top reaching into the heavens." Some interpreters have understood this notice to mean that the inhabitants of this city are attempting to invade heaven. This does not seem to be the case, however, because the Hebrew word for heaven (*shammayim*) most often means "sky." That is, they're just building a very high tower. The type of tower the biblical author has in mind is likely the *ziggurat*, which were widespread throughout Mesopotamia. At the top of these stepped towers was a palace or temple to a god (see Figure 4-1). Therefore, the inhabitants of this city seem to compound their disobedience of not spreading out by building a temple to another god.

Figure 4-1:
The Tower of Babel described by the Bible probably looked something like this ziggurat.

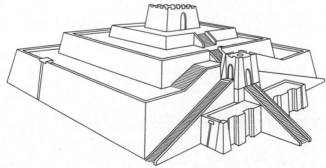

 One clear but subtle offense has to do with the inhabitants' own words, "Let us make a name for ourselves." This city and tower are ultimately for their own reputation and praise — a sort of deification of themselves. In response, God confuses their language, and soon, the inhabitants are unable to communicate with one another, forcing them to stop construction on the tower and scatter across the face of the earth (as God originally had commanded them). The city is given the name Babel because it is here that God *confuses* (Hebrew *balal*) humanity's language. This word play has even carried over into English, where "babble" means to speak incomprehensibly.

Making a name for yourself

Immediately after the Tower of Babel incident, the narrative shifts to one of those dangerous "who begat whom lists," taking us from Shem, Noah's eldest son, to one of the most important figures in the Bible: Abraham. You can read all about Abraham in Chapter 5, but for now, you don't want to miss this genealogy (really, this isn't just a couple of demented biblical scholars trying to draw you into our obsession). With this genealogy, the author makes an important theological point by way of word play. The Hebrew word for "name" is *shem*. So, by placing the lineage of Shem, which will culminate in Abraham, immediately after the inhabitants of Babel's failed attempt at making a shem (name) for themselves, the biblical author is arguing that a really great name comes at God's initiative and from doing what He commands. Confirming that the author is making this point is that he follows Shem's lineage with God's call to Abraham, which reads:

> *Go from your country . . . and I will make your name (shem) great!*

> —Genesis 12:1–2

And that is precisely what God does. But for that part of the adventure, you have to read Chapter 5 of this book.

I'm so confused! Babbling in Babylon

What isn't obvious in most translations of the Bible is that the word for Babel in the tower story is the same word that is translated later in the Bible as *Babylonia*. That is, an Israelite hearing the story of the Tower of Babel (Babylonia) would not miss its significance. This event took place in the same region where Babylon (a country that eventually would be a major political player during Israel's later history) would arise. Moreover, this would also be the place from which the founder of the Israelite people would come; namely, Abraham. Yet, as you may imagine, the Babylonians didn't understand their name to mean "confusion." In fact, in Akkadian, the language of Babylonia, it didn't. Babylon or Babel means "gateway of god." So, to the Babylonians, their name meant something far nobler. However, to the monotheistic authors of the Bible, Babylonia, and all that it represented, was a source of confusion.

Chapter 5

The Babylonian Hillbillies: The Adventures of Abraham and His Family (Genesis 12–25:18)

In This Chapter

▶ Discovering why God chose Abraham from all the people of the world

▶ Walking with Abraham and Sarah on the road to being blessed

▶ Understanding the sins of Sodom and Gomorrah

▶ Meeting the founding ancestor of the Muslim religion: Ishmael

▶ Finding out the Bible's definition of "the good life"

▶ Contemplating why God asked Abraham to sacrifice his son

*T*he Beverly Hillbillies is a "story 'bout a man named Jed," who struck it rich when his errant gunshot uncovered a vast oil reserve on his property. Soon, Jed and his family were off to Beverly Hills, California, where they would begin to live a life of plenty with their newfound millions.

In at least its basic outline, Jed's rags to riches tale isn't too unlike the biblical story of Abraham (or Abram, as he is called when we first meet him). Only, unlike Jed, this transformation is no accident. Abraham strikes it rich one day when God appears to him and asks him to play a leading role in the human drama unfolding on the world's stage. Heeding God's call, Abraham sets out on the journey of a lifetime — a journey that literally changes the world because from his descendants (both physical and spiritual), three of the world's major religions emerge: Judaism, Christianity, and Islam.

In this chapter, you look at Abraham's life and what it is about this "father of three faiths" that has left such an indelible mark on the religious landscape of our world.

Striking It Rich: God Calls Abraham

To understand Abraham's life, as well as the rest of the Bible, we need to listen in on God's first conversation with Abraham:

> The LORD said to Abram, "Go for yourself, from your country and your kindred and your father's house, to the land that I will show you. I will make you a great nation, and I will bless you and make your name great so that you will be a blessing. I will bless those who bless you, and I will curse those who curse you. And in you all the families of the earth will be blessed."
>
> —Genesis 12:1–3

That's quite a call! And God reiterates this promise on several occasions. While the list varies slightly each time, the basic components stay the same.

God promises Abraham that his descendants will

- Become a great nation
- Live in a bountiful land
- Be blessed
- Be a blessing to all the families of the earth

In demonstration of his faith, Abraham obeys God's call to leave his homeland, setting out on a most excellent adventure.

Accompanying Abraham on his momentous journey are his wife Sarah (or Sarai, when we first meet her), their nephew Lot, their servants, and all their belongings. At the time of their departure, Abraham is 75 years old, and Sarah is 65. Now, before you begin making plans to start your own nation in retirement, Abraham and Sarah will live to be 175 and 127, respectively. So perhaps we are to imagine them as being a little more "vigorous" (*sans* Viagra) than the average retiree. Yet, despite their vigor, Sarah is childless, a dilemma that will weigh heavy on her and Abraham's minds as they contemplate God's promise of numerous descendants.

If you're reading along in the Bible, you may notice that Abraham is initially called Abram and Sarah is called Sarai. Don't be confused. These are the same two people. God changes Abram's name, which means "exalted father," to Abraham, which means "father of many" in Genesis 17. This new name is quite appropriate because, in this same chapter, God promises Abraham a son (Isaac), whose descendants will one day give birth to a nation (Israel). The significance of Sarah's name change isn't quite as apparent because both Sarah and Sarai seem to mean "princess," although Sarah might be a title suggesting greater authority, such as "queen."

Abraham's Most Excellent Adventure to Canaan and Egypt (Genesis 12)

Abraham and his entourage travel along the well-worn Fertile Crescent that runs from Mesopotamia to Egypt, eventually stopping in Canaan at a place called Shechem (see Figure 5-1). Once at Shechem God appears to Abraham and tells him this is the land his descendants will inherit. In response, Abraham builds an altar — the first of many he will build in this new "Promised Land."

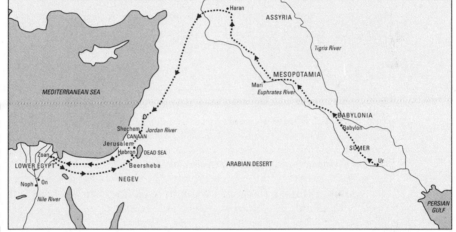

Figure 5-1: Abraham and Sarah's travels take them along the Fertile Crescent.

Abraham's initial stay in his Promised Land is actually quite short because a severe famine forces the people of Canaan to go to Egypt to find food. As Abraham and Sarah approach Egypt, Abraham realizes that, given Sarah's extreme beauty, the Egyptians might try to kill him to take her. You may be thinking, "She's 65 years old! And this was before Oil of Olay! How beautiful could she be?!" Actually, plenty of 65-year-olds in this world are beautiful. Moreover, Sarah is going to live to be over twice her present age, so we should probably imagine her to still look rather "young for her age."

In light of the present danger, Abraham says to Sarah: "Tell them you are my sister, and then it will go well with me." You may be asking, "But isn't that a lie?! What kind of role model is this?" Actually, this won't be the last time Abraham tries this "wife-sister act." In Genesis 20, Abraham tells a Philistine king, Abimelech of Gerar, that Sarah is his sister. To Abraham's credit, in this second wife-sister act we find out that Abraham is not a total liar, as Sarah is actually his half-sister, making what he says only a "half-lie" or, if you are an optimist, a "half-truth." But still, this behavior isn't very admirable. So, what's going on here?

Although later tradition would ascribe numerous noble acts to Abraham before he is called by God, the Bible doesn't indicate that there was anything particularly special about Abraham or any of his descendants that made God choose them. God seems to choose Abraham "just because." Yet, before you start thinking that character doesn't count, the Bible makes clear that God wants — even commands — that people do what's right, love their neighbors, tell the truth, pay their taxes (yes, sorry, that one's in the Bible, too). Moreover, before Abraham's death, he will be a changed man, trusting God with the impossible. But God's choice of Abraham "just because" is part of another message of the Bible: God is gracious and forgiving.

Despite the moral ambiguities of what her husband asks her to do, Sarah complies by telling the Egyptians that she is indeed Abraham's sister. The ruse works, and Pharaoh (the king of Egypt) welcomes Sarah into his harem. Abraham, for his good luck in having such a beautiful "sister," is rewarded by Pharaoh with all kinds of wealth and livestock.

Yet, the party is soon over when God sends "great plagues" against Egypt and Pharaoh realizes that he's done something wrong, and that this "something" has to do with Sarah. Summoning Abraham into his presence, Pharaoh asks him sternly, "What is this you have done to me? Why didn't you tell me she was your wife? Why did you say 'She is my sister', so that I took her to be my wife?" Without waiting for an answer (one of the perks of being a king), Pharaoh sends Abraham and Sarah on their way, allowing them to leave with all the wealth Abraham had accumulated while in Egypt — which just goes to show you, *it pays to lie*. Just kidding. Actually, what *does* this show us?

One reason Abraham and Sarah leave Egypt with great riches is that God has promised to bless Abraham. Although God may not approve of Abraham's ruse, He's not going to rescind His promise. Another reason Abraham and Sarah make out like bandits is that many of the events of their lives have meaning beyond their lives. In this particular case, Abraham and Sarah's sojourn to Egypt points forward to Israel's later slavery in Egypt where they will also be delivered by plagues and leave with great riches.

Abraham and Lot (Genesis 13–14)

Even though Abraham is willing to tell half-truths to others about his exact relationship with his wife, Abraham has several moral highlights in his early career of following God. Two of these moral moments occur in connection with his nephew, Lot, and give us a glimpse into the potential that God may have seen when He first called Abraham.

> ✔ **Abraham's generosity toward Lot:** Shortly after returning from Egypt, Abraham's and Lot's shepherds begin fighting over land rights. In an expression of exceptional deference, Abraham invites Lot to choose whatever real estate looks best to him. Whatever is left, Abraham says,

he will take. Lot chooses the beautiful, well-watered plains of Sodom and Gomorrah. Unfortunately, Lot doesn't realize that property values in this area are about to take a big hit because God will soon destroy these cities for their wickedness. But, without consulting a real estate agent, Lot takes his flocks and family, and they move to the region of Sodom and Gomorrah. It's no coincidence that after Abraham "gives away" part of his Promised Land, God appears to him again and says:

Lift up your eyes from where you are, and look north, south, east, and west. All the land that you see I will give to you and your descendants forever.

—Genesis 13:14–15

As the Bible says elsewhere, "Give, and you shall receive."

✓ **Abraham rescues Lot:** Abraham's second "moral moment" involving Lot occurs when Lot's new neighborhood becomes the stage for a massive battle between several warring kingdoms, and many of the inhabitants of Sodom, including Lot and his family, are taken away as war booty. When Abraham finds out about his nephew's demise, he gathers a band of warriors and rescues Lot, his family, and the others taken in battle, as well as all their stuff.

So, Abraham, like most uncles, is a decent guy after you get past his faults.

Melchizedek: The mysterious priest-king

While Abraham is heading home after rescuing his nephew Lot (Genesis 14), he is met by a very mysterious man, whose name is Melchizedek and who is both the priest and king of the nearby city of Salem. Without a word, this "priest-king" takes out some bread and wine and blesses Abraham. In response, Abraham gives Melchizedek a tenth of all he had gained in the battle when saving Lot. And that's it. End of story. So, who is this shadowy figure, and what's going on?

Later passages in the Hebrew Bible equate Melchizedek with God's promise to Israel that He would one day establish an eternal priesthood. (This promise was particularly comforting for Israel after the destruction of Jerusalem and the Temple.) Within Christian tradition, Melchizedek prefigures Jesus, who similarly initiates a feast involving bread and wine (the

so-called Lord's Supper or Eucharist), and who is presented as both a king (a descendant of King David) and a priest (offering the ultimate sacrifice: his life for the sins of the world).

In the more immediate context, however, Abraham's encounter with Melchizedek, like his experience in Egypt, seems to foreshadow Israel's future. Salem (Hebrew for "peace") is later equated with Jerusalem (Hebrew for "City of Peace"), the future capital of ancient Israel, and the city where both the *king* and *high priest* of Israel would one day reside. In addition, Abraham's giving Melchizedek a tenth of his war spoils seems to be a model for later Israel to follow in its own giving to God. In fact, this story, along with other biblical passages, are often used to set the modern-day standard of tithing. (A *tithe* is a contribution to God of one-tenth of your earnings.)

Cutting a Deal: The Abrahamic Covenant (Genesis 15–17)

Although God called Abraham, and has made several promises to him, He has yet to finalize the deal with a contract, or what the Bible calls a *covenant*. Abraham actually gets two "signed" contracts from God.

When you wish upon a star: Abraham's numerous descendants

In Genesis 15, God reiterates His promise to Abraham to give him numerous descendants, land, and blessings. But Abraham has heard this promise before, and points out to God an obvious flaw in the contract: "You have yet to give me any offspring." In response, God tells Abraham to step outside so He can teach Abraham a lesson. Thankfully for Abraham, God does not intend to teach him a physical lesson, but a spiritual one. God asks Abraham to look into the sky: "Count the stars, if you can. So will your descendants be." Rather than start counting, "Abraham believed God, and it was reckoned to him as righteousness" (Genesis 15:6). That is, because Abraham believed that God would come through on His promise, God considered Abraham morally upright, despite his many failings.

In the New Testament, the apostle Paul points to this episode of stargazing, and says that just as Abraham was considered righteous because he believed God, so all who wish to be righteous in God's eyes must do so "through faith, and not by works of the law" (Romans 3:28; 4:1–5).

God is now ready to "cut the deal," literally, as He asks Abraham to gather some animals and cut them in half, with their two halves facing each other. What's with the animals? In the ancient world, sacrifices often accompanied covenant ceremonies, not merely as an offering to God (or the gods), but as a symbolic gesture to say, "May I be like these animals should I not live up to my end of this agreement." In fact, the Hebrew word for "to make" a covenant (*karat*) is literally "to cut" a covenant.

Once the animals are prepared, God applies His anesthesiological skills on Abraham, causing him to fall into a deep sleep. While Abraham is "under," God tells him that his descendants will be enslaved for 400 years, but will eventually be delivered from their bondage by miraculous signs. This prediction refers to Israel's exodus from Egypt, and further confirms that during Abraham's life many of Israel's future experiences are foreshadowed.

Taking matters into your own hands: Hagar and Ishmael

Despite now having a "signed" contract, Abraham and Sarah begin to doubt whether God intends to provide a son for them through Sarah. As a result, Sarah offers Abraham her maidservant, an Egyptian named Hagar, saying, "Go, sleep with my handmaid — perhaps I can build a family through her." (In the ancient world, it was not uncommon in cases of barrenness for a man to bear children through a surrogate mother or concubine.) Abraham agrees.

When Hagar sees that she has conceived a child, she begins to despise Sarah, apparently feeling superior to her mistress for being able to become pregnant. Sarah, in turn, treats Hagar harshly, and Hagar runs away. Yet, in keeping with God's compassionate nature, He finds Hagar, desperate and alone, and, via an angel (the word angel means "messenger"), tells her to return to Sarah. Moreover, the angel tells Hagar that she, too, will have countless descendants. Finally, the angel tells her to name her son Ishmael, because "the LORD has heard your affliction." This is wordplay, as Ishmael means "God will hear," and it has been this conviction — that God hears the cries of the afflicted — that has led many throughout history to help those in need.

Cutting another deal: The Abrahamic Covenant of Circumcision

When you've been promised numerous descendants but have no children to show for it, you need reassurance that the deal is still on, especially as you get well into your nineties. And this is exactly what God gives Abraham and Sarah when He again appears to Abraham to reiterate His promise, only this time He adds (or really, "takes away") a little something:

> *Every male among you, when he is eight days old, must be circumcised.*
>
> —Genesis 17:10

Biblical circumcision is the process of cutting away part of the foreskin on the penis. (Ouch.) And lest we think that Abraham is excluded from this procedure because he is more than 8 days old, God makes it clear that there is no grandfather clause in this contract. In obedience to God's command, Abraham is circumcised, as is every male in his household — and many Jews, Christians, and Muslims have followed suit ever since. (For more information about the major world religions, get a copy of *Religion For Dummies,* by Marc Gellman and Thomas Hartman, published by Wiley.)

Why circumcision is made part of the Abrahamic Covenant is not entirely clear, although many cultures believe that this act of "pruning" increases fertility, which is interesting considering God's words to Abraham in the context of this command: "I will make you very fruitful" (Genesis 17:6).

Abraham's Three Mysterious Visitors (Genesis 18)

One day, while Abraham is hanging out at his tent, three mysterious men appear. In keeping with the ancient rules of hospitality, Abraham rushes out to meet these strangers, insisting they stay awhile. The three visitors agree.

Entertaining angels unawares

While eating, the visitors ask Abraham where Sarah is. Perhaps a little perplexed that these strangers know his wife's name, Abraham informs them that she is in the tent. One of the visitors then announces, "I will come back next time this season, and Sarah your wife will have a son." Wow. For guys who just showed up on the scene, they are pretty well informed.

Sarah, hearing the stranger's prediction, laughs in disbelief. The visitor sharply rebukes Sarah saying, "Is anything too difficult for the LORD?" This interchange is important because it reminds the reader (and Sarah) that God can do anything. Moreover, Sarah's laughter will help God decide on a name for this little lad. (See "Abraham: Father of Many Nations . . . and Faiths" later in this chapter.)

So, who are these guys who show up at your doorstep unannounced, start talking to you as if they know you well, and then reveal intimate details about your life? Probably your in-laws. However, in the present narrative, the identity of these strangers is both obvious and mysterious. First the obvious part: After the announcement that Abraham and Sarah will have a son by next year, two of these visitors are called "angels," so that makes identifying them easy. "But," you may be thinking, "Wouldn't Abraham have noticed the wing-bulge under the angels' garments?" Actually, no.

When angels visit humans in the Bible, they often look just like humans. In fact, it seems that angels don't have wings at all. That is, the television series *Touched by an Angel* has it right: Gabriel, Michael, Monica, Andrew, Tess, and the rest of the angelic crew don't have wings. Having said that, there are some "species" of angelic beings, such as seraphim, who do have wings (seraphim have six wings!). However, these angels are usually portrayed as staying in heaven.

Abraham's third divine visitor is a little more mysterious. He speaks as though he is God, and he is even called "the LORD." Yet, other biblical passages say that no one can see God and live. So, who is this visitor?

✔ Some have suggested that this third visitor is merely an angel (don't ever say "merely an angel," however, to an angel). *Angel* means messenger; therefore, this angel speaks as though he is God, just as royal messengers would often speak in the person of the king.

✔ Later Christian tradition would equate this third visitor with Jesus, in what theologians call his "preincarnate state," which means, literally, "before having flesh" (that is, before becoming a baby in a manger).

✔ Still others have suggested that this third visitor *is* God, but in a less concentrated form, lest His presence cause "permanent" damage (that is, death). This concept is known as a *theophany* — an appearance of God, which can be in any form, though is usually humanlike.

Whoever this third visitor is, he has not only come to deliver a birth announcement, he has come to check on reports of trouble in the neighborhood — in particular, Lot's neighborhood: Sodom and Gomorrah.

Bargaining with God

After two of Abraham's divine visitors depart, the third visitor, speaking as though he is God, informs Abraham, "I have come down to see if the outcry that has come to Me is as bad as I've heard." By saying that God "came down" to look into Sodom and Gomorrah's crimes, the biblical author doesn't mean that God's vision was impaired from heaven. Rather, the Bible intends to communicate that God renders judgment only after carefully investigating a matter — thereby establishing the model for human behavior.

Abraham, however, is not yet convinced of God's justice, as his response reveals:

> *Far be it from You to do this thing — killing the righteous with the wicked, treating the righteous and the wicked the same! Far be it from You! Shall not the Judge of all the earth do justice?*

> —Genesis 18:25

This discussion is precisely the one God wants to have with Abraham, especially because his view of God will inform the views of many to follow.

Hospitality in the ancient world

Abraham's encounter with the three heavenly sojourners was the moment that nearly everyone in the ancient world lived for: Strangers that you entertained are actually divine visitors. In many cultures, it was (and is) believed that the gods visit humans from time to time to test their virtue. Therefore, if you shunned a stranger, you were taking a big risk (just ask the prince in *Beauty and the Beast*). This belief helped to ensure that wayfarers were well cared for while traveling, since you never knew whether a stranger might be someone important (say, a god or angel) in disguise.

As a further expression of God's concern that Abraham understand that He is just, God allows Abraham to engage Him in some bargaining. Abraham asks: "Suppose there are fifty righteous people within the city. Will You still wipe out the place and not forgive it for the sake of the fifty righteous in it?" God assures Abraham that He will not destroy Sodom and Gomorrah if He finds fifty righteous people there.

Abraham, perhaps feeling like he aimed too high in his bidding, keeps lowering the bid, first by fives and then by tens, eventually stopping at ten. With each bid, Gods responds, "Sure — for that number, I will not destroy the city." And God departs, having demonstrated to Abraham that whether or not Sodom and Gomorrah survive, He is willing to bargain if that helps others see Him for who He really is.

Fire and Brimstone: The Destruction of Sodom and Gomorrah (Genesis 19)

After God's and Abraham's collective-bargaining agreement, the scene shifts to Sodom, where the two angels are just arriving at the city gate. Lot, whose presence at the gate suggests that he's become an important member of the city, sees these strangers and invites them to stay at his home. If this situation is a test of his hospitality, so far, Lot, like his uncle, is doing well.

Yet, after preparing a meal for his guests, things go sour — not the food mind you, but the circumstances. The inhabitants of Sodom, aware that Lot is entertaining strangers, gather around his house and demand that he bring them out "so that we may know" them. This request is reasonable. After all, these men are strangers from who knows where, and they very well could be spies sent by some enemy king wanting to attack the city. (Sodom had recently experienced such an attack. See "Abraham and Lot" earlier in this chapter.) So, it's no wonder that the people of Sodom are a little jittery about strangers.

But more seems to be going on here than just wanting to investigate why these strangers have come to Sodom. The most common meaning of the Hebrew word used for "to know" *(yada')* is simply to have factual knowledge about something. However, another meaning is "to have sex with" (for example, "Adam knew his wife, Eve, and they had a son"). We realize that the latter meaning is intended in the present case because of Lot's response to the crowd's request:

> *No, my friends, do not do this wicked thing. See, I have two daughters who have never slept with a man. Let me bring them to you, and you can do to them whatever you want. Only do not do anything to these men, for they have come under the protection of my roof.*

—Genesis 19:7–8

A pillar of the community

To understand the fate of Lot's wife, it helps to know the presumed location of Sodom and Gomorrah. Tradition places the former sites of these cities near the Dead Sea, which is the lowest body of water on earth. In fact, the salt content of the Dead Sea is about 30 percent, making it impossible for anything to live in it (hence, the name). Yet, because of this high salt content, salt deposits appear all along its banks.

Therefore, one walking through this region would notice a lot of "pillars of salt." Apparently, one of these pillars was thought to be Lot's wife. Even today, if you go on a tour in this region, your guide likely will point to one of these pillars and tell you that it's Lot's wife (though, notably, the guide will point to a different one with each group — tour guide humor, if you will).

This is a strange offer if all they wanted to do was ask a few questions. But another, more pressing question arises: "What kind of father would offer his daughters to a sex-craved, ravenous crowd?" The answer is quite simple: Lot.

In defense of Lot, some interpreters have understood his offer to be extremely noble, perhaps one of the noblest acts in all the Bible! By this understanding, Lot's offer is an example of tremendous self-sacrifice, the ultimate in hospitality, as he is willing to sacrifice his own daughters for the protection of his guests. Others, however, have viewed Lot's actions as cowardly. He should have protected his guests *and* his daughters, or at least died trying.

Whatever Lot's motives for offering his daughters, the crowd refuses the offer and moves toward his door to secure by force what Lot wouldn't give freely.

The angels intervene by striking the crowd with blindness. Then, turning to Lot, the angels tell him to gather his family and escape from the city, "for the LORD is going to destroy it." Lot makes haste to tell his future sons-in-law of God's intentions, but they think he's joking and refuse to follow him. Lot, now with only his wife and two daughters, flees from the city with the angels.

The LORD then sends down "fire and brimstone" to destroy Sodom and the other cities of the plain. (It is from this narrative that we get the phrase "fire and brimstone," which describes someone who [over-]emphasizes God's judgment in his or her preaching.) While Lot and his family are still running for their lives, one of the angels warns them, "Whatever you do, don't look back!" As anyone knows, the last thing you do if you don't want someone to look at something is to say, "Don't look!" Remarkably, only one of them does — Lot's wife — and she instantly turns into a pillar of salt.

The story of Sodom and Gomorrah has given rise to the word "sodomy," which refers to homosexual behavior, since the inhabitants of Sodom want to have relations with the men (really "angels") visiting Lot. However, most biblical passages that reflect on the sins of Sodom and Gomorrah don't mention their sexual practices, but list offenses such as their mistreatment of the poor and their neglect of justice (see, for example, Isaiah 3:8–15).

Lot and his daughters eventually make it to a mountainous cave, where they find refuge from the destruction below. In a story that they didn't teach you in synagogue or Sunday school (and perhaps for good reason), Lot's older daughter suggests to her sister, "Let's get father drunk with wine and sleep with him." You can almost see the look in the younger sister's eyes as she says, "Um, goood ideaaa, sis," while reaching for her cell phone to call 911.

Actually, the older sister does have a "good" reason: "There is no man around here to sleep with." As far as she knows, all the eligible bachelors just died in the "big catastrophe," including the most important to them: their fiancés. Sleeping with their father, they feel, is the only way to preserve the family line. That night, the two sisters get their father extremely drunk — so drunk, in fact, that the text says, "[Lot] did not know when [the older sister] lay down and when she got up" (Genesis 19:33). The next night, the younger daughter takes her turn, and both become pregnant.

So, what's going on here? And why is this in the Bible? No doubt, this narrative offers a number of lessons to learn, including the negative effects of excessive alcohol consumption and, perhaps, the corrupting influence of a bad environment on one's family. (The adage, "You can take the family out of Sodom, but you can't take Sodom out of the family," comes to mind.) But this narrative has another reason for being in the Bible that doesn't have to do so much with lessons as it does with relationships between future nations.

From these incestuous relationships come two sons, that is brothers, we mean grandsons . . . *drats,* these blended families!

- ✔ The older daughter names her son Moab, which sounds like the Hebrew words for "from my father" (appropriately enough).

- ✔ The younger daughter names her son Ben-Ammi, which is Hebrew for "son of my people" (not so revealing a name, for which Ben-Ammi was *extremely* grateful during his junior high years).

Although this narrative may seem peculiar to us (and well it should), it's significant for later developments in the biblical story because Moab's and Ben-Ammi's descendants — the Moabites and the Ammonites, respectively — play an important role in the later history of Abraham's descendants, the Israelites. The Moabites and the Ammonites were their "next door neighbors" to the southeast and east, respectively. Thus, if you were to ask an ancient Israelite who the Moabites and Ammonites were, they would say, "You mean those sons-of-an-incestuous-relationship-between-our-founding-father's-nephew-and-his-daughters?!" Hardly the stuff for good relationships, but it *does* establish a relationship, and the Israelites expect these relationships to guarantee peace between these countries.

Abraham: Father of Many Nations . . . and Faiths (Genesis 21)

A year after laughing at the strangers' prediction that Sarah would have a son, Abraham and Sarah find themselves laughing again, but this laughter reflects their being tickled at the news of having a healthy baby boy. As a result of all this laughter surrounding the birth of their son, Abraham and Sarah, following God's instructions, name their son "laughter" or "he will laugh," which is Yitzak in Hebrew and Isaac in English.

With the birth of Isaac, the old rivalry between Hagar and Sarah soon reappears, manifesting itself, of all places, at Isaac's "weaning" party. That's right, in many cultures (both ancient and modern), people celebrate the cessation of breastfeeding (perhaps you had a similar celebration). Yet, before imagining cute little Isaac in his baby carriage cooing as he listens to everyone celebrating on his (and Sarah's) behalf, Isaac would have been fully aware of what was going on. In many cultures (both ancient and modern), a child is commonly weaned anywhere from 3 to 6 years old.

During the celebration, however, something goes wrong. Although the exact nature of the offense is unclear, Ishmael did something toward Isaac that upset Sarah enough that she asks Abraham to send Hagar and her son away, never to return. Yet, Ishmael isn't just Hagar's son, he is Abraham's son, and Abraham doesn't want to see him go. While contemplating what to do, God appears to Abraham and assures him that Ishmael and Hagar will be okay, and that Ishmael's descendants will someday become a great nation. With this assurance, Abraham says farewell to Hagar and his beloved son.

What's in a name?

Isaac's naming points out an important aspect of names in the Bible and in many ancient (and modern) cultures: Names have meaning. True, all names have meaning. Perhaps you even know the meaning of your name. But in many cultures, names have *meeeeaning* (if you know what we mean). That is, people's names are actually words in their present language, so anyone hearing their name immediately knows what it means. Thus, when someone met Isaac, he or she would know instantly that his name meant "laughter." Moreover, a person would know that his name reflected something important about him, such as a character quality, the hopes and dreams of his parents, his religious beliefs, and so on. A name would actually be a great conversation piece ("Why did your parents name you 'laughter'?"). So, while in many cultures to forget a name is, at worst, embarrassing, in other cultures, and in the world of the Bible, to forget a name would mean to forget something important about that person.

This isn't the last we see of Ishmael (or his descendants, who are called the *Ishmaelites* in the biblical text). Later in the Bible, when Abraham dies, Ishmael returns to help Isaac bury their father. And Ishmaelites appear now and again in the biblical text. Although not recorded in the Bible, according to the Koran, the Holy Book of Islam, Abraham visits Ishmael at Mecca (in modern-day Saudi Arabia), where they build an altar together, called the Ka'aba. Today the Ka'aba serves as the most holy site of the Muslim religion (see Chapter 24).

Asking the Unthinkable: The Near Sacrifice of Isaac (Genesis 22)

Back in Genesis 12, God initiates His relationship with Abraham by calling him to leave his homeland and "Go for yourself, to the land I will show you." In Genesis 22, Abraham receives a similar, but far more troubling, call:

> *Take your son, your only son, whom you love, Isaac, and go for yourself to the land of Moriah. There you will sacrifice him as a burnt offering on one of the mountains that I will show you.*

> —Genesis 22:2

The similarities between Abraham's first and last calls are purposeful. Not only do both contain the words "go for yourself," but both calls narrow in focus from the general to the specific. In Abraham's first call, God tells Abraham to leave his country, then his relatives, and then his father's house. This narrowing focus seems to be the Bible's way of communicating that God is aware of the price He is asking Abraham to pay in leaving his family.

With this in mind, look at the narrowing focus of God's second call to Abraham:

> *Take your son,*
> *your only son,*
> *whom you love,*
> *Isaac.*

Ishmael has left, so God simply could have said, "Take your son" or, to cut to the chase, "Take Isaac." But God's narrowing command demonstrates that He is intimately aware of what He is asking Abraham to do — and He cares.

The journey

When Abraham receives the call to sacrifice his son, the text simply reports: "Abraham got up early the next morning, saddled his donkey, took two servants and his son Isaac, and after cutting enough wood for the burnt offering, set out for the place God had told him" (Genesis 22:3). You may ask, "Why would Abraham bargain over the fate of Sodom and Gomorrah and not over the fate of his own son?" The text doesn't say. Yet many scholars feel that it is precisely because of Abraham's experience in the Sodom and Gomorrah incident that makes it unnecessary for him to bargain here. Abraham now knows that no matter what God does, He does it for a reason. So, Abraham silently obeys.

Abraham and Isaac eventually arrive at the place where God wants "the deed" done. Abraham takes the wood for the sacrifice and, in ironic fashion, places it on Isaac for him to carry — the one who will soon be placed on it. Abraham then takes a torch and knife, and with these accoutrements of sacrifice, they begin the arduous journey up the mountain.

As they make their way, Isaac breaks the silence with a question: "Father . . . I see the fire and the wood for the burnt offering, but where is the lamb?" Abraham, apparently wanting to be truthful, but not wanting to say too much, responds: "God will provide for Himself the lamb for the burnt offering, my son." Abraham's answer is actually profound on a number of levels:

- ✔ First, God *was* the one who provided the "lamb" for the offering by giving Abraham and Sarah the son they otherwise would never have had.

- ✔ Second, for those who know the end of the story, God *will* provide the lamb, or more specifically, a ram, to offer in Isaac's place.

- ✔ Third, because there is no punctuation in the original Hebrew, Abraham's response could be rendered: "God will provide for Himself the lamb for the burnt offering: (namely) my son."

Perhaps the author intends that we understand Abraham's response with all these possible meanings.

Eventually they reach the location for the sacrifice, and Abraham builds an altar for the sacrifice.

With no apparent discussion or explanation, Abraham binds Isaac and places him upon the altar. In fact, Isaac's silence through this whole ordeal has baffled many. Did Isaac passively accept his father's binding? Did Abraham explain to his son what he was doing and why? Later interpreters imagined all sorts of conversations taking place between Abraham and Isaac in their "last" moments together. Yet, notably, the Bible does not tell us what, if anything, was said between Abraham and Isaac during this ordeal.

Abraham's action of binding (*'aqad* in Hebrew) Isaac before going through with the intended sacrifice has given rise to the Hebrew name for this story: *The Aqedah* (in English, *The Binding*).

Rock of ages

The mountain upon which Abraham offers his son Isaac as a sacrifice is called Mount Moriah. This mountain is identified later in the Bible as the place where the Temple in Jerusalem is eventually built. Today, the Dome of the Rock, one of the most holy sites of Islam, stands over what is believed to be *the* rock upon which Isaac was almost sacrificed, and the rock from which Muhammad, the prophet of Islam, is said to have ascended into paradise (see Chapter 24).

Saved in the knick of time

After Isaac is upon the altar, Abraham raises his knife and plunges it into . . . wait, was that a voice? Yes. Listen closely.

> *Abraham! Abraham! . . . Do not lay your hand on the boy. Do not do anything to him, for now I know that you fear God because you have not withheld from Me your only son.*

> —Genesis 22:12

Whew! That was close. And for Abraham's willingness to offer up his son as a sacrifice, God reiterates His promise to Abraham of many descendants and blessings (Genesis 22:16–18).

So, then, why did God ask Abraham to sacrifice Isaac? After all, if this was simply a test of Abraham's faith, then why not ask Abraham to jump off a cliff, or slide down the pyramids . . . or even sacrifice *himself?*

While many proposals have been put forth, the ultimate reason God would ask Abraham to sacrifice Isaac is that Isaac, more than anything or anyone else, embodies God's promises to Abraham. Without Isaac, there is no heir, no nation, no promises, and no blessings. By asking Abraham to sacrifice Isaac, God is asking Abraham to demonstrate his complete trust in Him for his future. Abraham demonstrates his complete trust, and for this he not only receives God's promises but also experiences the "good life."

When we first meet Abraham, he lies to protect his life, risks Sarah's well-being to enrich himself, uses a surrogate mother to bypass God's promise, and questions God's sense of justice over Sodom and Gomorrah. Now, near the end of his life, Abraham is a different person. He realizes that the good life or having a great name comes not from doing whatever it takes to get ahead, but from trusting in God and doing what's right (see Chapter 4). More precisely, from the Bible's perspective, one cannot truly achieve the good life without living a good life (that is, doing what's right, trusting God, loving others, and so on.) One may make it to the "top of the heap," but, as good as that sounds when sung by Frank Sinatra (who, by the way, could make "Who Let the Dogs Out?" sound inspiring), it is of no real value if "the heap" is made up of broken promises, broken relationships, and broken commandments. Abraham has undergone character development — an important part of any good work of literature, and of any good life.

One Wedding and Two Funerals (Genesis 23–25:18)

The Abrahamic narratives end with perhaps the saddest and happiest moments of Abraham's life: Sarah's death and Isaac's marriage. Then, after an adventurous and full life, Abraham himself moves on to the ultimate "Promised Land."

Sarah's death

Shortly after Isaac's near sacrifice, Sarah dies. Later interpreters suggested, in fact, that it was the stress of this event that eventually did her in. We can only imagine. In the wake of Sarah's death (no pun intended), Abraham purchases a plot of land for her burial. Actually, all of Genesis 23 is devoted to this "land deal." Some people have wondered, "Why does the Bible spend so much time describing a business transaction?" The answer is: "Because this is no ordinary business transaction." It is at this point in the Abrahamic narratives that we realize that even though Abraham has been guaranteed the "Promised Land," he technically owns none of it. This "deal" marks the initial purchase, the "down payment" as it were, on the whole property.

The land and cave that Abraham purchases are near the city of Hebron (southwest of Jerusalem), and it is in this cave — called the Cave of Machpelah — that all the patriarchs and most of the matriarchs will be buried. Today, this cave is still honored as a holy site by Jews, Christians, and Muslims.

Isaac gets hitched

Abraham, now advancing in years, is concerned about finding a wife for Isaac. Part of his concern is that he doesn't want Isaac to marry a local girl, but rather someone from his own clan. As a result, Abraham instructs his servant, Eliezer, to go back to Abraham's homeland (Haran) and see if he can find a wife for Isaac. Although the servant is skeptical at the prospects of success, Abraham assures him that "God will give you success". And God does. When the servant arrives at Abraham's ancestral home, he sees a beautiful woman named Rebekah at a well (wells were ancient pick-up joints — which is why we call bars "wells" or "watering holes"). The servant prays that if she is the one, she will offer him and his camels a drink. And she does.

Soon, negotiations for Rebekah's marriage are under way with her father, Bethuel (Abraham's nephew and Lot's cousin), her mother (unnamed), and her brother, Laban (who will become important later — see Chapter 6). But Rebekah is not totally left out of the negotiations, as she is asked: "Will you go with this man?" "Yes, I will go," Rebekah says. And off they go.

Shortly after Isaac and Rebekah meet, Isaac brings Rebekah into his mother's tent "and she became his wife, and Isaac loved her." The story closes with the following notice: "And Isaac was comforted in the matter of his mother's death." As you might have guessed, Freud loved this stuff.

Abraham's death

With the marriage of Isaac complete, Abraham's hopes for the future are assured. Abraham can now leave this world knowing that the promises God made to him so many years ago will now come to pass. His descendants will one day become a great nation; they will possess the land on which he is now living; they will be blessed; and they will bless all the people of the world. With these assurances, Abraham dies at the age of 175 years old — "an old man and full of years" (you can say that again!).

Abraham's other children

In addition to Ishmael and Isaac, Abraham actually has a number of other children. According to Genesis 25:1–4, after Sarah's death, Abraham marries a woman named Keturah, who goes on to have six sons. In addition, Genesis 25:6 says that Abraham had other sons by "his concubines." Although these children don't play a central role in Genesis, their descendants pop up now and then later in the biblical text. For example, one of Abraham's sons by Keturah — Midian — seems to be the ancestor of the Midianites, one of whom, a woman named Zipporah, marries the great Israelite leader Moses (see Exodus 2 and Chapter 7 of this book).

Chapter 6

The Birth of a Nation: Isaac, Jacob, and Their Many Children (Genesis 25:19–50)

. . . .

In This Chapter

▶ Seeing how one generation's sins affect the next

▶ Discovering why God blesses liars, cheats, and thieves (but don't try this with your own life)

▶ Witnessing the births of the twelve tribes of Israel

▶ Understanding the real story behind Joseph and his Technicolor dream tunic

. . . .

Dysfunctional families in the ancient world were no different than their modern counterparts — and few families rivaled the dysfunction of ancient Israel's ancestors. Whether it's the poor parental practice of favoring one child over another or the equally destructive behavior of betraying one's own sibling, the progenitors of the Israelites do it all. But for all their dysfunction, this clan of misfits eventually comes out on top due to divine intervention.

In this chapter, you trace the lives of Isaac, Jacob, and Jacob's children, as you watch them overcome insurmountable odds to become a great nation.

The Birth of Nations: Esau and Jacob (Genesis 25:19–26)

Isaac, the son of Abraham and Sarah (see Chapter 5), and Rebekah, Isaac's wife, have trouble conceiving a child. As this was before in-vitro fertilization, Isaac prays to God for a child, and Rebekah becomes pregnant. Rebekah, however, begins experiencing extreme discomfort during her pregnancy, and so she asks God what's going on. God informs her that she's having twins.

That's painful enough. The reason this particular pregnancy is producing such discomfort is that her twins represent "two nations." As God puts it:

> *Two nations are in your womb, and two peoples will come from your belly. One will be stronger than the other, and the older will serve the younger.*

—Genesis 25:23

Although this information probably provided little physical relief, at least Rebekah now knows that her suffering is not in vain.

Eventually, the time comes for Rebekah to give birth to these "nations." The first baby to come out is quite hairy, so hairy that Rebekah and Isaac name him "Hairy," which the biblical author says in Hebrew is Esau. Yet, even before Esau is removed fully from the womb, his younger brother seizes his ankle, and is therefore given the name "Seizer," which in Hebrew is Jacob. This name, as it turns out, is not only a fitting description of Jacob's reflexes, but also of his "graspy" or rapacious nature.

As the little lads grow up, they pursue very different interests. Esau loves the open country and spends most of his time hunting, while Jacob prefers to stay "among the tents" and cut out recipes from his *Cooking Heavy* magazine. Because of their divergent interests, their parents soon pick favorites (never a good idea): Isaac favors Esau, while Rebekah favors Jacob.

Stew of Trouble: Esau Sells His Birthright (Genesis 25:27–34)

One day, while Jacob is at home trying out a new recipe, his brother bursts into the room: "Quick! Let me have some of that red stew! I'm starving!" Jacob, being the selfless brother that he is, responds, "First, sell me your birthright." Say what?! What kind of a brother is this? And what is a birthright? Jacob, as we've already noted, is a heel . . . or at least a heel-grabber. Birthrights, however, are important for understanding what follows.

A *birthright* entitled a child — usually the firstborn son — to the majority share of the family's wealth. Although popularly understood to mean that the owner of a birthright received a "double portion," in truth, birthrights often entailed much more.

Esau declares, "What good is my birthright if I starve to death?" Thus, for some stew, Esau gives up his birthright. And because this particular bowl of stew is red, Esau is given the nickname "Red," which, in Hebrew, is Edom.

Beyond demonstrating the importance of valuing one's birthright, the author of this story provides his audience with an explanation for the political landscape surrounding ancient Israel of a later period. The descendants of Esau, who will be called the Edomites (after Esau's nickname, Edom, and in recognition of the reddish clay that characterizes this region), would become one of Israel's main rivals on their southern border. Thus, God's prophecy to Rebekah that struggling within her womb "are two nations" would one day come to fruition, as Israel and Edom would, in fact, "struggle" with one another for domination of this region.

Isaac and Rebekah's "Wife-Sister Act" (Genesis 26)

Genesis 26 flashes back to before Esau and Jacob's birth to show what's at stake in their "battle for the birthright": wealth and a peace treaty with a powerful kingdom.

During a severe famine, Isaac and Rebekah go in search of food. Eventually they end up at the doorstep of Abimelech, the king of Gerar. Because Isaac fears that Abimelech might kill him to take his beautiful wife, Isaac says that Rebekah is his sister. Surprisingly, Abimelech buys it, even though this seems to be the *very same king* Isaac's parents, Abraham and Sarah, deceived years earlier with their wife-sister act when they were in need of food (see Genesis 20 and Chapter 5 in this book).

Things initially go well for Isaac and Rebekah until one day when Abimelech notices Isaac and Rebekah "playing together." Although the exact nature of this play isn't described, that it is *not* croquet is certain, because Abimelech realizes that Isaac and Rebekah are not brother and sister, but husband and wife! Yet, rather than punish Isaac for lying, Abimelech makes a treaty with him, giving Isaac international amnesty and permission to live anywhere in Abimelech's domain Isaac chooses.

Beyond showing that the behavior of parents is often passed down to their children (not a minor lesson, indeed), this story explains why Isaac's descendants, the Israelites, should live in peaceful coexistence with Abimelech's descendants, the Philistines (from which the word Palestine derives). Their ancestors made a promise "not to harm" one another, even agreeing to "treat each other well," and it is the expectation of the biblical author that Israelites and Philistines continue to honor this agreement.

Jacob Steals Esau's Blessing (Genesis 27–28:9)

Eventually, Isaac becomes an old man — so old that "his eyes were weak and he could no longer see." Realizing that he needed to get his affairs in order before dying, he calls Esau, his firstborn and favorite son, to his side:

> *I am now an old man and I do not know when I will die. Therefore, get your weapons — your quiver and your bow — and go out on the range, and hunt some wild game for me. Prepare for me the flavorful meal I like and bring it to me so that I can eat and so that I can bless you before I die.*

> —Genesis 27:2–4

In addition to a birthright, a *blessing* was one of the most sought-after possessions that a son could obtain from his father. Blessings are more than just well wishes. They carry with them a prophetic element, becoming a prediction of what will happen in the life of an individual or his descendants.

Esau, having already given up his birthright, is anxious to secure his father's blessing. Therefore, he quickly puts his hunting skills into motion, and sets out to capture a meal.

Rebekah, who overhears Isaac and Esau's conversation, tells Jacob to retrieve two goats so that she can prepare them as a meal for Isaac. Jacob, pretending to be Esau, will then bring the meal to his father, and thereby receive his father's blessing. Jacob, who is a skilled liar, immediately perceives a flaw in his mother's plan: Esau is hairy, while he is smooth. When his father touches him, Isaac will uncover their deception and curse Jacob instead of bless him. Rebekah, in an act of maternal self-sacrifice, tells her son, "Let the curse fall on me." Jacob, a man who puts the needs of others — especially his mother — above his own, says, "Okay." And off he goes to get the meat.

To complete the deception, Rebekah takes the skin from one of the goats and places it on the arms and neck of Jacob, so that he will feel hairy like his brother (Esau must have been one hairy dude!). In addition, Jacob puts on Esau's coat so that he will smell like his brother (as a hairy man who spends a lot of time outdoors, we don't need to tell you what he must have smelled like).

When Jacob enters with a meal, Isaac is baffled: "How is it that you were able to find the game so quickly, my son?" Jacob's reply shows how low he will go in order to get what he wants: "The LORD your God gave me success."

What in the name of God?! Yes, that's right, Jacob lies *in the name of God*! Now that's low (and in violation of several commandments, by the way). Yet, more important for the author's purposes, Jacob refers to the LORD as "your (Isaac's) God," not "my (Jacob's) God." Embracing Isaac's God as his own becomes an important theme in the development of Jacob's character. At this point, Jacob has little use for God, except to use His name to trick his father.

After Isaac finishes the meal, he blesses Jacob, thinking him to be Esau. Thus, Jacob succeeds in stealing both his brother's birthright and blessing.

Heading Out of Dodge: Jacob Flees for His Life (Genesis 28:10–22)

After getting over the initial shock of having lost both his birthright and his blessing to his conniving brother, Esau swears revenge. After dad is gone, he determines, brother is a goner. Rebekah, perceiving Esau's intentions, convinces Isaac to allow Jacob to go to their ancestral homeland and find a wife from their kin, as Rebekah could not bear the thought of her son marrying a local Canaanite girl. Isaac agrees, and sends Jacob on his way.

Climbing Jacob's ladder to success

Jacob quickly leaves Beersheba, which is in the far southern part of the Promised Land, and heads north to his ancestral homeland of Paddan Aram, in what is today northeastern Syria. While on his way, Jacob stops to catch up on some much needed rest. While sleeping, Jacob has a dream in which he sees a stairway (or ladder, as some translations render it — giving us the phrase "Jacob's ladder") extending from heaven to earth, and all along this stairway Jacob sees angels "ascending and descending between heaven and earth." About midway up this "stairway to heaven," Jacob sees Led Zeppelin; and, at the very top, Jacob sees God, who declares:

> *I am the LORD, the God of your father Abraham and the God of Isaac. I will give you and your descendants the land on which you are lying. Your descendants will be like the dust of the earth, and will spread out to the west and east, north and south. All peoples on the earth will be blessed through you and your descendants. I am with you and will watch over you wherever you go, and I will bring you back to this land. I will not leave you until I have done what I have promised you.*
>
> —Genesis 28:13–15

Now, that's quite a deal for someone who just lied in the name of this God. You may be thinking, "Where do I sign up?" However, the more virtuous among us may be thinking, "This isn't fair." And you'd be right. This isn't fair. However, the Bible is trying to make a point about God's character. He is faithful, keeping His promises regardless of the individual behavior of those involved. Because

God promised Abraham and Isaac that their descendants would be blessed, and because God said that this blessing would come through Jacob, God intends to keep His word.

Jacob's bargain with God

When Jacob wakes up, he realizes that he's on no ordinary plot of real estate. In recognition of this fact, he takes the rock that he used as a pillow the night before and sets it up as a pillar. Then he anoints the rock with oil.

Anointing with oil designates something or someone as belonging to God. In the case of individuals, anointing prepares people for divine use as priests or kings. In the case of objects, anointing prepares items for use in worship. By anointing this rock, Jacob is attesting to the fact that God has been there, making this place "holy," or set apart for God's purposes. In fact, this spot will become an important religious site later in the Bible. In recognition of its importance, Jacob names the place "Bethel," which means "house of God."

Jacob, not one to throw his allegiances around lightly, makes a deal with God:

> *If God will be with me and will watch over me on this journey I am taking, and give me food to eat and clothes to wear, and if I return safely to my father's house, then the LORD will be my God, and this stone that I have set up as a pillar will be a house of God, and I will give to Him a tenth of all I have.*
>
> —Genesis 28:20–22

In essence, Jacob says that God must fulfill three criteria before Jacob will allow Him to be "his God" (talk about nerve): protection, provision, and a peaceful return.

Believe it or not, God will honor this "deal." The question is, will Jacob?

Love at First Sight: Jacob and Rachel (Genesis 29:1–30)

When Jacob arrives in Paddan Aram, the land of his ancestors, he comes to a well, where he notices a strikingly beautiful shepherdess named "Lamby" (which in Hebrew is Rachel). After some small talk, Rachel takes Jacob home to introduce him to her father, Laban, who, as we soon find out, is a man of comparable character to Jacob. Jacob also meets Rachel's older sister, Leah, who "had weak eyes," the meaning of which is not entirely clear, but seems to mean that she was less attractive than her younger sister (she wore Coke-bottle glasses?).

Jacob, always one to appreciate a person's inner qualities, falls in love with Rachel and offers Laban seven years of work in exchange for her hand in marriage. Laban agrees, and in one of the Bible's more romantic moments, we read that "Jacob served Laban seven years, but they seemed like only a few days to him because of his love for Rachel" (Genesis 29:20). Now that's love.

When Jacob's seven years of service are over, Laban holds a giant wedding feast. After the ceremonies and celebrations are complete, Jacob and his bride retire to their honeymoon suite (read: tent). The next morning, Jacob awakes and, leaning over to kiss his beautiful new bride, discovers that the woman next to him is wearing Coke-bottle glasses! Understandably angry, Jacob confronts his father-in-law, "What is this you have done to me? I served you for Rachel, and you have deceived me by giving me Leah!"

Laban, who graduated a class or two ahead of Jacob in the "University of Deception," informs him, "It is not our custom to give away the younger daughter in marriage before the firstborn" (Genesis 29:26). Now, most translations obscure what is going on here by rendering the Hebrew word for "firstborn" as "the older" to make it parallel with Laban's earlier reference to "the younger." This is a mistake.

The biblical author quite purposefully uses the word "firstborn" when describing Leah in order to make a point: It is precisely over the rights of the firstborn that Jacob deceived his own brother, Esau. Now Jacob is being paid back in kind for that deception.

Jacob makes a new deal with Laban, saying that he will serve him for another seven years for Rachel's hand in marriage. Laban agrees. Now, you may be saying, "Wait a minute here! What's with the two wives? Doesn't the Bible teach against polygamy?" Well, yes and no.

In the Bible, it's not unheard of for a man to have more than one wife, or at least to have children by more than one woman. Having said that, monogamy does seem to be the norm, and even seems to be the original plan of God at creation ("a man will cling to his wife [singular] and the two [not three or more] will become one flesh"). But a number of men, even those "approved" by God (for example, King David), will have more than one wife, although it almost always gets them into trouble.

Sibling Rivalry: The Birth of Jacob's Children (Genesis 29:31–30:24)

In addition to giving Jacob two wives, Laban gives his daughters two maidservants. Rachel's maidservant is Bilhah, and Leah's is Zilpah. These names, though bordering on the unattractive, are not mere Bible trivia, for they play an important role in the birthing of the Israelite nation.

Initially, Rachel is unable to bear children, while Leah has little difficulty becoming pregnant and eventually gives birth to four boys: Reuben, Simeon, Levi, and Judah. Leah's fertility, in fact, is attributed to an act of God, because "He saw that she was unloved by her husband." In other words, God cares for those who have been rejected or forgotten by others.

Rachel, in a desperate move to secure children of her own, offers Jacob her maidservant, Bilhah. Jacob, however, isn't one to compromise on his convictions, and he stands his moral ground — for a few seconds anyway — and soon Bilhah has two sons: Dan and Naphtali.

For reasons that aren't explained, Leah is unable to become pregnant again, and so she offers Jacob her maidservant, Zilpah. However, Jacob will only go so far, which, as we soon find out, is "all the way," and Zilpah bears two boys: Gad and Asher. Leah, too, is able to conceive again and bears three more children: Issachar, Zebulun, and Jacob's only daughter, Dinah.

In the midst of all this competition, God sees that Jacob has been neglecting Rachel (granted, he's been a busy man). In response, God enables Rachel to become pregnant, and she bears a son, whom she names Joseph. (Rachel will also have another son, Benjamin. See the section, "Jacob Embraces God and Loses His Father and Wife," later in this chapter.)

When the smoke clears, Jacob has twelve sons and one daughter. Since Jacob's twelve sons will go on to become the ancestors of the twelve tribes of Israel, and since birth order is important for understanding each tribes' future (see the section, "Once and Again: Jacob and Joseph Reunite," later in this chapter), Table 6-1 provides a breakdown for quick reference. (**Note:** Because only Jacob's male children result in tribes of Israel, Dinah is not numbered.)

Table 6-1	Jacob's Wives and Their Children		
Leah	*Bilhah*	*Zilpah*	*Rachel*
1. Reuben	5. Dan	7. Gad	11. Joseph
2. Simeon	6. Naphtali	8. Asher	12. Benjamin
3. Levi			
4. Judah			
9. Issachar			
10. Zebulun			
Dinah			

Jacob Strikes It Rich and Steals Away (Genesis 30:25–31:55)

Jacob, despite having a big family, has no personal wealth. Therefore, he makes a deal with Laban. He suggests that he serve Laban for another six years in exchange for livestock. Laban agrees.

Partly due to his own ingenuity and partly because of divine intervention, Jacob soon becomes a very rich man. Laban and his sons become extremely jealous, especially because they feel that Jacob's wealth came at their expense. Jacob, always the perceptive one, realizes that it's time for him to leave. Confirming this, God tells Jacob that it's time for him to go back home.

Jacob on the lam . . . again

While Laban and his sons are busy elsewhere, Jacob and his family sneak away and begin the long trek back to the Promised Land. Laban, however, soon finds out about their departure, and makes quick pursuit, eventually catching up with Jacob and his family. Angry with Jacob for his deception, Laban confronts him, asking why he had left without letting him say goodbye to his daughters and grandchildren. Now, before you start feeling too sorry for "Grandpa Labby," he actually intended to force Jacob and his family to return to Paddan Aram (or worse, to kill Jacob), but God appeared to Laban the night before and warned him against such action.

Laban, however, has another matter to settle with Jacob. It seems that someone stole his household gods, called *teraphim* in Hebrew. That's right, Laban and his family were idolaters, and household gods were important because they were thought to bring blessing to one's home and family. Moreover, household idols were connected with inheritance rights, so their theft was akin to stealing another's birthright (hmmm, stealing someone's blessing and birthright . . . sounds familiar).

Jacob, believe it or not, did not steal Laban's idols. Rachel did. Jacob, unaware of Rachel's crime, invites Laban to search their belongings. Jacob even goes so far as to say that whoever stole Laban's idols deserves to die. Whoa! Wait a minute! Is this the same guy who, 20 years earlier, had taken his brother's blessing and birthright? Yes, it is — and it is here that we discover that Jacob has undergone character development during his years of hard labor under Laban. He now has firsthand knowledge of what it is like to be cheated and deceived, and he realizes how much pain it causes others.

Laban begins searching for his missing idols, coming last to Rachel's tent (the Bible is good at drama). Rachel, as a last-ditch effort not to be caught with the stolen goods, places the idols underneath her saddlebag and then sits on it. As her father searches her tent, Rachel realizes that her posture might raise suspicions and says, "Forgive me father for not standing up, but the way of women is upon me." Now, "the way of women" is a Hebrew euphemism for, well, "the way of women" that happens monthly. Laban, having raised two daughters, knows all too well not to mess with "the way of women," and quickly scurries out of the tent, without finding his stolen teraphim.

May God watch between us: Jacob's and Laban's peace treaty

When Laban comes back to Jacob empty-handed, Jacob is livid, both because Laban had mistreated him for the past 20 years and because he had falsely accused him of stealing his idols. After rebuking Laban for his unjust ways, Jacob and Laban make a covenant with one another, agreeing that they will not enter into one another's land to harm the other. As a memorial to their agreement, they erect a pile of stones, and Laban declares, "This heap of stones is a witness between you and me today. May the LORD watch between us while we are apart." Because the Hebrew word for "a witness heap" is *gal-ed*, Jacob names this place Galeed or, as it is later called, Gilead.

Although this covenant ceremony has significance for Jacob and Laban, it will have even greater significance for their descendants because the hill country of Gilead marks the approximate boundary between ancient Israel and the neighboring nation of Aram (modern-day Syria and parts of northern Jordan). Jacob's and Laban's promise not to transgress this boundary marker "to harm the other" is intended to be honored by future generations.

Settling an Old Score: Jacob Meets Esau . . . and God (Genesis 32–33:17)

From his covenant ceremony with Laban, Jacob continues toward his homeland. While still a way off, Jacob receives notice that his brother, Esau, is approaching with 400 armed men! This is real trouble. The last time Jacob saw Esau, Esau was plotting Jacob's murder. In order to soften his brother's wrath, Jacob sends his wealth and family ahead of him. Jacob then decides to stay on the other side of the Jabbok River, where he will spend the night before his fateful meeting the next day.

Wrestling with God: Jacob's name change

That night, just before going to sleep, Jacob wrestles, not with his thoughts or the guilt of his past, but with a mysterious man who shows up out of nowhere. In fact, Jacob and this stranger fight all night, and when the stranger realizes that he can't overpower Jacob, he gives Jacob a Spock-like Vulcan grip on the hip, popping it out of its socket. Although injured, Jacob doesn't give up. When Jacob's opponent asks Jacob to cease and desist, Jacob replies, "I will not let you go until you bless me." In response, the stranger declares, "Your name will no longer be Jacob, but Israel, because you have struggled with God and man and have prevailed" (Genesis 32:28). Then the stranger leaves, leaving us to wonder: Who is this mysterious man, and what's going on here?

As in the case of Abraham's mysterious visitors (see Chapter 5), this stranger has been identified with an angel, God, and, in Christian tradition, even Jesus. The new name this stranger gives Jacob may provide at least one clue to his identity. *Israel* is said to mean "he will struggle with God." Because Jacob can identify the men he has struggled with during his life (Esau and Laban), he identifies this stranger as God Himself. As Jacob puts it, "I have seen God face to face and have lived." He then names the place "face of God," which in Hebrew is *Peniel.* For Jacob, then, he has just encountered God.

But why would God wrestle with Jacob, let alone let him prevail? Although these questions are matters of ongoing theological debate, perhaps the best explanation is that this story seeks to demonstrate that God is willing to stoop to Jacob's level by engaging him in a language he can understand: struggling. And now that God and Jacob have "wrestled things out," Jacob realizes God is on his side, and he is ready to face whatever comes — even his brother.

Letting bygones be bygones

When Jacob and Esau finally meet the next day, their encounter is described in dramatic detail (if you're squeamish, we suggest you close your eyes). The Hebrew literally says:

> *Jacob looked up and saw Esau coming at him with 400 men . . . and Esau ran toward Jacob to engage him, and [Esau] reached out his arms and seized Jacob, and he wrapped his arms around his neck and he . . . and he . . . [are you looking — we thought so] . . . and he kissed him.*

—Genesis 33:1, 4

That's right. Esau gives Jacob a big wet one, and then they weep together. It is a very touching scene. In addition, the Bible once again demonstrates its literary artistry by leading the reader to believe up until the last moment that

Esau is approaching Jacob to strangle him. Instead, it is the "strangling" embrace of brotherly love. Esau has forgiven Jacob for everything. Moreover, God has blessed Esau with a large family and plenty of possessions. Even though their descendants, the nations of Israel and Edom, will one day fight with one another, there is hope that they, too, will be reconciled, just as their ancestors, Jacob and Esau, eventually embraced each other as brothers.

Jacob Finds God and Loses His Father and Wife (Genesis 33:18–20; 35)

After his encounter with Esau, Jacob makes his way safely back to his homeland. If you recall (see the section, "Jacob bargains with God," earlier in this chapter), this is the last of the three conditions Jacob established with God at Bethel before leaving for Paddan Aram.

Jacob said that he would embrace God as "his God" if God

- **Protected him:** God certainly protected Jacob, delivering him from his father-in-law and from the potential vengeance of his brother.

- **Provided for him:** God provided for Jacob, who left home with nothing, but returned with a large family and considerable wealth.

- **Peaceful return:** God has now brought Jacob back to his homeland.

Now it's Jacob's turn to live up to his end of the bargain. Yet, how he does this is often missed by readers, as it is quite subtle, but unmistakable.

Upon returning safely to his homeland, Jacob builds an altar, which he names *El Elohe-Israel.* In English this literally means, "God is the God of Israel." Jacob *is* Israel, as he just received a name change during his wrestling match with God. Therefore, the name of this monument means, in effect, "God is now my God." The God of Abraham and Isaac has proven Himself worthy of Jacob's devotion, and Jacob builds an altar acknowledging this.

Not long after Jacob's return, Rachel dies while giving birth to their last son: Benjamin. Shortly after this, Jacob experiences another painful loss: the death of his father, Isaac. Esau joins Jacob in burying their father in the cave at Machpelah, where Abraham and Sarah are also buried.

The action in the remaining chapters of Genesis shifts from Jacob's life to the life of his children — and it's not very pretty.

The rape of Dinah

Amidst the Jacob narratives is a very disturbing story about his only daughter, Dinah, who is sexually accosted by a Canaanite man named Shechem (Genesis 34). In revenge, Dinah's brothers trick Shechem and the inhabitants of his city (also called Shechem) by saying that Shechem can marry Dinah if he and his fellow Shechemites are circumcised. When the Shechemites are incapacitated by their surgery, two of Dinah's brothers — Simeon and Levi — kill them and, with the other brothers, loot the city. When Jacob finds out what his sons have done, he is outraged, saying that when word gets out that they mercilessly killed the men of Shechem that the surrounding cities will kill them. The sons, however, are unmoved by this logic: "Should he have treated our sister like a prostitute?" And with this question the story ends. No response from Jacob, no final resolution, no moral to tie it altogether. So what is this story about?

The ambivalence of the story's ending seems to be precisely what this story is about. The only innocent person in this narrative is Dinah. Shechem is guilty of forcing himself upon Dinah. The Shechemites are guilty of wanting to take Jacob's wealth once Shechem marries Dinah. Jacob's sons are wrong for exacting more judgment than the Shechemites deserve. And even Jacob seems at fault for not confronting Shechem for his actions toward his daughter. Thus, the moral of the story is that life is complicated, and oftentimes there is no clear-cut "good guy" or "bad guy." If this is all we learn from this story, then we have learned a great deal.

Joseph and the Amazing Technicolor Dream Tunic (Genesis 37)

Joseph, Jacob's first son by Rachel, becomes his favorite. In recognition of this fact, Jacob gives Joseph a special tunic or coat that is described by a Hebrew word whose meaning we do not know. Most translations render the Hebrew as "multicolored," and, more recently, the renowned biblical scholars Andrew Lloyd Webber and Tim Rice have rendered it as "technicolor," which is as good a guess as any.

Jacob's favoritism toward Joseph stirs the ire of Joseph's ten older brothers. Compounding their hatred, Joseph has a couple of dreams that suggest that they'll one day bow before their younger sibling. (As a matter of principle, it isn't a good idea to tell your siblings that they'll one day bow before you.) The death knell for any hopes of reconciliation between Joseph and his brothers occurs when Joseph reports to their father that he saw them goofing off when they were supposed to be watching their father's flocks. Therefore, it should not surprise us that the next time Jacob sends Joseph to check on his brothers, they plot to kill "this dreamer." Reuben, the oldest brother, however, convinces them not to shed their own brother's blood but rather to throw him into a nearby cistern where he would die of "natural" causes. The brothers agree, and when Joseph arrives, they seize him, remove his technicolor tunic, and throw him into a well.

Reuben, as it turns out, had proposed this alternative not to kill Joseph, but to rescue him. His plan backfires, however, when Judah, who also wants to save Joseph's life, convinces the brothers to sell him as a slave to a passing caravan of traders. The brothers agree, and Joseph is sold into slavery.

The brothers, now realizing that they need to cover up their wrongdoing, take Joseph's multicolored dream coat, tear it, and cover it with the blood of a slaughtered goat. Bringing his coat to their father, the brothers simply say, "Recognize this." Jacob did, and he assumes that Joseph met his end by being torn to pieces by wild animals.

Notice what has just happened. Jacob has just been deceived by a coat and a slaughtered goat, precisely the items Jacob used to deceive his own father when stealing his brother's blessing. Jacob's past sins are once again coming back to haunt him. (For the full story on how Jacob stole Esau's blessing, see the section titled, "Jacob Steals Esau's Blessing" earlier in this chapter.)

A Righteous Ruse: Judah and Tamar (Genesis 38)

Imbedded in the Joseph narrative is a peculiar but important story involving Jacob's fourth son, Judah. Judah has three sons, two of whom die while married to the same woman (at different times, of course), whose name is Tamar. Feeling that Tamar may be responsible for his sons' deaths, Judah sends her back to her father's house, telling her that he will "call her" when his youngest comes of age.

The practice of a brother marrying his deceased brother's wife in order to bear a son for his brother is called *levirate* marriage — an institution that sought to preserve the family line and name of the deceased.

Judah, however, has no intention of giving his last son in marriage to Tamar, which she soon realizes. Posing as a prostitute, Tamar positions herself along a road she knows Judah will travel. When Judah sees this prostitute, he says, "Come now, let me sleep with you." Say what? Is this the Bible? It is.

The key to understanding Judah's sleeping with a prostitute is the notice that he is on his way to shear his flock (Genesis 38:12). In the ancient world, shearing was a springtime affair, and was accompanied by fertility rituals. One such ritual was having sex with a sacred prostitute. This "act" was thought to ensure fertility for the coming year, as humans were acting out on the human level what they hoped the gods were doing on the divine level: making the earth (which is often likened to a womb) fertile with rain (which is often likened to "seed" or semen). It seems, then, that Judah, in soliciting sex with this prostitute, is just "doing what everyone else is doing." Although the Bible speaks out against such behavior, it seems that Jacob and his sons are still learning about what God requires.

Judah, not realizing he has just slept with (and impregnated) his daughter-in-law, continues on his way to shear his sheep.

When Judah later finds out that his daughter-in-law is pregnant, he is outraged and insists that she be executed for sleeping around. While Tamar is en route to the executioner, she sends Judah some items she had been given from the man by whom she became pregnant: Judah's seal, cord, and staff (ancient credit cards). Judah, realizing he has been caught at his own game, declares, "She is more righteous than I, since I would not give her my son Selah in marriage" (Genesis 38:26). We have to hand it to Judah, for all his faults he is at least willing to admit when he is wrong — and bettered.

Rising to the Top: Joseph in Egypt (Genesis 39–41)

Joseph is sold into slavery to a man named Potiphar, who is an important official of the pharaoh (or Egyptian king). Despite Joseph's difficult circumstances, the Bible says several times, "the LORD was with Joseph" and "in everything Joseph did he prospered." Joseph's golden touch soon comes to Potiphar's attention, and he puts Joseph in charge of his entire household.

Unfortunately, Joseph also comes to the attention of Potiphar's wife, as Joseph is "well built and handsome." As a result, Potiphar's wife beckons Joseph, "Come to bed with me." Joseph, being a pillar of virtue and a man of uncompromising morals, actually refuses! (Yes, there are some upstanding people in the Bible, in case you were beginning to wonder).

Joseph's resolve to do what's right is matched only by Mrs. Potiphar's resolve to have her man. One day, when no one is at home, she approaches Joseph and invites him to take advantage of the situation. Joseph again refuses, and flees the scene, but not before Potiphar's wife grabs his cloak and tears it off — and Joseph loses yet another coat.

Potiphar's wife, seeing that she has Joseph's coat, decides to feign that Joseph tried to accost her. Believing his wife, Potiphar sends Joseph to jail. However, even in jail, the biblical author reminds us, "the LORD was with Joseph." Soon Joseph finds himself second-in-command of the "country clinker."

Jailhouse blues: Joseph goes to jail

Joseph isn't the only fallen official in prison. With him are Pharaoh's butler, baker, and candlestick maker (actually that last guy isn't there, but we couldn't resist). That both the butler (or "cupbearer") and baker are in prison suggests that Pharaoh came down with an acute case of indigestion, or worse, food poisoning.

Poisoned food was one of the easiest ways to bring down a mighty monarch. Therefore, those in charge of food preparation were among the most important and trusted officials in a king's retinue. Any mishaps, even a suspicious-tasting piece of fruit, could be deadly — if not for Pharaoh, for those in charge of food preparation.

To make matters worse, the cupbearer and baker have been having nightmares in jail (wouldn't we all?). Joseph's ability to interpret dreams is about to serve him well.

✔ **The cupbearer** has a recurring dream where he sees a vine with three branches bearing grapes. In his dream, he takes the grapes, squeezes them into a cup, and then presents that cup to Pharaoh. Joseph informs the cupbearer that the three branches represent three days, at which time he will once again be in the service of Pharaoh. Joseph, realizing that the cupbearer will soon have an audience with the king of Egypt, asks the cupbearer to mention his gift of interpreting dreams to Pharaoh.

✔ **The baker**, optimistic that he, too, will get a positive interpretation, tells Joseph his dream. Three baskets of food are on his head. As he is carrying them to Pharaoh, birds descend and eat from them. Joseph informs the baker that the three baskets are also three days, at which time he will be hanged, and birds will feed on his flesh (of all the luck). Joseph doesn't bother asking him to mention his gift to Pharaoh.

Three days later, which, as we find out, is Pharaoh's birthday, the baker and cupbearer are summoned from jail. The baker is sent to the gallows to be hung, and the cupbearer is sent to the Gallo's to purchase wine for Pharaoh's party. However, the cupbearer fails to mention anything to Pharaoh about Joseph, and Joseph remains in jail.

Get out of jail free! Joseph interprets Pharaoh's dreams

Two years later, Pharaoh has some nightmares of his own. Seeing Pharaoh's duress (and no doubt thankful that it's not indigestion), the cupbearer tells Pharaoh that he knows someone who can help. Joseph is summoned from jail and, after a shower, shave, and shine, is brought into Pharaoh's presence.

Pharaoh asks Joseph if it's true that he can interpret dreams. Joseph replies, "No, but God can." With this, Pharaoh tells him his dreams:

- ✔ In the first dream, seven healthy cows are standing by the Nile River. Suddenly, seven sickly cows come out of the river and eat the healthy cows.

- ✔ In the second dream, seven healthy heads of grain grow strong and tall. Suddenly, seven withered heads emerge from the ground and consume them.

Struggling not to lose his lunch, Joseph gives the following interpretations.

- ✔ The seven healthy cows and seven heads of grain refer to the same thing: seven years of plenty.

- ✔ The seven sickly cows and seven withered heads of grain signify the same thing: seven years of famine.

Joseph advises Pharaoh to appoint an official to oversee food storage during the seven years of plenty so that, during the seven years of famine, Pharaoh and his people will have enough food. Now, one doesn't become pharaoh by not being able to read the writing on the wall (especially since the writing is all over the walls in Egypt — in a script called *hieroglyphs* or "holy writing"). For Pharaoh, the choice is obvious. He appoints Joseph as second ruler over all of Egypt (yes, there was a "glass ceiling" in Egypt, too).

Spies Like Us: Joseph's Brothers Come to Egypt (Genesis 42–45)

Soon, the seven years of plenty pass, and the seven years of famine set in — hard. The famine is so widespread, in fact, that those living outside Egypt are forced to come to Egypt to buy food. Such famines are well-attested in the ancient record, as are migrations by people from Canaan (later Israel) to Egypt for food and trade. The regular inundations of the Nile River, which allowed for farming even during periods of drought, made Egypt the "breadbasket" of the ancient world.

Among those who come to Egypt are Joseph's ten older brothers. When Joseph sees his brothers, he recognizes them immediately; but they don't recognize him. Several factors account for this. First, Joseph was about 17 years old when he was sold into slavery, and now, he's at least 37 years old. Second, Joseph "walks like an Egyptian," being dressed in Egyptian garb and even having an Egyptian name, Zaphenath-Paneah. Third, Joseph "talks like an Egyptian," even using an interpreter when speaking with his brothers. Pretty clever.

Figure 6-1 shows part of a painting found on a tomb in Egypt. The painting shows Semitic people coming to Egypt for trade around 1900 B.C.E. This painting gives you a good idea of what Jacob and his family may have looked like, especially in comparison to Egyptians (the clean-cut individual on the far right).

Figure 6-1:
A painting of
Semitic
people and
an Egyptian
(far right)
found on a
tomb in
Egypt.

©Erich Lessing/Art Resource, N.Y.

Joseph's dreams come true

When Joseph's brothers first meet the second-greatest man in all of Egypt, they bow, and you, the reader, are reminded of Joseph's dreams, where Joseph saw a day when his brothers would bow before him. Then, for reasons that aren't entirely clear (revenge? a test?), Joseph not only hides his identity but accuses his brothers of spying. They assure him that they are not spies. As proof, they tell Joseph, "Your servants were twelve brothers, the sons of one man, who lives in the land of Canaan. The youngest is now with our father, and the other one is no more." No more indeed! Perhaps because they just reopened an old wound, or perhaps because Joseph sees they still have not admitted their guilt in his being "no more," Joseph puts them in prison.

Three days later, Joseph decides that he wants them to prove their claim of not being spies by producing this "youngest brother," but insists that one of the brothers — Simeon — remain in jail to ensure their return.

Joseph puts Simeon in jail because his oldest brother, Reuben, tried to save his life 20 years earlier. Simeon, as the second born, is therefore the most responsible for Joseph's being sold into slavery.

The brothers return to their father, who is extremely upset to hear that Simeon is in jail. However, he refuses to allow Benjamin out of his sight, for fear that he may lose him just as he lost Joseph twenty years earlier. Yet, soon, the food they purchased runs out, and Jacob realizes that he has no other choice but to let them return to Egypt with Benjamin.

When Joseph sees his only full brother, Benjamin, he becomes deeply moved and quickly leaves the room to find a solitary place to weep. After washing his face, he reenters the room and bids his guests to join him for a banquet. The brothers are baffled when Joseph seats them according to birth order. Moreover, Joseph gives Benjamin five times as much food as the others.

After the banquet, Joseph realizes that he has no other reason to detain his brothers in Egypt. Unwilling to let them go, however, Joseph secretly places one of his cherished cups into the bag of Benjamin and then later accuses the brothers of stealing it. The brothers protest, saying that whoever has stolen the cup will die, and the rest will become Joseph's slaves.

When the cup is found in Benjamin's bag, Joseph demands that Benjamin be made his slave. Judah, however, protests, making a counteroffer that he be made his slave, saying that their father would die if he lost his favorite son. Joseph, seeing that one of his brothers is now willing to sacrifice himself, even for a favored son, is overcome by emotion. Commanding the Egyptians to leave the room, Joseph embraces his brothers and, weeping, says, "I am Joseph, the one you sold into Egypt! Don't be distressed or angry with yourselves. God sent me here ahead of you to save lives" (Genesis 45:5).

Joseph has come to realize that all his trials, even his brothers' treachery, were for a bigger purpose. As Joseph will say later to his brothers, "What you intended for evil, God intended for good: the saving of many lives" (Genesis 50:20). Now that's noble. After his brothers get over their shock, they return Joseph's embraces and tears, and they agree they must tell their father at once.

Getting permission to leave: Jacob says farewell to Canaan

When Jacob's sons tell him that Joseph is alive, he, too, is overcome by emotion, and he immediately sets out for Egypt. While on his way, Jacob stops at Beersheba, where both his grandfather and father built an altar to God. This will be the last time he will see the Promised Land, and, in fitting style, he offers a sacrifice on the altar of his ancestors. That night, God speaks to Jacob in a night vision:

> I am God, the God of your father. Do not be afraid to go down to Egypt, for I will make you a great nation there. I will go down to Egypt with you, and I will surely bring you back again. And Joseph's own hand will close your eyes.

> —Genesis 46:3–4

With this assurance, Jacob leaves for Egypt.

Once and Again: Jacob and Joseph Reunite (Genesis 46–49)

Upon arriving in Egypt, Jacob has a joyous reunion with Joseph. In addition, Jacob has opportunity to meet Joseph's employer, Pharaoh, whose first question to Jacob shows how little tact guys who think they're gods can have: "How old are you!?!" Apparently, Pharaoh wants to know his secret (death and the afterlife were a major preoccupation of the Egyptian pharaohs, as the pyramids attest). Jacob's answer to Pharaoh's question borders on the comical: "The years of my sojourning are 130. My years have been few and difficult, but they do not compare with the years of my fathers' sojourning." (Having a father and grandfather who lived to be 180 and 175, respectively, can give someone such an inferiority complex!)

Jacob blesses his grandsons

Jacob's move to Egypt allows him to meet his grandsons by Joseph. Yes, Joseph married while in Egypt — to the daughter of an Egyptian priest, no less. When Joseph brings his two sons to Jacob for his blessing, Joseph is careful to bring his eldest son, Manasseh, up to Jacob's right hand, and his youngest son, Ephraim, to Jacob's left-hand, as it was thought that the right hand dispensed the greater blessing. Jacob, however, crosses his arms, thus giving the greater blessing to the younger son. Joseph protests, but to no avail, as Jacob clearly has a thing for the younger son getting the blessing.

In Israel's later history, the descendants of Joseph's younger son, Ephraim, would become a greater tribe than the descendants of Joseph's elder son, Manesseh. However, both tribes would be considered important — and in this sense, both are "blessed."

Jacob blesses his sons

Before his death, Jacob blesses all 12 of his sons. Because Jacob's 12 sons will go on to become the twelve tribes of Israel, his blessings provide a glimpse into the future of those tribes.

Reuben is the first to be blessed, and because he is the eldest son, we expect he will be given the most promising blessing and inheritance. As Jacob says, "You are my firstborn, my strength, and the first demonstration of my virility." But, surprisingly, listen to what Jacob says next, "but you will not excel, because you went up onto your father's bed, onto my couch, and defiled it."

Say what!?! What is Jacob talking about? Jacob is referring to an obscure episode back in Genesis 35:22. There you find out that Reuben slept with Jacob's concubine, Bilhah. For this he loses the blessing of the firstborn.

Simeon and Levi are the next two sons according to birth order. These two are also denied Jacob's blessing. It seems that their acts of violence against Shechem were not forgotten by their father (see the sidebar, "The rape of Dinah" earlier in this chapter). As a result, Jacob declares:

> *Simeon and Levi are brothers, their swords are weapons of violence. Let me not enter into their counsel, let me not join their assembly, for they killed many in their anger, and hamstrung oxen in their wrath. Cursed be their anger, so fierce, and their wrath, so cruel! I will scatter them in Jacob and disperse them in Israel.*

—Genesis 49:5–7

In fulfillment of Jacob's words, the later tribes of Simeon and Levi will, in fact, be dispersed throughout the other tribes of Israel, having no discernible tribal territory of their own.

The elimination of Jacob's first three sons from the line of blessing means that the rights and privileges of the firstborn should fall to the fourth son, Judah. And, despite his "indiscretion" with Tamar (see "A righteous ruse: Judah and Tamar," earlier in this chapter), they do.

Jacob promises Judah that he will be the preeminent one among his brothers and that "the scepter will not depart from Judah, nor the ruler staff from between his feet." This prophecy does come to fruition. The most preeminent king of Israel ultimately comes from the tribe of Judah: King David, whose dynasty lasts for over 400 years.

So Long, Farewell: Jacob and Joseph Die (Genesis 50)

Just prior to his death, Jacob instructs his sons not to entomb him in Egypt, but to bury him in the cave of Machpelah in the land of Canaan that he may be beside his grandfather and grandmother, his father and mother, and his one wife, Leah. With this parting instruction, Jacob dies. In fulfillment of Jacob's words, Joseph has the priests of Egypt mummify his father, and then he takes his father's body to Canaan where he is buried with his ancestors.

Then, at the close of the Book of Genesis, Joseph also dies, but not before giving his brothers departing instructions:

> *God will surely come to your aid and take you out of this land to the land He promised on oath to Abraham, Isaac and Jacob . . . When He does, then you must carry my bones up from this place.*

> —Genesis 50:25

With this promise of future deliverance, Joseph dies at the ripe old age of 110, and he, too, is mummified and then buried in Egypt.

Joseph's parting words — that God one day will fulfill His promises to Abraham, Isaac, and Jacob — remind you that, although the drama is far from over, all the major players and plot tensions have been introduced, and that what awaits you in the remaining books of the Bible is the resolution of these tensions.

Chapter 7

Holy Moses! Exploring Exodus, Leviticus, Numbers, and Deuteronomy

- -

In This Chapter

▶ Exploring the life of Moses — from rags to riches, to rags to riches

▶ Experiencing Israel's escape from Egyptian slavery

▶ Examining the Ten Commandments and Israel's other laws

▶ Entering the Tabernacle — God's mobile home

▶ Wandering in the wilderness with the Israelites

- -

*E*xodus, Leviticus, Numbers, and Deuteronomy (four books that, with Genesis, make up the "Five Books of Moses" or *Torah* — see Chapter 1) cover one of the Bible's most remarkable spans of time and distance. The 120 years and 400 miles from Moses' birth in Egypt to his death on Mount Nebo (modern Jordan) witness Israel's escape from Egyptian slavery, their miraculous crossing of the Red Sea, the establishment of a covenant with God on Mount Sinai, and their journey to the edge of the Promised Land. All these ingredients come together to create a drama more timeless than Egypt, more powerful than the Nile River, more majestic than Pharaoh (as Egyptian kings were called), and more amazing than buying a ticket to an all-night marathon of Bible movies. (Okay, we realize that last one may not rank high on everyone's list.) In this chapter, we explore the events and accomplishments that make up the life of Israel's great deliverer and lawgiver: Moses.

A Mosaic of Moses' Early Life

When the curtain closes on the book of Genesis, the Israelites are prospering in Egypt through the esteemed position of Joseph, Abraham's great-grandchild and Jacob's favored son. When the curtain opens on the Book of Exodus, however, time has passed and the tables have turned dramatically. The descendants of Jacob's 12 sons, who now make up the twelve tribes of Israel, find themselves languishing in slavery. Making matters worse, a population explosion among the Israelites concerns the Egyptian king (or Pharaoh) who orders that all Israelite newborn males be killed. Fortunately, the two midwives for the Israelites don't take orders well and spare the babies. Frustrated, Pharaoh instructs his own people to cast all Israelite baby boys into the Nile.

Into this context, Moses is born — an individual who would one day change the fate of a nation — actually, many nations.

The birth of Moses (Exodus 1–2:9)

Moses is the youngest of three children born to Jochebed (mom) and Amram (dad), members of Israel's priestly tribe, the Levites. Moses' older brother, Aaron, will one day become Israel's first High Priest, and his sister, Miriam, will one day lead Israel in worshiping God after their exodus from Egypt.

Moses' prospects for the future, however, are quite dim, due to Pharaoh's orders to kill all newborn boys. To give Moses a chance, and in ironic obedience to Pharaoh's order, Jochebed places her infant son into the Nile River, only she does so inside a reed basket to keep him afloat. As further irony, Moses' basket is eventually discovered by Pharaoh's daughter who takes pity on him and pulls him out of the water, naming him Moses, a name that comes from a Hebrew word meaning "to draw out." (To convey this in English, we might say, "She named him Drew because she drew him out of the water.")

Moses was a common name in ancient Egypt, as it means "begotten of" in Egyptian. For example, the name Ramoses (or Rameses) means "begotten of Ra" (the sun god). Thus, Moses' name had significance in both Hebrew and Egyptian.

Moses' sister, who'd been keeping watch over the basket, approaches Pharaoh's daughter and offers to find an Israelite woman to nurse the baby. The princess agrees, and Moses' sister takes him to their mother, where he remains until he's weaned (perhaps as old as 3 to 6 years — a typical period for nursing in the ancient world).

Rolling down the river to greatness

Moses' river adventure isn't as unique as one might imagine. About 1,000 years before Moses, the Mesopotamian king, Sargon the Great, is said to have been born to a high priestess, who places him in a reed basket in the Euphrates River to conceal his illegitimate birth. A humble gardener rescues the baby and raises him, but when Sargon discovers his true identity, he becomes king. What makes Moses' river adventure unique is that he's born in obscurity but raised as royalty.

Moses' lost youth (Exodus 2:10)

After Moses is weaned, his mother returns him to Pharaoh's court, where he's raised in the luxury of the earth's wealthiest nation. Interestingly, the biblical text doesn't give us the details of Moses' youth. Later interpreters, however (including the most learned of the bunch, Hollywood scriptwriters), have come up with some very creative ideas about these "missing years". Typically, Moses is paired with the Egyptian crown prince, Rameses II, the most likely candidate to be the pharaoh of the exodus. According to these accounts, Rameses and Moses grow up together in the Egyptian palace. Although both stepbrothers are gifted, Moses usually has the physical and mental advantage over Rameses. This non-biblical story makes Pharaoh's ultimate defeat during the exodus all the more dramatic.

Moses, the murderer, marries in Midian (Exodus 2:11–22)

As an adult, Moses witnesses an Egyptian taskmaster beating an Israelite slave. Scanning the area for potential witnesses, Moses strikes and kills the Egyptian and buries him in the sand. The next day, Moses breaks up a fight between two Israelite men. The aggressor taunts Moses: "Do you intend to kill me as you killed the Egyptian?" Realizing that his crime is well known, Moses flees Egypt, making his way eastward to Midian, a country of tent-dwelling nomads spanning the Sinai and northwest Arabian Peninsulas.

At Midian, Moses rests at a well (the prime pick-up joint in the ancient world). And sure enough, Moses meets his future wife there after rescuing her and her sisters from some hooligans (an ancient version of a bar fight). The sisters, and more importantly, their father Jethro (a Midianite priest) are impressed with their strange visitor. In just two verses (Exodus 2:21–22), Moses meets Jethro (also called Reuel), marries Jethro's daughter Zipporah, and has a son named Gershom. Moses remains in Jethro's camp until the age of 80. Then, when most people would be enjoying retirement, Moses takes up a second "career" — leading people out of slavery.

We're Outta Here! The Exodus from Egypt

While Moses is in Midian, the Israelites continue to suffer in Egypt as slaves. Although Moses seems to have put the Israelites' suffering out of his mind, God hasn't, and He decides to use Moses to rescue His people.

My God is bigger than your gods

The plagues God sends upon Egypt are called *judgments* against Egypt's gods (Exodus 12:12). Interestingly, the first plague of turning the Nile River to blood and the last plague (before the decisive death of the firstborn) of darkening the sun went after two of Egypt's most powerful gods: Hapi, the Nile River god, and Ra, the sun god. Which gods, if any, the other plagues were directed at is not so easily identifiable.

Also showing that Israel's God is "bigger" than the Egyptians' gods is the role of Pharaoh's magicians in the plague narratives. At first, the magicians are able to duplicate Moses' plagues (whether by tricks or supernatural power isn't specified). By the third plague (gnats), however, the magicians are no longer able to match Moses' wonderworking, even admitting, "This is the finger of God!" (Exodus 8:19). By the sixth plague (boils), the magicians are so afflicted by the plague that they can't even show up for the contest.

The burning bush (Exodus 3–6)

One day, while Moses is watching his father-in-law's flocks, he approaches a mountain named Sinai, where he sees a bush burning that's not consumed. Curious, Moses moves closer, and then he hears a voice: "Take off your sandals, for the place where you are standing is holy ground." Moses obeys, and God continues by informing Moses that He has heard the cry of the Israelites and has picked Moses to deliver them out of bondage. Although Moses is considered Israel's greatest prophet, Moses initially comes up with several excuses for why he isn't the right man for the job, including:

- ✔ No one will listen to him, whether Israelite or Egyptian, because of his history with both groups.

- ✔ The Israelites won't believe that God has appeared to him because he doesn't know God's personal name.

- ✔ He's "heavy of mouth and tongue," which probably doesn't mean that Moses has a speech impediment (as is commonly thought) but that he speaks like a foreigner.

In response to Moses' excuses, God assures Moses that He will be with him and will give him the words to say. Moreover, God gives Moses some miracles to perform to convince his skeptics, including a staff that turns into a snake, a vanishing and reappearing skin disease on his hand, and the ability to turn water into blood. (Houdini, eat your heart out.)

As for His personal name, God says to Moses in Exodus 3:14, "I am who I am. Thus will you say to the Israelites, 'I am' has sent me."

"I am" in Hebrew is *ehyeh*. Yet, when God tells Moses what to call Him before the people, God uses the third person "He is," which, in Hebrew, is *Yahweh* (Actually, we aren't entirely sure how God's name was pronounced because the Hebrew text originally had no vowels). Most English translations render God's personal name as "the LORD" (with all capital letters).

Out of excuses, Moses begs God to send anyone but him, to which God tells Moses that his brother, Aaron, will assist him on this "mission impossible." Reluctantly, Moses complies. (After all, it's tough to win arguments with omniscient deities.)

The plagues that freed a nation (Exodus 7–10)

Moses, now accompanied by his brother Aaron and armed with a few "magic tricks," returns to Egypt to free the Israelites. After convincing the Israelites that God has appeared to Moses and intends to release them from their bondage, Moses and Aaron deliver God's message to Pharaoh: "Let My people go!" Pharaoh refuses, saying he doesn't even know this God of whom they speak. In addition, for even having the audacity to ask to leave, Pharaoh increases the Israelites' work burden. The people, in turn, become angry at Moses, saying that they wish he'd never returned to "deliver" them. (This complaint is the first of many that the Israelites will file against Moses.) Confused, Moses and Aaron go back to God, who assures them that everything is on schedule and working according to plan. With renewed confidence, Moses and Aaron return to negotiate with Pharaoh. Pharaoh still refuses to release the Israelites, but he soon realizes that God means business, because He brings a number of plagues upon Egypt. Here's a brief rundown of the Ten Plagues:

1. **The Nile River,** Egypt's primary water source, turns to blood (Exodus 7:14–24).

2. **Frogs** come up from the Nile River and invade the land (Exodus 7:25–8:15).

3. **Gnats** emerge from the ground and swarm Egypt (Exodus 8:16–19).

4. **Flies** swarm the land, except Goshen, where the Israelites live (Exodus 8:20–32).

5. **A mysterious disease** afflicts most of Egypt's (but none of Israel's) livestock, which drop dead (Exodus 9:1–7).

6. **Boils** break out on both the Egyptians and their animals (Exodus 9:8–12).

7. **A hailstorm** erupts and destroys much of Egypt's crops and livestock (Exodus 9:13–35).

8. **Locusts** devour Egypt's remaining crops (Exodus 10:1–20).

9. **Darkness** covers all Egypt except Goshen for three straight days (Exodus 10:21–29).

10. **Egypt's firstborn,** including both livestock and humans, are killed by God's destroying angel (11:1–12:50).

Who hardened Pharaoh's heart?

In ancient Near Eastern thought, mental activity was based in the heart, and emotions were centralized in the liver and kidneys. Thus, when Pharaoh "hardens his heart," it means his mind remains stubborn. Yet, sometimes, the text reports that Pharaoh hardened his own heart and at others that God hardened his heart. So, who hardened Pharaoh's heart? The answer, it seems, is "both." God ultimately is in control of human hearts and, additionally, He needed a stubborn Pharaoh to show the world His incredible powers.

Although elsewhere in the Bible, angels wield swords to protect God's people or destroy their enemies, Exodus 12 doesn't specify by what method this destroying angel kills the Egyptians' firstborns. The firstborn, especially first-born males, held a special status in the ancient world. These children inherited more than their younger siblings and carried the family's promise of longevity. Thus, biblically speaking, the death of the firstborn is far worse than the death of the other children. Moreover, the death of the Egyptian males seems to be "divine justice" for the Pharaoh's earlier decree to have all Israelite baby boys drown in the Nile River.

Participating in the first Passover (Exodus 11–13)

As protection from the tenth plague — the killing of all firstborn children and animals — God tells the Israelites to take the blood from a sacrificed lamb and smear it upon the doorposts of their homes. That night, God, accompanied by His destroying angel, *passes over* (hence the name of the holiday) the Israelites and slays the firstborn sons of Egypt. This event forms the basis of the Passover holiday. (For more on Passover, see the section titled, "A guide to Israel's holy days" later in this chapter.) Not one house in Egypt is spared. Even Pharaoh's son, the crown prince, dies.

That very night, while still mourning the death of his son, Pharaoh summons Moses and Aaron and tells them that the Israelites can leave Egypt. The Israelites quickly gather their belongings, and are even given wealth by the Egyptians, and they hurry out of Egypt. This is the exodus (from a Greek word, meaning "exit"). However, the Israelites aren't out of trouble yet.

Crossing the Re(e)d Sea (Exodus 14–15)

Led by God, who manifests Himself as a huge pillar of cloud during the day, and a large pillar of fire by night, the Israelites, who now number well over 1 million people according to the Bible, leave Egypt and head into the wilderness.

However, their exit doesn't pass without incident (or notice, as you can imagine). When news reaches Pharaoh that his Israelite slaves are wandering about in the wilderness, God hardens Pharaoh's heart once more, and Pharaoh decides to get his slaves back. With his force of chariots, Pharaoh pursues and catches up with the Israelites at the shores of a body of water alternately referred to in translations as the Red Sea and the Reed Sea.

The reason for the discrepancy between the Red Sea and the Reed Sea is that the Hebrew Bible calls this body of water *yam suf* (sea of reeds), while the Greek translation of the Hebrew Bible, the Septuagint (see Chapter 1), calls it *thalassa erythra* (red sea). Many scholars believe the Bible is referring to the Red Sea (or the Gulf of Suez), but some have suggested that it is referring to one of the many fresh-water lakes (with abundant reeds) now covered by the Suez Canal. Either way, what happens next is by any reckoning a miracle.

The people, seeing that they are trapped between this large body of water and the Egyptian army, cry out to Moses. Moses, in turn, tells them to remain silent "and watch the deliverance of God" (Exodus 14:13). Moses then raises his staff and the waters part, allowing the Israelites to cross on dry ground. Pharaoh's forces, who up to this point have been held at bay by God via a pillar of fire, are finally allowed to give pursuit. Yet, once the Israelites are safe on the other side, Moses lowers his arms, and the waters sweep over the Egyptian army, drowning them.

After being delivered from Pharaoh's army, the Israelites worship God with a song led by the brother-sister duo of Moses and Miriam — a song recorded in Exodus 15 called the "Song of the Sea." Soon the Israelites are on their way to Moses' old stomping grounds, Midian, where Moses will receive the laws to govern this new nation conceived in liberty (see Figure 7-1).

When did the exodus take place?

At present, there is no extra-biblical historical or archaeological evidence to corroborate the specific events described in Exodus. Therefore, we aren't entirely sure when to date the exodus. Some scholars hold to a fifteenth century B.C.E. date for the exodus, based on literal readings of passages such as 1 Kings 6:1, which states that the exodus occurred 480 years prior to Solomon's construction of the Jerusalem Temple (around 960 B.C.E.). This would place the exodus around 1440 B.C.E. Yet, many scholars feel that the exodus occurred at some point in the thirteenth century B.C.E., when the pharaohs, including Seti I and his son Rameses II, undertook massive building projects in the eastern Nile Delta (including the store cities of Pithom and Raamses) as described in Exodus. Furthermore, an inscription from Rameses II's son, Merneptah, dating to 1208 B.C.E., records the earliest historical reference to Israel outside of the Bible. In this inscription, Merneptah brags of defeating a number of his Canaanite enemies, including a people not yet settled named "Israel." Thus, by the thirteenth century B.C.E., "Israel" refers to a people located in Canaan, but who had not consolidated into a Kingdom.

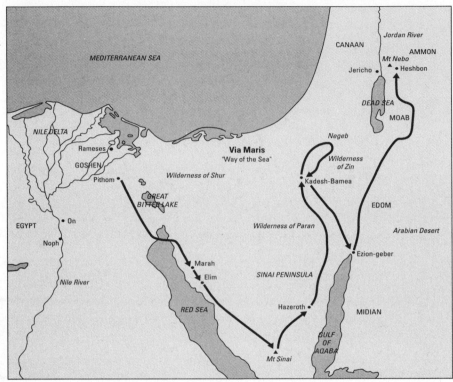

Figure 7-1:
The possible
route of the
exodus.

Are we there yet? The Israelites' constant complaining (Exodus 16–17)

Shortly after the miraculous events at the Red Sea, Moses leads the people on a three-month trek through the desert to Mount Sinai, where God first appeared to Moses in a burning bush. While on the way, the people, far from showing their gratitude for having been freed from slavery, grumble to Moses about everything from where they'll find their next meal to why Moses led them out of slavery to die in the wilderness. In each case, Moses brings their complaint to God, who provides for their need. As the peoples' complaints and God's provision are repeated in the Book of Numbers (a book discussed later in this chapter), here's a breakdown for ease of reference:

✔ The people complain that they don't have enough food. In response, God causes a sticky bread-like substance to fall from the sky. Not knowing what this stuff is, the people call it "What is it?" or *manna* in Hebrew. Manna will be part of the Israelite's daily diet during the 40-year wilderness wanderings.

✔ The people complain that they don't have enough meat. In response, God causes quail to land in the Israelite camp. The people gather the birds and have a barbeque each evening for 40 years.

✔ The people complain that they don't have enough water. In response, God instructs Moses to strike a rock with his staff, and water gushes forth from the rock for the Israelites to drink.

Receiving the Ten Commandments and Israel's other laws (Exodus 20)

After the Israelites arrive at Mount Sinai, they become frightened when they hear God's thundering voice and ask Moses to serve as a mediator between them and God. Moses then ascends Mount Sinai to receive Israel's law.

By tradition, the Laws received by Moses on Mount Sinai number 613. Yet, the most famous and important of these laws are the Ten Commandments, which God inscribes with His finger upon rock tablets.

Following is a brief rundown of the Ten Commandments and what they mean:

✔ **You shall have no other gods before Me.** This commandment, enjoining Israel to singular devotion to God, is intimately tied to their being delivered by God from Egyptian bondage. In fact, Jewish tradition reckons God's statement just prior to this command ("I am the LORD your God, who brought you out of Egypt, out of the land of slavery") as the first of the Ten Commandments. The thrust of this commandment is: Since God delivered you from slavery, you should be loyal to Him.

✔ **You shall not make idols.** Traditionally this commandment has been understood to mean that Israel couldn't make representations of humans or animals. Thus, Jewish artistic expression of a later period often lacked human or animal subjects. However, it seems more likely that this commandment prohibits the making of human or animal objects for worship. The reason for this prohibition is that an image or idol could never capture all that God is. Moreover, images of God already exist: humans, who the Bible says are made "in the image of God" (Genesis 1). Thus, making images of God devalues both God and humans.

✔ **You shall not lift up God's name in vain.** This injunction most likely prohibits people from making oaths in God's name. Yet, the phrase "in vain" means "for nothing," and, therefore, some scholars (and parents) understand this commandment to refer to using God's name in any inappropriate manner, such as when swearing or "cussing." Today, many devout Jews (and some Christians) don't use God's name at all to ensure that they don't break this command. Moreover, some people, when writing, replace the "o" in the word God with a hyphen (G-d).

✔ **Keep the Sabbath.** Because God rested on the seventh day of Creation, humans are ordered to mirror God's behavior. The Hebrew Bible takes this very seriously. As evidence of this, a man is killed for gathering wood on the Sabbath (Numbers 15:32–36).

✔ **Honor your father and mother.** Honoring your parents means to respect and care for them (such as providing for them in old age). This commandment is the only one with an accompanying promise: ". . . that your days may be long in the land the LORD your God is giving you." Although this promise would eventually be understood to refer to an individual's life, in its original context, this promise guarantees the nation of Israel a long tenure in their Promised Land if they obey this commandment (and presumably the others, as well).

✔ **You shall not murder.** The sixth commandment is often misunderstood to prohibit killing of any kind. However, the Israelites had several crimes that were punishable by death, and they were allowed to kill during times of war. This commandment prohibits *murder* — that is, the intentional killing of another person without cause.

✔ **You shall not commit adultery.** In the Hebrew Bible, adultery consists of sexual relations between a married man and a married woman (married to other people, of course). Sexual relations between a married man and an unmarried woman isn't technically adultery because polygamy is allowable in the Hebrew Bible (see Chapter 6 of this book).

✔ **You shall not steal.** This one's pretty easy, meaning the same thing then that it does today: Don't steal.

✔ **You shall not bear false witness.** This commandment, though more generally referring to lying in any situation, more specifically refers to accusing a person falsely in a legal context. In biblical times, as today, lying while "on the stand" was a major problem. To combat false testimony, ancient Israel had this commandment (plus a requirement of two witnesses) to convict a person. Nevertheless, people are wrongly prosecuted and even killed at times in the Bible as a result of dishonest testimony.

✔ **You shall not covet.** Unlike the previous nine, violations against the tenth commandment are unverifiable (except to God). Although unverifiable, this commandment is an important part of the Ten, because it seeks to address the impetus or motive contributing to the violation of the other commandments.

The Ten Commandments in context

Scholars have discovered that the covenant embodied in the Ten Commandments bears a striking resemblance to other ancient Near Eastern legal agreements, known as *suzerain-vassal* (or master-servant) *treaties*. In other words, when God establishes His covenant with Israel, He does so using a legal language that they could understand.

Adultery and the "Wicked Bible"

In 1631, King Charles I of Britain ordered 1,000 Bibles from a reputable English printer. All was well, except for one mistake: The printer left out the word "not" in the seventh commandment (to read "You shall commit adultery" in error). The king was not amused, and he ordered all the texts recalled and destroyed. This edition became known as the "Wicked Bible," and only a few copies remain around today, each worth a fortune.

Meanwhile, back at camp: Aaron and the golden "calf" (Exodus 32)

While Moses is on Mount Sinai receiving the Law for 40 days, the people grow impatient and ask Aaron to build them "a god to lead us." Aaron, being the pillar of virtue that he is, asks the people to give him their gold jewelry, with which he builds a golden bull. This idol isn't a calf, as is popularly believed. Calves are small, newborn animals that have trouble standing. Rather, the statue that Aaron creates is of a 1-year-old bull, a true symbol of virility and a common way to represent one's god in the ancient world. That is, if you wanted to show your god was a "real" (that is, *studly*) god, you presented him (or her) as a bull or riding on top of a bull.

Thus, in Aaron's defense, he may possibly have understood the golden bull to be a symbol of Israel's God, who showed His prowess against Egypt's gods. This would explain why Aaron would acquiesce to this idol-making and still feel like he could say, "Tomorrow, a festival to the LORD!" Regardless of Aaron's intentions, God sees in the people's actions a direct violation of commandments one (no other gods) and two (no idols), and He informs Moses that He intends to destroy the Israelites for their sin. Moses begs God to reconsider, saying that by destroying the Israelites, the Egyptians would assume that He couldn't deliver His people into their Promised Land. Persuaded by Moses' appeal, God changes His mind and spares Israel.

Having effectively represented the people before God, Moses descends from the mountain to represent God before the people. When he sees the golden bull and the people engaged in idolatry and revelry, he throws the tablets bearing the Ten Commandments to the ground, breaking them into pieces, which symbolizes the Israelites' breaking their covenant with God. Moses then destroys the idol by burning it and grinding it into dust, which he sprinkles on water and makes the people drink. The instigators are punished, but, in the end, God forgives the people and renews the covenant.

Does God change His mind?

The notice that God "changed" His mind about wiping out the Israelites for building the golden bull raises an important theological question: Does the biblical author really imagine that God changes His mind? Some scholars argue that the biblical author means exactly what he says: God changed His mind. However, some argue that, because other passages explicitly say that God doesn't change His mind (Numbers 23:19), this notice is an example of *anthropomorphic* language, where God's actions are described in human terms. By this reading, the reason for saying God "changed" His mind is to show that God is willing to engage in reasoned dialog and even be "persuaded" by the requests of His people.

God's mobile home: The Tabernacle (Exodus 25:1–31:11; 35:30–40:38)

Nearly one-third of Exodus is devoted to describing the form and function of the Tabernacle — a portable tent structure that becomes God's "residence" on earth. Although the Bible goes out of its way to say that God can't be limited to one geographical locale, the Tabernacle becomes a place where God's presence (also called His "glory") is uniquely manifest on earth, and where the people can offer Him worship and sacrifices. Moreover, the layout and content of the Tabernacle symbolize various facets of God's relationship with Israel (see Figure 7-2).

Here's what you would find at the Tabernacle if you lived during Moses' day.

The Tabernacle was a large rectangular tent (15 feet high, 45 feet long, and 15 feet wide) enclosed by a 75-x-150-foot courtyard. The worshiper brought an offering to the entrance of the courtyard, where he was met by a priest. In the case of an animal offering, the worshiper would place his hands upon the animal's head and confess his sins, symbolically transferring his wrongdoing to the sacrificial victim. The priest then took the animal to the Bronze Altar for sacrifice. Also in the courtyard was the Bronze Basin, which was filled with water and used by the priests for making themselves ritually pure before rendering service to God.

REMEMBER

The priest's role as mediator intended to convey that God is holy (or morally separate) from humanity. Even the priests needed to make themselves ritually pure via sacrifice and washings before offering sacrifices on behalf of others.

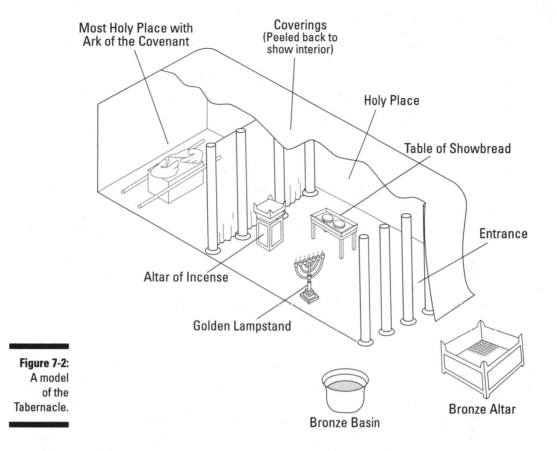

Figure 7-2:
A model
of the
Tabernacle.

An Old Testament God of wrath?

We often hear people say, "The God of the Old Testament is a God of wrath, while the God of the New Testament is a God of love." Ironically, the inaccuracy of this statement is nowhere more apparent than in the context of God's punishing the Israelites for worshiping the golden bull. In the wake of this event, God "reintroduces" Himself to Moses — a reintroduction that intends to remind Moses (and the reader) that God is first and foremost a God of love and forgiveness:

The LORD is a merciful and gracious God, slow to anger, and abounding in loving kindness and faithfulness, keeping steadfast love for thousands, forgiving iniquity and transgression and sin, but who will by no means clear the guilty, visiting the iniquity of the fathers upon the children and the children's children, to the third and the fourth generation.

—Exodus 34:6–7

That's right. According to Exodus 34, the God of the Hebrew Bible is seven parts love and forgiveness and only one part judgment (not "wrath" — there's a difference).

As you entered the Tabernacle proper (although only priests could enter), here's what you'd see:

- ✔ **The Table of Showbread,** which daily held 12 loaves of bread (one each for the twelve tribes of Israel) and which served as an offering to God and gave testimony to God's continual provision for His people.

- ✔ **The Golden Lampstand (or Menorah),** a seven-branched candelabrum, which always remained lit as a symbol of God's enduring covenant with Israel.

- ✔ **The Altar of Incense,** which not only covered the smell involved with sacrifice, but also symbolized the sacrifices and prayers that ascended to God on behalf of Israel.

A curtain separated the front room of the tent (called the Holy Place) from the back room (called the Most Holy Place or the Holy of Holies). The back room was God's "throne room," the sacredness of which was represented by the most sacred relic in the cult: the Ark of the Covenant, which rested in the center of the room. Only the High Priest could enter the Holy of Holies, and he could only do this once a year on the Day of Atonement (see "A guide to Israel's holy days" later in this chapter).

The *Ark of the Covenant* was a box made of acacia wood, covered with gold foil, and the lid was solid gold with two biblical *cherubim* (creatures with the body of a lion, the face of a human, and the wings of an eagle) facing one another at each end. Inside the Ark were a pot of manna, reminding Israel of God's provision; Aaron's staff, reminding Israel of Aaron's leadership; and the Ten Commandments, symbolizing God's covenant with the Israelites.

After the Tabernacle is completed, the pillar of smoke and fire symbolizing God's presence, which has been leading the Israelites since their departure from Egypt, fills the Tabernacle. From now on, when God wants the Israelites to move to a new location, the cloud lifts from the Tabernacle and leads the way.

Laws for Holy Living: The Book of Leviticus

The third of the Five Books of Moses, Leviticus, is the keystone of the Torah. Not only does Leviticus sit at the literary center of the books of Moses, it also provides Israel with the laws that set them apart as God's special people. The name "Leviticus," in fact, derives from its focus on laws and ritual, which were largely carried out by the priestly tribe of the Levites.

Sacrifice in the ancient world: The importance of being earnest *and* "ritually correct" (Leviticus 10)

Although being sincere when offering a sacrifice or performing a ritual was important in ancient Israel, so was carrying out that ritual in the proper manner. Anyone who changed a ritual in any way, especially adding anything that hinted of the practices of ancient Israel's polytheistic neighbors, was punished severely. Even Aaron's two oldest sons are killed by God for making an offering of "strange" or "foreign" incense.

Yet, for all its importance, Leviticus today is often a misunderstood book — not because it's difficult to interpret (though, at times, it is), but because it spends so much time focusing on how to properly perform various sacrifices, what one can and cannot eat, and what to do if a wound turns a certain color. To the modern reader, such details are mundane and even gross (and they are, we admit). But for priests whose job it was to offer proper sacrifices to God, instruct the people on what foods were clean or unclean, and to diagnose diseases, the book of Leviticus was an essential resource.

Understanding sacrifice in ancient Israel (Leviticus 1–9)

Leviticus begins by describing the various sacrifices priests were to offer. This priority on sacrifice is purposeful since Israel's sacrificial system provided the people with a way to obtain forgiveness from God and to express gratitude to God for His provision. Related to God's provision, sacrifice also provided the priests and people with food. In fact, far from being a savage practice, as people today tend to think of it, ritual sacrifice underscored the seriousness of taking an animal's life for food. (By comparison, the modern practice of saying, "I'll take that cheeseburger to go" does little to acknowledge the loss of life that accompanies eating meat.)

Leviticus describes five categories of sacrifice:

✔ **The Burnt Offering (Leviticus 1):** This offering was the most basic sacrifice for sin — the Hebrew word for it literally means "that which is offered up." Depending on what one could afford to give, the burnt offering consisted of a young bull, a 1-year-old lamb, or a bird (dove or pigeon). The animal was entirely roasted, the smell of which traveled skyward as a "soothing odor" to God. This sacrifice was offered twice daily — once in the morning and once in the evening — and was accompanied by offerings of cereal and wine. The priests offered additional animals and libations for the Sabbath and the beginning of new months.

✓ **The Grain Offering (Leviticus 2):** This offering was a way of thanking God for His provision of food. As the name implies, the grain offering consisted of grain (or fine flour), as well as olive oil, incense, and unleavened bread. Part of the offering was presented to God, with the rest of the offering going to the priests for food.

✓ **The Peace Offering, or "Sacrifice of Well-Being" (Leviticus 3):** This offering was a way of expressing one's desire for peace or fellowship with God. There were three types of peace offerings: the thanksgiving sacrifice (which included cakes of bread in addition to the animal), the votive sacrifice (repayment of a vow), and the freewill sacrifice (not limited to festive occasions).

✓ **Purification Offering, or "Sin Offering" (Leviticus 4:1–5:13):** The purification offering atoned mostly for unintentional sins, especially when no restitution could be made. Here, the status of the offender was taken into consideration, as well as his or her intentions. Thus, priests and rulers needed to offer larger sacrifices than laity, and purposeful or careless sins cost more than those committed accidentally.

✓ **Reparation Offering, or "Guilt Offering" (Leviticus 5:14–26):** The reparation offering was a sacrifice given to cover offenses against a fellow Israelite or God and required that the offender make restitution.

Is that kosher? The biblical diet (Leviticus 11)

Leviticus, beyond concerning itself with proper sacrifice, goes to great pains to describe what one could and could not eat. The dietary laws recorded in Leviticus 11 (and again in Deuteronomy 14) classify food as "clean" (or *kosher*, a Hebrew word that means "proper") or "unclean." In general, roadkill was out, as were all animals that died a natural death. Also, animals had to be at least 8 days old. Other than these general categories, the Bible breaks down the animals according to species: mammals, water creatures, birds, and creeping things.

Mammals

If an animal is a *ruminant* (it has an extra stomach and chews cud, allowing grass to be digested), and if it is an *ungulate* (it has a cloven hoof), and if that hoof is split rather than solid, we're talking barbeque! The Israelites ate mostly sheep and goats, but they also consumed cattle and hunted wild fauna, such as deer and ibex. The Bible lists a few examples of non-kosher animals, such as camel, which chews cud, has a split foot, but no hoof, rabbit, which appears to chew cud (but doesn't), and has no parted hoof, and pig, which has a split hoof but doesn't chew cud.

Why Kosher?

Kosher is a Hebrew word meaning "proper," and it refers to items that, according to the Law of Moses, are acceptable for use or consumption. Most often, however, *kosher* refers to things people are allowed to consume. Scholars have proposed a variety of solutions to explain why the Bible approves of some foods and not others. The most common proposal is that the Bible's dietary laws are intended to protect Israel from sickness or disease. However, this explanation doesn't account for all the data. For example, eating a beetle (not kosher) is no more risky than eating a cricket (kosher). Therefore, perhaps the best explanation for the Bible's dietary laws is that they made Israel culturally distinctive. Along with dress and language, diet is among the best markers of culture, and Israel's dietary laws set them apart from their neighbors.

Water creatures

The Israelites didn't spend much time in the water. So although they had dozens of words pertaining to sheep and goats, only one word in the Hebrew Bible exists for all types of water creatures: *dag*. A whale is a *dag*, as is a lobster, a squid, and a tuna. Nevertheless, if a creature lives in the water, it must have scales and fins in order to be kosher.

Birds

Instead of listing characteristics that a bird must possess in order to be kosher (as is done with the other categories of food), the Bible simply lists birds that are forbidden to eat, such as owls, eagles, hawks, and bats. (We know that a bat isn't a bird, but the official category in Hebrew is "flying thing," which a bat certainly is.) The prohibited birds all eat flesh, so birds that feed primarily on grain were considered kosher. Most often, ancient Israelites ate pigeons. Chickens aren't mentioned in the Hebrew Bible because domestic chickens only arrived in the area about 500 B.C.E.

Creeping things

This category includes reptiles and insects. No reptile was permissible to eat, but some insects were. If the insect had wings and walked on its legs, and if it had a leg joint above its body to hop, it was okay. Thus, locusts were acceptable, as were crickets and grasshoppers. Some locusts in this part of the world are the size of a double cheeseburger and would have taken several bites to consume. (Yes, we know . . . try to restrain yourself.)

A guide to Israel's holy days

The biblical calendar is necessarily sacred as it commemorates God's activity in history, such as the creation of the world and Israel's exodus from Egypt. Therefore, Leviticus goes to great lengths to specify how and when to commemorate various holidays or "holy days." The following sections describe some of Israel's most sacred days.

The pilgrimage feasts

Three holidays in the Israelite calendar called for a pilgrimage to Israel's central altar (at first, the Tabernacle, but eventually, the Temple built by Solomon in Jerusalem; see Chapter 10): Passover, the Feast of Weeks, and the Feast of Booths. (See Chapter 27 for more information on the Bible's feasts and holidays.)

- **Passover, or Feast of Unleavened Bread:** Passover is a spring holiday (April/May) that commemorates Israel's exodus from Egypt. In the original Passover, the Israelites were instructed to slaughter a lamb and apply its blood to the door frames of their homes so that God and His destroying angel would "pass over" their homes on their way to kill the firstborn of Egypt. The Passover is followed by the Feast of Unleavened Bread, where the Israelites are forbidden to eat anything with leaven in it. This feast commemorate the Israelites' hurried departure from Egypt when they didn't have time to leaven their bread.

- **Feast of Weeks, Shavuot, First Fruits, or Harvest (Greek Pentecost):** Seven weeks and a day (50 days) after Passover is the Feast of Weeks (May/June), a harvest festival for the wheat and barley that was planted in the fall. On this holiday, sacrifices were offered, both of animals and of the harvest, in recognition of God's provision.

- **Feast of Booths/Tabernacles, Sukkot, or Feast of Ingathering:** The final agricultural holiday before winter, Booths (Hebrew Sukkot), celebrates the harvest of grapes and olives (September/October). It's a weeklong joyous occasion, where participants live in temporary structures, or booths, to commemorate the Israelites' wilderness wanderings. As with the other pilgrimage feasts, Booths involves sacrifices given in gratitude for God's provision of food and, in this particular case, freedom.

Why kosher delis don't serve cheeseburgers

If you've been to a kosher restaurant or keep kosher yourself, you know that consuming milk and meat products together is a no-no. This prohibition ultimately derives from the command "You shall not boil a kid [baby goat] in its mother's milk" (Exodus 23:19 and 34:26, and Deuteronomy 14:21). Scholars disagree about the meaning of this prohibition. Some argue, based on parallels in other ancient cultures, that this command prohibits a pagan ritual in which baby goats were sacrificed by being boiled in milk. Other scholars claim that the command reflects the Bible's concern for the ethical treatment of animals. According to this view, the Bible prohibits boiling a kid in its mother's milk because it's cruel. Whatever the exact meaning, Jewish tradition has understood this prohibition to mean that you can't consume milk and meat products together — in other words, no cheeseburgers.

The Day of Atonement

The Day of Atonement (*Yom Kippur* in Hebrew) is the most solemn day of the calendar and takes place in the fall, five days earlier than Sukkot. It is a day of fasting and self-reflection, in which the priests and the society purge themselves of the past year's sins. During the Day of Atonement, the Tabernacle (and later the Temple) is purified, and only on this day is the High Priest allowed to enter the sanctuary's Holy of Holies, where the Ark of the Covenant resided, in order to offer a sacrifice for the sins of the whole nation. See Chapter 27 for more information on this holy day.

The Sabbatical Years

Just as the people rested every seventh day, so the land was to lay fallow every seven years, in what were known as Sabbatical Years. The Israelites were not allowed to plant, harvest, or even prune during this year. Moreover, several social reforms occurred during these special years, including providing food for the poor and canceling debts (if only we could get credit card companies to sign up for this one).

The Year of Jubilee

The year after seven Sabbatical Years was known as the Year of Jubilee, named after a Hebrew word for a ram's horn, which was blown as a trumpet at this and other celebrations. During the Year of Jubilee, the people were reminded that God, not they, owned all they had. Moreover, all Israelites enslaved due to debt were freed, and all land that was sold to pay off debts during the past 50 years was returned to the original owners.

Law and order: Israel's legal system

In addition to ritual laws and holy days that center around the Israelites' worship of God, Leviticus contains a variety of ethical laws that focus on the Israelites' relationship with one another. Many of the ethical laws in Leviticus may sound familiar to you. This familiarity is due, in large part, to the Bible's influence on our modern legal system, as well as on our moral code. Here's a sampling of Leviticus' ethical teachings:

> Don't oppress your neighbor or steal from him.
> Don't withhold the wages due to a worker overnight.
> Don't curse a deaf person or put a stumbling block in front of the blind.
> Don't show favoritism toward the poor or the rich, but judge fairly.
> Don't take revenge or bear a grudge but love your neighbor as yourself.

> —Leviticus 19:13–15, 18

An eye for an eye, a tooth for a tooth

Several of Israel's laws end with the phrase "an eye for an eye, a tooth for a tooth" (see, for example, Leviticus 24:20). This law is known in Latin as *Lex Talionis* (or "law of retaliation"). Today this law is often misinterpreted to mean that the Bible condones vengeance. However, the purpose for the law "an eye for an eye, a tooth for a tooth" isn't to encourage retaliation, but to limit it. The difference is subtle but important. For example, if Moe gives Curly an eye poke, Curly may be tempted not only to poke Moe's eye, but to slap him on the forehead and give him a "nyuk, nyuk." "An eye for an eye" limits Curly's right to retaliation to just the eye. This law helped to keep ancient feuds, as well as Three Stooges' abuses, from spiraling out of control.

Many of Israel's laws are influenced by the people's experience as slaves in Egypt. In particular, several laws seek to protect strangers from abuse or mistreatment. For example, Leviticus says,

> *You shall treat the stranger who lives with you as a citizen. You shall love him as yourself, for you were once strangers in the land of Egypt.*

—Leviticus 19:34

With these ethical laws to guide them, Israel hoped not only to avoid the oppressive practices of their neighbors but also to distinguish themselves as God's holy and righteous people.

40-Year Nomads: The Book of Numbers

The Book of Numbers gets its name from two censuses and other numbers recorded in its pages. Mostly, however, Numbers is about events that occur during the 40 years of wandering in the wilderness under Moses. Like the Book of Exodus, Numbers records the peoples' many complaints and rebellions against God and God's appointed leader, Moses. Numbers also recounts the passing of Miriam and Aaron, Moses' sister and brother, and prepares the reader for Moses' imminent death.

Israel's continued rebellions (Numbers 12–14, 21, and 25)

Much of the Book of Numbers recounts the remaining years of the wilderness wanderings under Moses, years that are wrought with rebellion. Here are a few of the highlights (maybe lowlights is a more fitting description):

✓ **Aaron and Miriam's rebellion (Numbers 12):** The rebelliousness of the Israelites even extends to Moses' own family. Aaron and Miriam turn on their brother because he's married a "Cushite woman." For this affront, God punishes Miriam by turning her skin leprous white. Who this Cushite wife is isn't clear. Because Cush can refer to an area inside Midian, some have argued this refers to Moses' Midianite wife, Zipporah. However, more often in the Bible, Cush refers to the area south of Egypt, in what is today Sudan. If this is the case, part of Aaron and Miriam's disdain may have been directed at her darkened skin, making Miriam's punishment of ultra-white skin all the more ironic.

✓ **Spies like us (Numbers 13–14):** Before attempting to conquer the Promised Land, Moses requests that each of the twelve tribes of Israel appoint one man to travel into Canaan and do a bit of James Bond reconnaissance. The spies return with amazing tales of an abundant land truly flowing "with milk and honey." But because of the size of the enemy, most of the spies feel that any attempted campaign will end in disaster. However, two spies, Caleb and Joshua, argue that God will give them victory. Unfortunately, the Israelites go with the majority report, and decide not to enter the Promised Land. In response to their lack of faith, God tells them that everyone 20 years of age and older will die in the wilderness, but their children, along with Caleb and Joshua, will one day enter the Promised Land.

✓ **Korah, Dathan, and Abiram (Numbers 16):** These three men lead a rebellion with 250 men, all of whom question Moses' and Aaron's right to lead the people. In response, God causes the earth to open, which swallows the three ringleaders and their families. God then makes fire to come down from the sky, which consumes the remaining 250 rebels. The lesson: Don't mess with God's appointed leaders.

✓ **Aaron's blooming staff (Numbers 17):** Aaron's fellow priests question his right to be the High Priest. In order to determine God's view on the matter, Moses takes the staffs of Aaron and his opponents and places them in the Tabernacle. The next day, when Moses retrieves the staffs, only Aaron's has blossoms, confirming that God has chosen Aaron.

✓ **Fiery serpents (Numbers 21):** The people become fed up with wandering in the wilderness and complain to Moses about their lack of food and water. As punishment, God sends "fiery" snakes with lethal venom among the people. In response to the peoples' pleas and Moses' prayers, God instructs Moses to build a copper snake and hold it up so people could see it. If, after being bit, the people looked at the snake, they would be healed.

Moses' bronze serpent is mentioned two more times in the Bible: once in the Hebrew Bible, when King Hezekiah (715–687 B.C.E.) destroys Moses' bronze serpent because it has become an object of worship in Jerusalem's Temple (2 Kings 18:4), and again in the New Testament, when the author of the Gospel of John compares Moses' lifting up the serpent in order to bring physical healing to the Israelites with Jesus' being "lifted up" on the cross to bring spiritual healing (forgiveness of sins) to the world (John 3:14–15).

✔ **Cleaning God's house (Numbers 25:14–18):** A number of Israelite men participate in cultic prostitution with foreign women. During this raucous affair, a man and woman enter the Tabernacle and begin having sex (not a good idea). While they're in the act, Aaron's grandson, Phinehas, takes his spear and, well, he makes the first "Shiksa-Bob." For his act of defending the sanctity of God's tent, Phinehas is blessed with a covenant that his descendants would serve before God forever.

Moses' indiscretion: The Promised Land denied (Numbers 20:2–13)

Even Moses commits a sin that is so egregious that he's prevented from entering the Promised Land (Numbers 20). The transgression occurs at a place called Meribah, where the people again complain to Moses about a lack of water. God instructs Moses, "Take the rod and assemble the congregation, you and Aaron your brother, and tell the rock before their eyes to yield its water" (Numbers 20:8).

Moses gathers the people and then says, "Hear now, you rebels; shall we bring forth water for you out of this rock?" (Numbers 20:10). Then Moses hits the rock with the rod, and water issues forth. Yet, as the people are quenching their thirst, God speaks to Moses and Aaron, "Because you did not believe in Me, to treat Me as holy in the eyes of the children of Israel, therefore you will not bring this assembly into the land that I have given them" (Numbers 20:12). So what went wrong?

Balaam and the smart ass (Numbers 22–24)

A number of the nations the Israelites encounter in their wanderings fear them for what Israel did to Egypt. As a result, kings repeatedly refuse Israel permission to pass through their territory. The King of Moab even hires a soothsayer named Balaam to put a curse on Israel. Yet, every time Balaam tries to carry out his task, God forces him to bless Israel instead. Despite God's interference, Balaam doesn't give up and is soon off again to go curse Israel. While on the way, his donkey strays off course and then eventually lies down despite Balaam's continual beatings. Finally, the donkey turns to Balaam and asks, "What have I done to make you want to beat me?" Balaam is taken aback because donkeys don't usually initiate conversations. God then opens Balaam's eyes to see a sword-wielding angel who's blocking the donkey's path. The donkey's actions, as it turns out, had saved Balaam's life. Balaam and his donkey proceed, though Balaam is only able to bless Israel.

A large plaster inscription was excavated in northern Jordan that records additional exploits of Balaam, showing that he was quite a famous prophet in antiquity.

Part of the problem is that Moses *struck* the rock instead of *speaking* to it, which, when accompanied with the words "shall *we* bring forth water," made it look as though he was partly responsible for the miracle. This is not merely an oversight on Moses' part — God describes his sin as "rebellion," akin to the people's constant complaining. And for this rebellion, Moses will never set foot in the Promised Land.

Moses' Farewell Address: The Book of Deuteronomy

The Book of Deuteronomy records Moses' farewell address to the next generation of Israelites just outside ancient Israel's Promised Land. Deuteronomy actually means "second (or repeated) law," as the book is both a recap of the events of the past 40 years, and a renewal of Israel's covenant with God. This renewal is embodied in the most important law of Israelite religion, which is called the *Shema* in Hebrew, from its opening word meaning "hear" or "listen up."

> *Hear O Israel, the* LORD *our God, the* LORD *is one! You shall love the* LORD *your God with all your heart, with all your soul, and with all your might.*
>
> —Deuteronomy 6:4–5

As is evident in the Shema, Deuteronomy emphasizes the importance of God's love for Israel and of Israel's need to love God in return. In fact, Deuteronomy has been called "the book of love." The word used for this love is Hebrew *hesed*, which derives from covenant language used in the broader ancient Near East, and which is probably best translated as "unwavering commitment" or "steadfast devotion."

Could you repeat that? Deuteronomy's "second" law (Deuteronomy 1–33)

Deuteronomy is a great speech, but much of it is a repetition of events and laws recorded earlier in the Bible. Thus, Deuteronomy 5 again records the Ten Commandments, as well as other laws found in Exodus, Leviticus, and Numbers. Yet, Deuteronomy also contains some innovations:

- ✔ The reason for keeping the Sabbath is no longer because God rested on that day during Creation, but because the Israelites found rest when they were released from slavery.

- ✔ Deuteronomy places more emphasis on centralized worship at a single sanctuary "at the place God will choose" (ultimately Jerusalem). This mandate is important because when the Israelites spread out in their Promised Land, it will be more difficult to bring sacrifice to God's altar.

- ✔ Deuteronomy places more emphasis on remembering God's words and acts, and passing these traditions on to the next generation. Parents are commanded to teach their children about God in every context of life — "when you sit at home or walk along the road, when you lie down or when you get up" (Deuteronomy 6:7).

The Israelites are even instructed to bind God's commands on their hands and foreheads, as well as to write them on the doorposts of their homes. Today many devout Jews take these commands literally by tying *phylacteries* (small boxes containing portions of the Bible) on their left arm and forehead, or by attaching *mezuzot* (small wooden or metal containers holding portions of the Bible — usually the Shema) on the doorframes of their homes.

The end of an era: The death of Moses (Deuteronomy 34)

Deuteronomy's (and, thus, the Torah's) ending is a cliff-hanger, with much left unresolved. Most notably, the Israelites have yet to enter their Promised Land. However, Moses has brought them a long way; from bondage in Egypt as slaves to free people with a law code of their own. Moreover, the Israelites are camped on the plains of Moab, immediately east of the border of Canaan. Only the Jordan River separates them from the Promised Land.

As Moses' final act on behalf of Israel, he transfers power to his trusted and faithful friend, Joshua. Then, at the age of 120, Moses climbs Mount Nebo, where God shows him the land of Canaan. With the assurance that the Israelites will soon enter their Promised Land, Moses passes away.

Deuteronomy ends with a tribute to the Hebrew Bible's greatest prophet:

> *And there has not arisen a prophet since in Israel like Moses, whom the* LORD *knew face to face.*

> —Deuteronomy 34:10

The intimate bond shared between Moses and God is further communicated in the notice that God Himself buries Moses. As a consequence, the exact location of Moses' grave remains secret.

Chapter 8

An Experiment in Theocracy: Joshua, Judges, and Ruth

The biblical books of Joshua, Judges, and Ruth chronicle Israel's history from Moses' death to the onset of the monarchy. Under the leadership of Joshua the Israelites successfully enter and conquer their Promised Land (ancient Canaan). After Joshua, Israel is ruled by judges, not in the modern sense of stoic figures in black robes, but in the ancient sense of charismatic figures who, though perhaps hearing a case or two, would lead the Israelites in battles against their enemies. The Book of Ruth focuses on the life experiences of one family during the period of the judges, who overcomes extreme hardship to become an influential member of ancient Israelite society.

During this period, Israel is loosely organized in a tribal *theocracy*, where God is viewed as the ultimate ruler of the confederacy. These are wild times for Israel, because it lacks a central governing authority to punish crimes and maintain order. However, wild times mean colorful characters and stories, and Joshua, Judges, and Ruth certainly do not disappoint.

Exploring the Book of Joshua

The Book of Joshua acquires its name from its main character. Joshua was Moses' right-hand man, accompanying him on Mount Sinai as he received the Law from God, and assisting him in battle against Israel's enemies. Joshua had also been one of two spies (Caleb was the other) who believed that God would deliver the Promised Land to Israel, despite the size of the foe. This courage, spirituality, and military prowess come in handy as Joshua leads the next generation of Israelites into their Promised Land.

Preparing to enter the land (Joshua 1)

When we pick up the action of Joshua, the Israelites are encamped on the border of the Promised Land, just east of the Jordan River. Joshua tells them to get ready, because in three days they will cross the Jordan, and when they do, there's no turning back. The people reply:

> *All that you have commanded we will do, and wherever you send us we will go. Just as we obeyed Moses in all things, so we will obey you.*

—Joshua 1:16–17

Although these words may seem a small consolation in light of just how infrequently the people really listened to Moses, this is a new generation, and they actually will end up obeying (most of) what Joshua commands.

Two spies and a prostitute (Joshua 2)

Prior to entering the Promised Land, Joshua sends two spies ahead to Jericho to gather strategic information. Upon entering the city, and in true James Bond fashion, the two spies go to the house of a prostitute named Rahab. (After all, if you want insider information, what better place to go than the local brothel?)

When the king of Jericho receives news of the Israelite infiltrators, he sends his soldiers to Rahab's house. Rahab lies to the soldiers, however, saying the two spies already left the city, all the while hiding them on her roof. The reason for Rahab's traitorous actions is that she has heard about God delivering the Israelites from their Egyptian bondage and from their enemies during their wilderness wanderings. For Rahab, the conclusion is obvious:

> *For the LORD your God is God in heaven above and on earth below.*

—Joshua 2:11

Rahab is now a believer in this God, which was one of the desired outcomes expressed by God when He delivered Israel from its Egyptian slavery — non-Israelites would also believe in Him. Therefore, Rahab asks the spies to return her favor of lying on their behalf by sparing her and her family when (not *if*) they conquer the city. The spies agree and, that night, Rahab lowers them from the city wall, and they eventually make it back to the Israelite camp. In the New Testament, Rahab's heroism is held out as an example of faith for others to emulate (Hebrews 11:31 and James 2:25).

Crossing o'er Jordan and preparing for battle (Joshua 3–5)

After the spies return, the Israelites prepare to enter the Promised Land. The final barrier to their entry, the Jordan River, actually proves insignificant because its waters miraculously roll back when the priests carrying the Ark of the Covenant (see Chapter 7) enter the river.

Israel's miraculous crossing of the Jordan River not only provides continuity between the leadership of Moses and Joshua (because this mirrors Israel's crossing the Red Sea — see Chapter 7), but it also serves to underscore that Israel's upcoming battles will be accomplished not by military prowess but by God's power.

So that future generations would remember God's miraculous acts on behalf of Israel, God commands that a representative from each tribe collect a stone from the dried riverbed to be made into a memorial. As Joshua says,

> For your children will ask in time to come, "What do these stones mean to you?" And you will say to them that the waters of the Jordan were cut off in front of the Ark of the Covenant of the LORD. When it crossed over the Jordan, the waters of the Jordan were cut off. And these stones will be a memorial to the children of Israel forever.

> —Joshua 4:6–7

Making up for past sins

When the Israelites enter their Promised Land, the *manna* (or divinely provided bread; see Chapter 7) that has fed them for 40 years ceases, because now they will eat the produce of this land "flowing with milk and honey." Also making this a momentous occasion, and as further preparation for battle, Joshua has all the Israelite males circumcised. Apparently adding to the sins of the former generation, they neglected to circumcise their sons. This new generation's obedience in this regard symbolizes their renewal of their covenant with God. In recognition of this renewal, the place of their circumcision is named Gilgal, from a Hebrew word meaning "to roll," because "God rolled back the reproach of Israel."

Meeting the commander-in-chief of God's army

As Joshua is looking over Jericho in preparation for the impending battle, he is startled by a man standing in front of him with a drawn sword. Already outmaneuvered, Joshua realizes diplomacy is his best option: "Are you for us or for our enemies?" The man's answer is perhaps more startling than his sudden appearance: "Neither. Rather I have come as the commander of the LORD's army." Realizing this is a divine visitor, Joshua falls on his face and asks what God would have him do. Rather than give Joshua a battle strategy, the divine visitor responds: "Take off your sandals, for the place where you are standing is holy ground" (Joshua 5:15). That's it. No discussion, no insider scoop, just take off your sandals. So what's going on here?

The main point of this encounter, on the eve before Israel engages the enemy, is manifold. First, God is with Joshua, just as He was with Moses — this event mirrors Moses' sandal incident at the burning bush (found in Exodus 3, as well as in Chapter 7 of this book). Second, God will be fighting on behalf of Israel. Finally, and most importantly, this war isn't about the Israelites. As the commander says, he is fighting on "neither" side, which reminds the reader that this battle is ultimately about God's purposes:

✔ Concerning the Israelites, God is fulfilling a promise made long ago to Abraham — that his descendants would one day live in the Promised Land.

✔ Concerning the inhabitants of Canaan, God is fulfilling another promise He made to Abraham — that He would one day judge the Canaanites for their many sins.

And the walls came a tumblin' down: The defeat of Jericho (Joshua 6)

The Israelites are now ready to take Jericho, and get the conquest underway, but there is a major problem: The heavily fortified walls of Jericho separate the Israelite army from their first victory.

The walls of Jericho were renowned in the ancient world. Apparently, as one of the oldest cities of human civilization, Jericho had learned over the millennia that nothing speaks "keep out" like tall walls. The irony is that as Joshua looks at the tightly shut walls of Jericho, God says, "See, I've delivered Jericho into your hands" (Joshua 6:1–2).

In keeping with this "achieve the impossible" optimism, God gives Joshua very unorthodox battle plans: Have the soldiers and seven priests with trumpets parade with the Ark of the Covenant once around the city every day for six days. Then, on the seventh day, the group should march around the city seven times, and then sound all the trumpets and everyone should shout at the top of their lungs. Yeah, that makes sense. And the inhabitants of Jericho will laugh so hard they'll fall off the wall, right? Thankfully, Joshua knew that God knew what He was doing and didn't ask questions. And sure enough, after the seven-day ritual and primal scream, the walls collapse and the Israelites take Jericho.

A temporary setback: Stealing from God (Joshua 7–8)

Things are going great for Israel in the war department. After the miraculous defeat of the Canaanites at Jericho, Israelite spies are sent northwest to reconnoiter the city of Ai. Due to Ai's diminutive forces, Joshua decides that only a limited army is needed to conquer. Nevertheless, they suffer an unexpected and terrible defeat.

Joshua is distressed when the bad news reaches him, and he asks God how this could have happened. God tells Joshua the defeat came because of a serious covenant violation — one of the Israelite soldiers took some of the war spoils at Jericho that belonged to God. Joshua summons the people and, using *lots* (biblical dice), discovers that a man named Achan stole some gold, some silver, and a beautiful robe from Jericho, and then buried the treasures inside his tent. For this sort of violation, in which religious laws of war are breached, the punishment is severe. Achan is "cut off" (Hebrew *keret*), meaning that he, along with his family and livestock, are stoned to death and buried along with his possessions (including the stolen items).

This religious purge does the trick, and the Israelites are successful in defeating Ai on their second try.

The Gibeonites' trick and the total conquest (Joshua 9–12)

With Israel back on track after the setback at Ai, Israel's conquest is rapid, using a divide-and-conquer strategy by attacking Canaan's midsection, and then campaigning south and north. Yet, when the residents of Gibeon, a city near Jerusalem, hear of Israel's victories, they understandably fear for their lives and come up with a tricky strategy of their own. The Gibeonites dress up like poor travelers and approach Joshua at Gilgal. They pretend to have traveled a great distance, so as to make Joshua think they are not inhabitants of the Promised Land. Without consulting God, Joshua and the Israelites make a treaty with the Gibeonites, promising never to destroy them. After three days, however, the Israelites discover their ruse, but they are unable to harm the Gibeonites due to their oath. So Joshua decrees that, from then on, the Gibeonites would become Israel's servants.

After the episode with the Gibeonites, Joshua performs one miracle so amazing that the Bible mentions "There has been no day like it before or after, when the LORD listened to the voice of a man" (Joshua 10:14). That miracle occurs when Joshua orders the sun to stand still to give the Israelites more time to finish a battle against a coalition of Canaanite kings. Because Joshua's order occurs some 3,000 years before Copernicus, the biblical author describes this miracle by saying "the sun stood still and the moon stopped" (Joshua 10:13), showing that truly nothing is impossible for God. With this extended time, the Israelites are able to defeat the coalition.

After this miraculous victory, the Israelites, in short order, defeat the kingdoms of southern and northern Canaan. Joshua 11 ends with the report:

> *Thus, Joshua possessed the entire land as the LORD had said to Moses, and he gave it as an inheritance to Israel according to their tribal allotments. Then the land had rest from war.*

> —Joshua 11:23

Biblical war rules

Conquering Jericho and other Canaanite cities are not ordinary battles where, if successful, the soldiers divide the war spoils, including taking any desirable women or children for slaves. Instead, these are wars of "destruction" (from the Hebrew word *herem,* often mistranslated as "holy war"), which have their own special laws as recorded in Deuteronomy 20. During these wars of destruction, God Himself partakes in the fighting. Because God is fighting, soldiers must be both morally and ritually pure. In addition, soldiers who are fearful (or lack faith) are not allowed to fight. Moreover, if the war is fought against a city within the borders of the Promised Land, then to erase the influence of foreign religion, the destruction must be total. Men, women, children, and even livestock are to be destroyed. This divinely sanctioned genocide is disturbing, but the Bible presents this as a unique period in ancient Israel's history. What's more, this war is not about personal enrichment, nor is it about one side being more righteous than the other, but it is about God judging the Canaanites for their many sins and keeping His promises to Israel's ancestors. As Moses reminds the Israelites while they are still wandering in the wilderness:

When the LORD your God drives out your enemy before you, do not say to yourself, "The LORD has given me this inheritance because of my righteousness." It is rather on account of the wickedness of these nations . . . and to fulfill the promise He made to your ancestors Abraham, Isaac, and Jacob. It is not because of your righteousness . . . for you are a stiff-necked people.

—Deuteronomy 9:4–6

New homes and renewed covenants (Joshua 13–22)

The distribution of the land of Canaan among the twelve tribes of Israel is carried out by Joshua and the priest Eleazar (Aaron's son) by using sacred dice called Urim and Thummim. The locations of the tribal territories are depicted in Figure 8-1.

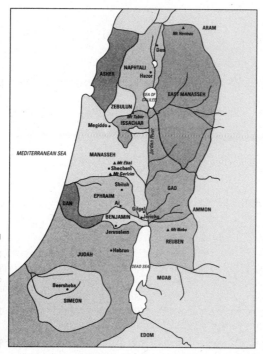

Figure 8-1: The territories of the twelve tribes of Israel.

Although Israel is traditionally reckoned as 12 tribes, in truth, there are 13. This is because the inheritance of Joseph, one of the 12 sons of Jacob, actually is divided amongst his two sons: Manasseh and Ephraim.

So then, who gets left out when the land is divided into 12 tribal allotments? Levi. Only, they aren't really left out. The Levites serve as priests for the tribes so they are given a total of 48 cities among the 12 tribal allotments. This ensures that there is a "priestly presence" in each tribe. Moreover, 6 of these 48 cities serve as "cities of refuge," where someone can go for protection and justice, particularly in cases where someone unintentionally kills another (see Joshua 20-21).

Joshua's covenant renewal and farewell (Joshua 23–24)

Near the close of Joshua, the Israelites gather one last time to renew their covenant with God. Moreover, Joshua delivers his farewell speech, admonishing the people to remain loyal to God:

> And now then, fear the LORD, and serve Him in sincerity and in truth; and turn away from the gods which your ancestors served beyond the River, and in Egypt, and serve the LORD. And if it is evil in your eyes to serve the LORD, choose this day whom you will serve, whether the gods your fathers served in the region beyond the River or the gods of the Amorites in whose land you dwell; but as for me and my house, we will serve the LORD.
>
> —Joshua 24:14–15

Joshua ends with three funerals (but no wedding). Joseph's mummy, which the Israelites carried up from Egypt, is finally buried as he had asked the Israelites to do hundreds of years before (Genesis 50:25). Then, Joshua and the priest Eleazar die, both being buried in Ephraim.

As for the survivors, they initially follow Joshua's instructions by obeying God, as does the next generation, but this obedience doesn't last too long, as the Book of Judges makes plain.

Understanding the Book of Judges

Some of the all-time greatest TV shows resemble Judges, because every episode follows the same plot structure. Take, for example, the cartoon *Scooby Doo.* In each episode a villain tries to fool others by posing as a paranormal phenomenon, which would have worked if it hadn't been for those meddling kids and their dog. In the same way, the cycle of Judges is quite apparent:

1. **A new generation of Israelites neglects God and worships other deities.**

2. **God punishes them through foreign oppression.**

3. **The people repent and beg God to save them.**

4. **God delivers the people militarily through a judge.**

5. **The villain is then unmasked, and snarls in Hebrew: "I would have gotten away with it if it hadn't been for those meddling kids and their dog."**

Actually we made up that last part — there are no masks in Judges, but there are plenty of villains, hijinks, and even some paranormal phenomena.

It is easy to misunderstand Joshua 1–12 to mean that the conquest of Canaan is rapid and complete. However, the later chapters of Joshua and the book of Judges make clear that many local inhabitants remain in the land — inhabitants whose religious practices will lure Israel away from its singular devotion to God.

Judge not, lest you be judged: Being a judge in the ancient world

During the period of the judges, Israel is fairly decentralized, with individual tribes administering their own affairs. However, on occasion, a serious enough foreign threat arises, and to meet the crisis God appoints an official known in Hebrew as *shofet* (a broad term often translated as "judge"). The term *judge* can be misleading, however, because hearing judicial cases was only a small part of their job description. A more apt title that encompasses all their roles is commander-in-chief, because a biblical judge oversees both the military and government during a time of crisis. However, the power of a shofet is less than a king's, because when the crisis abated or the judge died, the position would expire rather than be passed on to a descendant. Moreover, although judges oversaw one or more tribes during a crisis, no judge ever leads all of the tribes at once.

The Judges hall-of-fame (Judges 1–16)

Traditionally the 12 individuals in the Bible known as judges are divided into two categories: major and minor. The major judges are so-called because they have quite a bit written about them. By comparison, the minor judges have very little recorded about them, at most three verses. For ease of reference, Table 8-1 lists the major and minor judges, where in the Book of Judges they appear, and the nation or king that is oppressing Israel when God calls a particular judge into action.

Table 8-1			The Major and Minor Judges		
Major Judges			**Minor Judges**		
Judge	*Text*	*Oppressor*	*Judge*	*Text*	*Oppressor*
Othniel	3:7–11	King Cushan-rishathaim of Mesopotamia	Shamgar	3:31	Philistines

(continued)

Table 8-1 *(continued)*

Major Judges			Minor Judges		
Judge	*Text*	*Oppressor*	*Judge*	*Text*	*Oppressor*
Ehud	3:12–30	King Eglon of Moab	Tola	10:1–2	None listed
Deborah	4–5	King Jabin of Hazor	Jair	10:3–5	None listed
Gideon	6–8	Midianites	Ibzan	12:8–10	None listed
Jephthah	10:6–12:7	Ammonites	Elon	12:11–12	None listed
Samson	13–16	Philistines	Abdon	12:13–15	None listed

Othniel: The first judge

A couple of generations after Joshua, the Israelites begin worshiping other gods. As judgment, God allows a Mesopotamian king named Cushan-rishathaim to enslave the Israelites for eight years. The people cry out, and God selects as the Israelites' first judge a man named Othniel, who is the younger brother and son-in-law of Caleb (Caleb and Joshua are the spies during the wilderness wanderings who had faith that God would give Israel the Promised Land; see Chapter 7). Othniel defeats Israel's enemy in battle, bringing peace to Israel for a generation.

Ehud: Dirty jobs require getting dirty

Israel once again forsakes God, who in response sends Eglon, a Moabite king, to conquer and oppress it. Eighteen years later, Israel cries out to God in repentance, and He appoints a man named Ehud to deliver it. As Ehud is employed as a guard to oversee the safe delivery of the Israelite tribute to Moab, he is granted a private audience with the king to deliver a secret message. The guards, doing their duty, check to make sure Ehud has no weapons, and then let him in the king's private chambers. However, what the guards fail to realize is that, being left-handed, Ehud carries his weapon, which in this case is an 18-inch dagger, on the opposite side of most fighters, allowing him to enter the king's presence secretly armed.

During their meeting, the king sits down in what most translations say is "the upper room of his summer palace," but which most scholars believe actually refers to his private bathroom. While the king is getting up from his "throne," Ehud enters the bathroom, locks the door behind him, and gives the king his "message." The stab wound results in the king losing control of his bowels, which are emptied on the floor (note the King James translation: "and the dirt came out").

The king's servants soon arrive and, after opening the door, find their liege dead on the floor and Ehud gone. The Moabite army pursues Ehud, but the Israelite forces under his command defeat them.

If you're wondering how Ehud escaped the king's bathroom, he seems to have gone through the plumbing — a fairly common battle tactic in antiquity, and a favorite way to "dethrone" an indisposed monarch or baron in the Middle Ages. (Hey, overthrowing kingdoms is a dirty business.)

Deborah: Judge, prophetess, warrior

Deborah is one of the most remarkable people in the Bible. She is described as a prophetess, a judge who decides legal cases, and a military leader. As evidence of her influence, when she tells Barak, the Israelite military general, that God wants him to go to war against Jabin, the Canaanite king of Hazor and their oppressor of 20 years, Barak responds, "I won't go unless you go with me." Deborah's response is evidence of her prophetic abilities and the Bible's open discussion of established gender roles, "I'll go, but know that the glory for delivering Israel will go to a woman." Surprisingly, the woman Deborah refers to is not herself, but an unlikely heroine, whose actions are praised and used to mock the exploitation of women in the ancient world.

Deborah and Barak meet the enemy, and despite the fact that the Canaanite king had the benefit of 900 iron chariots and a skilled general named Sisera, his troops are routed. In order to allude capture, Sisera runs into the tent of a woman named Jael, who belongs to a neutral tribe in the Canaanite-Israelite wars. Jael invites Sisera to have a drink of milk and then tells him to rest. When Sisera is asleep, Jael takes a tent peg and drives it into his skull.

The prose narrative of this victory is followed by a poetic description known as the Song of Deborah. In it, Jael's actions are praised, even contrasting her active role in helping to win the battle with the passive role of the Canaanite women, who look out their windows for the returning armies carrying their spoils, including "a girl or two for every man" (Judges 5:30). Ironically, Sisera is not bringing subjugated women home, but rather is lying dead at the feet of a woman who subjugated him in her home.

Deborah's and Jael's victory becomes the turning point in Israel's battles with the Canaanites, as Israel grows "stronger and stronger against Jabin, the Canaanite king, eventually defeating him" (Judges 4:24).

Gideon: A wimp turned warrior

The Israelites turn again to other gods, and this time a people known as the Midianites devastate them through raiding parties. The Israelites call out to God in repentance, and again God sends a deliverer. Only this is not your average hero. When we meet Gideon, he's threshing wheat, not on a hilltop, where the wind could carry the chaff away, but in a winepress, for fear he would be spotted by the enemy.

Ironically, the angel whom God sends to commission Gideon says: "Hail, mighty warrior! The LORD is with you!" (Judges 6:12). God obviously sees something in Gideon we don't. Gideon, in keeping with his timid character, offers several excuses to get out of being a judge, but eventually he's convinced that he's the right one for the job.

Gideon's first task is to destroy his hometown's altar to Baal, the Canaanite storm god, which just happens to be on his father's property! After Gideon does it, the residents call for his death. However, Gideon's father calms the crowd and says that if Baal is a real god, then he can contend for himself. This explains why Gideon's other name is Jerubbaal, which means "let Baal contend."

As further evidence of Gideon's uncertainty in his new job as "mighty warrior," God commands him to go to battle against the Midianites. Gideon, however, is unwilling unless he can be sure God is with him. As a test, Gideon sets a fleece on the threshing floor, saying that if in the morning the fleece is wet and the ground is dry, he'll be successful in battle. The next morning it is exactly as he said. But you can never be too sure about these things, so he asks for the reverse sign the next morning — dry fleece, wet ground — and it happens. With no more excuses, Gideon goes to battle.

After Gideon gathers an army of 32,000 men, God informs him that the troops are too numerous. God wants the upcoming victory to be credited to divine power rather than human force. Eventually God whittles the number down to 300. In the end, the 300 don't even have to raise a sword — God instructs them to surround the enemy camp at night and, at Gideon's signal, expose lighted torches by breaking ceramic jars, yelling, and blowing trumpets. It works, and the Israelites have a resounding victory.

So why did God choose an excuse-making, father-worships-foreign-gods, wimpy kind of guy to deliver Israel? God's choice underscores what is one of the main themes of the Book of Judges — actually, of the whole Bible: God is the ultimate ruler and deliverer of Israel. As Gideon says when the people ask him to be their king:

> *I will not rule over you, nor will my son rule over you. The LORD will rule over you.*

> —Judges 8:23

Jephthah: The consequence of a hasty vow

The next to subjugate the Israelites are the Ammonites, their neighbors to the east (see Figure 8-1). In response to Israel's repentance and cries for deliverance, God appoints a skilled warrior named Jephthah to deliver them.

Did I say something wrong? Minding your shibboleths

Although today the word *shibboleth* refers to a password or a regional dialect, it is actually a Hebrew word meaning "ear of wheat" that comes from Judges 12. Jephthah and the people of Gilead, after receiving death threats, go to war against the Israelite tribe of Ephraim. Gilead wins the battle and secures the fords of the Jordan River, controlling the only road for the scattered Ephraimite soldiers to return to their homes. Whenever a soldier appears, Jephthah's men question if he is from Ephraim. Of course, the soldier always says no, but the Gileadites test him by making him say *shibboleth.* If the soldier pronounces the word *sibboleth,* apparently the regional dialect of Ephraim, then he is immediately killed.

Before the conflict, Jephthah makes a vow in God's name: "If You will give the Ammonites into my hand, then whatever comes out of the door of my house to meet me . . . I will offer as a burnt offering" (Judges 11:30–31). To an ancient Israelite audience, this would seem like a reasonable vow, because animals often lived in pens on the ground floor of homes. Thus, whatever animal happened to mosey out the door upon Jephthah's return would be the one he'd sacrifice. Jephthah is, in fact, successful, and he goes home to fulfill his vow. However, to his horror, the first "creature" to come out the door is his only child — a daughter, who rushes out to congratulate him.

Jephthah is despondent, but his daughter insists that he keep his vow to the LORD. Her only request is that she be allowed to spend two months with her friends mourning her childlessness in the hill country. The text reports that from this event comes a custom where each year the young maidens of Israel roam about for four days in her memory.

Now, you may be saying, "Wait a minute! You mean to tell me that God was okay with this kill-your-daughter-because-of-a-vow stuff?" Well, the text doesn't say, exactly — but we're going to go out on a limb here and say "no." Vows are very important in the Bible, especially when made to God, but not murdering others is also up there on the morality scale. Moreover, child sacrifice is repudiated in the Bible and is one of the chief reasons why God allows Israel to make war with the Canaanites. Finally, some have noted that Jephthah's vow was a mistake in the first place, because God is already said to be with him. If Jephthah had the faith to believe this, and not make a hasty vow, then this whole situation would have been avoided.

Samson: A buffed Nazirite duff

The lead role in *Samson and Delilah* (1949) is brilliantly played by the larger-than-life Victor Mature. He could lift heavy objects, and when it came to acting like he couldn't pronounce words exceeding three syllables, well, let's just say that he had us all fooled. And this is exactly how the Bible portrays Samson: stronger than an ox, but not the sharpest tool in the Israelite shed.

The story of Samson begins when Samson's mother is visited by an angel who informs her that, though barren, she will have a son. Only there's a catch: He is to be "a Nazirite from the womb."

Nazirites are so named because they are "dedicated" (Hebrew *nazir*) to God, and as a result they are forbidden to come into contact with dead bodies, drink fermented beverages, or cut their hair, among other things (see Numbers 6).

Because Samson is to be a Nazirite from the womb, his mother must also abstain from these things. Yet, after Samson is out of the womb, he does nothing but break these vows. For example, on one occasion, Samson kills a lion with his bare hands, and then on a return trip to the scene of the crime he takes honey from a hive that bees made in the lion's carcass. Now that's at least two Nazirite strikes, because he touches a dead animal and eats a fermented substance.

When Samson isn't eating sticky stuff from dead animals, he's roaming the countryside sleeping with prostitutes and getting in fights. For instance, Samson kills 1,000 men with a donkey jawbone (it's worth watching *Samson and Delilah* for this scene alone!) and carries a city gate 40 miles when escaping from the Philistines.

The only vow Samson does keep is not cutting his hair, which is the source of his strength. But even this vow eventually goes out the window when Delilah, the original *femme fatale,* convinces Samson to reveal the secret of his strength. When he finally does, she informs the Philistines, who are paying her a handsome price for this secret. While Samson is asleep on Delilah's lap, the Philistines enter the room, cut his hair, and tie him up. Once Samson is captured, the Philistines poke out his eyes (a common procedure to prevent prisoners from rebelling), and tie him to a grinding mill that he pushes in circles to make flour. Thus, the man who roamed the countryside freely, following the desires of his eyes, now has no eyes and is forced to walk in circles. But he's not finished yet.

As the text informs us, "his hair began to grow." Soon Samson has a full head of hair, and his unsuspecting captors parade him in front of the Philistines during a festival at the temple of their god Dagon (the god of grain). The Philistines marvel at Samson's size and gloat over his demise. Then, to thank their god for this victory, they enter Dagon's temple to party. Meanwhile, Samson, who is standing between the two pillars supporting the roof, prays to God for one last moment of glory. In answer to his prayer, Samson's strength returns, and he collapses the building, killing himself and all the Philistines inside.

Beyond its entertainment value, the story of Samson conveys at least two important lessons. First, God can even use someone's selfish impulses, such as Samson's lusts, to accomplish His will. Second, the Samson narratives are a tragic portrayal of the endless cycle of retaliation. When Samson or the Philistines are asked why they carry out such horrible actions against each other, they repeatedly reply, "I only did to them what they did to me" (Judges 15:11).

In the end, everyone is dead.

Where's the exit? The downward spiral of a nation (Judges 17–21)

The last chapters of Judges record some of Israel's darkest days as a nation without a stable government. One episode in particular illustrates the debauchery and lawlessness of the last days of the judges.

A Levite and a *concubine* (sort of like a wife, only a concubine has less status and fewer rights) decide to spend the night in a town called Gibeah in the tribal territory of Benjamin. An elderly man invites them to stay at his house, but that night the people of the city surround the house and demand that the elderly man produce the stranger so that they may have sex with him (much like the sin of Sodom in Genesis 19 — see Chapter 5 in this book for more discussion on Sodom). To placate the crowd, the old man, like Lot in the Sodom story, offers his daughter, but the crowd demands the male stranger.

Seeing no other way out of this predicament, the Levite grabs his concubine and sends her out of the house. She is raped all night, and in the morning she collapses dead at the doorstep. The Levite takes her corpse home, where he cuts her into 12 pieces and sends one piece to each of the tribes of Israel. This unusual mail delivery causes a stir throughout Israel, and the people demand that the guilty people in Benjamin be brought to justice. However, the Benjaminites refuse to extradite the men, and a civil war ensues. Although initially successful, the tribe of Benjamin is almost killed into extinction by the other 11 tribes. Once the war is over, and in order to ensure the tribe's survival, the Benjaminites are given permission by the other tribes to steal wives from a neighboring non-Israelite town.

This final story in the Book of Judges shows that Israel is in desperate need of a king, as the repeated refrain reminds us at the end of the book: "In those days there was no king in Israel. People did what was right in their own eyes" (Judges 21:25). Israel will get its desired king in the Book of Samuel (see Chapter 9), but in the end it won't help the national morale *or* morality.

Gleaning Wisdom from the Book of Ruth

Ruth is one of the great heroines of the Bible, and her character reminds you that not everyone during the period of the judges was morally challenged.

Because the Book of Ruth is set during the time of the judges, it appears immediately after the Book of Judges in most Christian Bibles. However, in the original Hebrew ordering and in modern Jewish Bibles, Ruth is located immediately after Proverbs or Song of Songs, respectively in the section called the Writings (see Chapter 1).

Ruth is a tale of heartbreak, loyalty, and love, and it offers a glimpse into the extreme hardships of poverty in the biblical world. Moreover, it seeks to present an alternative view to the harsh ethnic and cultural exclusivity common in the ancient (and modern) world.

How sweet it was to be loved by you (Ruth 1)

The opening lines of Ruth reveal the tragedies and hardships inseparable from biblical life for the poor. During a famine in Israel, Elimelech and his wife, Naomi, leave their home of Bethlehem and travel east to Moab in search of food. Their two sons, Mahlon and Chilion, accompany them. In time, Elimelech acquires a small piece of property, but soon thereafter he dies. Meanwhile, the two sons take Moabite wives: Mahlon marries a woman named Ruth, and Chilion weds a woman named Orpah. This arrangement lasts about ten years, until both of the husbands die.

Naomi, now widowed and childless, decides to return to Bethlehem, hearing that her former home now has food. Though saddened by the thought of departure, Naomi tells her daughters-in-law to return to their mothers' houses. Initially, both girls want to travel west with Naomi, but after much coaxing, Orpah returns home. Ruth, however, grabs her mother-in-law and says:

> *Do not beg me to leave you, to return from after you. For where you go, I will go, and where you stay, I will stay. Your people are my people, and your God is my God. Where you die, I will die and there I will be buried. Thus may the LORD do to me and more so if even death parts me from you.*

> —Ruth 1:16–17

In the end, Naomi succumbs, and the two march off to Bethlehem and arrive at the onset of the barley harvest (March/April). Naomi, whose name means pleasant or sweet, asks the townspeople to call her Mara, meaning bitter, "because the Almighty has dealt very bitterly with me" (Ruth 1:20).

Picking up the pieces and choosing the right stock (Ruth 2–3)

Thankfully, Naomi has a land-owning relative named Boaz, which means that with permission they will be able to come into the field after the harvesters and *glean*, or pick up, any barley kernels left behind. Off of these gleanings they will live for the next year. Boaz grants Naomi permission, and Ruth makes the most of the opportunity. She hopes that while gleaning, Boaz will see her and fall in love. Boaz takes the bait, and asks Ruth not to glean from any other field except his (ancient pickup lines still had a way to go).

Ruth is treated well by Boaz, and Naomi grows excited at the possibilities. However, when the wheat harvest (April/May) arrives Naomi grows impatient at the slow growth of this budding love affair and concocts a plan to get the two together. She tells Ruth to dress up in her best clothes and then go to Boaz when he is lying down at the threshing floor. When she arrives, she is to uncover his feet and then lie down — actions that would communicate to Boaz her interest in him.

Ruth follows the instructions, and in the middle of the night, Boaz awakens and discovers his feet uncovered and a woman lying there. Ruth then asks Boaz to cover her with his clothes, which is akin to asking to wear someone's letterman jacket. Boaz is impressed that Ruth has taken a fancy to him, because he is an older man. But there is a huge problem. Despite their desire to marry, there is a relative more closely related to her former husband, and by law this relative — known as a *kinsmen redeemer* — has first dibs on Ruth. Boaz vows to settle the matter the next day.

With this sandal 1 thee wed (Ruth 4)

In the morning, Boaz goes to the city gate, the center of business for an ancient town, and meets with the relative who has the legal right to inherit Elimelech's land and marry Ruth. Unfortunately for Boaz and Ruth, the relative decides to fulfill his role as kinsmen redeemer by buying the land and marrying Ruth.

All hope seems lost for Boaz's and Ruth's love affair when suddenly Boaz informs the man that there is one more catch to the deal: He must take care of the widow Naomi, and the first son born of his union with Ruth must be given the name and inheritance rights of Ruth's dead husband. This practice, recorded in Deuteronomy 25:7–10, is known as *levirate marriage* (*levir* is Latin for "husband's brother"), and is intended to ensure that someone's lineage doesn't die out. The man doesn't sign up for that deal, and he tells Boaz to go ahead and redeem the property and to marry Ruth. To close the deal with

Boaz, the man removes his sandal and hands it to Boaz — a way of guarantee-ing a pledge at this time.

Ruth and Boaz marry, and Ruth eventually conceives and bears a son: Obed. Naomi, now too old to bear children, helps raise Obed. In fact, the neighbor-hood women call the boy the son of Naomi.

Thus, the story of the woman who asked to be called bitter has a sweet ending. But that's not the end of the story, because from Obed will come a boy named Jesse, and from Jesse will come a boy named David, the eventual, and arguably greatest, King of Israel. Because of this connection between Bethlehem and David, several prophets in the Hebrew Bible identify this town as the place where a king would eventually arise and deliver Israel. And, in the New Testament, the gospels of Matthew and Luke appeal to these prophe-cies as evidence that Jesus, who is born in Bethlehem, is the Messiah.

Ruth ends with a *genealogy* (a recorded history of the descent of a person or family from an ancestor or ancestors) that extends from Judah's son, Perez, to David. And as far as genealogies go, it contains two unusual aspects. Not only is Ruth, a Moabite woman, included, but so also is the strange fling between Tamar and her father-in-law, Judah (see Genesis 38 and Chapter 6 of this book). Tamar is also a non-Israelite, and later tradition placed Rahab, the prostitute from Jericho, in this same genealogy. Thus, David's (and later Jesus') family tree is a testimony to the ethnic diversity that makes up the descendants of Abraham.

Chapter 9

The King and "I Am": 1 and 2 Samuel

From Michelangelo's *David* to Steven Spielberg's *Raiders of the Lost Ark,* the characters and stories of 1 and 2 Samuel continue to find expression in our world. Part of this enduring appeal is a consequence of the period covered by these books: Israel's transition from tribal rule to a centralized monarchy. Such transitions are seldom easy, and rarely, if ever, "pretty." As a result, the Books of Samuel are filled with all the things that make for front-page news and blockbuster movies: scandal, betrayal, murder, and redemption.

In this chapter, you meet the individuals and experience the events of 1 and 2 Samuel in order to understand their contribution to the biblical drama, as well as to appreciate their impact on ancient and modern religious belief.

Introducing Israel's Last Judge: Samuel

1 and 2 Samuel ultimately get their name from these books' first protagonist. This is a fitting tribute to a man whose impact on the religious and political life of Israel reverberates throughout its history. Apart from the great figure of Moses, Samuel's tenure as prophet, priest, and judge is unique. Samuel witnesses the demise of a priestly dynasty, and the birth of a political one. Even in death Samuel remains God's prophet, and his legacy leaves an indelible mark on Israel's national identity.

Samuel's birth (1 Samuel 1)

When 1 Samuel opens, we find ourselves on a religious pilgrimage to God's sacred tent (called the Tabernacle) with a man named Elkanah and his two wives, Peninnah and Hannah (yes, "two wives" — we discuss the Hebrew Bible's perspective on polygamy in Chapter 6). Adding to the normal tensions of any family vacation (including a chorus of "Are we there yet?" from the children), Peninnah, who has many children, passes the time by ridiculing her childless "co-wife," Hannah. So upon their arrival, a miserable Hannah slips away from the family to pray at the entryway of the Tabernacle.

In her prayer, Hannah promises that if she has a child, she will dedicate him to God. Although she only mentions that a razor will never touch his hair, the dedication she refers to is a "Nazirite vow" (see Numbers 6), which includes, among other things, refraining from alcohol. Therefore, it's ironic that while Hannah is praying, the High Priest (Israel's religious overseer) at the Tabernacle, Eli, comes up to her and accuses her of being drunk. Why? People in the ancient world usually prayed audibly, especially at holy sites. Eli, however, observes Hannah's lips move, "but he couldn't hear her voice."

In an example of wordplay, Hannah assures Eli that she is not drunk but is rather "pouring out" her soul to God. Realizing that Hannah is telling him the sober truth, Eli says, "Go in peace, and may the God of Israel grant your request." Hannah takes this as confirmation that God has heard her prayer, and leaves rejoicing. Soon afterwards Hannah does conceive, and gives birth to a son whom she names Samuel, which appropriately means "God hears."

After Samuel is weaned (perhaps as old as 3 to 6 years), Hannah takes him to the Tabernacle and gives him to Eli for the service of God. For her devotion, God eventually rewards Hannah with five additional children. Yet, this is not the last time Hannah will see her beloved Samuel. Every year when Hannah makes religious pilgrimage to the Tabernacle, she brings him new clothes. Now that's a good mom.

Samuel's call (1 Samuel 2–3)

Had Hannah known the kind of environment into which she was placing her son, she may have had second thoughts. The Bible informs us that Eli's two sons were "wicked men." Not only do they eat sacrifices intended for God, but they have sex with women at the entrance of the Tabernacle. Now that's bad. Eli, too, is less than admirable. Although he disapproves of his sons' actions, he fails to remove them from their priestly offices and even becomes fat on their stolen sacrifices. As a result, one day a mysterious "man of God" shows up at the Tabernacle with some bad news: Eli and his children will soon die.

Barrenness in the biblical world

It is commonly thought that a woman's worth in the ancient world was based largely on her ability to bear children. Yet, in the Bible, the women who are unable to bear children are often times more loved than the women who can. In the case of Hannah, it is actually her husband, Elkanah, who feels insecure and "devalued" by her discontent at not having children: "Aren't I worth more to you than ten sons?" he asks. Despite Elkanah's attestations of love, Hannah wants a child of her own.

Also interesting is how often in the Bible women who are initially barren end up giving birth to children who play important roles in Israel's history: Abraham's wife, Sarah, gives birth to Isaac, who embodies the fulfillment of God's promises to her and Abraham that through them a great nation would be born (see Chapter 5); Isaac's wife, Rebekah, gives birth to Jacob, whose children go on to become the progenitors of the twelve tribes of Israel (see Chapter 6); Jacob's wife, Rachel, gives birth to Joseph, whose actions in Egypt secure the survival of Jacob's other sons, and of many peoples besides (see Chapter 6); and, in the present narrative, Elkanah's wife, Hannah, gives birth to Samuel, who goes on to become one of Israel's greatest leaders. This pattern continues in the New Testament, where the barren Elizabeth gives birth to John the Baptist, the forerunner of Jesus' ministry (see Chapter 18); and Mary, who is not *merely* barren, but a virgin, gives birth to Jesus, who, according to the New Testament, is Israel's long-awaited savior (see Chapter 18). In fact, Mary's words of praise after hearing she will bear Jesus (Luke 1:46–56) borrow heavily from Hannah's prayer of praise for her son (1 Samuel 2:1–10). Thus, in the Bible, a woman need not be a mother to be of value, but if God wants you pregnant, nothing can prevent it.

Samuel, by contrast, demonstrates that he is a person worthy of his calling. As the text reports, "Samuel continued to grow in physical stature and in favor with the LORD and with people" (1 Samuel 2:26). As an expression of this favor, one night Samuel is awakened by a voice calling his name. Running to Eli, Samuel says, "Here I am." Eli, though no doubt a loud snorer, replies, "I didn't call you. Go back to sleep." This routine happens three times, and finally Eli realizes that God must be calling his young protégé. After telling Samuel what to do if he hears the voice again, Eli sends him back to bed. When Samuel does hear the voice again, he answers, "Speak, for Your servant is listening." God informs Samuel that He will soon cut off Eli's priestly dynasty. The next morning, Eli insists on hearing what God had told Samuel. Eli, for all his faults, receives the news quite nobly: "He is the LORD. Let Him do what is good in His eyes" (1 Samuel 3:18).

Beraters of the Lost Ark

Meanwhile, on the larger sociopolitical stage, Israel is at war with its archenemies, the Philistines, who have just defeated Israel at a place called Ebenezer (yes, where Scrooge gets his name, though Dickens spells it differently). The

Israelites realize that to defeat their enemy they need to pull out the big guns, which means bringing the Ark of the Covenant into battle.

Battling with the Ark (1 Samuel 4)

The Ark of the Covenant was the visible manifestation of God's presence among His people, and was believed to make Israel invincible in war. Thus, when the Philistines hear the shouts from the Israelite camp upon its arrival, they say, "A god has come into their camp!" Although fearful, the Philistines determine to fight bravely and march out to meet their fate. To the shock of everyone, including the Philistines, they rout the Israelites and loot their camp — including the Ark.

When Eli, who is now 98 years old, obese, and blind, hears the news of the Israelites' defeat and the death of his sons, he is devastated. However, when he hears of the Ark's capture, it is more than he can handle and he falls back in despair, breaks his neck, and dies. When Eli's daughter-in-law hears the news of her husband's death and of the Ark's demise, she goes into premature labor and dies, but not before giving birth to a son, who is given the name Ichabod (from whom Ichabod Crane gets his name), which means "no glory" — the glory of Israel, the Ark of the Covenant, is gone.

Israel is now at one of its lowest points since its slavery in Egypt. Its longtime religious leader is dead, and its most sacred relic is in the hands of its bitterest enemy.

Traveling with the Ark (1 Samuel 5–6)

To better understand what happens to the Ark after its capture, its important to know that Philistia was composed of a Pentapolis (Greek for "five cities"): Ashdod, Ashkelon, Gaza, Gath, and Ekron. Each of these cities had its own "king" and central temple. The Philistines, now in possession of the Ark, first take their prize to Ashdod, placing it in the temple of their god, Dagon.

Scholars once identified Dagon as a fish god, based on the similarity of his name and the Hebrew word for fish, *dag*. Representations of fish-headed figures found in Mesopotamia seemed to confirm this impression. However, it's now clear that Dagon was not a "fish head" but the god of grain, and the father of Baal, the Canaanite storm god. Like many gods of antiquity, Dagon had connections with fertility (although fish fertilizer can be quite effective).

The Ark's placement in Dagon's temple symbolized Dagon's supremacy over Israel's god, as it was believed one's god gave victory in war. However, in demonstration of God's supremacy, the next morning the priests of Dagon find Dagon's idol lying on its face in front of the Ark. Puzzled, the Philistines restore the statue to its upright position. The next morning, Dagon is again prostrate in front of the Ark, only this time his head and hands are broken off, symbolizing his powerlessness before the Ark. Because there were no college fraternities at this time to blame, the Philistine's knew that Dagon's humbling must be due to the power of Israel's deity. As further demonstration of God's power, the Philistines break out with tumors or, as the King James Version translates it, "hemorrhoids." With Preparation-H in short supply, the people of Ashdod wisely give the Ark to their neighbors in Gath, who soon also have difficulty sitting down for extended periods of time. They conclude that the Ark would make the perfect gift for their friends in Ekron. Ekron, however, has caught on to this trick and refuses Gath's "generous" offer.

The Philistines soon realize that they and their gods are no match for the Ark, and they decide to return it to Israel. Placing the Ark on a cart drawn by two cows, the Philistines send the Ark on its way. When the Israelites see it coming, they rejoice, and upon its arrival, priests take the Ark and place it on a large stone. Then, using the cart as wood for a fire, the priests offer sacrifice to God by slaughtering the two cows (some thanks). Yet, because this was before the movie _Raiders of the Lost Ark,_ the Israelites didn't fully appreciate the Ark's power, and 70 curious villagers decide to take a peek inside (bad idea), and they're struck dead.

Eventually, the Ark is transported north to Kiriath-Jearim, where it resides for 20 years until David transports it to Jerusalem, its last known resting place (see Chapter 10 for the scoop on what became of the Ark of the Covenant).

Saul, Israel's First King

With Eli's death, the care of the Tabernacle, as well as the religious and political leadership of Israel, falls to Samuel. And Samuel performs all of these tasks admirably. However, Samuel's sons, like his predecessor's sons, are "morally challenged." In particular, they accept bribes to influence their legal decisions. Not wanting to be ruled by Samuel's corrupt sons, and wanting "to be like all the other nations," Israel demands a king.

Ask and ye shall receive (1 Samuel 8)

Samuel is scandalized by the thought of appointing a king, likening the Israelites' request to turning their backs on their true king — God. Yet, when Samuel takes the request to God, he gets a surprising answer:

> _Listen to the voice of the people . . . because they are not rejecting you, but Me as king over them. Just as they've done from the day I brought them out of Egypt, when they abandoned Me and served other gods, so they're doing now._
>
> —1 Samuel 8:7–8

Therefore, Samuel acquiesces to the people's (and God's) request, but not before warning the people about the downside of kings: Kings will recruit your sons for the royal army, require your daughters to serve in the royal harem, and demand you to work on the king's royal building projects. As usual, the people don't listen, and, in the end, they get just what they ask for.

Saul's coronation (1 Samuel 9–12)

The Bible records two stories of how Israel's first king, Saul, is chosen:

- **Lost Donkeys (1 Samuel 9–10):** God informs Samuel that a young man who is looking for his father's donkeys will come to him for information. When he does, Samuel is to anoint the man as king.

- **Dice (1 Samuel 10):** Samuel gathers the people together and chooses a king by casting *lots* (sacred dice used to determine God's will).

The people are happy with the choice of Saul. He is described as tall and handsome (1 Samuel 9:2), but looks can be deceiving, and a central theme in the Books of Samuel is that a person's value stems from inner qualities. After becoming king, Saul's reign starts well — he defeats most of Israel's enemies — but then things take a turn for the worse.

Saul's censure (1 Samuel 13–15)

Just as there are two stories of how Saul became king, so there are two stories of how Saul loses God's favor and, ultimately, the crown.

- **Patience is a virtue (1 Samuel 13:1–15):** Before engaging the Philistines in battle, Samuel tells Saul to wait for him to return to offer a sacrifice. Saul waits, but then becomes nervous as he sees the troops growing restless. Feeling that he can't wait any longer, he offers the sacrifice himself. At that very moment, Samuel arrives, and Samuel is extremely put out at what Saul has done. Not only did Saul overstep his prerogatives as king (sacrifice was a priest's domain) but the fear that precipitated his action demonstrates he doesn't believe that God is the one who gives Israel its victories. As a result, Samuel tells Saul that his days as king are numbered.

- **How not to obey God (1 Samuel 15:1–35):** Because the Amalekites had attacked the Israelites unprovoked during their wilderness wanderings under Moses (see Chapter 7), God commands the Israelites to attack and kill all of the Amalekites — men, women, children, and even livestock. Israel is victorious, but Saul disobeys God by keeping the Amalekite king, Agag, alive, as well as some of the best livestock. When Saul sees Samuel approaching after the battle, Saul exclaims, "Behold, I have done all that the LORD has commanded!" (Just for future reference, don't ever lie to a prophet.) Samuel replies, "Then what is this bleating of sheep that I hear?" In response, Saul claims the soldiers took the livestock (another lie), and besides, the animals are for sacrifice (three lies, and you're out). Neither God nor Samuel is happy with Saul's prevaricating, and Samuel declares:

Does the LORD delight in burnt offering and sacrifices as much as in obeying the voice of the LORD? Behold, to obey is better than sacrifice! To give attention [is better] than the fat of rams!

—1 Samuel 15:22

These words express what becomes a constant theme among Israel's prophets: Right actions (obeying God) are more important than ritual acts (sacrifice).

As Samuel turns to leave, Saul grabs his robe, tearing it. (Again, for future reference, don't ever touch a prophet's threads.) Samuel interprets this symbolically: God will "tear" Saul's kingship from him. Demonstrating he still cares more about his own reputation than obeying God, Saul begs Samuel to stay and honor him "before the people." Surprisingly, Samuel agrees, but first he must take care of some unfinished business. Summoning the Amalekite king, Samuel delivers some pre-death trash talk that would make even Arnold Schwarzenegger blush: "Just as your sword has made women childless, so shall your mother be childless among women!" Then Samuel kills the Amalekite king with a sword. Although Saul has now lost God's favor and the backing of Samuel, he remains king for some time. But, to borrow from expressions deriving from the Bible, "the writing is on the wall" and his "days are numbered" (Daniel 5).

Déjà vu: Why are there so many duplicate stories in 1 and 2 Samuel?

Several stories in 1 and 2 Samuel have duplicates. For example, there are two stories about how Saul is chosen as Israel's first king (losing donkeys in 1 Samuel 9 and chosen by sacred dice in 1 Samuel 10), and two stories about Saul losing God's favor as king (offering unsanctioned sacrifice in 1 Samuel 13 and sparing an enemy king in 1 Samuel 15). And there are many other examples. Why this repetition? Most scholars think that the stories found in 1 and 2 Samuel were originally discrete traditions that were only later compiled into a single history.

Most scholars refer to this compiler as the Deuteronomistic Historian, because his theological views, when he expresses them, reflect teachings from the Book of Deuteronomy. However, this historian didn't view these duplicate stories as unrelated or contradictory. For example, the historian uses the cases of Saul being twice rejected as king to demonstrate that Saul habitually disobeyed God, which provided all the more reason for God's selection of David as the next king.

Charting David's Rise to Power

God informs Samuel that, because of Saul's disobedience, it is time to look for a new king. God sends Samuel to Bethlehem, a small village in Judah, where he is to find a man named Jesse, whose son will be Saul's successor.

When Samuel finds Jesse, he asks to meet Jesse's sons. Seeing Jesse's eldest, who is both tall and handsome, Samuel is certain he's the one. God, however, tells Samuel that He doesn't measure a person by his or her stature or appearance, "but the LORD looks at the heart" (1 Samuel 16:7). Soon all of Jesse's sons are paraded before Samuel, but none match the job description. Samuel, perhaps feeling he has the wrong Jesse, asks, "Are these all your sons?" Jesse informs Samuel he has one more son, but he's the youngest and out watching the sheep. "Go get him," Samuel requests. When David arrives, God tells Samuel, in effect, "He da' man," and Samuel anoints him as Israel's next king.

Biblical *anointing,* which is the act of pouring spiced olive oil on a person's head, is a way of designating someone or something for God's service. In the case of David, God chooses him to be Israel's next king. However, David must wait several years before officially taking the throne.

You play a mean harp, David (1 Samuel 16)

Like Elvis, David's musical talents elevate him from obscurity to the limelight, where he will one day be the undisputed king. David's ability to play the *lyre,* an ancient string instrument resembling a small harp, was renowned throughout Israel, and tradition claims that David wrote many of the Bible's *psalms,* which are religious poems set to music (see Chapter 15).

The Bible says that, because of Saul's wrongdoings, God sends an evil spirit to torment him. As music "soothes the savage beast" (this is not in the Bible, but certainly apropos here), Saul seeks a musician to calm his nerves. Ironically, the musician called to assist the king turns out to be David, the boy who would one day be king. David's playing has the desired effect, and for his service David is rapidly promoted to become Saul's armor bearer.

Slaying Goliath (1 Samuel 17)

The story of David and Goliath, in which a young boy defeats a mighty warrior, has become the epitome of the victorious underdog. Here's the story.

The Israelites are in yet another battle with the Philistines. Only this time, there is no fighting going on. The reason? The Israelites are afraid because the Philistines' have changed the terms of engagement. The Philistines offer to become Israel's slaves if they can defeat their champion in one-on-one combat. The only problem is that their champion, whose name is Goliath, is huge. We mean really huge. According to the Hebrew Bible, Goliath is about 9 feet, 9 inches — making even the tallest NBA superstar look puny in his presence. (The Greek text places Goliath's height at a "miniscule" 6 feet, 9 inches — still a pretty mean center on most ancient NBA teams.) Goliath, realizing his advantage, taunts Israel everyday, badmouthing both the nation and God. Desperate, Saul offers to anyone who might kill Goliath his daughter in marriage, wealth, and even tax-exemption. Even with the tax break, no one accepts, and Goliath taunts Israel in this regard for 40 days.

Meanwhile, back in Bethlehem, Jesse summons David from the flocks to look into the welfare of his brothers, who are serving in the Israelite army. When he arrives at the Israelite camp and hears Goliath's taunts he is outraged that no one has enough confidence in God to stand up to this "uncircumcised Philistine" (now that's hitting below the belt). David asks Saul to let him take Goliath's challenge. Admiring David's courage, Saul agrees and gives David his royal armor — an ironic gesture, for those who know David will one day be king. For now, however, Saul's battle duds are way too big for the young David, and he decides to face Goliath *sans* armor (and, according to Michelangelo, *sans* clothes — an interesting battle tactic; see Chapter 25).

But David does not go without a weapon. He's carrying a sling, which, far from being a child's toy, was ancient "heat." A skilled slinger could hurl a 5-pound stone at speeds of up to 200 miles per hour, and armies in antiquity used several contingents of slingers during battles. Moreover, David's aim was dead-on because, as a shepherd, he often used a sling to kill predators. Gathering five stones from a nearby brook, David goes out to meet Goliath.

As Goliath sees the armor-less David approach he can't believe his eyes: "Am I a dog, that you come at me with sticks?" David replies:

> *You come at me with a sword, spear, and javelin; but I come at you in the name of the* LORD *of hosts, the God of Israel's armies, whom you've defied!*
>
> —1 Samuel 17:45

David certainly wins the battle of words, but the battle of brawn has yet to take place. Running toward Goliath, David puts a stone in his sling and, after achieving the desired velocity, lets it fly, hitting Goliath squarely in the forehead. Goliath falls, and while the giant is unconscious, David rushes over to him, picks up his mammoth sword, and cuts off his head.

When the Philistines see their champion is dead, rather than live up to their end of the bargain by becoming Israel's slaves, they run for their lives (and their freedom). However, the Israelites make pursuit and rout them.

David takes Goliath's head and armor as war trophies (not the prettiest trophy case, you can imagine, but memorable), and eventually he deposits the sword at the Tabernacle (God's sacred tent) as a testimony to God's role in giving him the victory. David, in contrast to Saul, is one who trusts in the LORD.

Who really killed Goliath?

One question that arises from the biblical text is "Who killed Goliath?" David, of course, is the most famous giant slayer. But according to 2 Samuel 21:19, a man named Elhanan also killed Goliath. So, who dunnit?

Three explanations have been given for this apparent discrepancy:

✔ Both David and Elhanan killed giants from Gath named Goliath (very unlikely).

✔ A man named Elhanan killed Goliath and later tradition linked the event to the more famous David (possibly).

✔ David and Elhanan are one and the same person, "David" being a throne name, and "Elhanan" being his real name (compare the case of David's own son, King Solomon, whose "real" name is Jedidiah).

Because Angela Lansbury is no longer taking cases, we'll let you decide.

Foreskins and fathers-in-law (1 Samuel 18–24)

After David defeats Goliath, the Israelite women go around the streets singing, "Saul has slain his thousands, and David his ten thousands." Though Saul is praised, David is more so, and kings, like aged Broadway stars, don't like to share the spotlight. So one day, while David is playing his lyre, Saul picks up his spear and throws it at David, but misses his target. Saul then comes up with a more cunning plan to kill his rival.

Finding that perfect gift: David proves his love for Michal

Saul tells David that he wants him to marry his daughter, Michal. But before giving his daughter away, Saul asks David for a "bride price" — a little demonstration of David's ability to provide for the family. "Bring me 100 Philistine foreskins," Saul requests. Saul's plan is that David will die trying. But much to Saul's chagrin, David returns with 200 Philistine foreskins! (Our wives, to their relief, only got rings.) David then marries Michal.

Actually, collecting male genitalia (or, alternatively, heads, hands, or scalps) after a battle was a common way in antiquity to prove you had taken a man's life (because few men part with these items willingly).

Man on the run: David flees from his father-in-law

Saul continues his attempts to kill David, but the combination of David's agility and the help of others — even Saul's children, Michal and Jonathan — David always escapes. In one incident, Saul falls for the oldest trick in the book. Michal puts a pillow and clothes under the blankets and says that

David is sick in bed while David escapes out the back (1 Samuel 19:11–17). In another incident, Saul goes into a cave to relieve himself before continuing his hunt for David. David, as it turns out, is in the cave, and quietly sneaks up to Saul and cuts off the end of his . . . are you ready for this . . . garment. By not killing Saul, David shows he has no ill will toward his father-in-law. Also, David sets a good example. As David says, "The LORD forbid that I should lay a hand on . . . the LORD's anointed" (1 Samuel 24:6). Saul, for all his faults, is God's chosen king. David will be king one day, and he doesn't want to set a bad example of how to treat kings you don't like.

Although Saul says he's sorry for trying to kill David, it is only a matter of time before he is at it again. In one bloody event early in this process, Saul finds out that David has been to the Tabernacle where he and his men were given food and a weapon (Goliath's sword, which David had deposited there). The priests are unaware that David is on the run, as he tells them he's on a mission from Saul. However, Saul thinks they are working in collusion with David, and he orders that all the priests be killed. Saul's army, however, is unwilling to do it. But an Edomite named Doeg, who has no allegiance to this deity, doesn't hesitate to do the deed. Only one priest escapes: Abiathar, the son of the High Priest. As he has nowhere else to run, Abiathar, like Friar Tuck of Robin Hood lore, joins David and his merry band of outlaws.

The adventures of David and his merry men (1 Samuel 25–30)

Because of David's status as an outlaw, he is forced to rob from the rich and give to the poor — the poor, in this case, being David and his followers.

Fools and their money: David meets Abigail

The most famous case of David's Robin Hood antics involves a rich man named Nabal, who refuses to pay David for protecting his flocks (a sort of ancient "protection" racket). In response to his refusal, David vows to kill those in Nabal's house who "urinate against the wall" (1 Samuel 25:22), an expression referring to men of military age (because men employed walls for partial privacy when going to the bathroom). When Nabal's wife, Abigail, hears of her husband's foolish response to David's request, she intercepts David and flatters him, presenting him with gifts. She tells him that her husband is just like his name: Nabal, which means "fool." David is persuaded by Abigail's words and returns to his camp.

When Abigail arrives home, she puts off telling her drunken husband of his near-death experience until "the wine left him," a euphemism for urination. When she does tell him, he has a seizure and dies. Thus, David's words that those who urinate against the wall will die come true, only in an unexpected way. As Abigail is now "available," David marries her. (Yes. David had more than one wife. One of the perks of being the up-and-coming king.)

David and his merry men become mercenaries

But marriage doesn't settle David down — he remains on the run for some time, even living for a year and four months with Israel's archenemy, the Philistines. Although this may be viewed as traitorous activity, the biblical authors present David as having little choice in the matter — this is one of the few places he can escape from Saul's murderous intentions. David and his men even go on several raiding parties into Israel. However, the Bible is careful to point out that David actually tricks the Philistines in this regard. Instead of attacking Israel, David and his men go elsewhere and then bring back war spoils they claim are from Israel. But when the Philistines begin making war preparations for a massive attack against Israel, David finds himself in somewhat of a bind because he doesn't want to attack his own people. Thankfully, not all the Philistine kings trust David, and they refuse to let him participate in the war, lest he change sides in the heat of battle. Although David is spared, Israel will not be.

How the Mighty Have Fallen: The Deaths of Samuel, Saul, and Jonathan

Samuel eventually dies, and the whole country mourns his passing (1 Samuel 25:1). Adding to their grief, a huge battle against the Philistines looms on the horizon and, without Samuel, Saul is unable to determine whether God intends to give the Israelites victory. Saul realizes there is only one way to get an answer: Ask his old buddy Samuel. You're thinking, "But you just said he's dead?" True, he is, but this doesn't seem to matter, because in the ancient world (as well as today) there are those who claim to be able to contact the dead. The real problem in Saul's case is that he outlawed contacting the dead some years ago. Saul doesn't want to be seen going against his own law. Therefore, he disguises himself and secretly visits a medium at the city of Endor (not the Ewok planet).

The "witch of Endor," as she is sometimes called (though not in the Bible), summons Samuel, but when she sees him she realizes that the man making this request is Saul, and she fears for her life. Saul assures her that he won't kill her and asks her to tell him what she sees. She says it's Samuel, who has a question for Saul: "Why have you disturbed me!?!" (Apparently the afterlife isn't too bad.) When Samuel hears the reason — that Saul wants to know the winner of the upcoming Israelite-Philistine bout — he reminds Saul that God has rejected him as king and concludes, "Tomorrow you and your sons will be with me." Needless to say, this is not very good news to Saul.

The Bible and the afterlife

The story of Saul conjuring up Samuel's ghost is very important for understanding conceptions of the afterlife in ancient Israel, a topic that is noticeably underplayed in the Hebrew Bible. The abode for the deceased in the Hebrew Bible is typically called *Sheol,* a word that seems to derive from a word meaning "to ask." Thus, some have suggested that the dwelling of the dead is named after the practice of seeking advice from the deceased (as Saul does with Samuel). Although the exact character of Sheol is not entirely clear, it seems to have been a shadowy place where spirits dwelled — not too unlike the Greek notion of Hades, which is the word used to translate Sheol in the Greek translation of the Bible. Samuel's statement that Saul and his sons would be with him (1 Samuel 28:19) seems to suggest that spirits dwell together in Sheol, though Samuel's words may simply be a euphemism for death.

That Samuel's spirit could be called back to this world indicates that humans maintain their identity and self-consciousness after death. Although later writings in the Hebrew Bible develop the notion of the afterlife (for example, see Daniel 12:1–2), it is not until the Apocrypha and the New Testament that we get more detailed descriptions of life after death. In these works hell is described as a place of fire and torment, while heaven is a place of beauty and peace. Taking the biblical evidence together, some theologians understand Sheol to be the place for souls to dwell after death but before the "final resurrection" of the dead, when everyone will be judged and the wicked will go to eternal condemnation while the righteous will go to eternal life.

The next day, and in keeping with Samuel's prediction, the Israelites are routed by the Philistines, and many of Saul's sons, including Jonathan, the crown prince, die in battle. Saul himself is mortally wounded and asks his armor bearer to finish the job so that the Philistines won't capture and torture him. The armor bearer refuses to kill God's anointed king, and Saul is forced to take his own life by falling on his sword. When the Philistines arrive, they cut off Saul's head and take it and his armor to the temple of their god.

Thus, at the end of 1 Samuel, Israel is at a critical juncture in its national history. Their last judge, Samuel, is dead, as is their first king and most of his sons. What happens next will be crucial for the nation's survival.

Building a Dynasty

At the beginning of 2 Samuel, David finds out about Saul's and Jonathan's death and famously laments, "Oh, how the mighty have fallen!" (2 Samuel 1:25). And of Jonathan in particular, David says, "I grieve for you, my brother

Jonathan. You were precious to me. Your love was exceedingly wonderful to me, surpassing the love of women" (2 Samuel 1:26) — so close was their bond of friendship.

Things now get pretty messy as David sets out to secure his throne.

David secures his throne (2 Samuel 1–4)

The man who brings the news of Saul's death, along with Saul's crown and royal amulet, expects David to reward him. After all, he's literally giving David the crown of Israel. He even tells David that *he* ultimately killed Saul, because when he found Saul he was barely alive and asked to be killed before the Philistines came upon him. Despite the "favors" performed by this man, David commands that he be executed for killing "God's anointed."

Although Saul is dead, David does not immediately become king over Israel, because the northern tribes make Saul's son, Ishbaal (sometimes called Ishbosheth), their king. Eventually, though, Ishbaal's general, Abner, realizes that David is the better man and offers to bring Ishbaal's forces to David. David's general, Joab, however, feels Abner is too dangerous to be trusted and kills him in treachery.

Not long after this, Ishbaal also meets his end when two soldiers sneak into his room while he's asleep and cut off his head. As in the case of Saul's death, when the men report to David what they did, rather than reward them, David has them killed for their treachery. Yet, because of their treachery, David is now the undisputed king of Israel.

David's political savvy (2 Samuel 5–10)

David's first strategic move as king of both Judah and the northern tribes of Israel is to move his capital from Hebron, which is in Judah, to Jerusalem, a city previously not belonging to either Judah or the northern tribes and which was on the border between both the north and the south. Thus, David's choice of Jerusalem as capital is somewhat analogous to the choice of Washington D.C. as the capital of the United States. In both cases, the capital is on the border of the north and south and did not belong to any one tribe or state. David also solves a religious dilemma. Two groups of priests wanted the esteemed position of Israel's High Priest. One group, whose leader was Abiathar, seems to have traced its lineage back to Moses. The other group, whose leader was Zadok, traced its lineage to Aaron. David solves this problem by appointing both priests as High Priest.

David's culminating strategic move is to transfer the sacred Ark of the Covenant and Tabernacle from Kiriath-Jearim to Jerusalem. However, this is tricky, and David runs into some problems.

Shame on Baal: Biblical name changes

Saul's son and successor is called Ishbosheth in the Books of Samuel. Yet, in the Books of Chronicles he is called Ishbaal. So what's his name? It's Ishbaal, a name that means "man of Baal." Because Baal was the name of the Canaanite storm god, the compiler of the history of Samuel changed his name to Ishbosheth, which means "man of shame." Does this mean Saul worshiped Baal? Maybe. But, because "Baal" can also mean "lord" or "master," these names may also refer to Israel's God. To a later editor, however, using the title Baal for God was distasteful given its connection to the Canaanite storm god.

Transferring the Ark

The procession accompanying the transfer of the Ark to Jerusalem is filled with music, shouting, horns, song, dance, and partial nudity — courtesy of David. But before getting to the nudity, tragedy strikes the parade when the Ark begins to totter on the cart carrying it and a man named Uzzah reaches out his hand to steady it. For his concern, he is struck dead by God. This puzzling event even enrages David, but the message is clear: "Don't mess with the Ark." Uzzah, as innocent as his actions may have been, did not take the holiness of the Ark seriously enough. Moreover, as its travels in Philistia demonstrated earlier, the Ark of the Covenant is more than capable of taking care of itself. So Uzzah should have let it be.

Okay, now to the nudity. When David decides to resume the parade (three months later), he puts on an *ephod* (a sacred undergarment resembling a nightshirt), and dances before the Ark with all his might. When the parade finally enters the city, the Ark is taken to the Tabernacle, and a feast is held. That evening, when David returns home, Michal, David's wife, is not in a partying mood: "How the king of Israel has distinguished himself today, by exposing himself today before the eyes of his virgin maids as a vulgar man would shamelessly uncover himself!" (2 Samuel 6:20). Apparently, David's dancing in only a night shirt revealed more than Michal wanted him to reveal. David, who feels innocent in the matter, rebukes Michal for her affront of his character. The story concludes, "And Michal, the daughter of Saul, had no child until the day of her death" (2 Samuel 6:23). That is to say, because she is so concerned about David exposing himself, he will never do so again in her presence.

Building houses for God and David

David, now residing in a beautiful palace, decides he wants to upgrade God's house from a mobile home (Tabernacle) to a state-of-the-art estate (Temple). As it turns out, though, God prefers the Tabernacle, and, furthermore, David's hands are too bloody from all his wars to build such a sacred building. However, God appreciates David's intentions, and, in a play on words, God tells David that although he won't build God a house, God will build him a

The Davidic Covenant and the Messiah

God's promise to David that his dynasty would last forever is cut short when, in 586 B.C.E., the Babylonians destroy Jerusalem. As a result, later prophets understood God's promise to mean that He would again raise up a descendant of David to rule over Israel, only this new king would usher in a kingdom that, as God promised, would never end. This belief became known as the Messianic Expectation, from the Hebrew word *meshiach,* which means "anointed one."

"house" in the form of a dynasty. God even promises David that his dynasty "will endure forever" — a promise referred to as the Davidic Covenant.

David's Fall from Power

David is now at the top of his game, having received an eternal covenant from God and having securely established his kingdom by unifying its religion and leadership and defeating Israel's enemies. But, as the old saying goes, "The bigger they are, the harder they fall." And David falls hard.

David and Bathsheba (2 Samuel 11–12)

The story of David and Bathsheba begins with a notice intended to prepare the reader for trouble: "It was spring, when kings go out to war" (2 Samuel 11:1). David, however, stays home, sending his general Joab in his place. Spring is also the time when birds and bees are in full swing, and trouble is on the horizon — the kind of trouble that arises from greed, lust, and arrogance.

Late one afternoon, David strolls along the palace roof and spies a beautiful woman bathing. This is not an ordinary bath, but a ritual bath a woman takes after menstruation. This is vital information for the story, because she is clearly not pregnant *at this point*. David asks his assistant who the woman is, and he is informed that her name is Bathsheba (*bath* is Hebrew for daughter, having nothing to do with her activity when David sees her). She is the wife of a man named Uriah, one of David's trusted soldiers now out in the field.

David summons Bathsheba to his chamber, and one thing leads to another, and he breaks two of the Ten Commandments: David covets his neighbor's wife and commits adultery. David soon adds a third violation to the list.

Covering one's sins: David tries to hide his crime

Shortly thereafter Bathsheba sends a message to David: "I am with child." David quickly devises a plan, and truth be told, it's a clever one.

David summons Uriah home from the battlefield. After asking him about the war, David instructs Uriah to go home and "wash your feet" (2 Samuel 11:8), here a euphemism for sexual intercourse. Instead, Uriah sleeps at the door of the palace and does not go home. When questioned about this the next day, Uriah tells David that he won't go home and enjoy himself while Israel and the Ark remain on the battlefield. (Finally, we meet a righteous person in the Bible, and he's ruining everything!) Actually, Uriah's statement is an unintended rebuke, because David is at home and not fighting. Moreover, he's not just enjoying himself while others are out fighting for his kingdom, he's enjoying himself with the wife of one of those fighting for his kingdom.

Rather than give up on his plan, David gets Uriah drunk, thinking the alcohol will loosen him up a little, and will result in Uriah going home to sleep with his wife. But still, Uriah will not go home.

This story is filled with irony, because Uriah, a Hittite (non-Israelite), knows God's rules better than David. Soldiers fighting for God need to be ritually pure, and this specifically means no sexual relations (Leviticus 15:19–24).

Because Uriah won't go along with David's plan, David writes a letter instructing Joab to place Uriah on the front lines, then have the other troops withdraw, exposing Uriah to the enemy. When Uriah arrives back at the front, he gives Joab the letter, who does as it instructs.

When Bathsheba finds out that her husband is dead, she mourns for the requisite time and then marries David. Their child, a son, is eventually born, and David, it seems, has gotten away with murder *and* adultery.

"You da' man!": Nathan confronts David

One day, David's trusted prophet, Nathan, comes to him to inform him of a tremendous injustice that has taken place in his kingdom. It seems a rich man with countless sheep killed the only sheep of another man in order to feed a visitor. Making it worse, the man with the only sheep dearly loved it, even treating it as a member of the family. David is outraged, and says that the rich man who took the poor man's sheep deserves to die. Nathan looks David straight in the eye and says, "You're that man!" (2 Samuel 12:7). David unknowingly condemned himself, the parable's rich man. David had many wives, but he took Uriah's only wife.

David stands in shock as Nathan continues to deliver God's message. David's dynasty will continue, but he will receive a threefold punishment:

- ✔ The sword will never leave David's house, meaning that David's family will be undone by violence.

- ✔ Someone will take David's wives and sleep with them in public, because David took his neighbor's wife in secret.
- ✔ The child (unnamed) from his adulterous affair will die.

The third punishment comes true first, though Bathsheba and David will have another son, Solomon. The next two punishments come to fruition shortly afterwards, as David's family gradually falls apart.

Fighting for David's throne (2 Samuel 13–21)

Similar to sausage production, the politics of an ancient monarchy are more appealing when you are unaware of what's on the inside. In the narratives following David's "indiscretion" with Bathsheba, readers are offered a rare glimpse into the inner workings of a royal family. And it's not pretty.

The rape of Tamar

David's oldest son, Amnon, is the crown prince, but he will not live long enough to reach the throne. His trouble begins with his infatuation for his beautiful half-sister Tamar, which makes him "sick" with love. Amnon's cousin, Jonadab, who is described as very wise, gives some very unwise advice. He instructs Amnon to feign illness and then ask his father to allow Tamar to nurse him back to health. When they are alone together, Jonadab schemes, Amnon is to sleep with her (read: rape her). Amnon foolishly does as Jonadab instructs. However, when David learns of Amnon's actions, he does nothing, leaving the punishment to another: Tamar's full-brother, Absalom.

Two years later, Absalom decides to throw a party, only this is no ordinary celebration, but rather, a sheep-shearing festival! Think about this for a minute (but only for a minute): abundant alcohol, hundreds of raucous young men with shears, and thousands of sheep. These parties were so out of control that they made the wildest fraternity parties of today seem as tame as tea and crumpets at four. Amnon gets drunk, and not ordinary drunk, but sheep-shearing-festival drunk. Then, according to plan, Absalom's men jump Amnon and kill him. Fearing reprisal from his father, Absalom flees Israel. However, eventually David and Absalom are reconciled, and Absalom returns to Jerusalem.

Rebellious children and parents in denial

Absalom doesn't waste time in Jerusalem waiting for David to die so he can become king. He rises early every morning and stands at the city gate, the center of action for a biblical city. When people pass by on their way for a judgment from King David, Absalom promises them that if he were king they would receive a more favorable decision. Eventually, Absalom steals the hearts of the Israelites from David with these tactics and his good looks.

In fact, along with Samson (Chapter 8 in this book, Judges 16 in the Bible), Absalom has some pretty famous biblical hair. It is described as both beautiful and abundant, so much so, in fact, that when they cut it annually it weighs 200 shekels (5 pounds). Just as hair proved vital in the downfall of Samson, Absalom's beautiful locks prove to be his undoing.

After winning the hearts of the majority of Israel, Absalom declares himself king, and David is forced to flee Jerusalem. As one of his first "acts of state," Absalom sets a tent up on the palace roof in Jerusalem (the same spot from which David first saw Bathsheba) and sleeps with David's concubines in broad daylight. This action fulfills Nathan's prophecy that because David took another man's wife in secret, someone would take his in public.

Eventually, though, David's forces defeat Absalom's, and Absalom is forced to flee from battle. However, while Absalom is escaping by mule, his long hair gets tangled in a tree, and he is left hanging there. When Joab finds Absalom, he orders him killed, even though David gave strict orders that no harm should come to his son.

When David hears of Absalom's death, he is very upset, and famously mourns, "O my son Absalom, my son, my son! Would I had died instead of you, O Absalom, my son, my son!" (2 Samuel 18:33).

David's latter days (2 Samuel 22–24)

Near the end of 2 Samuel, we are treated to a beautiful song composed by David (2 Samuel 22) — a song that finds echoes in many of the psalms ascribed to this king (see Chapter 15). Then we hear David's parting words, as he reflects upon his life and reign (2 Samuel 23). This seems a fitting end to the story of David, only it's not the end.

As 2 Samuel draws to a close, David makes a very bad decision — he takes a census of Israel. Why is this a bad decision? David's census is for the purpose of determining the number of able-bodied soldiers in Israel, which reflects a lack of trust in God as Israel's ultimate protector. Even Joab, the commander of David's army, warns David not to take a census. But David insists. In response, God sends a deadly plague against Israel, thereby weakening the very thing David is trusting in: the population.

When God things happen to bad people

1 and 2 Samuel leaves you asking why God would choose a man as king, even promising him an enduring dynasty, whose track record is far from, let us say, clean. The answer seems to be found early in David's life, when God first tells Samuel He is looking for another king. As Samuel tells Saul, "The LORD has chosen someone after His own heart" (1 Samuel 13:14). It seems then, for all his faults, David has a "heart" for God.

In support of this conclusion, we see a marked difference between Saul's and David's responses when confronted for their sins. Whereas Saul prevaricates to avoid guilt and cares more about being "honored before the people" than doing right (outward appearances), David simply says, "I have sinned against the LORD" (inward attitude). Although David is far from perfect, he ultimately wants to please God, and his tainted example has served as an example to others that "if God could love and forgive a sinner like David, perhaps there's hope for me."

To end the plague, David purchases a plot of land that has a threshing floor and offers a sacrifice. Because threshing floors symbolized bountiful crops, they were commonly converted into holy ground, so David's choice of this location is not entirely random. After the sacrifice is made, the plague ends. Beyond providing a lesson about trusting in God's protection and provision, this story explains how the future site of the Temple was purchased — a temple David's son and successor, Solomon, will soon build (see Chapter 10).

2 Samuel 24:1 says that God incited David to take a census. Why? The Bible only says that God was angry at Israel, but doesn't say why. Interestingly, 1 Chronicles 21:1 says that Satan was the one who incited David to take the census! So who dunnit? Some scholars think that changing God to Satan is 1 Chronicles's way of clearing God's name. That's possible. However, another explanation is that God is the ultimate cause of David being incited, but Satan is God's vehicle. According to the Book of Job, Satan must ask God permission before messing with people on earth. Perhaps we are to imagine a similar scenario here, where God uses Satan for His purposes. In the present case, God wants to test David's faith — and David fails. However, to David's credit, even before God's judgment, he realizes he has done wrong and repents (2 Samuel 24:10).

When the curtain closes on 2 Samuel, David sits securely on his throne in Jerusalem. Yet, this security has come at a price, because three of his sons (Amnon, Absalom, and Bathsheba's first son) are now dead as the fallout from his adulterous affair with Bathsheba. And the killing is not over, as further civil war and political assassinations will continue in the opening chapters of the next book: 1 Kings.

Chapter 10

A Tale of Two Kingdoms: 1 and 2 Kings and 1 and 2 Chronicles

• •

In This Chapter

▶ Intellectualizing with Solomon

▶ Surviving the division of a nation

▶ Fighting Baal and King Ahab with the prophets Elijah and Elisha

▶ Overthrowing governments with Jehu

▶ Reforming the nation with Hezekiah and Josiah

▶ Destroying Jerusalem with Nebuchadnezzar

▶ Witnessing ancient spin doctors in the Books of Chronicles

• •

The Books of Kings and Chronicles continue the drama of ancient Israel's monarchy. At the conclusion of 2 Samuel, David is sitting on the throne as king over a unified nation. In addition, he has secured the location and supplies for God's "house" — the Temple. At the beginning of 1 Kings, David successfully passes the throne to his son, Solomon, who fulfills his father's dream of building the Temple. What's more, Solomon surpasses his father's dreams by making Israel one of the wealthiest and most powerful nations in the world. But then things take a drastic turn for the worse.

When Solomon dies, the kingdom splits into two kingdoms — Israel and Judah. Then, after two centuries of political coups and spiritual conflict, the northern kingdom of Israel falls to the mighty Assyrian Empire in 721 B.C.E. Less than 150 years later, the southern kingdom of Judah meets its end at the hands of the Babylonians, who conquer Jerusalem and destroy Solomon's Temple in 586 B.C.E.

Although filled with tragedy, the Books of 1 and 2 Kings and 1 and 2 Chronicles give us some of the most memorable episodes and colorful characters found in the Bible. This is the tale of two kingdoms.

The "Golden Age" of Solomon

Solomon is David's second son by Bathsheba, their first son having died as punishment for their adulterous (and murderous) affair — see Chapter 9. Solomon's reign has been called the "Golden Age" of ancient Israel. Yet, how Solomon ascended to the throne was anything but "golden."

Solomon's succession (1 Kings 1)

When 1 Kings opens, David is old and can no longer fulfill his royal duties, including performing sexually (or as the King James translates it, "he gat no heat"). That may sound weird (especially in the King James), but leadership in antiquity was intimately tied to virility. Therefore, a beautiful girl named Abishag is brought to David's bed, but as the text reads " he was not intimate with her" (1 Kings 1:4). David's sons immediately begin maneuvering for the throne.

Adonijah, David's eldest surviving son, is the most obvious choice to be the new king, but Solomon also feels he has a claim. Bathsheba, who has a vested interest in seeing her son, Solomon, on the throne, reminds David of an oath he allegedly made saying Solomon would be the next king. David, perhaps feeling he's having a "senior moment," declares Solomon king.

Meanwhile, just outside Jerusalem's walls, Adonijah is declared king by his own supporters. However, when they hear of David's choice of Solomon, they abandon their cause. Adonijah, seeing his desperate predicament, rushes to God's altar and clings to it. Adonijah's actions reflect what was commonly understood in the ancient world as an appeal for mercy.

Solomon promises not to kill his older brother on one condition: he must never again conspire for the throne. Adonijah agrees, and he and his supporters are spared (for the moment). Soon, Solomon is summoned to his father's deathbed to receive his parting instructions. In a scene that is reminiscent of *The Godfather*, David tells Solomon to kill two men:

- **Joab,** David's general, who killed two men who were under David's protection. He also backed Adonijah in his recent bid for the throne.

- **Shimei,** the previous king's (Saul) kinsman, who turned against David during a coup (see Chapter 9). Although Shimei "repented" of this "folly" when David regained the throne, he still couldn't be trusted.

David's instructions may sound harsh. However, David knew that transitions between monarchs were precarious times for a nation and that treacherous people were capable of treacherous actions during such transitions.

On a more positive note, David also tells his son to love and obey God, for in doing so his kingdom will prosper, and he will be blessed (1 Kings 2:1–4). Then David, the shepherd boy who became a king, dies.

Solomon's wisdom (1 Kings 2)

After David's death, Solomon takes quick action to secure his throne. Beyond following David's final instructions to kill Joab and Shimei, Solomon also kills his brother, Adonijah. "Now wait a minute," you may be saying, "David never said anything about that!" True, but, as we say today, Adonijah "asked for it." Having lost the kingdom, Adonijah asks Solomon for a "consolation prize": the beautiful Abishag. Solomon sees this request as another bid for the throne, because, if Adonijah can perform sexually with Abishag, with whom the previous king, David, couldn't "get heat" (that is, perform sexually), then Adonijah will have demonstrated his capacity to rule. Therefore, Solomon denies the request, and orders Adonijah's execution.

There remains only one other important participant in Adonijah's failed bid for the throne: the High Priest Abiathar. Yet, rather than kill Abiathar, Solomon pardons him due to his former status as High Priest. The key word here is *former*. Solomon deposes Abiathar and banishes him to Anathoth, a small town just close enough to Jerusalem to keep an eye on him, but just far away enough to keep him out of the affairs of state.

Acknowledging Solomon's wise request (1 Kings 3:1–15)

Solomon now sits securely on the throne. In addition, he follows his father's advice to love and obey God. Then, one night, God appears to Solomon and says, "Ask for whatever you want from Me" (1 Kings 3:5). Rather than ask for a long life, riches or power, Solomon asks for wisdom "to rule Your people and to distinguish between good and evil." This request so pleases God that He not only gives Solomon wisdom, but He gives the rest as well: longevity, wealth, and power. Solomon doesn't let his newfound gifts go to waste, but becomes a prolific author, songwriter, and scholar. Yet, the story that best exemplifies Solomon's wisdom involves two prostitutes and a baby.

Dividing the truth with Solomon's wisdom (1 Kings 3:16–28)

One of the most important duties of any king in the ancient world was to preside over difficult legal cases. And one day, Solomon is presented with a doozy. Two prostitutes come to Solomon with a baby, both claiming to be the mother. One prostitute explains that the other accidentally rolled over on her own child and suffocated him, and then exchanged babies with her while she was asleep. The other prostitute said that was a lie, as the living baby was definitely her own. Because this is before DNA testing, Solomon comes up with another plan: "Let's cut the baby in two, then you can both have half." While the one woman acquiesces, the other speaks up, "Please! Give her the baby. Only don't harm the child!" (1 Kings 3:26). Giving the baby to the woman who just spoke, Solomon says, "You're the real mother."

Solomon's building projects: the Temple and other treasures (1 Kings 5–7)

After securing his reign, Solomon fortifies his kingdom. He rebuilds the wall and gate systems of several cities and establishes regional centers from which he and his officials can administer the nation. Additionally, he builds stables to house his abundant horses and chariots. Solomon also increases maritime trade to the south by constructing a fleet of ships on the Red Sea. Yet, most of Solomon's time and money is spent on building projects in his capital city of Jerusalem. Solomon enlists the help of Phoenician craftsmen and purchases other goods from his ally, King Hiram of Tyre. Solomon spends the next 13 years constructing his elaborate palace, and 7 years building a Temple for God next door. (The palace's location near the Temple symbolized Solomon's privileged status as God's appointed ruler.) When the Temple is completed, the priests move God's cultic equipment from the Tabernacle to the Temple, and a feast is held for 14 days in celebration.

Although the Temple is called God's house, it is only symbolically or mystically so. As Solomon says in his prayer at the Temple's dedication:

> *Yet will God really dwell on earth? The highest heavens cannot contain you, much less this Temple I have built.*

—1 Kings 8:27

Solomon's last days (1 Kings 9–11)

Solomon marries literally hundreds of foreign princesses to build peaceful relationships with the surrounding nations. When combined with his other wives and concubines, Solomon's spouses number 1,000, which is just asking for trouble. And sure enough, trouble comes as Solomon gets older. First, Solomon gradually loses his commitment to *monotheism* (the belief that there is only one God), and begins succumbing to the religions of his foreign wives. This doesn't sit well with God, who vows to take all but one tribe away from Solomon's kingdom. Yet, because God so loved Solomon's father, David, He postpones punishment until Solomon's reign is over.

Check out the new digs

The Temple and its furniture symbolized Israel's special relationship with God. In the court of the Temple stood a large altar for sacrifices, which the priests offered for Israel's sins and to express thanks to God. The large water basin or Sea was used for ritual cleansing of the priests and altar, as both needed to be pure in the presence of God. Inside the Temple, in the room called the Holy Place, stood ten tables with offerings of bread, acknowledging God's ongoing provision of food. Also in this room were ten lamps, which burned continually, a symbolic

expression of God's enduring covenant with Israel. The most sacred room, called the Most Holy Place or the Holy of Holies, was situated in the back of the Temple and symbolized God's throne room. Inside were two massive statues of *cherubim* (biblical monsters — part lion, eagle, and human; see Chapter 3), overlaid with gold and which figuratively stood guard above the *Ark of the Covenant,* the golden box housing the tablets of the Ten Commandments (discussed in detail in Chapter 7).

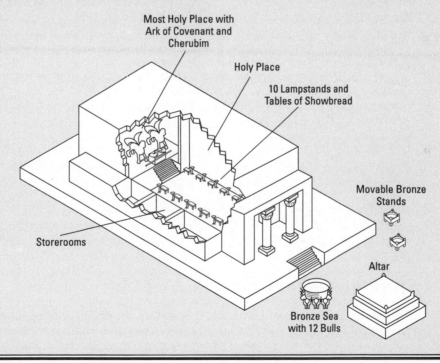

Most Holy Place with
Ark of Covenant and
Cherubim

Holy Place

10 Lampstands and
Tables of Showbread

Movable Bronze
Stands

Storerooms

Altar

Bronze Sea
with 12 Bulls

Sheba visits Solomon

One of the most famous people to visit Solomon is the Queen of Sheba (1 Kings 10), who journeys northward to see if all she heard about Solomon and his wisdom and wealth is true. Hollywood repeatedly portrays the Queen of Sheba as a European woman wearing a leopard-skin bikini. Nevertheless, Sheba is located in the southwestern Arabian peninsula in modern Yemen (or nearby in Ethiopia), and capitalized on the lucrative spice and incense trade that originated in that area. The sap from various desert trees in Sheba produces incense such as myrrh and frankincense, and the bark from Sheban plants composes cinnamon and other spices. The Bible's account of the queen's procession to see Solomon lists quite a parade — she and her traveling companions bring along with them camels, spices, gold, and precious stones, which she presents to Solomon. He in turn pays her "whatever she desired."

Beyond his many wives, close examination of the biblical record reveals that Solomon makes some other mistakes. Solomon's administration oppresses the northern tribes for the benefit of his own tribe of Judah. Solomon's large-scale building projects cost a fortune, and increased taxes are a necessity. To collect funds, and also to increase his power base by weakening tribal alliances, Solomon creates 12 administrative districts based not on the traditional tribal borders but rather on geographical features and towns. Solomon also requires each of these districts to provide forced laborers one month out of the year in order to work on his various building projects. This "redistricting" and forced labor is difficult to accept, especially considering the Israelites' past history as slaves in Egypt. Moreover, Judah isn't taxed at all, though they receive the largest benefits (fortifications) from the tax.

Further angering the northern tribes, Solomon sells 20 towns from northern Israel to the Phoenician king Hiram. And, although the northern tribes once hosted the Tabernacle, now the Jerusalem Temple permanently houses the Ark of the Covenant, thus diminishing their religious influence. If things weren't bad enough, during the latter portion of Solomon's reign, several neighboring kingdoms that David conquered break away from Israelite control. Moreover, the northern tribes threaten to withdraw their support from Solomon and follow their own leader, Jeroboam, an official appointed by Solomon to supervise labor. Solomon makes an unsuccessful attempt to kill Jeroboam, who flees to Egypt, where he remains until Solomon's death.

Solomon, after a long and eventful reign of 40 years, passes away, leaving his throne to his son Rehoboam.

Witnessing the Division of Israel

Solomon's son and successor Rehoboam doesn't seem to have inherited his father's brains. In fact, due to his foolishness, the nation divides in two.

Snips and flails and scorpion's tails: Rehoboam divides a nation (1 Kings 12)

Rehoboam travels north to reaffirm his position as its new king. However, the northern tribes want to know if he will continue Solomon's policy of overtaxing and overworking them. Rehoboam meets with his advisors, and while his elders wisely tell him to promise the north anything it wants in order to secure his power, the younger advisors instruct him to show these rebels who's the boss. Rehoboam foolishly listens to the younger crowd and tells the northern tribes: "My father made your yoke heavy, but I will add to your yoke; my father beat you with whips, but I will beat you with scorpions!" (1 Kings 12:14). In response, the northern tribes secede from the union, which ushers in the Period of the Divided Monarchy (928 B.C.E.–721 B.C.E.).

✔ Israel, as the northern kingdom is now called, consists of the northern ten tribes of Israel (see the map in Figure 10-1). Numerous dynastic transitions over the next 200 years result in a variety of capital cities, but most predominant is Samaria, which becomes an alternate name for this kingdom.

✔ Judah, as the southern kingdom is called, remains comparatively stable. The capital of Judah remains in Jerusalem, and the dynasty established by David is one of the longest in history, lasting for over 400 years.

Figure 10-1:
A map of Israel, the divided kingdom.

During the Period of the Divided Monarchy, there are nearly 40 kings who rule Israel and Judah, and keeping them straight is no easy task. We deal only with the most prominent kings here — the ones you ought to know. As a reference, we supply all the kings in the following table. ***Note:*** Sometimes the reigns overlap due to co-regencies (ruling together), and all dates are B.C.E.

Kings of Judah	Kings of Israel
Rehoboam (928–911)	Jeroboam I (928–907)
Abijam or Abijam (911–908)	Nadab (907–906)
Asa (908–867)	Baasha (906–883)
Jehoshaphat (870–846)	Eliah (883–882); Zimri (882)
Jehoram or Joram (851–843)	Omri (882–871)
Ahaziah or Jehoahaz (843–842)	Ahab (873–852)
Athaliah (842–836)	Ahaziah (852–851)
Jehoash or Joash (836–798)	Jehoram or Joram (851–842)
Amaziah (798–769)	Jehu (842–814)
Azariah or Uzziah (785-733)	Jehoahaz (817–800)
Jotham (759–743)	Jehoash or Joash (800–784)
Ahaz (743–715)	Jeroboam II (788–747)
Hezekiah (715–687)	Zechariah (747); Shallum (747)
Manasseh (687–642)	Menahem (747–737)
Amon (641–640)	Pekahiah (737–732)
Josiah (640–609)	Pekah (735–732)
Jehoahaz (609)	Hoshea (732–722)
Jehoiakim (608–598)	
Jehoiachin (597)	
Zedekiah (597–586)	

Idol time: Jeroboam and the golden calves (1 Kings 13–14)

Israel's first king, Jeroboam, immediately begins building his kingdom. First he constructs a palace. Then, motivated by a fear of losing his subjects when they travel to Jerusalem for the major religious festivals, he builds two cult centers within his borders. One is at the northern extremity of Israel at the site of Dan; the other is in the south at Bethel, right on the border between Judah and Israel (refer to Figure 10-1). At both sites, he sets up a golden calf (actually a young bull, a common symbol of virility in the ancient Near East). Then, just as Israel's ancestors had done after Aaron built a golden calf (see Chapter 7), Jeroboam declares, "These are your gods, O Israel, who brought you up out of the land of Egypt!" (1 Kings 12:28).

Perhaps Jeroboam, like Aaron, understood these bulls to symbolize God's virility and strength. Regardless of his intent, the biblical authors consistently refer to these ovine figures as idols and as a "sin," perhaps because in popular religion the young bull was understood to be a symbol of the Canaanite storm god Baal. Whatever the reason, all subsequent kings of Israel are condemned for their preservation and support of these alternate sites of worship.

Cut to Judah: Shishak's campaign (1 Kings 14:25–28; 2 Chronicles 12)

During this same period of turmoil (and perhaps because of it), Pharaoh Shishak I (931–910 B.C.E.) invades Judah, apparently in an attempt to break Judah's monopoly on trade routes. He plunders and pillages over 150 cities before returning to the Nile Valley. Although Jerusalem does not occur on Shishak's own lists of conquered cities, it would seem that King Rehoboam had to pay a considerable sum to spare his capital. According to the Bible, "[Shishak] took away the treasures of the LORD's house and the treasures of the king's house; he took away everything" (1 Kings 14:26). This verse has caused some scholars to speculate on the fate of the Ark of the Covenant. (See the "What happened to the Ark of the Covenant?" sidebar in this chapter for more information on this topic.)

What happened to the Ark of the Covenant?

The Ark of the Covenant, the most sacred relic in ancient Israel, simply disappears without direct mention in the historical record. We know it moved from the Tabernacle to Solomon's Temple in 960 B.C.E., and we are fairly sure that it wasn't among the relics taken to Babylon in 586 B.C.E. Several possibilities for how it vanished have been proposed:

✔ Because Shishak "took away everything" from the Temple, some scholars (and Steven Spielberg in *Raiders of the Lost Ark*) theorize that Shishak took the Ark to his capital city of Tanis in the eastern Nile Delta of Egypt.

✔ According to 2 Maccabees 2:1–7 in the Apocrypha, the prophet Jeremiah hid the Ark of the Covenant on Mount Nebo, the same

place from which Moses spies the Promised Land immediately before his death.

✔ The Talmud suggests that King Josiah of Judah hid the Ark in one of the many storerooms beneath the Temple in Jerusalem.

✔ Many Ethiopian Christians believe that the Ark resides today within the Church of Mary Zion in Aksum. This belief is based on a classic Ethiopic text that records that King Solomon and the Queen of Sheba had a son named Menelik who brought the Ark to Ethiopia.

Where the Ark really is, if it still exists, remains a mystery (though we're partial to Spielberg's contention that it resides in a U.S. government warehouse in an unmarked crate)

Israel's Kingdom from Jeroboam to Ahab

The politics of ancient Israel are messy even by antiquity's standards. Rarely does a dynasty last beyond a couple of generations.

- Jeroboam I rules from 928 to 907 B.C.E. and passes the crown down to his son, Nadab in 907.

- Nadab is assassinated in 906 B.C.E. after a reign of only two years.

- Nadab's assassin and usurper, Baasha, kills all of Jeroboam's male descendants to better ensure his reign from 906 to 883 B.C.E.

- Baasha's son and successor Elah rules for two short years (from 883 to 882 B.C.E.) before he is assassinated along with his male descendants. Elah is killed by his servant Zimri, the commander of the Israelite chariots, who seizes power by killing Elah while the monarch is drunk.

- Zimri's coup lasts a mere seven days, however, as the military backs another commander, Omri, and burns the usurper Zimri in his house.

- Omri's dynasty is one of the longest, lasting 40 years, and includes Omri (ruling from 882 to 871 B.C.E.), Ahab (ruling from 873 to 852), Ahaziah (ruling from 852 to 851), and Jehoram (ruling from 851 to 842).

The time of Omri's dynasty is marked by frequent wars and coalitions to stop expanding neighbors. This threat seems to produce the political marriage between Ahab, as crown prince, and the Phoenician princess Jezebel, whose idolatrous exploits bring them into conflict with God's prophet, Elijah.

Ahoy there, King Ahab! (1 Kings 16–22)

The tenth king of Israel, Ahab, and his wife, Jezebel, are among the most vilified characters in the Bible. This is for good reason: They both commit horrible crimes against their subjects for personal gain. They also endorse the worship of the Canaanite god Baal and Baal's divine girlfriend, Asherah.

Ahab, like most of the kings of Israel before and after, worships a variety of deities. However, even worse than his apostasy is a crime he commits against a neighbor. Next door to Ahab's palace lives a man named Naboth, who owns a vineyard. Ahab wants Naboth's vineyard because it is choice land. However, Naboth refuses to sell it. Ahab is so upset after being rebuffed that he returns home and refuses to eat. Jezebel tells Ahab to relax, saying she will take care of everything. Jezebel pays two of her subjects to lie, saying that they overheard Naboth cursing the king and God. Because these are capital offenses, Naboth is summarily executed, and his property goes to Ahab.

Ahab and Jezebel would have gotten away with this crime were it not for God and His prophet Elijah. God tells Elijah to confront Ahab, who is presently looking over his newly acquired property. When Elijah finds Ahab in Naboth's vineyard, he tells him that both he and Jezebel will die for what they've done. Elijah pulls no punches: "In the place where dogs licked up the blood of Naboth, so dogs will lick up your blood. Yes, yours!" (1 Kings 21:19). This eventually will come to pass, but before their undoing, Ahab and Jezebel make a lot more trouble for Israel. Yet, as in the case of Naboth's vineyard, at each step of the way they have to reckon with God's prophet, Elijah, and his dutiful understudy, Elisha.

Elijah and Elisha's excellent adventures

Elijah and Elisha are extraordinary prophets, and their journeys and battles epitomize a complete devotion to God. Elijah is initially called by God to travel across the Jordan River into the desert where he is fed by ravens. Soon thereafter, Elijah travels to Phoenicia where he multiplies food and brings a widow's son back to life. Yet, it is when God sends Elijah to the Israelite king Ahab for a showdown at Mount Carmel with the Canaanite god Baal that he distinguishes himself as a prophet to be reckoned with.

Elijah versus the prophets of Baal (1 Kings 18)

Distraught over Israel's apostasy under Ahab and Jezebel, Elijah gathers all of Israel to Mount Carmel where he has scheduled a competition. The god who can send lightning down from heaven to consume a sacrifice is the god worthy of Israel's worship. The people agree.

Now this fire from the sky stuff should be easy for Baal, because, as the god of storm, lightning is his specialty. Despite this advantage, the prophets of Baal try all morning with prayer, ritual dance, and even bodily mutilation to get their god to respond. Nothing works. Exhausted and humiliated, the prophets give up, and Elijah takes center stage.

Pouring water on his sacrifice three times in order to show that God can start a fire even with dampened wood, Elijah then begins to pray. Suddenly, fire descends from heaven and consumes the sacrifice. It is a fantastic victory for God and Elijah, and all the people acknowledge that "The LORD, He is God!" At Elijah's command, all the prophets of Baal are seized and killed. Elijah then runs faster than Ahab's chariot back to the royal city of Jezreel where he heralds the news. Jezebel, fed up with Elijah's "God-talk" and angered over the loss of her prophets, vows to kill the prophet. Remarkably, the man who just stood up to the prophets of Baal, flees for his life.

Elijah's Moses-like exodus (1 Kings 19)

Elijah travels south to Mount Horeb, another name for Mount Sinai, where God gave Moses Israel's Law (see Chapter 7). Along the way, Elijah is miraculously sustained for 40 days without food, which is reminiscent of Israel's earlier wilderness wanderings of 40 years under Moses. At Mount Horeb, Elijah experiences an earthquake, a great wind, and fire, which is also reminiscent of what the Israelites experienced here when Moses met with God. However, God is said not to be in any of these phenomena. The reason? These phenomena have become too closely associated with the storm god, Baal. God, therefore, reveals Himself to Elijah in the sound of a thin whisper. Then God asks Elijah, "What are you doing here?" Without waiting for an answer, God tells Elijah to perform three tasks:

- ✔ Anoint an Israelite military commander named Jehu as Israel's king.
- ✔ Anoint the next king of Israel's neighbor, Aram.
- ✔ Appoint Elisha as his successor.

Elijah performs the third task first, and the other two are left to Elisha, who takes Elijah's place in dramatic fashion.

Swing low, sweet chariot: Passing the torch to Elisha (2 Kings 1)

Elijah eventually finds Elisha, and they travel together for a short time. Wanting some privacy from an entourage of prophets who are following them, Elijah takes off his cloak and touches the Jordan River, which miraculously parts so they can cross over (again similar to Moses, who parted the Red Sea). On the other side of the Jordan, Elijah says farewell to his friend, and a fiery chariot descends from heaven and takes Elijah away in a whirlwind (2 Kings 2:11).

As you may imagine, the passage of Elijah's miraculous departure in a chariot of fire is very big with believers in alien abductions. This passage also had importance for the authors of the Bible. In the Hebrew Bible, the prophet Malachi says that Elijah will return and prepare the way for God's coming. In the New Testament, John the Baptist is said to fulfill this prophecy by preparing the way for Jesus' ministry.

Now going solo, Elisha crosses back over the Jordan River into Israel, and picks up where Elijah left off in working wonders on behalf of God (see 2 Kings 2–13). Among Elisha's miracles are a floating axe-head, getting two bears to maul 42 youths for making fun of his baldness, multiplying food, and reviving a dead man. Ahab, Elijah's old nemesis, dies in battle, and just as Elijah predicted, dogs lick his blood.

Israel's Kingdom From Ahaziah to Jehu

The hostile politics between Israel and Judah are postponed by a marriage alliance between Ahab's sister, Athaliah, and the crown prince of Judah, Jehoram (also known as Joram). Athaliah and Jehoram have a son, Ahaziah, who eventually becomes king of Judah. He then joins forces with his cousin, Joram (different from Judah's Joram), who is the King of Israel, and they fight against Aram, Israel's neighbors to the north. However, during the battle, Joram is wounded and retreats with Ahaziah to recuperate at Jezreel (2 Kings 8). It is while Ahaziah and Joram are at Jezreel that one of the bloodiest revolutions in the Bible takes place, and the sins of Ahab and Jezebel are finally paid in full.

Jehu's political coup and religious reform (2 Kings 9–10)

Jehu, as the commander of King Joram's army, remains near the frontlines of the battle while his king recuperates at Jezreel. As he is meeting with his officers, a prophet sent by Elisha walks into the room and anoints him king. The prophet then informs Jehu that he is to be God's chosen vessel for punishing Ahab's descendants for Ahab's and their sins. When word of this event reaches the Israelite troops under Jehu's command, the camp expresses their support. Jehu quickly mounts his chariot and sets off to Jezreel.

When Joram and Ahaziah see Jehu approaching, they send a horseman to find out his intentions. The horseman never returns — instead, he joins Jehu's side. When another horseman does the same thing, the two kings themselves set off toward Jehu. When they meet, Joram and Ahaziah inquire, "Is it peace, Jehu?" When Jehu's treachery becomes apparent, it is too late. Jehu, citing the religious heresy of Joram's mother, Jezebel, shoots an arrow through Joram's heart. Ahaziah turns to flee, though he also is mortally wounded. Jehu then enters Jezreel to begin securing his reign.

Jezebel, held up in Jezreel, does not live long. When she sees Jehu approaching, she paints her eyes and adorns her head. These actions have long been misinterpreted as her attempt to seduce Jehu and save her life. Jezebel is, in fact, meeting her impending death with dignity.

When Jehu arrives, he tells those with Jezebel to throw her out the window. When she hits the ground, Jehu's horses trample her, and then Jehu and his troops enter the palace to eat. When they return to bury Jezebel, however, they find only her head, hands, and feet, because dogs have eaten her — just as Elijah had prophesied for her sin in killing Naboth.

Jehu's usurpation is not secure until he can eliminate all of Ahab's relatives and supporters, which he does in short shrift by beheading them. If you're disturbed by all this bloodshed, you aren't alone. The biblical prophet Hosea later condemns Jehu's slaughter as excessive (Hosea 1:4).

Jehu does not confine his purge of the corruption in Israel to only the political realm. One day he calls all the priests of Baal together for a major celebration. When they are all gathered in the temple of Baal, Jehu declares, "Let's have a sacrifice to Baal!" At this, Jehu's soldiers come rushing in and slaughter the priests and Baal's temple is destroyed. In one of our favorite passages, the Bible says, "and the ruins of the temple of Baal have been used as a latrine until this day" (2 Kings 10:27). Jehu's reign lasts 28 years (842–814 B.C.E.), and his dynasty lasts for five generations, when his great-great-grandson, Zechariah, is assassinated in 747 B.C.E.

Cut to Judah: Athaliah, the woman who would rule Judah (2 Kings 11)

While Jehu is "cleaning house" in the north, King Ahaziah's death in the south results in a revolt that nearly ends the Davidic dynasty. Ahaziah's mother, Athaliah, takes the opportunity of her son's death to kill all the male heirs to the throne, thus making herself ruler of Judah. Unknown to Athaliah, however, Ahaziah's sister, Jehosheba, who is also the wife of the High Priest, hides one of her infant brothers in the Temple. After Athaliah rules for six years, the High Priest, Jehoida, gathers together an armed guard and brings the now 7-year-old son of Ahaziah out of the Temple, declaring him king. When Athaliah hears the commotion, she enters the Temple courts crying, "Treason! Treason!" Those are her last words. The soldiers execute her, and the young lad, Joash by name, is anointed king. Under the direction of the High Priest, Joash institutes many religious reforms. But these changes would be short lived because subsequent kings would return to the worship of other gods.

Experiencing Israel's Destruction

Israel and Judah fight on and off during the next 100 years (between the mid-ninth and mid-eighth century B.C.E.). These conflicts reduce the stability and power of both nations, but especially Israel.

In 733 B.C.E., an Assyrian monarch named Tiglath-pileser III conquers many of Israel's cities and, as was Assryria's policy, deports many of its inhabitants. As a further demonstration of Assyria's dominance, Tiglath-pileser III appoints a new king of Israel, Hoshea. But Hoshea soon makes a horrible mistake. Thinking that Egypt will provide military assistance, he rebels against Assyria. Assyria, as you may imagine, is not too happy about this and decides to make an example of Israel. Under Assyria's next two kings — Shalmaneser V (727–722 B.C.E.) and Sargon II (722–705 B.C.E) — every major Israelite city is captured or destroyed. Then, in 721 B.C.E., the nation of Israel itself falls.

Many of Israel's inhabitants are exiled, never to be heard from again. Because the northern kingdom of Israel consisted of ten tribes, these become known as the "Ten Lost Tribes of Israel."

Although you may think that the fall of Israel would be welcomed news to Judah in light of their strained relationship, it actually is a huge shock. The Israelites were, after all, Judah's "brothers to the north." Sure they disliked each other, but they never really wished each other dead. In addition, Israel's fall leaves Judah feeling vulnerable. Not only is there one less buffer state between Judah and its Mesopotamian enemies but the ten northern tribes, who had equal claim to God's promises, are gone. If God allowed Israel to be defeated for its repeated violations of God's commands, would He do the same if Judah should continue in its unrighteous ways?

With these questions in mind, it comes as no surprise that Hezekiah, the king ruling Judah about the time of the fall of Israel, decides it's time to follow God.

Too Little, Too Late: Judah's Reforms

Two kings of Judah — Hezekiah (715–687 B.C.E.) and Hezekiah's great grandson, Josiah (640–609 B.C.E.) — are hailed by the biblical authors as unrivalled for their devotion to God. However, even their pious efforts won't be enough to save Judah.

The reforms of Hezekiah (2 Kings 18)

Hezekiah demonstrates his faithfulness toward God by destroying the alternate sites of worship in and around Jerusalem. He even destroys the bronze serpent made by Moses in the wilderness to heal the people of poisonous snake bites (Numbers 21:6–9) because it has become an object of worship. As further demonstration of Hezekiah's heart for God, he allows the prophet Isaiah free access to the royal court to provide counsel and to inform him of God's words and how they relate to matters of state.

Despite Hezekiah's reforms, these are difficult times for Judah. Shortly after destroying Israel, the Assyrians besiege Judah and capture some 46 cities. In fact, pictorial representations of the capture of one of these cities, Lachish, has been discovered on the walls the Assyrian royal palace in Nineveh (modern-day Iraq).

However, the "trophy" the Assyrians want most on the palace wall is not Lachish, but Judah's capital, Jerusalem.

Jerusalem on the brink of destruction

While the Assyrians are still attacking Lachish, the Assyrian king Sennacherib sends messengers to King Hezekiah to tell him to surrender or else face certain defeat and death. As Sennacherib's general puts it, "None of the gods of the surrounding nations were able to protect them. And your god will not be able to protect you." As we might say today, "Them are fightin' words" — only the one who will be fighting for Hezekiah is God Himself.

When Hezekiah gets a letter from Sennacherib repeating this same threat, he goes into the Temple and spreads the letter before God. After praying and asking God to protect His own honor and reputation, the prophet Isaiah shows up with a message from God. In short, God tells Hezekiah that everything is going to be okay. God will deliver Jerusalem from the Assyrians, forcing the king to return home.

Hark the herald angels slaying: God delivers Jerusalem

According to 2 Kings 19, the night before the Assyrians attack, an angel goes through their camp and kills 185,000 soldiers. With the loss of his fighting force, Sennacherib is forced to return home. Interestingly, the Greek historian, Herodotus, writing several hundred years later, also describes the Assyrian army as being prevented from concluding their military campaign, although he ascribes it to a plague.

That Sennacherib was unsuccessful in conquering Jerusalem is confirmed by Sennacherib himself. In a royal inscription discovered by archaeologists, Sennacherib boasts that he laid siege to Jerusalem, and even "trapped Hezekiah in Jerusalem like a caged bird." However, the purpose of a siege is not to trap someone in his city "like a bird," but to *get in* to the city and *conquer it*. (Ancient kings, like modern politicians, were always trying to put a positive spin on their failed exploits.) Even though Sennacherib doesn't get into Jerusalem, both Assyrian records and the Bible agree that Hezekiah was forced to pay a heavy tribute to Sennacherib.

Manasseh's "very bad" reign (2 Kings 21)

Hezekiah's son, Manasseh, reigns for 45 years (from 687 to 642 B.C.E.), the longest of any king of Israel or Judah. However, he rescinds the religious reforms of his father, much to the dismay of the biblical authors. He practices sorcery and divination, as well as consults mediums. He even offers his own son as a sacrifice to a foreign god. Because of these heinous crimes, which the people willingly follow, God promises that Judah will soon be destroyed.

After Manasseh's death, his son, Amon, becomes king, but because of his unpopular reign he is assassinated by his own officials after ruling only two years (from 641 to 640 B.C.E.). Because of his "untimely" death, Amon's son, Josiah, is only 8 years old when he inherits the throne. Despite his youth, Josiah goes on to become one of Judah's greatest kings.

The reforms of Josiah (2 Kings 22–23)

Josiah's religious reforms are even more fervent than Hezekiah's. Part of the reason Josiah's reforms outdo his great grandfather's is because of a remarkable discovery early in his reign.

While the priests are cleaning the Temple due to its neglect and abuse during the years of Manasseh and Amon, they find a scroll — and not just any scroll, but the Law of Moses. Based on the reforms that follow, this scroll does not seem to be the entire Law of Moses, but primarily the laws contained in the Book of Deuteronomy. When Josiah hears the scroll read, he tears his clothes as a sign of deep repentance and then initiates a series of reforms, including destroying all the foreign altars erected by his predecessors. He even goes up into the former kingdom of Israel and destroys the altar at Bethel, which was built by Jeroboam some 300 years earlier. In fact, his actions fulfill a prophecy that was spoken at the time Jeroboam originally built the altar and its golden calf. When Jeroboam was dedicating the newly completed altar, a mysterious man showed up and said,

> *O altar, altar. This is what the* LORD *says: "A son will be born to the house of David, Josiah by name, and he will sacrifice on you the priests of the high places who make offerings here, and human bones will be burned on you."*
>
> —1 Kings 13:2

Now, three centuries later, this prophecy has come true. These and other reforms led the author of Kings to report that there was never a king like Josiah, "who turned to the LORD with all his heart and with all his soul and with all his might, according to all the Law of Moses" (2 Kings 23:25). Despite his successes, in 609 B.C.E. Josiah is killed during a battle with the Egyptians. So devastating is the loss of this righteous king to Judah, that the prophet Jeremiah writes songs lamenting his passing (2 Chronicles 35:25).

The End of an Era: The Fall of Jerusalem

Following Josiah's death, the kingdom of Judah becomes a pawn amidst the mega-powers of Egypt and Babylon. First the Egyptian pharaoh, Neco, imprisons Josiah's son, Jehoahaz, and places another of Josiah's sons, Jehoiakim, on the throne as Egypt's vassal. Egypt, however, gradually loses power as Babylon, led by its king, Nebuchadnezzar, gains strength through conquest. Eventually the Babylonian army approaches Jerusalem, and Jehoiakim, seeing the writing on the wall, switches alliances. This arrangement lasts for three years, but when Nebuchadnezzar retreats after failing in his attempt to invade Egypt, Jehoiakim rebels. In response, Nebuchadnezzar attacks Jerusalem in 598 B.C.E., and Jehoiakim dies during the struggle. Jerusalem's days are numbered.

Judah's last days (2 Kings 23–25:26)

Jehoiakim's son, Jehoiachin, is only 18 years old when he ascends to the throne. However, he rules for just three months before Nebuchadnezzar besieges Jerusalem, forcing the king to surrender. Although Nebuchadnezzar spares the city from destruction, Jehoiachin, along with his family and officials, are carried off to Babylon, as are many of the treasures from the royal palace and Temple. The Bible records that at this time 10,000 captives are exiled, and "none remained, except the poorest of the land" (2 Kings 24:14). The next decade is full of famine resulting from this conflict's devastation on the economy.

Nebuchadnezzar puts Jehoiachin's uncle, Zedekiah, on the throne. Ultimately, however, Zedekiah revolts, and Babylon responds with a vengeance. In 587 B.C.E., the Babylonian forces besiege Jerusalem. While Jerusalem's walls hold off the invading army for 18 months, inside the city things are falling apart as famine and starvation become widespread. Numerous atrocities occur during this period, including parents eating their own children in order to stay alive. Finally, in July of 586 B.C.E., Jerusalem's walls are breached. Zedekiah tries to escape but is captured. As punishment for his rebellion, the Babylonians kill his children before him, and then gouge out his eyes, so that the death of his offspring is the last thing he sees. Then Zedekiah is led away in chains to Babylon.

Within the next two months, Nebuchadnezzar implements another deportation of the population, and Jerusalem is destroyed, including the fortifications and, most importantly, God's Temple. For nearly four centuries, God's Temple stood in Jerusalem as the center of Israelite religion symbolizing its enduring strength. Now it is gone, with no indication that it will ever stand again.

Asking why in the face of disaster (2 Kings 25:27–30)

With the loss of their city and Temple, the Judahites are faced with the difficult question of how God could have allowed these tragedies to happen. After all, how could God let a nation that worships idols overthrow a nation that worships the living God? That, in fact, was the problem. Judah, and Israel before it, had neglected its worship of God. God had repeatedly warned both nations that if they didn't repent of their idol worship, with its accompanying immorality and injustice, He would send them into exile. They had not changed their ways, and now judgment had come.

As the Books of Kings comes to a close, Jerusalem is destroyed, the Temple has been razed to the ground, and the prominent members of Judean society are in exile. But there is some hope at the end of 2 Kings. We are informed that King Jehoiachin, who had been taken captive in the 598 B.C.E. campaign, is now doing well. Although still Nebuchadnezzar's prisoner, he is given a regular stipend and is allowed to dine at the king's table.

Perhaps hope is not lost after all.

Ancient Spin Doctors: Chronicles

As two witnesses are better than one, the Books of 1 and 2 Chronicles offer a welcomed second opinion concerning the history of Israel's monarchy.

Say that again? Chronicles recalls the past

In relation to the Books of Samuel and Kings, Chronicles spans from the last chapter of 1 Samuel (Saul's death) to the end of 2 Kings, and then a little beyond. More specifically, whereas 2 Kings ends with the destruction of Jerusalem and its inhabitants in exile (around 560 B.C.E.), 2 Chronicles contains the later Persian edict by King Cyrus giving those exiled permission to return to their homeland (539 B.C.E.). Yet, Chronicles is not simply a retelling of Samuel and Kings; it is a reinterpretation of the monarchy for a different generation living during very different times.

The Books of 1 and 2 Chronicles were actually not called Chronicles until hundreds of years after their completion, when the fifth century C.E. Church Father and Bible translator, Jerome, first applied the term to these books. In the original Hebrew Bible the title is The Events of the Days, "the days" being the period of the Israelite monarchy. In the Greek translation of the Hebrew Bible (the Septuagint), the Books of 1 and 2 Chronicles are called The Things Left Out. This title emphasizes the expanded and, in some cases, alternate version of the history of Israel's monarchy recorded in Chronicles.

The Chronicler's point of view

The author of 1 and 2 Chronicles (originally one book in Hebrew) is creatively called by scholars "the Chronicler." Although the author of Chronicles remains anonymous, Jewish tradition ascribes these books to Ezra, a scribe and priest who witnessed firsthand the Jews' return to their homeland (see Chapter 12). Although many did not take the Persians up on this offer, many did, including Ezra. Now that the Israelites were back in their homeland, they needed a "new" history to give the nation a "new" perspective on its past and a "new" direction for its future.

Most notably, the Chronicler does not concern himself with showing all the peccadilloes and problems of the past. These were important for the earlier history, because its author (traditionally the prophet Jeremiah) wanted to explain why God would allow His people to be conquered and sent into exile. In short, the authors of Samuel and Kings demonstrate that God did not abandon His people, but His people abandoned Him by breaking His commandments and following after other gods. As a result, the earlier work gave us the negative portrait of the monarchy and the nation as a whole.

The Chronicler, in contrast, though wanting to emphasize the importance of following God's commands, does not want to wallow in the past. Israel has been given a new beginning, a new chance to get it right, and in keeping with this new perspective, the Chronicler puts a new spin on Israel's past.

- ✔ The Chronicler spends a great deal of time and effort praising David and Solomon. For example, Chronicles makes no reference to David's affair with Bathsheba, or Solomon's violent ascent to the throne.

- ✔ As a priest, the Chronicler emphasizes the centrality of the Temple as God's chosen place of worship.

- ✔ Chronicles places more of an emphasis on the importance of prophets and prophecy in the administration of the state. For the Chronicler, prophets are essential for checking the power of the monarchy.

- ✔ Finally, in keeping with the Chronicler's desire to set a positive tone for the future, Chronicles does not belabor the nation's past sins, but focuses on spiritual renewal and God's forgiveness.

Thus, upon the completion of the Temple, God says to Solomon:

> *I have heard your prayer, and have chosen for Myself this place as a house for sacrifice. If I shut up the heavens so that there is no rain, and if I command the locust to eat the land, and if I send pestilence to My people, then if My people who are called by My name humble themselves, and pray and seek My face, and turn from their evil ways, then I will hear from heaven, and I will forgive their sin and heal their land. Now My eyes will be open and My ears listening to the prayer that is made in this place.*
>
> —*2 Chronicles 7:12–15*

Chapter 11

Strangers in a Strange Land: Israel in Exile with Daniel and Esther

*T*he ancient Israelites got around. Early in the Bible, Abraham traveled the entire Fertile Crescent, from Mesopotamia to the Nile Valley. Then, several generations later, Moses led the Israelites out of Egypt, through the Sinai, and to the edge of their Promised Land. Moses even named his first son Gershom, which means "stranger there," reflecting "I have been a stranger in a strange land" (Exodus 2:22). However, journeys like these were rare in antiquity. After all, travel agencies were nowhere to be found, and more importantly, strangers were usually enslaved or even killed if they entered a territory not their own. Yet, one of the remarkable results of the ancient Israelites' migrations is that they discovered firsthand the difficulties of getting around. As a result, they thought differently about strangers, as is evidenced in their laws: "Love the stranger, because you were once strangers in the land of Egypt" (Deuteronomy 10:19).

Despite the difficulties of getting around in the ancient world, the Israelites found themselves once again strangers in a strange land. Only this time they were not in Egypt or the Sinai, but back where it all had begun: Mesopotamia. That's right, just as God called Abraham to leave Mesopotamia and seek out his Promised Land, so now God was sending Abraham's descendants back to Mesopotamia, courtesy of the Babylonians. In this chapter you look at their adventures in this strange, yet familiar land, where they struggle to survive, and even thrive, while maintaining their unique identity and their faith in God.

Relocation, Relocation, Relocation

Babylonian kings are about as patient as sugar-eating squirrels, and after repeated rebellions by Judah, the sovereign of Babylon decided to put an end to this vassal kingdom by destroying its capital city of Jerusalem (586 B.C.E.). When he was done, the city and Temple that had been God's "home" and the focal point of Judah's political and religious life for 400 years now lay in ruins. But Jerusalem's destruction merely marks the beginning of Judah's struggle for its cultural survival. The leading citizens become slaves in Babylon, just as their ancestors did in Egypt. Far from their Promised Land, the exiles face the most serious threat to their survival as a people: assimilation. Virtually all displaced peoples in antiquity eventually assimilated into their new surroundings. This seems to be what happened to the northern kingdom of Israel when the Assyrians deported many of its inhabitants throughout their empire. The Ten Lost Tribes were "lost" precisely because many assimilated into the cultures that surrounded them.

So, how will Judah and its culture survive these perilous times? Books such as Daniel and Esther seek to answer this question. But they raise the bar of expectation for those in exile: Not only can you survive in a foreign land, you can *thrive*. Individuals such as Daniel and Esther demonstrate that the exiles can remain true to themselves and their cultural heritage, and still rise to the top and make a difference in the world.

The Book of Daniel

Daniel is born in Judah, but at an early age he is carried off into Babylonian exile, where, because of his abilities, he rises to prominence. But Daniel's high status makes his cultural peculiarities all the more obvious, and he and his three friends — Shadrach, Meshach, and Abednego — are threatened with death if they don't conform. But Daniel and his three buddies never succumb to these pressures, and God repeatedly delivers them. The book of Daniel contains some of the Bible's most amazing and famous adventures, stories written to offer courage to peoples persecuted for practicing their religion.

Reading Daniel can be a bit confusing because it doesn't follow a historical sequence, but is arranged topically and linguistically. For example, Daniel 1–6 contains stories about Daniel interpreting various signs and dreams, and he and his friends escaping various dangers, while Daniel 7–12 contains apocalyptic material (or visions of the end times). Also, Daniel 1–2:3 and 8:1–12:13 are in Hebrew, while Daniel 2:4–7:28 is in Aramaic — a language related to Hebrew and the *lingua franca*, or common language, of Daniel's day. So don't be confused if a king who died in the first half of Daniel is all of a sudden alive again in the second part!

Attending Babylonian University and interpreting dreams (Daniel 1–2)

Kings expect to be waited upon. And, because good help is hard to find in any day, King Nebuchadnezzar of Babylon orders that many of the Judean youths

Daniel's story: 400 years in the making?

The Book of Daniel is set in the sixth century B.C.E., but nearly all scholars believe that it wasn't completed until about 165 B.C.E. This determination is based on its language and its extremely detailed prophecies of events that occurred during the second century B.C.E. Of course, as a prophet, predicting the future was Daniel's job, and even if the Book of Daniel wasn't completed until long after Daniel's death, this doesn't diminish the fact that it preserves authentic traditions from Daniel's life.

among the exiles be trained as royal stewards. Such training included education in the language, literature, and culture of Babylon.

Among those enrolled in this "Babylonian University" are Daniel and three of his friends: Hananiah, Mishael, and Azariah. The first item on the agenda is to give these freshmen Babylonian names. Daniel, a Hebrew name meaning "God is my judge" is given the Babylonian name Belteshazzar, which means "Bel protects his life." Bel is a reference to the Babylonian chief god Marduk. Daniel's three friends Hananiah ("the LORD is gracious"), Mishael ("Who is like God?"), and Azariah ("the LORD is my help") are also given Babylonian names: Shadrach ("command of Aku," a Mesopotamian moon god), Meshach ("Who is like Aku?"), and Abednego ("servant of Nabu," the Mesopotamian god of learning), respectively. Already the cultural battle has begun, as their names now give recognition to other gods.

Daniel's diet for a small planet

Daniel's and his friends' educations involve three years of physical and mental conditioning. During this period, they're expected to partake in Babylonian cuisine. Yet, according to the biblical dietary laws, Babylonian meat and wine are not even close to being ritually pure (*kosher* in Hebrew; see Chapter 7). Thus, Daniel asks that he and his friends be able to eat only vegetables and drink only water. The problem with this request is that Nebuchadnezzar wants his stewards to be robust, because scrawny, wimp servants would compromise his reputation as a manly king. Still, Daniel's proposed diet is given a trial run, and, remarkably, after ten days Daniel and his friends look "better in appearance and fatter in flesh" than the others. With this winning diet and God's help in giving them "understanding and knowledge in all kinds of literature and learning," Daniel and his pals graduate atop their class, and the king rewards them with important jobs in the royal administration.

Dreaming about the future

All is well in the kingdom until King Nebuchadnezzar has a very disturbing dream. Because dreams were believed to be divine messages, the king seeks to know what this dream means for him and his kingdom. But there's a little catch: to guarantee that the interpretation he receives is from the gods, and because he can't remember the dream, Nebuchadnezzar demands that his wise men first tell him what he dreamed before they interpret it. Nebuchadnezzar's servants fail, saying that only the gods could perform such a difficult feat (precisely Neb's point). Nebuchadnezzar, unimpressed, orders all the wise men executed. As wise men, Daniel and his friends are among the condemned, but just before their execution, Daniel prays, and God reveals the dream to him, saving his and the other wisemen's lives.

So what was the king's dream? A very bright and scary metal image appears before the king. Its head consists of gold, its breasts and arms are silver, its belly and thighs are bronze, its legs are iron, and its feet are part iron and part clay. Suddenly, a stone appears "from heaven" and strikes the foot of the statue, causing the whole image to crumble. Then the stone becomes a giant mountain that fills the earth. And what does this mean? The metals represent future successive kingdoms. The head of gold is Nebuchadnezzar and the kingdom of Babylon, which will be replaced by "a kingdom inferior to yours" (hence, the silver). The belly and thighs of bronze represent another kingdom, which will "rule over the whole earth." Then a kingdom will arise that will "crush all the others," just as "iron breaks everything." The clay mixed with iron represents the division of this kingdom. Most scholars equate the silver with Media, the bronze with Persia, the iron with the Greek Empire under Alexander the Great, and the iron mixed with clay with the division of Alexander's kingdom among his generals. However, because in Daniel's other visions the kingdoms of Media and Persia are usually combined (because Media eventually assimilated with Persia), some have argued that the kingdoms need to be shifted up one, making the last kingdom the emerging Roman power. Whatever the case, the stone that destroys these empires is God's kingdom, "which fills the whole earth."

Nebuchadnezzar, justifiably impressed with Daniel's wisdom, worships Daniel's God, promotes Daniel, and sacrifices on his behalf.

Is it getting hot in here? Daniel's friends in the fiery furnace (Daniel 3)

Daniel 3 is about Daniel's three friends, who refuse to worship a huge, 90-foot-tall golden statue that king Nebuchadnezzar has erected. Their refusal takes some guts, because the king's order that everyone must bow to the statue came with a sizeable threat to those who wouldn't: they will "immediately be thrown into a fiery furnace" (Daniel 3:6). Despite this threat, Shadrach, Meshach, and Abednego refuse, because they bow only to God. The king is furious when he finds out about their defiance, and he asks angrily (and rhetorically), "What god can save you from my hand?" The three amigos have an answer: God will save them, and even if He won't, "we won't serve your gods or bow to the golden image you have built" (Daniel 3:18).

Well, this of course infuriates Nebuchadnezzar all the more, and he orders the furnace to be turned up sevenfold. The fire becomes so hot that the guards responsible for throwing the three men into the furnace are killed as they carry out their command. Then, straining to look into the furnace at the suffering of these three rebels, the king asks: "Didn't we throw three men into the fire?" (Kings are never short of rhetorical questions.) "Then why do I see four men walking about in the flames, untied and uninjured, and the fourth appears like a son of the gods?" At this, the king tells the three men to come out, and they emerge without even a singed eyebrow or the smell of smoke.

So, who is this one like "a son of the gods" who rescues the three men? As you may expect, several interpretations have been put forth, including God, an angel (which is what Nebuchanezzar later calls him), Jesus, and even Elvis, which inspired the *Burnin' Love* lyrics "Lord Almighty, I feel my temperature rising" (okay, that last one is not seriously debated among scholars . . . yet). Whoever it is, Nebuchadnezzar is impressed, promotes Shadrach, Meshach, and Abednego, and worships God.

Pride before a fall (Daniel 4)

Years later, Nebuchadnezzar has another dream and he can't make heads nor tails of it. In his dream, he sees a large tree that provides food and protection for humans and beasts alike. But then a heavenly being orders that the tree be chopped down, and only the stump remains. The stump is then turned into a wild animal. Understandably, all the king's wise men are stumped at the stump until Daniel shows up and saves the day. According to Daniel, the tree is the king, who, like the tree, has a vast kingdom that provides for his subjects. But this situation will soon change. God will make the king go mad because of his pride, and he will live in the wild and eat grass like an ox.

A year passes. Then Nebuchadnezzar, while walking on his roof, reflects on his many accomplishments and says, "Isn't Babylon great, a royal residence that *I* have built by *my* power and for the glory of *my* majesty?" Uh oh. There were a few too many *I*s and *my*s in that statement. In a scene reminiscent of *Beauty and the Beast,* God strikes the king with madness, driving him into the wild where he eats grass, grows long hair and nails, and listens over and over again to The Beatles' *White Album* (okay, we made up that last part). The spell is finally broken when a young woman named Belle falls in love . . . Actually, after seven years of insanity, Nebuchadnezzar repents of his pride and acknowledges God as the ultimate sovereign, and then regains his sanity.

The writing's on the wall: Belshazzar's feast and the fall of Babylon (Daniel 5)

With dad away in the Arabian desert, the king-in-residence, Belshazzar, decides to throw a party. All is fine until he decides to boast about Babylon's might by drinking wine from the gold and silver cups looted from the Jerusalem Temple. Bad idea. Those vessels were for one purpose only (God's worship) and for one place only (the Temple in Jerusalem). Suddenly a hand appears out of nowhere and writes mysterious words on the wall. The king, realizing this can't be good, offers a reward to anyone who can read it.

Although the penmanship was undoubtedly flawless, no one can make out the message until the queen remembers some guy named Daniel who did pretty well at things like this. Daniel is summoned and immediately recognizes the penmanship as God's, and then reads the writing on the wall: *mene, mene, tekel, uparsin.* These are Aramaic words deriving from metrology, and Daniel gives the following interpretation:

- ✔ **Mene** means "to count." Daniel says, "God has numbered the days of your kingdom and is bringing it to an end."

- ✔ **Tekel** means "to measure." Daniel states, "You've been weighed (on the moral scales) and have been found wanting."

- ✔ **uParsin:** The *u* is Aramaic for "and," and *parsin* means "to divide." Daniel informs Belshazzar, "Your kingdom is divided and will be given to the Medes and Persians."

The last line is particularly effective, because the words for "to divide" and "Persians" sound alike in Aramaic. Unfortunately, the king had little time to appreciate God's wordplay, because that night the Persians took over Babylon and killed Belshazzar, marking the transition from the Babylonian to Persian periods in ancient Near Eastern history. The year was 539 B.C.E., and soon Cyrus the Great, the king of Persia, would allow the exiled Jews and other groups to return to their ancestral homeland. However, most exiles, including Daniel and Esther, chose to remain in their new homes.

Lying with lions: Dan in the den (Daniel 6)

With Persia in and Babylon out, Daniel's new employer, King Darius, immediately recognizes his gifts and appoints him to one of the highest posts in the Persian administration. But the other administrators are jealous and set out to ruin Daniel. Unfortunately for them, Daniel has more moral resolve than Jimmy Stewart in *Mr. Smith Goes to Washington.* Realizing that the only way to bring a good man down is by exploiting his goodness, they decide to frame Daniel for his religious convictions. They convince the king to order an edict that no one can beseech any other god or human other than the king for a month. If they do, they'll be fed to the lions.

Daniel, fully aware of the edict, continues his practice of praying three times a day at his window (so he could face Jerusalem). Lingering in the shadows below are the officials, who report Daniel's behavior to King Darius and have him arrested. The king is distraught to learn that his friend Daniel is guilty, but because Persian kings could not change an edict (this would convey uncertainty to his subjects), he must comply.

Thus, Daniel is thrown into the lions' den, which is sealed to ensure no one tries to rescue Daniel. That night, the king is so upset that he can't sleep or eat. Fortunately for Daniel, the lions couldn't eat either, because an angel appeared and "shut their mouths." At daybreak, the king rushes back to the pit and finds Daniel miraculously unharmed. Darius then orders that those who led him to make this silly law, along with their families, be thrown to the lions. They are, and they are eaten "even before they hit the floor."

Daniel's visions (Daniel 7, 10–12)

Because the first half of the Book of Daniel consists of narrative stories, while the other half records Daniel's visions of things to come, debate arose about where to put Daniel in the Bible. Jewish tradition places Daniel with the Writings, while most Christian Bibles place him with the Prophets. Many scholars, however, place Daniel, along with Revelation in the New Testament, into a special genre of *apocalyptic literature*. The term "apocalyptic" means to reveal hidden knowledge, which is exactly what these types of literature purport to do. No matter where you put him, Daniel's visions became extremely influential in later Judaism and Christianity.

The following sections cover two of Daniel's most famous visions.

Of beasts and horns

Daniel has a dream where he witnesses four remarkable beasts: a winged lion, a bear, a four-headed winged leopard, and a "terrifying beast" with ten horns. Then, among the ten horns appears a "little horn," which cuts off some of the other horns. After this, Daniel sees God, here called "the Ancient of Days," on His throne in heaven. Ushered before God is "one like a son of man," who is given authority to establish an everlasting kingdom, which is soon to come.

So what does this vision mean? An angel tells Daniel that the four beasts symbolize empires that are to come. Although they remain unnamed, most scholars link the lion to Babylon, the bear to a joint Median-Persian empire, and the winged-leopard with four heads to Alexander the Great and his four generals (among whom Alexander's kingdom is divided after his death), and the "terrifying beast" to the Greek rulers of Mesopotamia, called the Seleucids after Alexander's general, Seleucus. (Some scholars, however, identify this last beast with a power yet to come, such as Rome.) Nearly all scholars agree that the "little horn" that appears on the beasts head is the Seleucid king, Antiochus Epiphanes, who, as Daniel describes, desecrated the Temple in Jerusalem and waged war with the Jews (see Chapter 16). The identity of one "like a son of man" is not specified. However, in later Jewish literature, the title "Son of Man" came to refer to the promised Messiah, who would deliver the Jews from their enemies and establish an eternal kingdom of righteousness and justice. In the Christian New Testament, the title "Son of Man" is applied to Jesus (see Chapter 19), who is also called the Messiah. Moreover, Jesus predicts another desecration of the Temple when describing the events of the end times (see Matthew 24:15).

On earth as it is in heaven

On the banks of the Tigris River, Daniel has a vision concerning the "end of days." The messenger (who seems to be the angel Gabriel of Daniel 8–9) tells Daniel that he would have arrived earlier, but there is a heavenly battle currently being waged between angels, with Michael representing the Jews and another heavenly patron representing Persia. Daniel's vision foretells successive kings and empires, and a war between the north (representing the Greek kingdom of the Seleucids in Mesopotamia) and the south (the Greek kingdom of the Ptolemies in Egypt). Finally the Seleucid king, Antiochus Epiphanes, will arise, persecute the Jews and profane the Jerusalem Temple, and be killed after campaigning south. Not long after these events God's kingdom will arrive, and, in the Hebrew Bible's most explicit reference to heaven and hell, Daniel writes: "Those who sleep in the dust of the ground will awake, some to eternal life, and some to eternal contempt" (Daniel 12:2).

The Book of Daniel ends with a promise to Daniel that the visions he has seen will come to pass, and that he will be among those who awake to eternal life.

The Book of Esther

Like the Book of Daniel, Esther records the difficulties of life in exile. But whereas Daniel is set in sixth century B.C.E. Babylon, Esther tells of events in the fifth century B.C.E. Persian capital city of Susa. The Book of Esther is a marvelous work of literature, remarkable for its use of irony and plot twists.

Miss Persian Empire (Esther 1–2)

The Book of Esther opens with a stag party thrown by the Persian king, Ahasuerus, usually identified with Xerxes I (486–465 B.C.E.). (Hebrew *Ahasuerus* is a transliteration of Persian *khshayarshan,* while Xerxes is the Greek form.) The king demands that his wife, Vashti, come out to the party "wearing the royal crown" so he can show her off to his guests. Vashti refuses, which terrifies the men. As one official puts it, "When the women of Persian and Median nobility hear of the queen's actions, they'll do the same thing. Then there will be no end to disrespect and discord!" (Esther 1:18). (Yes, the author of Esther was laughing too.)

With a woman's liberation movement on the horizon, the king deposes his wife and begins a search for a replacement. The king decides to hold a beauty pageant, only it is an ancient beauty pageant, where the rules are a little more risqué. Contestants are given one year of beauty treatments, and then for the "contest" they spend the night with the king in his chambers. That's right. No talent show, no "I'd end war and world hunger" speeches, just the evening wear competition. One contestant is Esther, a nice Jewish girl who is being raised by her cousin Mordecai. Their names, in fact, show the extent to which they have assimilated — Mordecai is derived from the Babylonian chief deity Marduk, and Esther from the fertility goddess Ishtar. (Esther also has a Hebrew name: Hadassah.) Esther wins the contest and becomes the queen of the Persian Empire, all the while keeping her Jewish heritage secret.

Esther saves the day (Esther 3–10)

A short time after Esther wins the sleepover beauty pageant, Mordecai learns of a plot to assassinate the king and informs him. The king averts death and records in the daily chronicles that Mordecai the Jew saved the monarch. But Mordecai soon runs into trouble when he refuses to bow to the king's highest official, named Haman, the story's villain. For Mordecai's insolence, Haman vows to destroy all the Jews and brings the matter before the king. However, rather than specifying the Jews, he refers to them as a "certain people." Xerxes signs Haman's edict and gives him the funds to carry out his plan.

Esther's bravery and Haman's humiliation

When Mordecai learns of the edict, he relays the disturbing news to Esther, asking her to intercede for her people before the king. She refuses, saying that the king hasn't summoned her and that anyone entering his presence uninvited is put to death. In response, Mordecai sends Esther this message:

> *Do you think that just because you are in the royal palace that you alone of all the Jews will escape? If you remain silent at this time, then deliverance for the Jews will come from another place, and you and your father's family will perish. But who knows? Perhaps you have achieved your royal status for such a time as this?*

—Esther 4:12–14

Esther replies, "I will go to the king, even though it is against the law. And if I die, then I die" (Esther 4:16). Esther does go to the king, who welcomes her, even offering her whatever she wants. Instead of laying all her cards on the table, she asks if the king and Haman would join her for dinner. He agrees. At dinner, Ahasuerus offers Esther anything she desires, and she coolly asks for another dinner with the same guests the following day. Haman, assuming this means a promotion is imminent, is thrilled. As he boasts with friends and family that night, he admits that the only thing robbing him of complete joy is that darn Mordecai, who still refuses to bow to him. His friends convince Haman to find an outlet for his dissatisfaction by having gallows built in front of his house so he can watch Mordecai hang on the day the edict takes effect.

Meanwhile, in the palace, the king has insomnia and asks that the daily records be read to him (that would put anyone to sleep). He discovers that Mordecai was never rewarded for saving his life. When Haman shows up the next morning, King Ahasuerus asks what he would recommend as a reward for one the king wants to honor. Haman, believing it is him, advises the king to give that man fancy clothes and jewelry and have him ride on the king's horse through the city while a high official goes before him declaring: "This is what is done for the person whom the king wants to honor." To his horror, Haman learns that the honoree is not him but Mordecai! Making matters worse, the king tells Haman to lead Mordecai through the streets shouting his suggested line. Haman is livid but must comply.

Haman's downfall and the Jews' deliverance

That night, at the second dinner party, Ahasuerus asks again for the chance to fulfill the queen's desire. Esther, to everyone's surprise, begs for the king to preserve her life and the life of her people. The king asks who would dare threaten her. Esther replies, "This vile Haman." The king becomes furious and leaves the room. In desperation, Haman falls on the couch beside Esther, pleading for his life. When the king returns and sees Haman on the couch next to his wife, he interprets this as his coming on to his wife — now Haman's doubly dead! The king only bemoans the fact that he doesn't have any gallows ready to hang him. One of the king's officials speaks up, saying he saw newly built gallows in front of Haman's house that would work perfectly!

However, the edict that the king ordered to kill the Jews can't be revoked. Therefore the king allows Mordecai to issue a new edict, allowing the Jews to defend themselves and encouraging others to support them. The Jews outside of the city of Susa win victory after the first day of battle, and one day later, even within Susa the victory is complete. The book ends encouraging all Jews to observe this day as a holiday, which is given the name Purim after the Hebrew word for lots (ancient dice) used by Haman to determine the day he would kill the Jews (for more on Purim see Chapter 27).

BIBLE TRIVIA

Barely a biblical book: The survival of Esther

The Book of Esther is a great example of narrative literature. But for all its literary merits and popularity, Esther almost didn't make it into the Bible because of controversy surrounding God's diminished role in the story. In fact, there is not one reference to God. Also, surprising is that religious customs such as prayer are absent. As an indication of its shaky status, fragments from every book in the Hebrew Bible except Esther have been discovered among the Dead Sea Scrolls (see Chapter 1). In the end, however, the book was included in both the Jewish and Christian Bibles as an example of how God, even when seemingly absent or silent, orchestrates events so that good wins out in the end.

Chapter 12

Home for the Holidays: Returning to the Promised Land with Ezra and Nehemiah

In This Chapter

▶ Returning to the Promised Land courtesy of Cyrus the Great

▶ Rebuilding the Temple with Zerubbabel

▶ Repairing Jerusalem's walls with Nehemiah

▶ Rediscovering Israel's biblical heritage with Ezra

The Jews of the fifth century B.C.E. had a hard time being optimistic. And who could blame them? Less than a century earlier, their beloved country, Judah, their capital city, Jerusalem, and their pride and joy, God's Temple, had all been destroyed by the Babylonians. Now in exile, their culture lay in danger of disappearing through assimilation. Theologically, they struggled with issues of *theodicy* — a fancy way of saying "Why did God let these terrible things happen to us"?

The Bible's answer to the question of "Why?" was that God hadn't abandoned His people, but that they'd abandoned Him through their continual disregard for His commandments. But things didn't have to stay this way. If they would turn back to God and mend their ways, God would restore them to their Promised Land. And this is exactly what happens! Thanks in large part to a Persian king named Cyrus the Great, who issues a decree allowing those in exile to return to their ancestral home, and thanks to those brave souls who took him up on his offer, Jerusalem and its Temple are eventually rebuilt, and the Jews find themselves again in their homeland.

In this chapter, you examine the Books of Ezra and Nehemiah, which chronicle the exiled Jews' return to Jerusalem as they discover anew that "there's no place like home."

Who wrote Ezra and Nehemiah?

The Books of Ezra and Nehemiah were originally a single book (called Ezra), and in many Jewish Bibles they're still reckoned as one book (usually called Ezra-Nehemiah). Christian scholars in the third and fourth centuries C.E. separated these books based on their different protagonists. One reason Ezra and Nehemiah have always been so closely connected is their similar vocabularies and theological outlooks. In fact, some scholars believe that not only Ezra and Nehemiah but also 1 and 2 Chronicles (see Chapter 10) were written or, more accurately, compiled by the same person (traditionally Ezra). 2 Chronicles even ends with the same passage that begins Ezra: Cyrus the Great's edict giving the Jews permission to return to their homeland.

Cyrus the Great's Great Idea

Cyrus the Great is one of the real heroes of antiquity. He not only overthrows the unpopular Babylonian Empire in 539 B.C.E., but he also encourages his new subjects to go back to their homelands and revive their former way of life. The Jews were no exception to Cyrus's rule. Thus, in 538 B.C.E., Cyrus permits any Jews who so desire to return to Judah and rebuild God's Temple. Here is Cyrus's edict, as recorded in the Bible:

> Thus says Cyrus king of Persia: the LORD, the God of heaven, has given me all the kingdoms of earth, and He has charged me to build Him a house in Jerusalem, which is in Judah. Whoever is among you of all His people, may his God be with him, and let him go up to Jerusalem, which is in Judah, and rebuild the house of the LORD, the God of Israel, He is the God who is in Jerusalem. And let each survivor, in whatever place he stays, be assisted by the men of his place with silver and gold, with goods and with animals, besides freewill offerings for the house of God which is in Jerusalem.
>
> —Ezra 1:2–4

Home is where the heart is: The Jews who stayed in Babylon

Even though Cyrus the Great allows the Jews to return to Jerusalem, not everyone packs up and leaves. In fact, relatively few do, and those who ultimately return don't do it all at once. Most Mesopotamian Jews are firmly established, having spent over half a century there already. Moreover, many followed the prophet Jeremiah's advice to buy property in Babylon and settle down (Jeremiah 29). Therefore, the majority of Jews remain in Babylon, which will become the dominant and most influential Jewish community from the period of the exile throughout the Greco-Roman Period. It is this community that produces the Babylonian *Talmud* (third to fifth centuries C.E.), a collection of Jewish laws and stories that is the most important book in Judaism outside of the Hebrew Bible.

There's no place like home: The Jews who returned to Judea (Ezra 1–2)

Those Jews who decide to return to Jerusalem do so initially under the leadership of Sheshbazzar, a member of Judah's royal family. Although the first wave of returnees (around 538 B.C.E.) doesn't seem to have been very large, they had the financial backing of those who remained in Babylon. They also brought back with them the Temple vessels confiscated earlier by the Babylonian king, Nebuchadnezzar, when he conquered and eventually destroyed Jerusalem (586 B.C.E.).

Aside from mentioning Sheshbazzar's departure from Babylon, the Bible provides very little information about his activity and accomplishments once back in Judea. Based on the evidence, it seems that Sheshbazzar and his fellow returnees began laying the foundations of the Temple (Ezra 5:16), but for unknown reasons, they're unable to complete the task.

The Second Temple: A Sight for Sore Eyes

Eighteen years after the initial return of the exiles under Sheshbazzar, work begins anew on the Temple. But this time the returnees are led by a man named Zerubbabel, the grandson of Jehoiachin, the king of Judah exiled and later favored by the Babylonians (see 2 Kings 25:27–30).

Picking up where others left off: Re-rebuilding the Temple (Ezra 3)

When Zerubbabel, with the approval of the Persian Empire, and the Jews accompanying him first arrive in Jerusalem (around 520 B.C.E.), they begin where the first wave of returnees left off: rebuilding the Temple. They start by rebuilding the central altar, which allows them to offer sacrifices to God. They then begin work on the Temple itself. When the foundation is laid, most of the people shout for joy. However, when those familiar with the first Temple see the diminished size of the new foundation, they weep, realizing that this Temple (creatively called the second Temple by scholars) will in no way compare to Solomon's glorious structure. Despite these mixed emotions, the people busy themselves with the construction of the new Temple.

Running interference: The Samaritans' opposition to the Temple (Ezra 4–6)

Although the Book of Ezra doesn't follow a strict chronological order, it is clear that at some point during the rebuilding of the Temple, the Jews' efforts are hampered by a people known as the Samaritans (see the sidebar "Who are the Samaritans?" in this chapter), who are upset by the Jews' refusal to let them help. In response, the Samaritans warn the local Persian administrator that if the Temple is rebuilt, the Jews will rebel as they did under the Babylonians. When the Persian administrator checks the royal records, he discovers that the Jews indeed have a history of rebelling against their overlords, and he insists that they stop work on the Temple.

Years pass, and the Temple remains unfinished. Realizing that the people need a little motivation, God calls the prophets Haggai and Zechariah to do their stuff (see Chapter 13). Haggai plays the role of the "bad cop," as it were, chastising the people for fixing up their own homes while neglecting the house of God. Zechariah plays the role of the "good cop," envisioning a day when the Judean monarchy will be restored. Motivated by the prophets' preaching, the people again begin rebuilding the Temple.

This time, some Persian officials approach the Jews, asking who gave them permission to start work on the Temple. To get to the bottom of things, the Persian officials contact the new Persian king, Darius, asking him to settle the matter. To the joy of the Jews, Darius proclaims that Cyrus's original decree allowing the Jews to rebuild their lives in Judea is still in effect, and that work on the Jerusalem Temple should not only be continued, but it should be funded by Persian imperial funds. Grateful, the people thank God and continue with their work. Finally, the Temple is completed and dedicated in 515 B.C.E., and the Jews celebrate the Passover holiday with sacrifices for the first time in 70 years.

Who are the Samaritans?

According to the Bible, the Samaritans of Ezra and Nehemiah's day consisted of people resettled by the Assyrians from southern Mesopotamia (2 Kings 17). That is, they weren't legitimate Israelites. The Samaritans, however, claimed descent from the Israelite tribes of Ephraim and Manasseh. Regardless of the Samaritans' origins, the returning Judeans believed them to be intruders, and, despite offers by the Samaritans to work in unison to rebuild Jerusalem, the returnees resist. In the New Testament, Jesus uses the story of a "Good Samaritan" (an oxymoron to most Jews of his day) to teach that one should love everyone (Luke 10:29–37).

Ezra the Priest: Can We Fix It? We'll Get Back to You on That

About 50 years after Zerubbabel's return and rebuilding of the Temple, Ezra comes on the scene. Ezra, as an expert in Israel's ancient legal code (or the Torah; see Chapter 7), is sent by the Persian king, Artaxerxes, to find out how things are going in Judea. Ezra and his fellow returnees travel with a letter from the Persian king (Ezra 7:12–26) that grants Ezra the authority to use money from the Persian treasury to tend to any unfinished business in rebuilding the Jews' lives in their homeland.

Changing leadership: The Jews swap a monarchy for a theocracy (Ezra 7–8)

When Ezra arrives in Jerusalem (around 458 B.C.E.), he discovers that the people aren't well informed about their religious heritage. Therefore, Ezra begins to teach the people about the Law of Moses, and he implements religious and civil reforms to ensure that they're following God's laws as recorded in the Bible. Although Ezra isn't a descendant of David, he is effectively made the leader of the Jewish community in Jerusalem by Persian royal commission. This arrangement dramatically alters the governing of the Jewish community, changing it from a *monarchy* (rule by a king) to a *theocracy* (rule by God). Although individuals calling themselves kings will later rule the Jews during the Hasmonean Period (from around 165 B.C.E.–63 B.C.E.; see Chapter 16), they, too, are descendants of the Jewish priesthood. And even after the Hasmoneans are replaced by Roman appointed rulers, the priests are looked to as the leaders of the Jewish community until the Roman destruction of the Temple in 70 C.E. Thus, the shift in Judean leadership initiated by Ezra continues for over five centuries.

Divorce, biblical style (Ezra 9–10)

Shortly after Ezra arrives in Judea to enact religious reforms, a large group of people approach Ezra and confess:

> *We have sinned against our God and have married foreign women from the peoples of the land. Yet now there is hope for Israel concerning this thing. Now therefore let us make a covenant with our God to eject all these women and those born to them, according to the counsel of my lord and those who tremble at the commandments of our God.*

> —Ezra 10:2–3

What's Aramaic doing in the Hebrew Bible?

The Hebrew Bible is written mostly in Hebrew (hence, the name). A few portions, however, are written in a language similar to Hebrew, known as Aramaic (named after the region of Aram [modern Syria] where it originates). The biblical passages in Aramaic include Artaxerxes's letter that Ezra carries as recorded in Ezra 7:12–26, as well as Ezra 4:8–6:8; Daniel 2:4–7:28; one verse from Jeremiah 10:11, and only two words in Genesis 31:47.

The Aramaic language came to dominate the ancient Near East after the Persian Empire took over the area because they used it in all of their legal documents. The use of Aramaic continued for some time — Jews in first-century Palestine, including Jesus, would've spoken in Aramaic.

Ezra is very disturbed to learn of the interfaith marriages, and forces the priests who have married local women to take an oath to immediately divorce their wives and families. Then, Ezra summons all the returned exiles to assemble within three days in Jerusalem. Heavy rains increase the drama, as the people gather and are drenched as they hear they must abandon their families. According to Ezra, some priests and laymen oppose the plan, but in the end all are forced to divorce their wives and children.

Ezra's insistence that these men divorce their foreign wives and their children may strike you as peculiar. To explain, divorce is largely discouraged, if not condemned, in the Bible (see Malachi 2:16; Matthew 5:31–32). Secondly, other biblical authors seem to be more tolerant of intermarriage between neighboring peoples. For example, all the kings of Judah, as descendants of King David, stem from the intermarriage of the Moabite woman Ruth and her Israelite husband (see Chapter 8). Nevertheless, in Ezra's defense, it's quite possible that such interfaith marriages would have destroyed the Jews' religious identity due to assimilation. So he insists that these men get divorced. (Making matters worse, the names of those who had intermarried are listed in the Bible — to be forever preserved for future generations!)

Nehemiah the Builder: Can We Fix It? Yes, We Can!

In about 445 B.C.E., the Persian king sends a man named Nehemiah to look into the welfare of Jerusalem. Actually, Nehemiah, who is the king's cupbearer (not the one who taps the king's keg, but an important royal official in charge of food preparation), *asks* the king for permission to return to his ancestral homeland. The reason: Nehemiah receives word that the walls of Jerusalem still lay in ruins, even though the Jews have been in their homeland for nearly 100 years. Because walls were a city's primary means of defense, Nehemiah knew that the rebuilding of Jerusalem's walls was essential for the protection of the Jews against their enemies.

Not only does the king give Nehemiah permission to go to Jerusalem, he gives Nehemiah an armed escort, as well as permission to use the empire's resources to rebuild Jerusalem's walls.

Rebuilding Jerusalem's walls (Nehemiah 3–4, 6)

When Nehemiah arrives in Jerusalem, he surveys the damage to the walls and begins to organize the people for work. Nehemiah wisely decides to have the people work on the walls by family groups, and near the location of their houses. Nehemiah's strategy ensures that the people remain motivated in their work, because rebuilding the walls means protection for their own homes.

However, once word gets out that the Jews are rebuilding the walls, the Samaritans raise opposition, and even threaten violence. The threat of attack requires that the Jews work on the wall with a tool in one hand and a sword in the other. There are even several attempts on Nehemiah's life. Despite these many obstacles, Nehemiah and his coworkers succeed in rebuilding the walls — and in record time: a mere 52 days (Nehemiah 6:15). Now with the walls completed, there is just one thing left to do (no, not "party" — well, actually, they do that, too): dedicate themselves and their newly fortified city to God.

Rediscovering the Torah at Water Gate (Nehemiah 8–9)

The defining moment for the former Jewish exiles and Richard Nixon both occur at a place called Water Gate. Coincidence? Well, yes, of course it is. Yet, although both would change the course of a nation, what happened at Jerusalem's Water Gate contained far less political intrigue.

Ezra reads the Law of Moses

Ezra's Water Gate is the name of one of the main portals in Jerusalem's walls, seemingly located by the fresh-water spring just southeast of the city. Near the Water Gate, at a public square, the former exiles gather in 445 B.C.E. to hear Ezra read the Law of Moses. Many of them are hearing these laws for the first time, and several of them no longer understand biblical Hebrew. As a result, while Ezra reads, others skilled in Israel's ancient legal code mingle among the crowd and answer any questions people have. Many Judeans weep as they hear of their ancestral heritage and laws they had long ago abandoned. Ezra consoles them and instructs them that they shouldn't mourn, but should celebrate the joyous occasion.

The people celebrate Sukkot

The following day, the people's leaders come to Ezra to study the words of the Torah more closely. Lo and behold, they discover that according to the biblical calendar, it is the holiday of Booths (also called Sukkot — described in Chapter 27 of this book). It's time to party!

During this weeklong celebration, Jews set up and inhabit makeshift shelters to commemorate their ancestors' exodus and wilderness wanderings under Moses (the holiday is recorded in Leviticus 23; see Chapter 7 of this book). Now, for the first time in years, Jews are celebrating the holiday of Booths, just as the Torah instructs. This story demonstrates just how close Judaism came to losing its biblical heritage.

The Temple during holidays

In the histories recorded in the Books of Ezra and Nehemiah, the Temple takes on special significance during certain days in the calendar. Thus, Zerubbabel rededicates the Temple during Passover, and one of Ezra's first reforms is to re-implement the holiday of Sukkot (sometimes spelled Succoth) near the Temple precinct. Other biblical books record similar features: The Temple is first dedicated by Solomon during the New Year festival; in the Apocrypha, the Temple is rededicated once again during the festival of Hanukkah; in the New Testament gospels, Jesus travels to Jerusalem before his crucifixion during Passover; and in Acts, the disciples speak in tongues at the Temple during Pentecost. These holidays at the Temple, in which people from all over Israel and Judah came to Jerusalem to celebrate *en masse* (or as a group), were often the settings for dynamic events that people would remember for generations, as well as providing us with some of the Bible's most memorable stories.

Chapter 13

More Than Mere Fortune-tellers: The Prophets

Today we call those who predict the future brokers. In the Bible, however, they are called prophets. Yet, predicting the future was only part of a prophet's job (and, unlike brokers, true prophets were strictly not-for-profit). In this chapter, you explore what it took to be a biblical prophet, and you meet those who fulfilled this important task.

Being a Biblical Prophet

The word *prophet* comes from the Greek word *prophetes,* which means "to speak on behalf of another." On the most basic level, then, biblical prophets are messengers who speak on behalf of God. In Hebrew, though, the most common word for prophet is *nabi'* (pronounced *na-VEE*), which means "one who is called." Thus, the emphasis in the Hebrew Bible is not so much on the prophet's role as a messenger but on his or her status as one called by God.

Describing a prophet's job

Being a prophet was not an easy job. Most often God's messages were about as popular as a pharaoh costume at a Passover party. In fact, only one prophet, Isaiah, actively seeks the job, while several others, including Moses, Jonah, and Jeremiah, complain that their vocation is a fate worse than death.

Some of the most common tasks biblical prophets performed include:

- **Predicting the future.** Predicting future events was a prophet's calling card. These predictions could range from picking the sex of an unborn child (ancient sonograms) to predicting the outcome of a battle. Typically, the ability to predict the future gave prophets credibility, and when they had an audience, they could tell their listeners what was really on their (or, more accurately, God's) mind.

- **Advising leaders.** Kings realized the importance of getting God's approval before embarking on a particular course of action, such as building a temple or going to war. Yet, most kings didn't want "no" for an answer, so they would usually hire "prophets," who were really nothing more than ancient yes-men. At times, however, and much to the chagrin of the king, a true prophet would show up on the scene and tell the king what God really thought about his plans or administration. As a result, kings and prophets rarely got along well.

- **Enacting change.** Prophets worked hard to get people to rectify their behaviors and beliefs. At times their messages were met with repentance and change, but most often their admonitions were shunned, and prophets found their very lives in danger.

- **Performing symbolic acts.** Because "a picture is worth a thousand words," sometimes prophets conveyed messages by dramatic action. For example, the prophet Ezekiel is asked to cook food over manure "briquettes" to symbolize Israel's moral uncleanness (Ezekiel 4); the prophet Hosea is asked to marry a prostitute to convey Israel's unfaithfulness (Hosea 1); and the prophet Isaiah is asked to go around naked for three years to depict Israel's impending judgment and shame (Isaiah 20). As you may imagine, there was not a long line in front of the Prophet Employment Agency.

- **Declaring oracles.** Perhaps the most common function of a prophet was to deliver God's messages. These messages, called *oracles*, usually begin with the words "Thus says the LORD . . . " Oracles most often warned people of the impending judgment they would face if they didn't reverse direction and amend their ways.

Examining a prophet's qualifications

Unlike other vocations in ancient Israel — such as the priesthood, where one needed to fulfill specific requirements before getting "hired" (such as being a Levite, male, and falling into a particular age bracket) — biblical prophets could be young or old, rich or poor, brainiacs or simpletons, male or female. In fact, some of Israel's most influential prophets were women, including Miriam, who led Israel in its worship of God after the exodus from Egypt (Exodus 15:20); Deborah, who led Israel to victory against the Canaanites (Judges 4:4); and Huldah, who advised one of Israel's greatest kings, Josiah

(2 Kings 22:14). The secret to God's choice is diversity, because God needs a wide range of people to deliver His diverse messages to the ever-changing circumstances of Israel's national existence.

Introducing the Major Prophets

Among the prophets, three are called "Major" (Isaiah, Jeremiah, and Ezekiel), and the other twelve are called "Minor" (Hosea, Joel, Amos, Obadiah, Jonah, Micah, Nahum, Habakkuk, Zephaniah, Haggai, Zechariah, and Malachi). These designations do not refer to their relative importance, but rather to the relative length of their writings.

The writings of the Major Prophets are quite long, each filling their own scrolls, while the Minor Prophets are considerably shorter, and are written all on one scroll. The Book of Daniel, though certainly containing prophecies, is not found with the Prophets in the Hebrew Bible, but with the Writings. However, in the Greek ordering, Daniel is placed with the Prophets, after Ezekiel, making him a kind of fourth Major Prophet. Because we are following the Hebrew ordering, we discuss Daniel in Chapter 11.

Isaiah

Isaiah is perhaps the best known and most influential of the biblical prophets. Part of the reason for his impact was that he lived during one of Israel's most trying periods (around 742–700 B.C.E.). During his tenure as prophet, the northern kingdom of Israel was destroyed by the Assyrians (721 B.C.E.), and Jerusalem narrowly escaped a similar fate. How could God allow His people to be destroyed by so wicked a nation as Assyria, which had an international reputation for violence and bloodshed? And what would be the eventual fate of Judah, who, though still standing, was teetering on the brink of destruction? For the answers to these questions, and to figure out what God wanted from and for His people, the nation looked to Isaiah.

The material in the Book of Isaiah, as with the other prophetic books, is not in chronological order. The prophetic books are collections (not histories) of messages and events surrounding a particular prophet. Therefore, don't be confused if things seem out of order (such as Isaiah being called as a prophet in Isaiah 6, even though Isaiah 1–5 already contain prophecies by Isaiah).

Calling Isaiah (Isaiah 6)

Isaiah's call to be a prophet is quite unique among the prophets, such as Moses and Jonah, because rather than skirting God's call, Isaiah enthusiastically volunteers his services.

JARGON ALERT

What are seraphim?

The heavenly creatures that purify Isaiah's mouth with a burning coal in Isaiah 6:1–7 are called *seraphim,* a designation derived from the Hebrew word for "fiery." This association seems to result from their shining like flames. Isaiah's seraphim have six wings: with two they cover their faces lest they look directly at God and die, with two they cover their "feet" (which most believe is a euphemism for male genitalia) so they remain modest, and with two they fly. It seems likely that Isaiah's seraphim are winged serpent-like creatures, who symbolically guard the sanctity of God's throne.

God appears to Isaiah in a vision where God is sitting on an elevated throne wearing a *mantle* (or robe) that fills the inner sanctum of the Temple (see Chapter 10 for more about the construction of the Temple). Because not just anyone can look upon God, Isaiah is made ritually pure by a six-winged angelic being called a *seraph* (see the "What are seraphim?" sidebar in this chapter) who takes a burning coal from God's altar and places it on Isaiah's lips. God then asks, "Whom shall I send [to my people]?" Isaiah responds, "Here am I, send me!" (Isaiah 6:8).

God's message for Isaiah in this particular case is that Judah will be destroyed. Moreover, God tells Isaiah to speak to the people in order to make their hearts "fat" so they won't understand, their ears "heavy" so they won't hear, and their eyes "shut" so they won't see. With their senses dulled, God can punish them without reservation. Yet, this seems a strange call by God given that a prophet's main job is to warn people so that they *will* listen and change their ways. So what's going on here?

Actually, getting people to change their ways is exactly the desired effect God wants in the present case. When those who truly want to please God hear that God has reached the point of not wanting His people to repent, they will repent all the more earnestly. But why has God reached this point?

The opening chapters of Isaiah show that although the people offer God sacrifices and prayers, they reveal their insincerity by neglecting the rights of the poor and disadvantaged. As God puts it,

> *Remove your evil ways from before Me, cease doing wrong, learn to do good, seek justice, correct the oppressor, defend the orphan, contend for the widow.*

—Isaiah 1:16–17

Israel has a lot to do, and it stands on the threshold of imminent judgment. How it responds to Isaiah's warnings will ultimately determine its fate.

Isaiah's most famous prophecies

Several of Isaiah's prophecies have had an enduring influence. Here are some of the most influential:

- ✔ **Swords to plowshares: the great day of peace (Isaiah 2):** In Isaiah 2:4, Isaiah predicts that in the "latter days" God will usher in a great age of judgment, followed by unprecedented peace. In beautifully crafted poetry, Isaiah predicts that God "will judge among the nations, and rebuke many peoples. And they shall beat their swords into plowshares, and their spears into pruning hooks; nation shall not lift up sword against nation, and they shall no longer learn war." It hasn't happened yet, but it's nice to imagine such a day. This passage, in fact, adorns the United Nations building in New York.

  A sword that was bent in a fashion similar to Isaiah's prophecy now resides in the Israel Museum. In 1979, following the peace treaty between Egypt and Israel, Prime Minister Menachem Begin gave the Egyptian President Anwar Sadat a replica of this sword, symbolizing their newfound peace.

- ✔ **The birth of Immanuel (Isaiah 7):** In Isaiah 7:14, Isaiah prophesies that a "young woman will conceive and bear a son, and his name will be called Immanuel." In its immediate context, Isaiah is advising King Ahaz not to get involved in a war because those pressuring him to do so won't be around much longer. In fact, they'll be gone "before the child knows how to refuse evil and choose good" (Isaiah 7:16) — in other words, the danger will pass in a few years. The child's name, Immanuel, which means "God is with us," intends to remind Ahaz that God will protect him during these trying times. Many scholars think that the "young woman" involved here is Isaiah's wife, who is elsewhere called a "prophetess" and who later gives birth to sons with important names.

  Isaiah's prediction took on *new* meaning in the New Testament, where it is applied to Jesus' mother, Mary, who, though a virgin, conceives Jesus by the power of God. One reason for the "flexibility" of Isaiah's prophecy is that, when the Book of Isaiah was translated into Greek (the translation used by most of the early Christians), the Hebrew word for "young woman" was rendered with the Greek word *parthenos,* which, though meaning "young woman," can also mean "virgin." Thus, the gospels of Matthew and Luke record that while Mary was still a virgin she conceived Jesus, demonstrating Jesus' divine status.

✓ **Isaiah and Handel's *Messiah* (Isaiah 9):** Nothing says Christmas like the smell of pine, the taste of eggnog, the sight of bills stacking up on the hearth, and the melodic sound of choirs singing Handel's *Messiah:* "For unto us a child is born, unto us a son is given, and the government will be upon his shoulders; and his name shall be called: 'Wonderful, Counselor, Mighty God, Everlasting Father, Prince of Peace.'" In truth, Handel didn't write these words, Isaiah did. With these words Isaiah predicts the birth of a child who will usher in a Golden Age of justice and peace. Isaiah's descriptions of this child, though grandiose, were not uncommon in ancient royal eulogies. Thus, some scholars believe they were composed for the coronation of a Judean king, perhaps King Hezekiah, who ruled during Isaiah's tenure as prophet (see Chapter 10). Yet, most interpreters, both ancient and modern, have understood these words to refer to the Messiah — an understanding that resulted in Handel's applying them to Jesus.

My two sons and their naked father (Isaiah 7–20)

Isaiah fathers two sons who, like Immanuel, receive symbolic names: Shearjashub and Mahershalalhashbaz.

✓ **Shearjashub** is not as bad as it sounds — it means "a remnant shall return," and could be understood to mean that, no matter how bad things get, there will always be a remnant of God's people. However, it could also mean that although a whole army will go into battle, only a remnant will return. That's bad.

✓ **Mahershalalhashbaz** means "the spoil speeds, the prey hastens." Positively, this indicates that Assyria will soon defeat the Syrian-Israelite coalition threatening Ahaz. Negatively, however, it means that the people of Judah will also be victims of Assyria's aggressions. That's really bad.

Later, Isaiah strips and walks around naked for three years. Although this must have been extremely difficult for Shearjashub and Mahershalalhashbaz to explain to their friends, the historical background for Isaiah's unusual behavior is the Assyrians' capture of the Philistine city of Ashdod (711 B.C.E.). The people of Ashdod had hoped that their powerful allies, Egypt and Cush (south of Egypt, now Sudan/Ethiopia), would defend them against this attack. They didn't. Thus, Isaiah removes his clothes to symbolize the "dress" of war captives to warn the people of Egypt and Cush that they, too, will fall to Assyria. In addition, Isaiah cautions Judah not to trust in Egypt as its military deliverer.

A close call for Jerusalem (Isaiah 36–39)

Nobody liked the Assyrians, though this didn't seem to bother the Assyrians much. They were constantly raping, pillaging, and plundering kingdoms both to enrich themselves and to ensure that people were too terrified to revolt. Because Israel did revolt, the Assyrians destroyed the northern kingdom in

A prophet for all seasons: Second and Third Isaiah

Because of differences in vocabulary, theological outlook, and historical perspective, many scholars believe that the Book of Isaiah records the words of more than one prophet. As the theory goes, Isaiah 1–39 records the words of the actual eighth-century prophet from Jerusalem. This material is characterized by stern warnings against Israel and Judah for their wrongdoings, with the threat of exile if they do not mend their ways. In Isaiah 40–66, by contrast, the prophet (whom scholars call "Second" or "Deutero" Isaiah) declares the end of God's wrath and the promise of return from exile. This prophet, according to this theory, lived in exile shortly before Babylon's fall in 539 B.C.E., after which the Jews are allowed to return to their homeland. Some scholars further divide chapters 40–66 into "Third" or "Trito" Isaiah (56–66), which, because of still other changes in vocabulary and outlook, is believed to have been written by a fifth-century Judean after the exiles returned to Jerusalem. Although all of this is theory, the important point is that the mood and message of Isaiah changes to address changing historical circumstances — making Isaiah "a prophet for all seasons."

721 B.C.E., and Judah almost fell 20 years later when the Assyrian king, Sennacherib, destroyed several cities and even besieged Jerusalem.

Fortunately for Judah, their king Hezekiah listens to Isaiah and repents on behalf of the nation. Thus, while Jerusalem is under siege by the Assyrians, the Bible records that an angel kills 185,000 Assyrian soldiers in their sleep, and Sennacherib is forced to return home.

The Suffering Servant (Isaiah 53)

Several passages in the Book of Isaiah describe the activity of an unnamed "Servant" of God. The best known of these is the "Suffering Servant Song" of Isaiah 53, which tells the story of an unattractive man filled with grief, and who is hated and rejected by others. He carries others' pain, but still they inflict pain upon him. God even inflicts pain upon this servant, placing the sins of everyone else upon his shoulders.

Because the Suffering Servant is unnamed, he has been linked to a number of figures from Israel's past, including the prophet Isaiah himself, Jeremiah, and even the nation of Israel. The New Testament writers understood him to be Jesus, who also suffers great physical and emotional pain, remains silent before his accusers, and is "pierced through (crucified) for our sins."

Although Isaiah's death is not recorded in the Bible, tradition maintains that King Hezekiah's son, Manasseh, the most evil of Judah's kings according to the Bible, executes him by sawing Isaiah in half, a tradition that seems reflected in the New Testament's notice of one of God's prophets being "sawn in two" (Hebrews 11:37).

Jeremiah

Jeremiah, also known as the "Weeping Prophet," is arguably the most depressed person in the Bible. You can hardly blame him: He's active from 626 to 580 B.C.E., seeing firsthand the destruction of Jerusalem at the hands of the Babylonians. Moreover, much of these horrors could have been avoided if the people would have listened to his admonitions to repent.

The fetal and frightful prophet's calling (Jeremiah 1)

Jeremiah was born in Anathoth, a small village 4 miles north of Jerusalem. He, like his father Hilkiah, was a priest, and he seems to have traced his heritage back to Moses, Israel's great deliverer and lawgiver (see Chapter 7 for more information about Moses). Thus, it is interesting that, although God says He appointed Jeremiah "from the womb," Jeremiah, like Moses, comes up with several excuses as to why he isn't fit for the job. For example, he reminds God that he is only a youth and, like Moses, he doesn't know how to speak. In response God tells Jeremiah what He told Moses: I will be with you and tell you what to say. Then, to symbolize how He will put words in Jeremiah's mouth, God touches his lips. Reluctantly, Jeremiah accepts his commission as God's prophet.

The yoke's on you, Hananiah (Jeremiah 27–28)

Some of the most memorable passages in Jeremiah relate to his ongoing battle with a false prophet named Hananiah. One of these bouts occurs when several of Judah's neighboring nations send emissaries to Jerusalem to celebrate the coronation of Zedekiah. In order to get their attention, Jeremiah puts on a *yoke,* or oxen harness, to symbolize that soon all of the nations in the area will be servants to Babylon. Jeremiah goes so far as to call the Babylonian king, Nebuchadnezzar, "God's servant." Moreover, Jeremiah warns the nations that if they don't submit to Babylon, God will punish them with the sword, famine, and pestilence.

The people, as you may imagine, don't want to hear this bad news, and Hananiah comes to their rescue. He says that Nebuchadnezzar's days are numbered. Moreover, he removes the yoke from Jeremiah and breaks it, symbolizing that God has broken the yoke of the king of Babylon. However, Jeremiah has the final word in this confrontation. He turns to Hananiah and tells him that, although he broke the wooden bars of the yoke, God will make new ones of iron. Furthermore, Jeremiah predicts that God will kill Hananiah within the year. Shortly thereafter, the false prophet dies.

Sour grapes of wrath (Jeremiah 31)

The famous expression "sour grapes" comes from Jeremiah. However, rather than having the contemporary meaning of pouting, in the Bible this expression has to do with accountability. Jeremiah says that one day soon the people will no longer say, "The fathers have eaten sour grapes, and the children's teeth are set on edge" (Jeremiah 31:29). This proverb was apparently repeated a lot during Jeremiah's day, since it is also quoted by Jeremiah's contemporary — the prophet Ezekiel (Ezekiel 18:2). This proverb expressed what seems to have been most people's view during the difficult times in which Jeremiah's generation lived: their present problems were the result of their ancestors' sins. Jeremiah assures the people that everyone is account-able for their own actions, and that children, though they may suffer from the effects of their parent's sins, will not be judged for them.

Jeremiah's new covenant (Jeremiah 31)

Perhaps the most moving passages in Jeremiah are those describing God's future plans for Israel — plans, as Jeremiah puts it, "to give you hope and a future" (Jeremiah 29:11). Among these plans, God intends to establish a new covenant with Israel where people will obey God's laws because they are written "on their hearts" and God will "forgive their wickedness and will remember their sins no more" (Jeremiah 31:33–34). This prophecy gave the Jews great hope following Jerusalem's destruction by the Babylonians in 586 B.C.E., and early Christians applied it to Jesus, whose death on the cross was believed to usher in a new covenant by providing forgiveness of sins (Luke 22:20).

Don't go to Egypt! Jeremiah's relocation and death (Jeremiah 42–43)

After the destruction of Jerusalem by the Babylonians, the survivors come to Jeremiah and admit that they should have listened to him and repented of their wrongdoing. They also ask him what they should do next. Jeremiah tells them that whatever they do, "don't go to Egypt" (Jeremiah 42:19). Showing that they really hadn't changed, the people respond: "Truly, you are a prophet of lies!" And with this, they grab Jeremiah and take him to Egypt with them.

Although the Bible does not say how Jeremiah died, later traditions say alter-nately that he died of natural causes or that he was stoned to death for his unpopular messages. Whatever the exact circumstances of his death, Jeremiah serves as an example of how hard a job it is to be called as a prophet of God.

The Weeping Prophet: Lamentations

Reading Lamentations, though we highly recommend it, is an extremely diffi-cult enterprise. The difficulty isn't because of length or vocabulary, but because of the content. Lamentations records the sad songs recalling the destruction of Jerusalem by the Babylonians in 586 B.C.E. Because Jeremiah, the "Weeping Prophet," lived through these terrible events, and because he is elsewhere said to have written laments (2 Chronicles 35:25), tradition holds that he authored these dirges. However, they are anonymous, which is perhaps fitting, because they express the sorrow of a nation.

In Christian Bibles, Lamentations is placed after the Book of Jeremiah because of its associations with this prophet. However, in the Hebrew Bible and modern Jewish Bibles, Lamentations (which is also called Eicha or "How" from its opening word) is placed among the Writings.

Lamentations opens with the words: "How lonely sits the city that was full of people." And the book only gets more depressing from there, as it describes how the Babylonian forces breached Jerusalem's walls, killed or enslaved the people, and burned the city. Those who survived the attack now have no food, and in desperation go so far as to eat their own children (Lamentations 2:20 and 4:10). Moreover, things that they formerly valued, such as gold and precious stones, don't matter anymore in the face of the horrors they have endured (Lamentations 4:1). Yet, amidst all this destruction and despair, there is still reason to hope in God:

> *For though He brings affliction, He will show compassion as a demonstration of the abundance of His unfailing love — for He does not willingly bring affliction or grief on anyone.*

> —Lamentations 3:32–33

Ezekiel

Like his contemporary Jeremiah, Ezekiel lived through the destruction of Jerusalem, though he did so from 1,000 miles away, in Babylon. Ezekiel was a prominent citizen of Jerusalem, a Temple priest, who was exiled to Babylon ten years before the demise of Jerusalem in 586 B.C.E. As a result, Ezekiel was the prophet to the exiles.

UFOs and Ezekiel's call (Ezekiel 1–3)

The Book of Ezekiel opens with an incredible vision in which God leaves Jerusalem and His Temple in a swift flying machine that is called a chariot but is more like a chair-throne borne up by some very unusual creatures. They are *cherubim* with lion's (or, in this particular case, possibly human's) bodies and eagle's wings, but unlike typical cherubim that have only a human head, these have four different faces: human, lion, ox, and eagle.

From his fiery chariot God sends Ezekiel to prophesy against Israel. God hands Ezekiel a scroll with the tragic events about to unfold written upon it and commands him to eat it, which he does (Ezekiel 3:3). Ezekiel then gets to ride in God's flying chariot to the exiles in Babylon. This marks the beginning of Ezekiel's career.

Ezekiel's vision underscores two important points. First, even though the people are in exile, God will continue to be with them. Thus, He flies in His chariot from Jerusalem to Babylon. Second, having eaten the scroll written by God, Ezekiel is now speaking for God, and his words are true.

Them bones, them bones, them dry bones (Ezekiel 37)

Ezekiel records a vision in which God leads him to a valley filled with dried bones. God asks the prophet, "Can these bones live?" Ezekiel wisely responds that only God knows the answer. Following God's instructions, Ezekiel prophesies to the bones that they will live, and then he hears an increasingly loud rattle. The dry bones begin to move, eventually coming together and re-creating skeletons. Then the skeletons grow tendons, muscle, and flesh.

You may think that this sounds more like a remake of *The Mummy* than the Bible. Actually, this vision is intended to provide the Israelite exiles with hope. Just as God reassembles the scattered remains of these skeletons and brings them back to life, so He will reassemble and revive Israel by bringing the exiles back to their homeland (make no bones about it).

A vision for the future: The Temple (Ezekiel 40–48)

On the 25th anniversary of Ezekiel's exile (572 B.C.E.), he has an amazing vision. He sees Jerusalem's future Temple, the measurements of which are quite large. Then, the glory of God, which Ezekiel saw depart from the former Temple when it was destroyed in 586 B.C.E., returns from Babylon and enters this new, idealized Temple. Now God will dwell with the people of Israel forever. There will no longer be a need for kings in this restored empire, and God will rule from what Ezekiel calls the "New Jerusalem."

Nothing is certain about Ezekiel's death, though according to legend he lived a long life in exile, died of natural causes, and is buried in a tomb near Babylon.

Meeting the Twelve Minor Prophets

Despite their small size, the text of the twelve Minor Prophets held an important place in Israel's holy writ. At least seven scrolls containing "the Twelve," as they are called, were found among the Dead Sea Scrolls (see Chapter 1). In addition, their wide-ranging prophecies greatly impacted later Judaism and Christianity.

Hosea

Hosea lived in the northern kingdom of Israel during the latter half of the eighth century B.C.E. These were turbulent years for Israel, because several kings were assassinated, and it seemed to be just a matter of days before an expanding Assyrian empire would destroy the nation. And, as if things were not bad enough, God tells his prophet, Hosea, to marry a prostitute. And, to make matters even worse, the prostitute he marries is named Gomer.

The reason God tells Hosea to marry a prostitute is because Israel has been "prostituting" itself by not obeying God's laws and by worshiping other gods ("husbands"). And in keeping with Israel's "adultery," Gomer is unfaithful to Hosea, and through these infidelities she bears three children: Andy, Barney and Floyd (sorry, couldn't resist). Gomer's children are Jezreel, Lo-ruhamah, and Lo-ammi. Just as the marriage is symbolic, so are these names:

- ✔ **Jezreel** refers to a famous valley and city in northern Israel where a bloody coup took place under Jehu (2 Kings 9 — see Chapter 10 in this book). The king of Israel during Hosea's life, Jeroboam II, is a descendant of Jehu, and Hosea predicts that this dynasty will soon come to an end, as will the nation (Hosea 1:4–5).

- ✔ **Lo-ruhamah** means "no mercy," and signifies that God will not have compassion on Israel, but will allow Assyria to punish it for its unfaithfulness to Him and its oppression of the poor (Hosea 1:6–7).

- ✔ **Lo-ammi** means "not my people," and signifies God's rejection of Israel as His people due to their wrongdoing.

Following the birth of their three children, Gomer leaves Hosea. God, however, tells Hosea to go out and rescue Gomer, and to bring her back into his home. This is intended to symbolize God's heart toward Israel. Though the Israelites have been unfaithful, God will one day rescue them and bring them home. And, in reversal of God's earlier rejection, Hosea sees a day when God will cleanse "Jezreel" of its bloodguilt, and once again show mercy to Israel, calling them "My people."

Joel

Because the Book of Joel offers no real clues as to when it was written, dates for this prophet range from the ninth to the fifth century B.C.E. Yet, knowing the date for this prophet is not essential for understanding his message.

Joel writes at length about an upcoming "great and terrible day of the LORD" (Joel 2:31), which will be a day of judgment for the whole earth. Prior to this judgment the sun will turn black, and the moon will turn to blood. Advancing armies, like giant swarms of locust (though some take these to be actual locusts), will destroy everything. But despite this impending doom, there is hope of deliverance if Israel changes its present course and returns to God:

> *Return to the LORD your God, for He is gracious and compassionate, slow to anger and abounding in lovingkindness . . . Who knows? He may relent and have compassion, and leave behind a blessing.*

> —Joel 2:13–14

Yet, even if Israel does return, God promises that there will be a day of judgment for those who don't. On that day, God will gather all the nations of the earth to the "Valley of Jehoshaphat," which means "Valley of the LORD's Judgment." Those who did not turn to God in repentance for their wrongdoing before that day will be judged. But "all who call upon the name of the LORD will be saved" (Joel 2:32).

Amos

Amos seems to be the earliest of the writing prophets, being active during the prosperous and peaceful years of the mid-eighth century B.C.E. In many ways, this made Amos's mission more difficult, because people are less inclined to heed the warnings of prophets when times are good.

Although Amos condemns the behavior of Israel's neighbors, including Syria, Philistia, Phoenicia, Edom, Ammon, and Moab (Amos 1:3–2:5), he is most critical of Israel, which, because of its privileged position as God's chosen, is more accountable than these other nations (Amos 3:1–15). According to Amos, God is a champion of social justice, defending the underprivileged and poor. In contrast, God detests Israel's religious hypocrisy, because the Israelites perform religious acts but fail to perform acts of kindness or justice. As God says,

> *Remove the noise of your songs. I will not listen to the music of your harps. Rather, let justice roll down like a river, and righteousness like an ever-flowing stream.*

> —Amos 5:23–24

Obadiah

Obadiah's prophecies make for the shortest book in the Hebrew Bible — a mere 21 verses. This brevity also makes its author one of the most enigmatic. What is clear is that Obadiah is angry with Judah's neighbor to the south, Edom. The Israelites thought themselves to be related to the Edomites. In fact, according to Genesis 25, the ancestors of Edom (Esau) and Israel (Jacob) were twins. Yet, following Judah's destruction by Babylon in 586 B.C.E., instead of helping its "brother," Edom gloated over Judah's defeat. Worse, the Edomites kicked Judah while it was down — looting and pillaging its cities. For this brotherly betrayal, Obadiah prophesies that Edom will soon meet a similar fate. As God says,

> *Because you were violent toward your brother, Jacob, you will be covered with shame and will be destroyed forever.*

> —Obadiah 10

Jonah

The Book of Jonah recounts the trials and tribulations of a hot-tempered Israelite prophet living in the eighth century B.C.E. At the story's onset, God tells Jonah to go to the Assyrian capital of Nineveh to declare that God will destroy it for its many sins. Yet, instead of traveling east to Nineveh, Jonah hires a boat and goes due west, to "Tarshish," an apparent reference to modern-day Spain. On the way, however, God sends a violent storm that threatens to destroy the ship. Eventually Jonah admits to the sailors that he is to blame for the storm, and that if they want to survive, they must throw him overboard. The sailors, not wanting to harm Jonah, try rowing to shore, but this fails. With no other recourse, the sailors pray to Jonah's God for forgiveness, and then heave-ho.

Jonah, now in the middle of the ocean without a life preserver, begins to drown. In desperation, he cries out to God, who hears his pleas and sends a giant whale named Monstro to save him. Actually, the Hebrew name for this creature is *dag gadol,* which literally means "big fish," and can therefore refer to anything big that lives in the water. (So calling this story "Jonah and the Whale" may be a bit of a misnomer.) Jonah remains in the big fish for three days, after which God tells the sea creature to vomit Jonah onto dry land, which it does, and God repeats His command to go to Nineveh. Wisely, Jonah heeds God's call and heads for Nineveh.

When Jonah enters Nineveh, he wastes little time before declaring God's message: "In 40 days Nineveh will be destroyed." Yet, rather than kill Jonah for his threat, the Assyrians repent. And not just a few of them, but everyone, including the king and even the animals, which the Assyrians dress in *sackcloth* (a coarse material worn to show extreme contrition and repentance). Seeing their repentance, God also "repents," forgiving the Assyrians for their many sins.

Jonah is livid. He did not come all this way just to see the bane of the ancient Near East forgiven. And at this point we realize why Jonah ran from God in the first place: He was not afraid of what the Assyrians might do with him, but what they might do with his message — repent! Jonah wanted to see the Assyrians destroyed. In anger, Jonah says to God, "I knew You were a gracious and merciful God, slow to anger and abounding in lovingkindness and repenting of evil!" (Jonah 4:2). Everywhere else these words appear in the Bible they are used to praise God. Here, Jonah uses them to accuse God.

In a huff, Jonah departs from the city and camps outside its walls, waiting to see if Nineveh or God will repent from their respective repentances. While Jonah is waiting, the weather grows extremely hot. Thankfully, Jonah finds refuge under the shade of a plant that God had made grow the night before. The next morning, however, God sends a worm that eats the plant, and Jonah again becomes extremely hot, both in temperature and temper. No longer wanting to live, Jonah begs God to kill him. In response, God says,

> *You pitied the plant for which you did not labor, nor did you make it grow. It was alive one night and dead the next. Should I not have compassion on the great city of Nineveh, in which there is more than 120,000 people who do not know between their right and their left, and many cattle besides?"*

—Jonah 4:10–11

And with that question, the Book of Jonah ends.

God's point is that Jonah cares more about seeing people get what's coming to them than seeing them turn from their wrong ways and receive forgiveness. Even the pagan sailors, who try to save Jonah's life, show more compassion toward this foreigner than he is willing to show toward other foreigners. God, however, is not like Jonah. He wants to show mercy. The Assyrians, as bad as they are, are still human and, therefore, worth rescuing. Even the animals are important to God. If Jonah can care about a plant that he neither created nor planted, can't God care about His creation by extending mercy rather than judgment?

Micah

Micah, like Isaiah, Hosea, and Amos, prophesied during the eighth century. And like his contemporary Amos, Micah chastises the urban elite for exploiting the poor (Micah 2:1–5). In what is one of the most famous passages in the book, Micah asks if he should perform sacrifices to God. The response he receives gets to the heart of the matter:

> *[God] has shown you, O man, what is good, and what the* LORD *requires of you: To do justice, and to love mercy, and to walk humbly with your God.*

—Micah 6:8

Because of the nation's sins, Micah sees a day when not only Israel will be destroyed but also Judah (Micah 3:12). For his "foresight," Micah becomes very influential later in Israel's history. When certain Judean officials are deciding whether to kill the prophet Jeremiah for predicting the fall of Jerusalem, they decide to spare his life because Micah had made a similar proclamation over a century earlier. Micah was also very influential in Christianity's early development. When the magi ask Herod where the "King of the Jews" was to be born, Herod's advisers find the answer in Micah:

> *And you, O Bethlehem of Ephrathah, though you are small among the rulers of Judah, from you will come one who will rule for Me over Israel.*

—Micah 5:2

And Christians have been singing "O Little Town of Bethlehem" ever since.

Nahum

Nahum means "comfort," which is ironic, because the Book of Nahum is perhaps one of the most violent books in the Hebrew Bible. Written in the late seventh century, Nahum celebrates the demise of the hated Assyrian empire. Just as the Assyrians raped, pillaged, and plundered others, so too will they be the victims of unthinkable violence. And Nahum's words come to pass, when the Medes, Persians, and Babylonians join forces and conquer Nineveh in 612 B.C.E., bringing an end to the Assyrians' "reign of terror." So in what sense is Nahum a book of comfort? Because the message of Assyria's destruction would bring comfort to everyone else in the ancient Near East:

> *When everyone hears the news of your fall, they will clap their hands, for who has not felt your endless cruelty?*

> —Nahum 3:19

Habakkuk

Habakkuk's oracles date to the late seventh century in Judah, a time when the Babylonians' power was growing. Although Jerusalem has yet to be conquered, Habakkuk knows its fall is imminent. Addressing the question of *theodicy* (why good things happen to bad people, and vice versa), Habakkuk asks why a just God is "silent while the wicked man swallows up those more righteous than he?" (Habakkuk 1:13). God remains silent. Yet, Habakkuk is determined to wait out God's silence, and remains in a watchtower until God answers him (Habakkuk 2:1). When God does respond, He tells Habakkuk that He will deal with the wicked in His own way and in His own time, "but the righteous shall live by his faith" (Habakkuk 2:4).

The Hebrew word for faith used in Habakkuk 2:4 is related to the word "Amen," and denotes not only belief in something but a complete reliance on or trust in something or someone.

In the New Testament, the apostle Paul quotes Habakkuk 2:4 twice (Galatians 3:11 and Romans 1:17) in order to demonstrate that even in the Hebrew Bible people were ultimately justified (made right with God) by their faith, and not by performing ritual acts or works of the law.

Zephaniah

Zephaniah was active in Judah during the reign of King Josiah (640–609 B.C.E.), but seemingly just before Josiah had enacted his famous religious reforms (621 B.C.E.; see 2 Kings 22–23 and Chapter 10 in this book). In fact,

Zephaniah may have been a relative of Josiah — the genealogy provided at the beginning of Zephaniah links him to Hezekiah, Josiah's great grandfather and the former king of Judah. (However, some scholars have suggested this is a different Hezekiah.)

According to 2 Kings, Judah was involved in unprecedented idolatry and apostasy before Josiah's reforms (see Chapter 10), which helps to explain why the major theme of Zephaniah is the coming "day of the LORD," when God would judge the world, including Judah, for its wrongdoing. Yet, through the gloomy clouds of judgment, a ray of light appears. Zephaniah predicts that after God's judgment, He will restore the people of Israel, and they will be "praised among all the peoples of the earth" (Zephaniah 3:20).

Haggai

The prophet Haggai lived during the Persian Period shortly after the first group of Judean exiles returned to Jerusalem (around 520 B.C.E.). The main focus of his prophecies is to motivate the Judeans to rebuild God's Temple. To this end, Haggai chastises the people for neglecting the Temple while beautifying their own homes:

> *Is it a time for you to live in your houses with roofs, while The House [the Temple] lies in ruins?. . . Go up to the mountain and bring wood and build The House, so that I will be pleased with it and will appear in My glory.*

> —Haggai 1:4–8

Despite their initial opposition to Haggai's message, the people eventually rebuild the Temple, completing it in the spring of 515 B.C.E. Although the Temple was nowhere near its former glory, this was a major accomplishment.

Zechariah

Zechariah was Haggai's contemporary, and, like him, admonishes the people to rebuild the Temple. Moreover, Zechariah envisions a day when a Davidic king would once again rule over Israel. He even predicts that the then governor, Zerubbabel, would one day be king (*Messiah,* in Hebrew), and that the High Priest, Joshua, would also wear a crown of leadership. All of this pointed to a day of future blessing, when God would fully restore Jerusalem:

> *I have returned to Jerusalem with compassion. My house will be built in it . . . My cities will again overflow with goodness, and the LORD will again comfort Zion and choose Jerusalem.*

> —Zechariah 1:16–17

Several of Zechariah's visions have significance for his contemporaries as well as for future generations. In one vision, Zechariah is a shepherd who is paid 30 pieces of silver for his services (Zechariah 11:12). Although this vision in its original context is intended as a rebuke of Israel for rejecting God as its Shepherd, this passage would later be associated with the price Judas receives for betraying Jesus (Matthew 26:15). In a second vision, Zechariah sees a day when the Messiah would come riding into Jerusalem on a donkey. The New Testament writers portray Jesus as fulfilling this prophecy when, during his Triumphal Entry (see Chapter 19), he rides into Jerusalem on a donkey on what is now celebrated as Palm Sunday.

Malachi

Malachi seems to have lived in Jerusalem during the early fifth century B.C.E. He repeatedly emphasizes that those guilty of sin and unfaithfulness to God will be punished on the upcoming "day of the Lord." As preparation for this day, Malachi predicts that Elijah (see Chapter 10) will return to earth in order to prepare the people for God's coming:

> *Behold, I am sending Elijah the prophet to you before the great and the fearful day of the Lord comes. And he will turn the fathers' heart to their children and the heart of the children to their fathers, lest I come and strike the land with complete destruction.*

> —Malachi 4:5–6

For Christians, John the Baptist fulfilled this prophecy by being the forerunner to Jesus (see Chapter 18), and Jews invite Elijah to Passover meals to hasten the day of the Messiah.

Chapter 14

Israel's Wisdom Literature and Love Poetry: Proverbs, Job, Ecclesiastes, and Song of Songs

- -

In This Chapter

▶ Living a better life with Proverbs

▶ Suffering and keeping the faith with Job

▶ Discovering the meaning of life with Ecclesiastes

▶ Falling in love with the Song of Songs

- -

"*W*isdom literature" is a category that scholars use for Proverbs, Job, and Ecclesiastes, but giving this genre a definition is extremely difficult. In fact, biblical wisdom literature is more unified by what it lacks. Unlike most biblical writings, wisdom literature does not refer to key historical events, such as the patriarchs, the exodus, or the monarchy. Wisdom literature is timeless. It constitutes a search for order or truth amidst life's mysteries. Basically, these writings seek to answer why we're here, how to make the most of our lives, and why things don't always go according to plan.

In this chapter, you take a look at Israel's wisdom literature, as it seeks to make sense of life. After this heady material, and to lighten the mood a little, we end this chapter by looking at a different form of wisdom in the book known as the Song of Songs, a steamy love poem about, well, steamy love.

Words to Live By: The Book of Proverbs

The word *proverb* comes from the Hebrew word *mashal,* meaning "to rule" or "to govern." Thus, proverbs are not just wise sayings, they are rules covering a broad range of topics that govern life — they're rules to live by.

At times Proverbs offers what seems to be contradictory advice. For example, Proverbs 26:4 recommends, "Do not answer a fool by his folly, lest you will be like him yourself." But the next verse goes on to say, "Answer a fool by his folly, lest he may be wise in his own eyes." Both of these statements are true. Therefore, it's necessary to use wisdom when taking the Bible's wisdom to heart. Also, Proverbs offers no guarantees. It describes what typically results from making both wise and foolish decisions.

Traditionally, all the proverbs are attributed to Solomon, but how many he actually wrote is widely debated. Some of the proverbs are specifically recorded with the heading "belonging to Solomon" (Proverbs 1:1, 10:1, 25:1), and Solomon, as testimony to his wisdom, is said to have composed 3,000 proverbs (1 Kings 4:32). Yet, even according to the Bible, Solomon didn't write all of the proverbs. For example, Proverbs 30 is attributed to the otherwise unknown "Agur son of Jakeh of Massa," and Proverbs 31 is ascribed to "Lemuel, king of Massa, which his mother taught him" — both of whom are also unknown. In addition, many proverbs are simply called "the sayings of the wise." In short, the Book of Proverbs is full of wise things said by many wise people, not just Solomon.

Cause, effect, and some sound advice

Most often, the Book of Proverbs places a direct relationship between effort and reward, cause and effect. For example, Proverbs 10:4 says, "A lazy hand creates poverty, but the hand of the diligent creates wealth." And Proverbs 6:6–11 tells the sluggard to quit sleeping so much and look to the diligent ant for a model of how to store up provisions for the future.

Beyond the importance of hard work, Proverbs praises honesty and justice, and condemns exploiting the poor (Proverbs 14:21, 28:8). It extols being kind to all, even animals (Proverbs 12:10), and warns those who would rejoice at the calamity of others, even one's enemies (Proverbs 24:17–18). Proverbs denounces the proud and arrogant (Proverbs 11:2, 21:4, 24), and commends humility and reverence for God. In fact, the famous lines "Pride comes before destruction, and a haughty spirit before a fall" come from Proverbs 16:8.

Examining the true source of wisdom

The central thesis of the Book of Proverbs is that true wisdom comes from fearing God. As Proverbs 9:10 puts it, "The fear of the LORD is the beginning of wisdom, and knowledge of the Holy One brings understanding."

Wise guys: Wisdom literature in the ancient world

Scholars have long noticed many similarities between the Book of Proverbs and other ancient Near Eastern Wisdom writings, most notably from Egypt and Mesopotamia. For example, Proverbs 22:20 asks: "Have I not written to you these 30 sayings of counsel and knowledge?" Scholars agree that this biblical passage refers to the 30 chapters of the Instruction of Amenemope, an ancient Egyptian wisdom text. Additionally, several passages in Proverbs and Ecclesiastes parallel an Aramaic Wisdom tale known as The Words of Ahiqar, an official in the Assyrian court of Sennacherib. For example, one of the most often quoted passages in Proverbs is, "He who spares his rod hates his son, but he who loves him seeks him with correction" (Proverbs 13:24). Similarly, Ahiqar advises, "withhold not the rod from your son, or else you will not be able to save him" (Ahiqar vi.81).

Now, by "fear of the LORD" the writers of Proverbs do not mean you should cower in fright before God (unless, of course, you've done something that should make you cower in fright before God). Rather, the "fear of the LORD" means to have an awe-inspiring reverence for God's own wisdom, justice, and love. That is, for the writers of the proverbs, God is both the *source* and *example* of true wisdom — fearing God ensures that you live circumspectly, with the constant awareness that "the eyes of the LORD are everywhere, keeping watch on both the wicked and the good" (Proverbs 15:3). According to Proverbs 16:2, God even perceives your thoughts and motives. Therefore, those who try to appear righteous are fooling themselves.

Introducing Lady Wisdom

Wisdom is personified in Proverbs 1:20 and 8–9 as a woman. She is named Lady Wisdom, or *Hochma*, which is Hebrew for "wisdom," and was later called Sophia, from the Greek word for wisdom. Lady Wisdom calls out to all those who would partake of the banquet she has prepared of wisdom's delights (truth, knowledge, justice, and so on).

In contrast to Lady Wisdom is Fraulein Folly, who also seeks to entice young men to partake of her banquet, though it is a shoddy substitute for true wisdom (including deceit, ignorance, injustice, and so on), and often nothing more than illicit sex. According to Proverbs 9:18, you don't want to go to Fraulein Folly's house, because its steps "lead down to Sheol (the underworld)." Lady Wisdom's house, however, is a seven-pillared structure (seven being the number of perfection), hewn out of solid rock, and filled with everything that is good and right. Quite the opposite of meeting their death, those who dwell with Lady Wisdom will have "years added to [their] life" (Proverbs 9:11).

Later Christian interpreters connected the description of Lady Wisdom with Jesus, because "she" is said to have accompanied God at Creation (Proverbs 8:22–31), which is said of Jesus in the New Testament (John 1:1 and Colossians 1:16–17). More recently, some have seen in Lady Wisdom a goddess figure, even connecting her with the mysterious "we" of the Creation account in Genesis 1 ("Let us make humankind in our image"). However, most have seen in Lady Wisdom not so much a divine being as a personification of a divine attribute — namely, God's wisdom.

Describing the ideal spouse

Related to Lady Wisdom near the beginning of the book, Proverbs concludes with an epilogue describing and honoring the noble wife. In this poem, where each line begins with a successive letter of the alphabet (known as *alphabetic acrostic;* see Chapter 15), the noble wife is described in ways that epitomize many of the qualities identified with wisdom throughout the book, including diligence, ingenuity, upright behavior, and faith in God. And like Lady Wisdom, she is described as priceless.

> *Who can find a good wife? Her value is far above jewels. The heart of her husband trusts in her, so that he has no lack of gain.*

—Proverbs 31:10–11

Translating Job is no easy job

The poetic sections of the Book of Job contain the most difficult Hebrew in the Bible. Usually when scholars want to know the meaning of a biblical word, they look to see how that word is used in other places in the Bible. Yet, sometimes words only occur once in the Bible (known by the Greek term *hapax legomenon*), making figuring out a word's meaning very difficult. The Book of Job has more "one-time words" than any other biblical book, making Job extremely difficult to translate. Because of its unique vocabulary, modern translations of Job differ widely, and even early translators had a hard time. For example, in the *Septuagint* (the Greek translation of the Bible), Job is 400 lines shorter than the Hebrew text, which has led some to hypothesize that the translators became so frustrated when trying to translate Job's unique vocabulary that they just omitted lines they couldn't understand.

Loving God for Naught? The Book of Job

The Book of Job is one of the most popular books in the Bible for the same reason that tourists flock to Vegas: gambling, suffering, and a chance at a happy ending. But beyond a happy ending, Job (the main character in the Book of Job, go figure) seeks to comprehend why suffering exists, especially for the righteous. This raises the question of *theodicy* (literally, "divine justice"), or why bad things happen to good people. Ultimately, the Book of Job extols the merit of maintaining your faith even through terrible times.

The author of this influential text remains unknown, though many scholars believe that the Book of Job was composed in two stages:

- The older material is the poetry in the middle sections (chapters 3–37).
- The more recent material consists of the prologue (chapters 1 and 2), the divine discourses, and the epilogue (chapters 38–42).

One reason why scholars believe that Job was written in two stages is because the poetry has a vocabulary that is remarkably different from the vocabulary of the prologue, divine discourses, and epilogue. For example, God's most personal name, LORD (or *Yahweh* in Hebrew), occurs only once in the middle sections (Job 12:9), but 31 times in the beginning and end. Yet, it is the story "as it is" that has had such an important impact on people's understanding of why evil exists and what the righteous should do during trying circumstances.

Job seems to be set in the early times of the Bible. Like the patriarchs of the Book of Genesis, Job lives more than 100 years, measures his worth in cattle, and acts as a priest for his family. The story makes no mention of either Israel or Judah. Instead, it takes place in the land of Uz, which, beyond being somewhere over the rainbow, is traditionally located to the southeast of Israel in Edom. Thus, the story creates irony by the fact that this most righteous of men is not an Israelite.

When bad things happen to good people

Job is described as "blameless and upright, one who feared God, and turned away from evil" (Job 1:1). Furthermore, he has all a biblical guy could want: 7 sons, 3 daughters, 7,000 sheep, 3,000 camels, 500 pairs of oxen, 500 donkeys, and many servants. Job is so righteous he even offers sacrifices to atone for the sins of his children. Then, through no fault of his own, things change for the worse.

Satan's bet and Job's very bad day (Job 1)

One day God is holding court in heaven, and is joined by the "sons of God" — a phrase meaning "angels." The last to present himself before God is one called *Ha-Satan,* meaning "the adversary" (see the nearby sidebar "Satan in the Bible"). God asks Ha-Satan, "Have you considered my servant Job, that there is none like him on the earth, a blameless and upright man, who fears God and turns away from evil?" Ha-Satan responds, "Does Job fear God for naught?" Ha-Satan suggests that Job worships God because of all the good stuff God gives him. He then bets God that if he is allowed to take away all of Job's possessions, Job will curse God. God agrees to the bet.

On what would turn out to be a very, very bad day, Job receives increasingly bad news from four successive messengers:

- ✔ He finds out that bandits took his oxen and donkeys and killed the servants watching them.

- ✔ He discovers that his sheep and some other servants were burned in a fire.

- ✔ He receives word that, during an army raid, his camels were stolen and those servants were murdered.

- ✔ He is horrified to learn that all ten of his children are dead after a house collapses on them.

Job is understandably distraught. He tears his robe, shaves his head, and falls to the ground — all as a sign of extreme remorse. Yet, for all his pain and misfortune, Job never curses God. Rather, he acknowledges God in the face of his sorrow: "Naked I came from my mother's womb, and naked I will return; the LORD gave, and the LORD has taken away; blessed be the name of the LORD" (Job 1:21). Consequently, Ha-Satan loses the bet.

Job's second test: Boils (Job 2:1–10)

Ha-Satan does not give up easily after losing his first bet with God. He soon challenges God again, only this time he asks for permission to harm Job personally. Then, he reasons, Job "will curse You." God accepts the challenge, and Job suffers physically, breaking out with sores from head to foot. Things are so bad for Job that he scrapes his skin with broken pottery to open the boils (ouch!) and sits in a pile of ashes.

Job's wife, who can't understand Job's patience while undergoing such misery, encourages Job to curse God and die. Always steadfast, Job responds to her, "Shall we accept good from God's hand, and not evil?" (Job 2:10).

Questioning Job's innocence (Job 2:11–42)

Then Job's friends, Eliphaz, Zophar, and Bildad show up. At first they do what good friends should do during trying times — not seek to give answers, just companionship. But after a week of commiserating, they start trying to solve

Satan in the Bible

Surprisingly, most of what people believe about Satan does not come from the Bible. For instance, the common image of Satan as a forked-tailed horned demon with a goat's body from the waist down derives more from the Greek god Pan than anything biblical. What, then, does the Bible say about Satan?

The Hebrew name Satan (pronounced *sa-tan*) actually means "adversary," and most often in the Hebrew Bible it is prefaced by the direct object, meaning "the adversary" rather than a distinct personal name. Satan's role grows more developed both in scope and magnitude through time, and, thus, in the earlier writings of the Hebrew Bible, Satan is presented not so much as an individual character but as an adversarial position occupied by both humans and angels. For example, the word satan is used for a human potential adversary in the Philistine army (1 Samuel 29:4), and two kings God raises to be Solomon's adversaries (1 Kings 11:14, 23). An angel of the LORD is called satan when he blocks the path of Balaam (Numbers 22:22, 32). Satan becomes more developed as a character in later writings of the Hebrew Bible, though he only appears a few times. He at times tempts humans to do bad things, as he incites King David to conduct a census (1 Chronicles 21:1). Satan also acts as a heavenly prosecuting attorney, bringing charges against sinners before God's heavenly court. For example, in Psalm 109:6 the author asks Satan to bring an enemy to trial. Also in Zechariah 3:1–2, Satan stands at the right hand of an angel to bring charges against the High Priest. Satan has a similar role in the opening chapter of Job, where he appears in the heavenly court with the "sons of God" (or angels) to bring charges against Job.

In the New Testament, Satan plays a much larger role. Here Satan, also frequently called the Devil (from Greek *diabolos,* also meaning "adversary") is a proper name for the one who opposes God. Satan is also identified in the New Testament with the deceitful serpent in Eden, and is given many other names including Belial, the evil one, the ruler of the demons, the enemy, the ruler of this world, and Beelzebul (Beelzebub, meaning "LORD of the flies," is a pun on the name Beelzebul, meaning "Prince Baal"). Many scholars attribute Satan's development from an adversary to the archenemy of God to the influence of the Persian religion Zoroastrianism. This religion is a lot like *Star Wars,* in which two opposing forces, one good and the other evil, struggle for control of the universe. Yet, the New Testament preserves the Hebrew Bible's notion of Satan as far inferior to God and needing to get God's permission before "raising hell" on earth (see, for example, Luke 22:31). Following the biblical period, Medieval theologians reinterpreted passages such as Isaiah 14 and Ezekiel 28, in which Babylonian and Phoenician kings are condemned for pride, as descriptions about Satan. In fact, the name Lucifer comes from a Latin translation of Isaiah 14:12, in which the Babylonian king is linked to a fallen Morning Star, called in Latin *lucern ferre* ("bearer of light").

the problem. Although they are sorry to see their buddy suffering so, they maintain a very strict cause-and-effect theology — Job must have sinned horribly to warrant such horrendous divine punishment. However, Job maintains his innocence throughout. And although he curses the day he was born, and even life itself, he never curses God. After going back and forth for a number of rounds, Job and his friends finally admit they have reached an impasse. They say Job has sinned big-time, and Job says he hasn't.

Finally, Job challenges God to a fair trial, suggesting that God must have made a mistake, because he did nothing wrong. At this, God appears "in a whirlwind" and gives Job his long-awaited answer — only He does so by asking Job a series of questions, beginning with, "Where were you when I laid the foundation of the earth? Tell me if you have understanding" (Job 38:4), and ending His first series of questions with, "Will the one who contends with the Almighty correct Him? Let the one who accuses God answer" (Job 40:2).

After another series of questions, Job realizes that his human brain is no match for God's infinite wisdom, and responds, "Truly I spoke about things I don't understand, things too marvelous for me to comprehend" (Job 42:3). In light of Job's repentance, God restores all that Job had lost, and then some. As the final chapter reports, "The LORD blessed the latter days of Job's life more than the first" (Job 42:12).

What to make of it all

Job is one of the most difficult books in the Bible to understand because it provides no clear-cut moral or answer to Job's problems. In fact, the book truly has more questions than answers. Yet, this is part of the message of Job. Life is complicated, and there will always be unanswered questions, inexplicable suffering, and unthinkable tragedy. The real question, therefore, is not *why* do the righteous suffer, but *how* will the righteous respond in their suffering? If people do right merely to be rewarded by God, then their righteousness is worthless (even Satan realizes this). And, if people abandon their faith because of hardship, then again, their righteousness is worth little. According to the Book of Job, genuine faith weathers even the most difficult of storms. As Job says, "Even if He should kill me, I still will trust in Him" (Job 13:15).

BIBLE TRIVIA

Behemoth and Leviathan (Job 40–41)

While God lists His accomplishments to Job, He discusses the creation of two remarkable animals: Behemoth and Leviathan. In modern vernacular, Behemoth refers to anything huge, and Leviathan to monsters that live in water. Many scholars think that God is referring to two animals fairly common in the biblical world: a hippopotamus and a crocodile. Like the hippo, Behemoth is described as a huge grass-eating animal living amongst the reeds in marshes, and not cowering under turbulent waters. Leviathan, like a crocodile, is a fierce animal with armor-like skin, sharp teeth, and strong jaws. Yet, given the descriptions of their enormous size, some have suggested these animals refer to mythical beasts (Leviathan is elsewhere connected with the deified ocean) or even dinosaurs!

Life Stinks and Then You Die: The Book of Ecclesiastes

Ecclesiastes, although hardly a cheerful book, is one of the most incredible and profound works in the Bible. It is about an erudite author's reflections concerning a remarkable quest for discovering meaning in life. In the end, he finds it, though not where you may expect.

The author of Ecclesiastes is identified as *qoheleth,* a Hebrew word meaning "preacher" or, more literally, "one who assembles." This gave rise to the title Ecclesiastes, which is a Greek word meaning "member of an assembly." Traditionally, the authorship of Ecclesiastes is attributed to Solomon, because the author refers to himself as "the son of David, king in Jerusalem." However, "the son of David" can refer to any king in Jerusalem, and scholars place the language used much later, during the second Temple period (see Chapter 12). Although likely not Solomon, qoheleth adopts the persona of Solomon as someone of unrivaled knowledge, wealth, and experience, who looks back over his entire life experience and claims that traditional paths to happiness are meaningless. (Ascribing wisdom books to Solomon was not uncommon; see Chapter 17 regarding the Wisdom of Solomon.)

One Hebrew word dominates Ecclesiastes: *hevel,* usually translated as "vanity." Thus, the book opens with the author reflecting, "vanity of vanities, all is vanity." Today, vanity connotes self-obsession, the type of person who likes looking in mirrors — the type of vanity in Carly Simon's song that you thought was written about you. However, hevel is more literally "a puff of air" or "a vapor," in other words, everything is illusive, transitory, or fleeting.

Ecclesiastes has many notions similar to the philosophy of *existentialism,* which, simply put, is the belief that all there is to life is our present existence. Thus, for the author of Ecclesiastes, purpose remains largely hidden within the universe or, as he describes it, "under the sun." The same fate of death comes to the righteous and the wicked. This even extends to the relationship between animals and humans:

> *For the humans and the animals have the same fate; as one dies, so dies the other. They all have the same breath, and humans have no advantage over the animals; for all is vanity.*
>
> —Ecclesiastes 3:19

The author unsuccessfully tries to find meaning in life from the traditional venues, including wisdom, gluttony, riches, building, and love. He finds that the pursuit of each of these is hevel. Adding to his discontent are all the injustices he sees in the world. For example, people are oppressed without hope of relief (Ecclesiastes 4:1), the wicked flourish while the righteous perish (Ecclesiastes 7:15), and noble acts are too soon forgotten (Ecclesiastes 9:15).

So, where do you find meaning in life? The author of Ecclesiastes realizes (as did the band The Byrds) that part of life's meaning derives from life's cycles. As the author puts it: "There is a season for everything, and a time for every matter under heaven" (Ecclesiastes 3:1). Moreover, although life can seem meaningless, "God makes everything beautiful in its time" (Ecclesiastes 3:11).

So, how are you to live your life? Although the author of Ecclesiastes gives a number of answers, including working hard (Ecclesiastes 9:10), doing good to others (Ecclesiastes 3:12), and fearing God (Ecclesiastes 8:12), the one answer he repeatedly gives is "Enjoy life!"

That is, the chief aim of life — given the inevitability of death — is to enjoy life before we grow old and no longer find pleasure in life (Ecclesiastes 12:1–7). But this is not "party hard and then you die" stuff, but rather "live life to the fullest while still living right." As the author says,

> *Follow the desires of your heart and your eyes, but know that God will bring you to judgment for all these things.*

> —Ecclesiastes 11:9

Then, for all its uncertainty, Ecclesiastes concludes with this certainty:

> *Here's the end of the matter: Fear God and keep His commandments, for this applies to everyone. For God will bring every deed to judgment, including all that is hidden, whether good or whether evil.*

> —Ecclesiastes 12:13–14

Wise words from Ecclesiastes

Ecclesiastes contains many of the Hebrew Bible's most famous quotations, including:

There is nothing new under the sun (1:9).

He who increases knowledge increases suffering (1:18).

There is nothing better for humans than they should eat and drink, and find enjoyment in their work (2:24).

Whoever loves money never has enough (5:10).

Naked a person comes from the womb, and naked he departs (5:15).

And our favorite . . .

Of the making of many books there is no end, and too much study wearies the body (12:12).

Follow the Bible's advice: Drink beer!

In Ecclesiastes 11:1–2, the author beseeches the reader to "Throw your bread upon the face of the water, because in many days you will acquire it. Give a serving to seven and also to eight, because you do not know what evil will be upon the land." This has traditionally been interpreted as a call for charity or international trade or even to diversify one's portfolio.

However, given that in the ancient Near East people most often threw bread into water to make beer, it is more likely that the author is recommending beer production and drinking with friends. This advice is similar to other passages in Ecclesiastes, where the author tells his audience to eat, drink, and enjoy life (3:12–13, 5:18–19, 9:7–10).

Biblical Pickup Lines: The Song of Songs

The Bible, although an excellent source for morality, also contains some of the world's greatest pickup lines. These lines are contained in an ancient, erotic love poem known as the Song of Songs, a title that means that of all the songs ever written, this one is *the* song.

The Song of Songs opens with the line "The song of songs, which is to Solomon," and as a result, the poem has traditionally been ascribed to King Solomon. This is also because Solomon is mentioned six additional times in the poem (Song of Songs 1:5. 3:7, 3:9, 3:11, 8:11–12). In addition, 1 Kings 4:32 says that Solomon composed 1,005 songs (Barry Manilow, eat your heart out). Thus, the book is alternatively known as The Song of Solomon, and even Canticles, after its Latin title meaning "song." Yet, it is more likely that the title means this is *about* Solomon, because most scholars date the final form of the Song of Songs to the fourth through third centuries B.C.E., at least 500 years after Solomon's reign. Whoever wrote it, the Song of Songs is well worth the read. In this poem, a man praises the beauty of his lover, named Shulammite (either a feminine form of Solomon or indicative of the town she comes from), and she, in turn, praises her lover. And so, on to the pickup lines.

After the title, the Song of Songs wastes no time getting to the heart of the matter: love. Solomon's lover begins,

> *Let him kiss me with the kisses of his mouth,*
>
> *for your love is better than wine . . .*
>
> *Take me with you, let us hurry,*
>
> *Let the king take me into his bedchambers.*

> —Song of Songs 1:2, 1:4

And after they're in the bedchambers, their banter only gets more vivid. For example, he says to her: "Your figure is like a palm tree, and your breasts are like its clusters. I say I will climb the palm tree and lay hold of its branches!" (Song of Songs 7:7-8). (Okay, you get the idea. It's no wonder that this book doesn't make it into children's Bibles.) While one might get away with the "figure like a palm tree" line, other lines probably wouldn't go over so well. For example, today it would not be a good idea to tell that special someone, "Your belly is like a pile of wheat" (Song of Songs 7:2) or "Your nose is like a tower of Lebanon, overlooking Damascus" (Song of Songs 7:4). Some lines comically indicate that dental health has dramatically improved, as the woman is described as being so beautiful, that her missing teeth are rarer than usual, as each tooth has a twin (Song of Songs 4:2, 6:6).

But, with that said, the Song of Songs contains some pretty beautiful passages that still are inspiring. For example, he says to his lover: "You have stolen my heart, my sister, my bride. You have stolen my heart with one glance from your eyes" (Song of Songs 4:9). *Sigh*.

So what is this love poem — in which God is not mentioned — doing in the Bible? Excellent question. Most scholars attribute its inclusion to the tradition that it was authored by Solomon, one of Israel's most revered kings. But, in order to cope with its erotic nature, many Jews and Christians came to understand the poem as allegory. Thus, for Jews this poem described God's love for Israel, and for Christians, it pictured Jesus' love for the church. Nevertheless, most today read the poem not as allegory but rather for what it is: a poem about the love between a man and a woman. That is, far from shying away from sexuality, the Bible embraces it. After all, as someone once said, "If God invented sexuality, He certainly has the right to talk about it."

Chapter 15

Rockin' the Temple: Music in Ancient Israel (Psalms)

*W*ords are often inadequate to express our deepest emotions. That's why there is music. Music allows us to convey feelings on a much more profound level than mere words. By way of example, imagine the lyrics to your favorite love song without the music — fairly empty in comparison (especially the *ooh baby*s). Thus, when ancient Israelites stood before God to express their emotions, they set their prayers to music, and 150 of these beautiful religious hymns are preserved within the Book of Psalms.

In this chapter, you discover Israel's musical heritage and sit in on an ancient jam session, as we rehearse some of Israel's most memorable songs.

I Write the Psalms: Feeling Bible Music

The name Psalms (or Psalter) comes from the Greek translation of the Hebrew Bible known as the Septuagint (see Chapter 1). In the Septuagint, these works are collected under the heading *psalmoi,* which means "songs of praise." The traditional Hebrew title for this book is *tehillim* (meaning "praises"), which is related to the Hebrew word *hallelujah* (meaning "praise the LORD").

The Book of Psalms reveals how ancient Israel prayed, and what the Israelites thought and felt about God through both difficult and good times. Yet, because these psalms express human thoughts and emotions, they still speak to us today.

Considering the creation of the psalms

Tradition holds that King David composed many of the psalms, a tradition that seems to be based on several factors:

- ✔ Aside from slaying Goliath, David is most famous for his ability to sing and play music. This is why David is frequently depicted in art as a king playing a stringed instrument known as a *lyre* (a harp-like instrument about the size of a ukulele).

- ✔ Even after David's death, David is remembered for establishing musical worship at the Temple (2 Chronicles 7:6).

- ✔ Nearly half of the psalms contain the heading "A Psalm of David."

Nevertheless, even psalms attributed to David need not be by King David. The name "David" can refer to his dynasty, and thus these psalms may have been composed by later kings in Jerusalem or even musicians patronized by Davidic kings. Alternatively, they may be songs in the style that David composed, or songs honoring David.

The Bible also ascribes psalms to other individuals, including David's son, Solomon, (Psalms 72, 127), Moses (Psalms 90), the sons of Korah, a priest from Moses' day (Psalms 42, 44–49, 84, 85, 87, 88), and three worship leaders appointed by King David: Asaph (Psalms 50, 73–83), Jeduthun (also known as Ethan; Psalms 39, 62, 77, 89), and Heman (Psalms 88).

Of the 150 psalms, only 34 lack superscriptions, which are called *orphan psalms* (for example, 91 and 93–97).

Dating Psalms is extremely difficult, and scholars continue to debate when individual psalms were composed. Some psalms, including Psalms 29 and 82, appear to be early compositions — perhaps even earlier than King David, who ruled around 1,000 B.C.E. Conversely, Psalm 74, which describes the Babylonian destruction of the Temple, and Psalm 137, in which the author laments Judah's exile in Babylon, were certainly composed after 586 B.C.E., when these events took place. Some Psalms even have historical notices as to when they were written, such as Psalm 51, which is a psalm of repentance ascribed to David, written after his adulterous affair with Bathsheba.

Regardless of the author and date, the psalms are both universal and timeless.

Examining the types

Psalms come in several types:

- ✔ **Liturgical:** Liturgical psalms are sung at particular moments in the religious life of ancient Israel. Such events may include the dedication of the Temple, psalms for holidays, and psalms for the coronation of kings.

✔ **Laments:** In laments, either individuals or the community inform God of their suffering and beg God to forgive and deliver them.

✔ **Thanksgiving:** Psalms of Thanksgiving praise God for good fortune.

✔ **Imprecatory:** A number of psalms are *imprecatory,* meaning they call on God to curse their enemies.

Appreciating the structure

Perhaps to mirror the five books in the Torah (Genesis, Exodus, Leviticus, Numbers, and Deuteronomy — covered in Part II), the 150 chapters of Psalms are traditionally divided into five books as shown in Table 15-1.

Table 15-1		The Five Books of Psalms	
Book	*Chapters*	*Author(s) Attributed To*	*Characteristics*
I	1–41	Almost all to David	Mostly individual laments.
II	42–72	Mostly David, the sons of Korah, and Asaph	Mostly temple liturgies.
III	73–89	Mostly the sons of Korah and Asaph	Mostly group laments and liturgies.
IV	90–106	Almost all untitled	Mostly Temple liturgies.
V	107–150	Mostly David and untitled	Most liturgical of all books. Contains the "great Hallel" (Psalms 113–118) used on pilgrimage holidays.

Each book concludes with a *doxology,* or liturgical formula for praising God. For example, Book I ends with the doxology: "Blessed be the LORD, the God of Israel, from everlasting to everlasting, Amen and Amen" (Psalms 41:13).

Psalm 119: The pinnacle of poetry

Check this out. Psalm 119 consists of 22 stanzas (for each of the 22 letters of the Hebrew alphabet). Each stanza consists of eight lines all beginning with the same Hebrew letter. Additionally, Psalm 119 repeats eight key words, all related to legality: law, statutes, precepts, commands, judgments, decrees, word, and saying. In six of the stanzas, all eight terms are used, and in all of the stanzas, at least six of these terms are used. It is truly the work of a genius.

Psalms records poetry that is sublime, but this does not mean that it rhymes. In fact, biblical poetry rarely rhymes (and mostly by accident), and it oftentimes lacks a discernable meter. So how do you know it's poetry? Largely by its *parallelism* and *alphabetic acrostics:*

- **Parallelism:** Hebrew poetry's most pervasive and distinct feature is parallelism, in which words and themes mirror those immediately before and/or after. For example, Psalm 72:1–2 translates:

  Give the king Your judgments, O God,
  and Your righteousness to the king's son.
  Your people He shall judge in righteousness,
  and Your poor in justice.

  Thus, "the king" is parallel to "the king's son," and "Your people" corresponds to "Your poor." Furthermore, "judgments," and "justice" are both parallel to "righteousness."

- **Alphabetic acrostics:** A number of Psalms contain what scholars call alphabetic acrostics. Within these literary gems, the first word of each line begins with a successive letter of the Hebrew alphabet. For example, the beginnings of an alphabetic acrostic in English would look something like this (and see if you can find the parallelism):

  Assist me, O God, in my work; dear Lord, *aid Your devotee in his toil.*
  Before I found Your truths; prior to uncovering Your laws:
  Comfort was lost on Your servant, Your subject could not rest.
  Death seemed inescapable, mortality appeared to be my fate.

  Acrostic poems in the Bible include Psalms 9–10, 25, 34, 37, 111–112, 145, as well as Psalm 119, the crowning achievement of all ancient Near Eastern poetry. (See the sidebar, "Psalm 119: The pinnacle of poetry," in this chapter.)

Musical Instruments in Ancient Israel

Have you ever attended a religious service that bans musical instruments? Religion in ancient Israel held quite the opposite attitude. The final Psalm in the Bible illustrates the vital role music and musical instruments played in ancient Israelite worship:

Praise Him with the sound of the trumpet. Praise Him with the harp and the lyre. Praise Him with the tambourine and dance. Praise Him with strings and pipes. Praise Him on the cymbals loudly. Praise Him with the cymbals resounding. Let everything that breathes praise the Lord. *Praise the* Lord!

—Psalm 150:3–6

The preceding passage refers to many of the instruments used in ancient Israel to accompany the psalms. From this and other passages, percussion instruments such as drums and tambourines seem to be the most abundant. Of the stringed instruments, the lyre is the most common. Double flutes consisting of parallel twin pipes are also common.

Interestingly, it seems that some instruments tended to be gender specific. Thus, women most often played the tambourines or timbrels (hand drums) and men performed with lyres. By way of example, Miriam and the women play timbrels after crossing the Red Sea (Exodus 15:20–21), while King David plays the lyre.

Unfortunately, these instruments rarely survive in ancient Israel's archaeological record. Only those composed of metal, clay, and bone have been discovered. Though rare, at times statues or paintings depicting figures playing instruments have been found as well (see Figure 15-1).

Figure 15-1:
Female Egyptian musicians playing ancient instruments.

How'd That Tune Go Again?

As important as these songs were to ancient Israel, very little survives about how the melodies went. Although musical accents are preserved above and below the biblical letters, the original meaning of these accents and certain terms having to do with the musical arrangement (such as "For the choir-master" and "in the style of Gath") are largely unknown. Many of these terms are thought to correspond to how the musical accompaniment should sound, and others pertain to once famous melodies. For example, many psalms are said to be set to the tune "Do not destroy" (for example, Psalm 59). No doubt this tune was beautiful, but, unfortunately, it's been destroyed. Other tunes

---

Psalms in their ancient Near Eastern context

Many Psalms in the Bible borrow heavily upon the writings and cultural concepts of their ancient Near Eastern neighbors. For example, many scholars are of the opinion that Psalm 29 was originally composed to glorify the Canaanite storm god Baal, and later transferred to Israel's God. Thus, in verses 3–7, God's voice "thunders" over the "waters" and "strikes with flashes of lightning" (common storm-god language). Additionally, scholars have long noticed the similarities of Psalm 104 to an Egyptian poem, known as the *Great Hymn to the Aten*, praising the sun god. Scholars debate whether Psalm 104 borrowed from the Egyptian hymn or whether both borrowed from a common source, but all agree on some relationship. Thus, in writing psalms, ancient Israel participated in a centuries-old tradition of composing poetry to honor the divine.

---

include "The Doe of the Morning" (Psalm 22), "A Dove on the Distant Oaks" (Psalm 56) and "The Lily of the Covenant" (Psalm 60). The meaning of a recurring musical notation, Selah, is also unknown, with guesses ranging from "pause" (for a musical interlude) to "crescendo" to "one more time!" (okay, that last one isn't really a competing theory).

Israel's Top Tunes: Psalms' Greatest Hits

Many Psalms remain the most famous and cherished writings within the Bible. We discuss several of the most influential in the following sections.

Psalms 9–10

Thought to be a single poem that was later divided, Psalms 9–10 record an individual's lament expressing his desire for deliverance from personal enemies.

> *Why, O LORD, do You stand far away? Why do You hide in times of trouble? In their pride the wicked pursue the poor. Let them be caught in the schemes that they have devised. For the wicked boast of the desire and of their soul, and the covetous curses and scorns the LORD.*

> —Psalm 10:1–3

Psalm 22

Psalm 22 is another lament in which a sufferer begs God to intervene.

> *My God, my God, why have You forsaken me, and why are You far from my deliverance, from the words of my groaning? O my God, I call by day, but You do not answer, and in the night, but I find no rest. Yet You are holy, enthroned on the praises of Israel. Our fathers trusted in You, they trusted and You delivered them.*

> —Psalm 22:1–4

The powerful words in the opening lines of Psalm 22, in Hebrew *eli, eli, lamah 'azavtani?* are quoted by Jesus (though, in Aramaic) immediately prior to his death on the cross, seemingly to emphasize his isolation in suffering.

Psalm 23

Inspirational Psalm 23 is the most famous Psalm in the English language, and masterfully likens our relationship to God as a sheep to a shepherd.

> *The LORD is my shepherd, I shall not want; He makes me lie down in green pastures. He leads me beside still waters; He restores my soul. He leads me in paths of righteousness for His name's sake. Even though I walk through the valley of the shadow of death, I will fear no evil; for You are with me; Your rod and Your staff they comfort me. You prepare a table before me in the presence of my enemies. You anoint my head with oil, my cup overflows. Surely goodness and mercy shall follow me all the days of my life. And I shall dwell in the house of the LORD forever.*

> —Psalm 23:1–6

Psalm 46

This Psalm describes the power of God and later forms the basis for Martin Luther's famous hymn "A Mighty Fortress."

> *The nations roar, the kingdoms totter; He utters His voice, the earth melts. The LORD of hosts is with us; the God of Jacob is a refuge for us.*

> —Psalm 46:6–7

Psalm 51

Tradition holds that David composed this psalm following his sin of adultery with Bathsheba and subsequent murder of Uriah. The author takes full responsibility for his wrongdoing and begs God for forgiveness.

> *Be gracious to me, O God, according to Your love, according to the multitude of Your many mercies. Blot out my transgression. Greatly wash me from my iniquity, and from my sin cleanse me. Because I know my transgressions, and my sin is before me forever. Against You, You alone, I have sinned, and done evil in Your eyes.*
>
> —Psalm 51:1–4

Psalm 137

This remarkable song, in which the author vibrantly recalls the pains of exile, has the added distinction of being the only Psalm ever recorded by Don McLean, Bob Marley, and the disco band Boney M.

> *By the rivers of Babylon, we sat down, also we wept, when we remembered Zion. On the willows there we hung our lyres. For there our captors asked us to sing a song, and our plunderers asked for mirth, saying, 'Sing to us a song of Zion!' How shall we sing the song of the LORD in a foreign land? If I forget you, O Jerusalem, let my right hand forget. Let my tongue cleave to my palate if I don't remember you, if I do not set Jerusalem above my highest joy.*
>
> —Psalm 137:1–6

Psalm 139

Psalm 139 is a powerful personal lament in which the author completely submits to God's omniscience.

> *O LORD, You have searched me and You know me. You know my sitting and my rising. You understand my thought from far away. You search my path and my lying down, and You are acquainted with all of my ways. For even before there is a word on my tongue, O LORD, You know it completely. Behind and in front You have closed me in and Your palm is laid upon me.*
>
> —Psalm 139:1–5

Such are the songs that ancient Israel sang when worshiping God, and that have since "made the whole world sing." We commend them to you.

Part III

Revealing the Bible's Hidden Treasures in the Apocrypha

The 5th Wave   By Rich Tennant

Though many questioned its claim to be divinely inspired, The First Book of Gossip was a popular item at food stands across Jerusalem during the first century B.C.E.

"Not another St. Elvis sighting...?"

In this part . . .

You discover why some Bibles are bigger than others by exploring the contents of the Apocrypha — books that are included in Catholic and Eastern Orthodox Bibles, but not in Jewish or Protestant Bibles. The Apocrypha contains fascinating history and timeless tales of great heroes, including Judah Maccabee, who leads a rebellion against the Greeks, and Judith, who cuts off the head of a potential paramour (most of us would have settled for a kiss). You even meet a dragon and an angel fond of fish.

Chapter 16

Rebels with a Cause: The Books of 1 and 2 Maccabees

. . . .

In This Chapter

▶ Spreading Hellenism with Alexander the Great and his successors

▶ "Hammering" the Seleucids with the Maccabees

. . . .

There's a huge difference between a *cannon* (a weapon that fires large metal balls) and a *canon* (a Greek word meaning "measuring rod," used to describe those books belonging in the Bible). However, both cannons and canons have played an important part in sparking religious conflict.

One source of contention when discussing the books that belong in the Bible is the *Apocrypha,* a Greek word meaning "hidden." You may be asking, "If the Apocrypha is so good at hiding, why all the controversy?" Well, the books making up the Apocrypha only hide from certain people's Bibles and not others. Roman Catholics and Orthodox Christians, for example, include most of these books in their Bibles, while Jews and Protestants don't include any. (For more on the history of the Apocrypha, and why it was ultimately not considered part of Jewish and Protestant Bibles, see Chapter 1.) Today, the canonical status of the Apocrypha remains one of the main differences among these groups.

The books of the Apocrypha were written mostly by anonymous Jewish scribes and sages living in Egypt, Israel, and Babylonia after the Hebrew Bible (or Old Testament) was completed, but before the New Testament was written. Because these books arose "between the testaments," they're sometimes called *Intertestamental Literature.* The Apocryphal books included in Catholic Bibles are called the *Deuterocanonical* (or *secondarily canonical*) books to distinguish them from the contents of the Jewish Hebrew Bible, but to affirm their status as part of the Old Testament.

Yet, whatever your religious heritage, the Apocrypha is well worth reading, and has a little something for everyone, including history, romance, music, philosophy, and prophecy. In this chapter and the next, you take a closer look at the Apocrypha and the historical circumstances from which it arose.

Filling the Gaps: Jewish History between the Testaments (586–4 B.C.E.)

When the curtain closes on the Hebrew Bible, Ezra and Nehemiah are instigating religious reforms in Jerusalem following the Jews' return from Babylonian exile. When the curtain opens on the Aprocrypha, the Jews are under Greek rule. Understanding how this transition took place is essential for understanding the message and meaning of the Apocryphal books.

From exile to return: The Jews come home

The Babylonian Empire, after destroying Jerusalem and deporting the Judean aristocracy to Babylonia in 586 B.C.E. (see Chapter 10), fell to the up-and-coming Persian Empire in 539 B.C.E. In a move of diplomatic genius, the Persian king, Cyrus the Great, wrote what has come to be called *The Edict of Cyrus,* permitting all peoples formerly displaced by the Babylonians to return to their homeland. For this, Cyrus achieved great popularity in the ancient Near East, and is even called the Messiah in the Bible (Isaiah 45:1).

Even though the Jews were free to return to Jerusalem, most Jews remained in Babylon, which became a center of Jewish learning and culture over the next several hundred years. But many Jews did return to Judea, including Ezra and Nehemiah (see Chapter 12). What they found was an unorganized Persian province that needed rebuilding. Under the governor Zerubbabel, the Jerusalem Temple was finally restored. While this went on, Cyrus's descendants expanded their empire to the west, and on one occasion, they set fire to the Greek capital of Athens. As may be expected, the Greeks didn't forget this attack, and when the time was right, they sought their revenge.

The rise and fall of Alexander the Great

Alexander was born the son of the Macedonian King Philip II, and he grew up receiving the best that Greek culture had to offer. Yet, because Greeks don't call Greece "Greece," but rather "Hellas" (not after Hellen, their famous ancestress whose face "launched a thousand ships," but an earlier Greek hero named Hellen), the culture that Alexander learned, embraced, and spread is known as *Hellenism.* And what a culture it was! In fact, Alexander's teacher was Aristotle, who's considered by many to be one of the greatest minds the world has ever known. Aristotle himself studied under Plato, who, in turn, studied under Socrates. Now that's one impressive academic lineage (unless, of course, you take the position of Vencini in *The Princess Bride,* who, in demonstration of his own intellectual prowess, called these three philosophers morons!).

Alexander was a brilliant military tactician and leader. And talk about ambitious — before Alexander reached the age of 33, he'd conquered the known world, taking over and expanding the Persian Empire from Greece to the Indus River Valley in India (see Figure 16-1). Alexander's empire brought Hellenism to the conquered territories, and for the first time, much of the world came to be dominated by one culture.

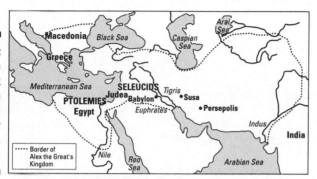

Figure 16-1: Map of the Greek Empire following Alexander the Great's conquests.

Alexander's not-so-great successors: The Ptolemies and Seleucids

Alexander didn't live long, however. Probably due to a combination of factors, such as battle wounds, exhaustion, and a drinking problem akin to Dean Martin's, Alexander met his untimely death in 323 B.C.E. Enigmatically, on his deathbed, he left his kingdom "to the strongest." Because Alexander's son was too young, Alexander's generals divided the empire among themselves. Two of these generals, Ptolemy and Seleucus, and their successors are important for Jewish history and the biblical story.

Ptolemy inherited Egypt, and his dynasty lasted until 31 B.C.E., when Cleopatra VII (the famous Ptolemaic queen) committed suicide. Seleucus inherited Mesopotamia and the surrounding territories, and his dynasty lasted until 65 B.C.E., at which time the Roman general, Pompey, dismantled it. But before the demise of the Ptolemies and the Seleucids, they were antiquity's version of the Hatfields and the McCoys, and, unfortunately for the Jews, Judea was both a battlefield and a pawn between these feuding empires.

The Ptolemies and Seleucids continued the policy of Hellenization begun by Alexander the Great to the extent that it interfered with local cultures, and in particular Jewish culture. This is most apparent during the reign of the Seleucid king, Antiochus IV or "Epiphanes," meaning "the manifest" (manifest as a god — yes, he was modest, too). Antiochus IV completely renovated Jerusalem, turning it into a Hellenistic city. This included building, among other things, a gymnasium, where youths and even priests competed naked. This thoroughly divided the Jews — some (mostly the common people) detested Hellenization while some (mostly the upper class) coveted it, because their participation in Greek culture reaffirmed their positions of power. Some Jewish men, apparently self-conscious at the gymnasium and public baths about being circumcised, even went so far as to be "uncircumcised" by sewing lamb's skin on their genitals. (Joey, in the hit sitcom *Friends,* tries a similar maneuver, though notably with Play-Doh.)

Understanding the Hasmoneans and the Books of Maccabees

The Apocryphal books of 1 and 2 Maccabees are the most informative for understanding the history of the Jews from the completion of the Hebrew Bible to shortly before the advent of Christianity. (We discuss the other books of the Apocrypha in Chapter 17.) Although 1 and 2 Maccabees cover roughly the same period, they do so from different perspectives, giving us a unique glimpse into the events and issues that shaped Judaism during this period.

First Maccabees and "The Hammerer": Not a wrestling superstar

First Maccabees recounts the history of the Jews, beginning briefly with Alexander the Great's death and the origin of the Seleucid Empire in 323 B.C.E., and then recounting the oppressions of the Seleucid king, Antiochus IV, which lead to a Jewish revolt (called the Maccabean Revolution) and the establishment of a Jewish dynasty (called the Hasmoneans). Although 1 Maccabees is written anonymously, most scholars agree that the author was a supporter of (and perhaps employed by) the Hasmoneans.

According to 1 Maccabees, Antiochus desecrated the Jerusalem Temple by offering a sacrifice to the Greek god Zeus on its altar. In addition, he forbade circumcision, outlawed traditional Jewish sacrifices, and disallowed the reading of the Law of Moses. Many Jews followed Antiochus's decrees out of fear, but a few heroically refused. One such refusal sparked a rebellion that eventually led to the independence of the Jews.

As part of Antiochus's religious "reforms," he decreed that people not only in Jerusalem but all over Judea offer pagan sacrifices as a demonstration of their loyalty to him. At Modien, a town about 15 miles northwest of Jerusalem, the honor of proving oneself a "Friend of the King" fell to a certain Mattathias. Mattathias, however, refused:

> *Even if all the nations under the king's power obey him, straying from the religions of their fathers and obey all of his commandments, yet I along with my sons and my brothers will live by our father's covenant. God forbid that we should abandon the law and the ordinances. We will not obey the king's words by straying from our religion either to the right or the left.*
>
> —1 Maccabees 2:19–22

With this said, Mattathias struck down a Hellenized Jew about to offer such a sacrifice, and he then killed the royal official implementing the king's decree. Mattathias, along with his five sons and others desiring religious freedom, fled into the wilderness. The revolt sparked by Mattathias's actions grew rapidly, with people from all over Judea joining his "rebel forces." However, Mattathias, who was already an old man, died shortly after the revolution began, and so the leadership fell to his son, Judah, whose nickname was *Maccabee,* which is Aramaic for "hammerer." And hammer he did.

Because Judah's nickname was Maccabee, the revolt led by him is called the Maccabean Revolt. Yet, because Judah and Mattathias's family name was the Hasmoneans, the revolt is also sometimes called the Hasmonean Revolt.

Judah (or Judas in Greek), as his nickname suggests, was a fierce fighter and a brilliant military strategist, using his knowledge of Judea's landscape to his advantage in defeating the Greeks. After several spectacular military victories, Judah was eventually able to retake Jerusalem (165 or 164 B.C.E.). Judah then commanded that the Temple be cleansed of all its pagan paraphernalia and be ritually purified in order to reinstate the proper sacrifices to God. When the Temple grounds were ready, the Jews celebrated the Temple's rededication on the 25th of Chislev — exactly three years after Antiochus had profaned the Temple. This celebration became known as *Hanukkah* (also spelled Chanuka or Chanukkah), from a Hebrew word meaning, appropriately enough, "dedication." After this celebration, it was determined that Hanukkah, or "The Feast of Dedication," should be celebrated every year, which it is, in the month of December. (For more information on Hanukkah and other Jewish holidays, see Chapter 27.)

Ultimately, Judas Maccabee died in battle. His brother, Jonathan, took over the leadership of the Hasmoneans for a short while, followed by yet another brother, Simon. Simon and two of his sons were murdered in 134 B.C.E., and his sole surviving son, John Hyrcanus, became the leader of the Jews. At this point in the Hasmoneans' history, 1 Maccabees ends.

Second Maccabees: Looking through priest-colored glasses

Second Maccabees isn't a continuation of the story of 1 Maccabees. Rather, 2 Maccabees is an independent work recounting much of the same history as 1 Maccabees.

Second Maccabees purports to be narrated by a High Priest named Jason who is living during the reign of Antiochus IV. Most strikingly (though not surprisingly given the author's priestly perspective), 2 Maccabees puts more emphasis on the actions of those who remained faithful to God's commands during so difficult a time. In one moving passage, a mother watches as her seven sons willingly endure torture and death rather than conform to Antiochus's demands. After the mother encourages her seventh son to do as his six brothers had done, the son turns to Antiochus and boldly says:

> *What are you waiting for? I will not obey the king's command, but I obey the command of the law that was given to our ancestors by Moses. But you who have brought all this evil against the Hebrews will not escape the hands of God. For we suffer because of our sins. And though the living LORD is angry with us for a little while to punish and correct us, yet He will again be reconciled with His servants. But you, unholy wretch, you most wicked of all men, do not be elated in vain or puffed up by uncertain hopes, when you lift your hand against the servants of God. You have not yet escaped the judgment of the almighty God, who sees all things.*

> —2 Maccabees 7:30–35

In addition to the story of the Hasmoneans in 1 and 2 Maccabees, two other books are known by the titles 3 and 4 Maccabees. Third Maccabees is a collection of three stories of Judaism's conflict with Ptolemy Philopator, a king based in Egypt who defeats the Seleucids. These stories bear a striking resemblance to Esther in the Hebrew Bible. Fourth Maccabees is a philosophic discourse on why physical passions are inferior to religious reason, and it is quite unique when compared to anything in the Bible. Of these two, only 3 Maccabees is considered canonical, and only among Eastern churches.

The Hasmonean dynasty, though plagued by internal and external struggles, continued to rule Judea. Yet, a new power was on the rise in the west: Rome. Rome's influence steadily increased until eventually Judea became a client state under Rome's direction. Finally, the Hasmonean rule ended in 37 B.C.E., when Rome appointed Herod the Great to govern what would soon become the Roman province of Judea. Herod married a Hasmonean woman named Mariamme to secure his reign, though the marriage didn't last long. In a fit of jealousy aided by apparent dementia, Herod killed Mariamme along with their children. With their deaths, the Hasmonean family line abruptly ended. Herod ruled Judea until 4 B.C.E., when he finally succumbed to a long battle with disease. It was during Herod's reign that a new "King of the Jews" would be born: Jesus, later called "the Christ" (see Chapter 18).

Chapter 17

The Apocrypha's Other "Hidden Treasures"

. . . .

In This Chapter

▶ Falling in love with Tobit's family and knowing why not to sleep under birds

▶ Losing your head with Judith

▶ Defending Susanna's honor

▶ Exposing Bel and killing dragons

. . . .

The *Apocrypha,* which gets its name from a word meaning "hidden" (due to its absence from Jewish Bibles and, perhaps, its hidden or arcane content), includes some of the Bible's most pious and scandalous literature (we realize there is a fine line between those two categories). Unfortunately, either due to a lack of knowledge or a lack of interest, few people have read these books.

In the previous chapter, you explore 1 and 2 Maccabees. In this chapter you look at the other books of the Apocrypha, where you discover some of the Bible's most intriguing "hidden treasures."

Play It Again Ezra: 1 and 2 Esdras

Although no order of the Apocryphal books is universal, the books most commonly known as 1 and 2 Esdras often appear at the beginning. Both books purport to tell the story and vision of Ezra (*Esdras* is Greek for "Ezra"), the priest who helped reestablish Jerusalem's religious life in the fifth century B.C.E. (see Chapter 12). Most scholars place the composition of 1 Esdras some time in the third century B.C.E., and 2 Esdras in the first century C.E.

BIBLE TRIVIA

1 and 2 Esdras are sometimes called 3 and 4 Esdras, because in the Latin Bible, 1 and 2 Esdras refer to the Hebrew Bible's Books of Ezra and Nehemiah, respectively.

1 Esdras

1 Esdras retells Judah's history from the reforms of King Josiah (around 620 B.C.E.) to the Jews' return from Babylonian exile (around 450 B.C.E.).

As a result, 1 Esdras duplicates much of the history recorded in 1 and 2 Chronicles, Ezra, and Nehemiah, though it spends more time describing the religious life of the returning exiles under the leadership of both Zerubbabel and Ezra (see Chapter 12). The main difference between 1 Esdras and the Hebrew Bible's Book of Ezra involves a story in 1 Esdras 3–5, which recounts a contest between Zerubbabel and two of the Persian king's bodyguards. Should Zerubbabel win, he will be granted permission to return to Judea and rebuild the Jerusalem Temple.

Here's what happens: Three of the Persian king's bodyguards attempt to solve the riddle of what is the strongest thing in the world. The first proposes wine, because under its influence mighty monarchs act just as foolish as inebriated commoners. The second bodyguard says that kings are the most powerful, because whatever they order is carried out. The third contestant, Zerubbabel, says that women are stronger, because they give birth to kings, but that the strongest thing of all is truth. The audience unanimously agrees, and they all shout, "Great is truth, and strongest of all!" (1 Esdras 4:41). Zerubbabel wins, and gets to return to Jerusalem to rebuild the Temple.

2 Esdras

In stark contrast to 1 Esdras, 2 Esdras records an apocalypse in which the angel Uriel informs Ezra of great mysteries in the world. In the context of these revelations, Ezra repeatedly asks how God could have allowed the Babylonians to destroy Judah. Did God allow this to happen because in some way the Babylonians are better than the Judeans? Uriel responds, "Your understanding has completely failed concerning this world, and do you think you can understand the way of the Most High?" (2 Esdras 4:2).

Similar to the Hebrew Bible's Book of Job, the answer to why tragedy occurs is complicated and multifaceted, and only God can understand all the reasons. But, in the end, God will ensure that everything works together for good.

The Tobit and the Lord of the Rings: The Book of Tobit

The Book of Tobit is named after, you guessed it, Tobit, who happens to be a pious Israelite man taken captive by the Assyrians and exiled to Nineveh.

Although the tale of Tobit is set in the eighth century B.C.E., most scholars date its composition to the late third or early second century B.C.E.

Tobit is happily married to a woman named Anna, and they have a wonderful son named Tobias. Everything is perfect, except that Tobit piously buries the dead, in direct violation of the Assyrian king's order. One night, while digging a grave, Tobit falls asleep, and when he awakens he discovers, to his horror, that all night birds have been defecating in his eyes. Besides the mess, this mishap causes Tobit to go blind, and he wants to kill himself.

At the same time of Tobit's despair, far away in the land of Media, a girl named Sarah prays to die because, though she has been married seven times, she is still a virgin. The reason for this state of affairs is that every wedding night an evil demon named Asmodeus slays her husband before their marriage is consummated. (Talk about bad honeymoon luck.) But God hears both Tobit's and Sarah's prayers and sends Raphael, the angel of healing.

Tobit postpones his suicide because he remembers that a man in Media owes him money. He sends his son Tobias to collect on the debt, and on the journey Tobias is accompanied by Raphael, who takes the form of a human named Azarias (meaning, appropriately enough, "the LORD is my help"). During their amazing adventure, Tobias nearly dies when a fish jumps out of the water and tries to swallow him. Ultimately, they kill and eat the fish, but they save the heart, liver, and gall bladder for future medicinal remedies.

Finally Tobias and Raphael arrive in Media, and stay at the house of Sarah's family. Sarah and Tobias fall madly in love and, despite her bad track record with husbands, they marry. On the wedding night, Sarah's father doesn't have too much confidence in Tobias's chances of survival, so he digs a grave for his soon-to-be son-in-law. But Tobias, heeding Raphael's advice, burns the fish heart and liver, and the smoke drives the demon Asmodeus away to Egypt where Raphael imprisons him. Everyone is ecstatic that Tobias survives the wedding night, and the two newlyweds travel back to Nineveh with the debt collected. Upon returning home, they rush to Tobit and rub the fish's gall bladder in his eyes, enabling him to see once again. The story ends with Raphael revealing his true identity, and Tobit, now rich and able to see his son and daughter-in-law's marital bliss, dies a happy man.

The moral of this story? We have no idea, except that no matter how bad it gets — even if you're blinded by bird poop and lose seven husbands (and avoid jail time) — things can work out in the end.

Don't Be Afraid: The Book of Judith

The Book of Judith is one of the most popular in the Apocrypha, and for good reason. It is a fantastic story with the message that you can overcome any obstacle with determination and faith. Although the story's setting is the sixth century B.C.E., it seems to have been composed in the second century B.C.E. to give courage to those persecuted by the evil Antiochus Epiphanes (for more information on Antiochus's religious persecutions, see Chapter 16).

The story begins by retelling how the Babylonian king, Nebuchadnezzar, after conquering Assyria, battled against the Medes without the assistance of his vassal kingdoms in the west. After his victory, he sends his general Holofernes west to punish the vassal kingdoms for not joining his coalition. Holofernes arrives at Bethulia, a city where many of the rebel Judeans live, and besieges the city. The Judeans are desperate, and many want to surrender.

When all hope seems lost, a beautiful, brave, and intelligent widow named Judith delivers a stirring speech and delays the Jews' capitulation. She and her female servant then leave Bethulia and march directly to Holofernes's camp. She flirts with the general for a few days and, winning his confidence, she gets him drunk at a banquet. While he is passed out, she takes his sword from the wall and, with two mighty strokes, severs his head. She returns with Holofernes's head to Bethulia, and the trophy motivates the Judeans to battle. Placing the head on the city's wall, early the next morning they launch a surprise attack and drive the enemy army away in a great victory.

Giving God Credit: Additions to Esther

Six additions placed at various points in the Greek translation of the Book of Esther are, in most Bibles containing the Apocrypha, separated and placed under one heading: Additions to Esther. Though set during the Persian Empire of the fifth century B.C.E., most scholars date these additions to the first century B.C.E. These writings seek to give the biblical story of Esther a more religious component. In the Hebrew Bible's Esther, for example, God is not mentioned, and religious practices, such as prayer, are only alluded to. In Additions to Esther, God's presence abounds, as do prophetic dreams and prayers. For example, in the Hebrew Bible, the Book of Esther ends with praise for Esther's uncle, Mordecai, for his role in saving the Jews from genocide. In Additions to Esther, however, Mordecai attributes their deliverance to God. Mordecai declares,

> The LORD has delivered His people; and the LORD rescued us from all of these evils. And God has done great signs and great wonders that have not been done among the nations.
>
> —Additions to Esther 10:9

Wisdom, What a Woman! The Wisdom of Solomon

The Wisdom of Solomon purports to be a prayer by the wisest person in the Bible: Solomon. Although most scholars date this book to the late first century B.C.E., its ascription to Solomon is understandable, given that much of this book expounds upon King Solomon's prayer for wisdom as recorded in 1 Kings 3:6–9 and 2 Chronicles 1:8–10. In this expanded version of the prayer, the author elaborates on how the just are rewarded, while the wicked are punished. Additionally, Solomon explains the folly of worshipping idols. Most famously, the author personifies wisdom as a beautiful woman, and frequently offers her praise. The author writes of wisdom:

> *The very beginning of [wisdom] is the most sincere desire for instruction, and the care for instruction is love of her, and love of her is the keeping of her laws, and giving heed to her laws is assurance of purity, and purity brings one nearer to God. So the desire for wisdom leads to a kingdom.*

—Wisdom of Solomon 6:17–20

Que Sira Sira: The Wisdom of Ben Sira

The Wisdom of Ben Sira is also known by its Latin title, Ecclesiasticus (meaning "The Church Book," because it was very important in the early church), and as The Wisdom of Jesus the Son of Sirach, after the Greek name of its author (Joshua in Hebrew is Jesus in Greek, but no relation to the Jesus of the New Testament). The Wisdom of Ben Sira was composed just prior to the Maccabean Revolt (in the second century B.C.E.) and was a very influential book in early Judaism and Christianity. It was translated into Greek by Ben Sira's grandson in about 130 B.C.E., though copies of the original Hebrew have been found at Masada and among the Dead Sea Scrolls. Like the Hebrew Bible's Book of Proverbs (see Chapter 14), Ben Sira commends the pursuit of wisdom: "He who devotes his mind to studying the Law of the Most High, and occupies himself with its meditation, will seek out the wisdom of all the ancients" (Ben Sira 39:1). Ben Sira's own wisdom is apparent in his erudite contrasts:

> *O death, how bitter is the reminder of you to a man who lives at peace with his possessions, to a man with no distractions, who has prosperity in all things; yea, to him that is able to eat meat. O death, how welcome is your sentence to the needy, and to those whose strength has failed, very old and distracted over all things, to one who despairs, and has lost his patience.*

—Ben Sira 41:1–2

If It's Not Baruch, Don't Fix It: The Book of Baruch

Although most scholars date the writing of the Book of Baruch to the early second century B.C.E., the book itself is set in the sixth century B.C.E. and is ascribed to Baruch, the son of Neriyahu, who was the prophet Jeremiah's scribe and who accompanied him into exile. The book combines prose and poetry and captures remarkably well the emotional roller coaster brought about following Jerusalem's destruction. The exiles go from suffering to guilt, repentance, devotion, and ultimately hope that one day soon God will intervene and allow the Jews to return to their Promised Land. Moreover, Baruch doesn't separate the Judeans into two categories — those who remained faithful to a particular interpretation of the Law of Moses and those who did not — but rather, all Judeans are asked, as a collective nation, to acknowledge their sin and repent. When this occurs, hope is on the way:

> *Take off the garment of your mourning and affliction, O Jerusalem, and put on the beauty of the glory that comes from God forever.*

> —Baruch 5:1

Cheer Up, Exiles! The Letter of Jeremiah

The Letter of Jeremiah, often appended to the Book of Baruch, claims to be an actual letter from Jeremiah, written in 597 B.C.E. to the Jews about to be taken captive to Babylon, though most scholars place its composition sometime in the fourth or third centuries B.C.E. It is primarily designed to give hope to the Jews being oppressed in exile, and to encourage them not to worship idols. The author writes of the folly of idols:

> *Gods made of wood and overlaid with silver and gold can't save themselves from robbers and thieves. . . . So it is better to be a king who shows his courage, or a household utensil that serves the need of its owner than to be these false gods. Better even the door of a house that protects its contents than these false gods.*

> —Letter of Jeremiah 6:57–59

The Rest of the Story: Additions to Daniel

Several Greek manuscripts of the Bible expand Daniel with three stories. In Catholic and Orthodox Christian Bibles these additions are printed where they appear in the Greek or Septuagint version of the Bible (see Chapter 1).

Within the Apocrypha they are printed separately and each given a distinct title. The following sections provide a run down of these additions.

Faith under fire: The Prayer of Azariah and the Song of the Three Young Men

The first addition is known as The Prayer of Azariah and the Song of the Three Young Men (or Jews). This poem was inserted immediately after Daniel 3:23, and records the prayer of the three Jewish men, Shadrach, Meshach, and Abednego (here called by his Hebrew name, Azariah), thrown in the furnace for not worshipping Nebuchadnezzar's golden statue.

The second and third additions to Daniel are known as The Story of Susanna and The Story of Bel and the Dragon. Although all three additions are set in sixth-century Babylon, most scholars date their composition to the late third or early second centuries B.C.E.

O Susanna, don't you cry for me: The story of Susanna

This single chapter of exploitation, lust, wrongful accusations, and courtroom drama is one of the greatest short stories ever composed. The heroine is Susanna, a beautiful and happily married Jewish woman living in Babylonian exile. Two Jewish elders are infatuated with her, and they concoct a scheme to force her to submit to their perverted wills. While she is bathing, they threaten to bring false charges of adultery against her unless she lies with them both. Preferring civil shame and even the death penalty over sinning before God, Susanna refuses their request even though the two men's false testimonies convict her to death at her trial. Susanna is not allowed to speak at the trial and simply puts her fate in God's hands.

Right before she is executed, God sends Daniel to save the day. In a cross examination that would put Perry Mason to shame, Daniel separates the two self-appointed witnesses and asks them under which tree Susanna embraced her fellow adulterer. They give conflicting testimonies, and the two elders are executed while Susanna is cleared of all charges. Talk about happy endings!

Bel and the Dragon

The third addition to Daniel is known as Bel and the Dragon, and it contains two fascinating tales that ridicule idolatry. In the first story, shortly after Cyrus the Great conquers Babylon, the king grows impressed with a statue of the god Bel, the chief god of Babylon. And who wouldn't be? The idol drinks from the Babylonian temple's table 50 gallons of wine per day to wash down 12 bushels of flour and 40 sheep. However, rather than worshiping this idol with an appetite, Daniel engages in some good old Scooby-Doo-style detective work and proves the priests are lying. He puts ashes all over the temple floor. The next day, when the wine and food are gone, Daniel points out to the king the many human footprints around the table. They discover a hidden door that the priests and their families used to enter the temple nightly and consume the wine and food. Cyrus, upset at being duped, has the priests and their families put to death. They would have gotten away with it, too, if it hadn't been for that nosy Daniel and his meddling friends!

The second tale also involves Cyrus failing to understand why Daniel is not so impressed with another Babylonian god. This time, however, it is not a statue but a "living god" in the form of a dragon. Daniel gets permission to slay the god, which he does through its stomach — not with a sword, but with food. He feeds the dragon a mixture of pitch, fat, and hair, causing the dragon's stomach to burst. But the Babylonians aren't too happy to see their god dead, and they force the king to hand over Daniel and then throw him in the lion's den. Of course, Daniel has experience in dealing with lions — plus, the Hebrew Bible's prophet Habakkuk happens to be there to help Daniel. As in the Book of Daniel, the king shows up to mourn his friend Daniel's passing. Upon seeing Daniel miraculously alive, the king pulls him out and feeds Daniel's enemies to the starving lions.

Okay, I Was Wrong: The Prayer of Manasseh

The Hebrew Bible has some pretty wicked rulers, but perhaps none is as awful as Manasseh, the king of Judah in the seventh century B.C.E., who sacrifices children to pagan gods. The Book of 2 Kings records that because Manasseh is so evil, God condemns the kingdom of Judah to destruction (2 Kings 24:3–4). Yet, 2 Chronicles provides the rest of the story, explaining that after Manasseh is taken captive to Babylon, he repents, and God puts him back on the throne of Jerusalem where he is from then on a pious leader. The Prayer of Manasseh purports to be the actual lament of the repentant king while in exile, though most date the text as it exists to the late second century B.C.E. It is beautiful and emotional poetry, in which a transgressor pleads for a second chance:

> *For I have sinned more than the number of sand in the sea. . . . And now I bend the knee of my heart, beseeching You for Your goodness.*

> —Manasseh 1:9–11

Part IV

Discovering What's New About the New Testament

The 5th Wave   By Rich Tennant

It's the carpenter's son! They say he's turning water into wine and causing the blind to see!

Oh great! I'm sure everyone's gonna be really thrilled to see my disappearing date pit trick.

THE AMAZING OMAR

In this part . . .

You experience the entire New Testament, from the birth of Jesus in the "little town of Bethlehem" to his crucifixion and resurrection in the "big city of Jerusalem." You watch as a bunch of uneducated fishermen and friends from the "backwaters" of the Roman Empire begin a movement that eventually takes over that empire. (Changing the world takes patience — the perfect job for a fisherman.) You witness Paul's transformation from Christianity's chief persecutor to its chief promoter. You get to read other people's mail (really, they want you to) with Christianity's early churches. And you peer into the "end of days" with the fantastical book of Revelation.

Chapter 18

From Birth to Baptism: Jesus Prepares for the Ministry (Matthew, Mark, Luke, and John)

*T*he narratives surrounding Jesus' birth have inspired countless works of art and music over the centuries, including those familiar carols that echo in churches and shopping malls during Christmas time. From "Angels We Have Heard on High" to "We Three Kings," Jesus' birth has come to embody the simple, yet profound, message of Christmas, which is: Shop until you drop. (No, wait, that's a later message.) The message of Christmas is: God's Son came to earth as a little baby to save humankind.

Less well known, although no less important, are the events of Jesus' life between his birth and the beginning of his ministry around the age of 30.

In this chapter you relive Jesus' early years — from his birth in the little town of Bethlehem to his baptism as an adult — in order to understand why he had such an impact on his world . . . and ultimately on ours.

Examining Our Sources for Jesus' Life

Although writings outside the Bible talk about Jesus (see the sidebar, "Other sources for Jesus' life," in this chapter), scholars have long considered the four New Testament gospels of Matthew, Mark, Luke, and John to be our most important sources for understanding Jesus' life and teachings.

The word *gospel* comes from the Anglo-Saxon *god-spell,* meaning "good tidings" or "good news," which, in turn, comes from the Greek word *euangelion,* also meaning "good news." (It is from *euangelion* that we get words like *evangelist* and *evangelical* to denote those who believe in and proclaim the gospel or "good news.") So what's the good news? According to the New Testament writers, Jesus' life and teachings are the good news.

Meeting the gospel writers

The New Testament gospels are ascribed to early leaders within Christianity. Matthew and John, for example, belonged to the inner circle of Jesus' closest

---

Other sources for Jesus' life and teachings

Several authors from the first and early second centuries C.E. mention Jesus, providing important confirmation for the general outline of Jesus' life. The Roman historian, Tacitus (around 120 C.E.), for example, refers to Jesus' being crucified under Pontius Pilate, and testifies to the existence of Jesus' followers in many parts of the Roman Empire. In addition, the Jewish historian, Josephus (around 85 C.E.), mentions Jesus' profound teaching and ability to perform miracles, and even reports the tradition that Jesus appeared to his disciples after his death.

In addition to these Roman and Jewish historical sources, other gospels of Jesus' life also exist. There is, for example, *The Gospel of Thomas* (reputedly written by Jesus' disciple by that name; see Chapter 19), which contains supposed sayings of Jesus, many of which are not found in the four New Testament gospels. The early Christian community ultimately rejected *The Gospel of Thomas* as a forgery because it was (rightly) thought to have been written long after Thomas's life, and because it promotes a belief system known as Gnosticism (see Chapter 22). Another gospel attributed to

Thomas, although written several centuries later, is called *The Infancy Gospel of Thomas*, which relays additional stories about Jesus' youth. In these stories, Jesus comes across as a wonderworking Dennis the Menace, even striking dead a neighborhood boy for annoying him. (Don't worry, Jesus brings the boy back to life when his father complains.)

Even before the discovery of these other gospels, scholars had long hypothesized that the New Testament gospel writers used a common source to reconstruct Jesus' life. This document scholars call *Q* from the German word *Quelle,* meaning "source." According to the most prevalent theory involving Q, Matthew and Luke used Mark and Q to construct their gospels. Although Q is a hypothetical document, the existence of works like *The Gospel of Thomas* make its existence a theoretical possibility, and sometimes it is the best explanation for the exact grammatical and structural parallels among the Synoptic Gospels (Matthew, Mark, and Luke). Of course, the Christian community has long acknowledged that the gospel writers had a common source for the life of Jesus: the life of Jesus.

followers, also called the twelve disciples (see Chapter 19). Mark and Luke, although not among "The Twelve" (as the disciples are sometimes called), were traveling companions of the apostle Paul, who was arguably the most influential Christian of the first century C.E. (see Chapter 21). In addition, tradition holds that Mark knew Jesus personally, even being present when Jesus was arrested just prior to his crucifixion (see Chapter 19).

Yet, the names attached to the gospels were not part of the original works, but were added later by the early church based on traditions about who wrote them, as well as from evidence deduced from the gospels themselves. That is, the gospels were originally written as anonymous documents — a common practice in the ancient world. One reason for writing anonymously, which likely applies to the New Testament gospels, was to focus attention on the subject of the work, and not the author.

Understanding the similarities and differences among the gospels

Matthew, Mark, and Luke share a number of similarities, even using the exact same words at times to relate a story or teaching of Jesus. As a result, these three works are called the *Synoptic Gospels,* from a Greek word meaning "to view together." The Gospel of John is unique, using very distinct language and theological concepts when describing Jesus' words and deeds. Yet, even the Synoptic Gospels, for all their similarities, have different perspectives on the life of Jesus. Knowing the different perspectives of the four gospel writers helps you to interpret their works and better understand Jesus' life.

- ✔ **Matthew** depicts Jesus as "the Fulfillment of the Law and the Prophets." That is, Matthew seeks to demonstrate that, far from being a break from the Jewish faith, Jesus' life and teachings were consistent with, and even brought completion to, the Hebrew Bible's message. Therefore, look for Matthew to include more prophecies than the other gospels, as well as to present Jesus as a kind of new Moses and perfect Israel.

- ✔ **Mark** portrays Jesus as "the Suffering Son of God." In particular, Mark attempts to show that, although Jesus should have been received with honor as God's Son, he was destined to die a humiliating death to pay for humankind's wrongdoing. Therefore, look for Mark to emphasize that Jesus was often misunderstood, and that Jesus wanted to keep his identity as God's Son a secret to those who didn't believe in him.

- ✔ **Luke** presents Jesus as "the Savior of the World." That is, according to Luke, Jesus' life and teachings were for everyone — Jew or non-Jew, rich or poor, male or female. Therefore, look for Luke to include more stories about Jesus interacting with outsiders, the poor, and women.

> ✓ **John** portrays Jesus as "the Eternal One from Heaven." In other words, John underscores Jesus' eternal existence and divine nature. Therefore, look for John to be more theological and philosophical than the others.

The gospel writers' different approaches to the life of Jesus often result in them including differing details, even when describing the same events or teachings. In this chapter (and the next), we highlight some of the more important differences among the gospels so you can better appreciate their varying approaches. However, in order to give you a coherent and full-bodied portrait of Jesus' life, we also weave these accounts together into one story.

In the Beginning: Contemplating Jesus' Very Early Life (John 1)

According to the Gospel of John, Jesus' story properly begins "In the beginning," before God created anything. In fact, the opening words from John's gospel come directly from the opening words of the first book of the Bible, Genesis. But rather than follow these words with a description of Creation (as Genesis does), John lingers for a moment in order to explain that Jesus was not only with God in the beginning, Jesus was (and is) God (John 1:1).

John's opening description of Jesus highlights two related themes of his gospel: Jesus' eternal existence and his divine nature. Yet, John's words also raise an important theological question: How can God and Jesus both be God? This question is further complicated (or clarified, depending on your perspective) by passages that similarly equate God's Spirit with God (see, for example, 2 Corinthians 3:17).

Although a debated issue during Christianity's early history, the prevailing view became that God exists in three persons: Father, Son, and Holy Spirit. According to this doctrine, which is called the *Trinity*, these are not three gods, but one God revealing Himself in three persons. Sound confusing? Don't worry, you're not alone. Even those who first formulated the doctrine of the Trinity called it a "mystery." But they also believed this doctrine was the best explanation of the evidence of the New Testament. The doctrine of the Trinity is important not only because it is the official stance of orthodox Christianity, but because it has tremendous implications for how you understand Jesus' life. According to this doctrine, God Himself came to earth in order to teach humankind about His truth and to show them His love. For this kindness, God was condemned as a heretic and rebel, and then crucified. Yet, as a further demonstration of His love, God forgave those who mocked and killed him. What's more, his death paid for the sins of the world.

Whether one believes in the Trinity or not, that's quite a story.

Reliving the Christmas Story

Rather than just appear on earth one day, or "beam down" (to use Trek-talk), Jesus is said to have entered this world in the most orthodox of ways: childbirth. Jesus' appearance on earth is known as the *Incarnation*, or what the Gospel of John calls Jesus' "becoming flesh." Interestingly, though, John doesn't describe the events surrounding Jesus' Incarnation. For this story, you need to turn to the gospels of Matthew and Luke, whose combined accounts give us what is now known as "The Christmas Story."

Receiving Jesus' birth announcement (Matthew 1 and Luke 1:26–38)

According to the gospels, Jesus' mother is a young woman named Mary. Although being of humble means, Mary and her fiancé, Joseph, are of noble birth, as they are descendants of the great Israelite king, David (see Chapter 9). This connection to David is important for the New Testament writers, because many Jews during Jesus' time were expecting a Davidic Messiah or king who would deliver them from their enemies (the Romans, during Jesus' day).

Messiah comes from a Hebrew word which means "anointed one." In Greek, this word is *Christos* — hence, the name Jesus Christ.

But there is something else about Mary that is exceptional — something that she's not even aware of at first. She is to become pregnant with Jesus while she is still a virgin. Mary finds out about her unusual pregnancy when she is visited by the angel Gabriel, who declares:

> *The Holy Spirit will come upon you, and the power of the Most High will overshadow you. Therefore, the Holy One who is conceived in you will be called the Son of God.*

> —Luke 1:35

Gabriel's declaration to Mary is known as the *Annunciation,* which is a fancy word meaning "the birth announcement" (only it is *the* birth announcement). Today you can visit The Church of the Annunciation in Nazareth, where this event is traditionally thought to have taken place.

Gabriel's announcement to Mary is recorded only in Luke's gospel. According to Matthew, an unnamed angel also appears to Joseph, who is contemplating breaking off his engagement with Mary after finding out she is pregnant. The angel informs Joseph that Mary's pregnancy has been divinely orchestrated, and that he is not only to marry Mary, he is to name their son Jesus, which means "the LORD saves" — a fitting name, since, as the angel tells Joseph, "[Jesus] will save his people from their sins" (Matthew 1:21).

Revisiting the manger scene: Jesus' birth (Luke 2:1–20)

As Mary approaches her due date, a most "unfortunate" thing happens. According to Luke, the Roman Emperor, Caesar Augustus, decrees that a census should be taken of everyone in his empire. In order to accomplish this, people have to go to their ancestral hometown in order to register their names.

O little town of Bethlehem

Because Joseph and Mary trace their lineage to King David, Augustus' decree requires that they make the approximately 80-mile trek from their home in Nazareth to David's hometown of Bethlehem (see Figure 18-1). Yet, this inconvenience is important, because it further connects Jesus' life with the expectations of a coming Davidic Messiah. As the angel Gabriel says to Mary:

> *The Lord God will give [Jesus] the throne of his ancestor David, and he will reign over the house of Jacob forever. And his kingdom will never end.*

> —Luke 1:32–33

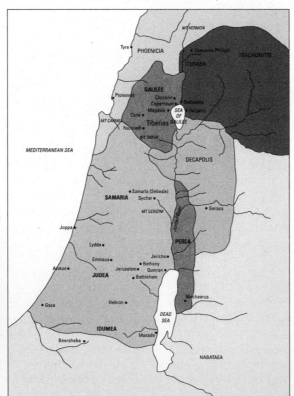

Figure 18-1: Map of Israel during Jesus' life showing the Roman divisions used for administrative purposes.

Away in a manger

Upon arriving in Bethlehem, Mary and Joseph cannot find lodging at the inn. Therefore, they are compelled to stay in an animal stable. Here Mary gives birth to Jesus, and places him in a *manger* (a feeding trough). At least this is how the story has traditionally been understood — but this may be wrong.

The Greek word *kataluma,* translated "inn," elsewhere means the guest room of a house. Therefore, many scholars believe that the overcrowded conditions are in a guest room of the home of one of Joseph's or Mary's relatives. Because Mary wants some privacy while giving birth to Jesus, she goes to the bottom floor of the home (many homes were multi-leveled in first-century Judea), where animals also lived (yes, animals lived *in* their owners' homes — so let the dog in for heaven's sake!). Therefore, imagining Joseph running frantically from hotel to hotel in search of a room, while Mary is out in the wood-paneled station wagon (read: brown donkey) shouting, "Hurry, Joseph, hurry! I think it's time! I think it's time!" is probably a mistake.

Today The Church of the Nativity in Bethlehem commemorates the place of Jesus' birth.

Angels we have heard on high

In keeping with Luke's emphasis on Jesus as the Savior of the *whole* world, including the poor and seemingly unimportant, he recounts that, upon Jesus' birth, an angel appears to some lowly shepherds in a nearby field, and says,

> *Behold! I bring you good news of great joy that will be for all people. For today in the city of David is born to you a Savior who is Christ the Lord.*
>
> —Luke 2:10–11

In this brief announcement, the angel says a lot. Not only does he mention the "good news" or gospel that will be for "all people," he also refers to the messianic expectation surrounding a descendant of David. The angel then tells the shepherds that they will find this Messiah "wrapped in swaddling clothes and lying in a manger." Suddenly, numerous angels appear in the sky, and begin declaring (*not* "sweetly singing") praise to God.

Today, outside of Bethlehem, is a low-lying valley called The Shepherds' Field, which marks the traditional location of this event.

The adoration of the shepherds

Quickly, the shepherds make their way to Bethlehem, where they find the infant child and worship him. Mary, who is amazed at hearing the report of the angel's announcement, "treasured all these things, pondering them in her heart." The shepherds then go back to their flocks, but not without telling everyone they encounter about the amazing things they had seen and heard.

Calculating the date of Jesus' birth

We do not know the exact date or year of Jesus' birth. The determination of B.C. ("before Christ") and A.D. (*anno Domini* or "year of our Lord") was calculated in the sixth century, and the scholar who did it, Dionysius Exiguus, missed by a few years (though he came remarkably close).

Most scholars place Jesus' birth around 6 or 5 B.C., because both Matthew and Luke say that Herod the Great, the Roman appointed ruler, was alive when Jesus was born (Herod died in 4 B.C.). (For the choice of December 25 as Jesus' birthday, see Chapter 27.)

Jesus' circumcision and dedication (Luke 2:21–40)

Eight days after his birth, Jesus is circumcised (ouch). This fulfills God's command as expressed to Abraham (Genesis 17) and Moses (Exodus 12) in the Hebrew Bible. Jesus is also given his name at this time, a tradition that similarly derives from Abraham, who circumcised and named his son, Isaac, at 8 days old (Genesis 21).

Even today, many Jewish parents circumcise and name their children on the eighth day, in a ceremony called a *bris,* from a word meaning "covenant." All of this underscores that Jesus is Jewish — a fact that is too often forgotten or overlooked in present-day discussions of Jewish-Christian relations.

Further underscoring Jesus' "Jewishness" is that, at 40 days old, he is brought to the Temple to be dedicated to God. This rite finds its origins in the Hebrew Bible, where, according to the Law of Moses (see Chapter 7), all firstborn sons are to be dedicated to God by sacrificing a lamb and a turtledove or pigeon. If you could not afford a lamb, you could sacrifice an additional bird.

That Luke only mentions the birds when quoting the Mosaic Law concerning offerings for newborns suggests that Jesus' parents don't have the means to offer a lamb. Luke's emphasis on Jesus' humble beginnings highlights his theme that Jesus' life and teachings are for everyone, including the poor.

Following these events, the gospel of Luke says that Mary, Joseph, and Jesus returned to Nazareth, where Jesus grew up.

"Now wait just a minute here!" you may be saying. "You skipped the part about the three wise men who worshiped Jesus alongside the shepherds and presented him with gifts of gold, frankincense, and myrrh! How could you forget something like that?" Actually, we didn't. We explain their absence (actually tardiness) from Jesus' birth story in the following section.

Adoration of the magi (Matthew 2:1–12)

No manger scene would be complete without the presence of the wise men (or magi, as they are sometimes called) bearing gifts of gold, frankincense (or incense), and myrrh for the newborn Jesus. There's only one problem: The wise men most likely weren't there.

The mysterious absence of the magi at Jesus' birth

As we've already noted, Luke wants to show that Jesus is the Savior of everyone, whether Jew or gentile, male or female, rich or poor. Therefore, Luke tells us about the lowly shepherds who come and worship Jesus, but says nothing about the wise men.

Matthew, though not disagreeing with Luke's emphasis, wants to present Jesus as the fulfillment of Old Testament prophecies concerning the Messiah. Because the Messiah was to be a descendant of David, the great king of Israel, Matthew emphasizes Jesus' royal origins by recounting the story of the wise men, who are *royal* astrologers who have followed a star that heralds the birth of a *king* in order to present him with *royal* gifts. It's hard to miss the point.

Yet, Matthew does not seem to present these wise men as arriving at Jesus' birth, but perhaps as much as two years later (see the section "Out of Egypt," later in this chapter). That is, even if we combine the accounts of Matthew and Luke, it probably would be inaccurate to place the shepherds and magi side by side. (So the next time you're at a friend's house at Christmastime, we recommend that you tactfully remove the wise men from the manger scene.)

While on the subject of the manger scene, and though it pains us to say this, the little drummer boy is absent from the gospel accounts of Jesus' birth.

The magi eventually make their way to Jerusalem to ask King Herod, the Roman appointed ruler of the Jews (see the sidebar "Meeting Herod the Great" in this chapter), where the king of the Jews has been born. Herod, as you might imagine, is not too happy to hear about this rival claimant to the throne, even if that rival may still be in diapers. When Herod's officials inform him that the Messiah is suppose to be born in Bethlehem, Herod passes this information on to the wise men, and he asks them to return with news of the child's exact whereabouts so he can also worship (read: kill) him.

The Slaughter of the Innocents

The wise men continue on their way to Bethlehem, where they find Jesus. However, after they present their gifts to Jesus, they are warned in a dream not to return to Herod because he only intends to kill this newborn king. When Herod finds out that the wise men have left his territory without reporting back to him, he becomes furious and dispatches his soldiers to kill all male children in the vicinity of Bethlehem who are 2 years old and younger — a choice informed by the time told him by the wise men, which suggests that Jesus is approaching 2 years old when the wise men appear. Although Jesus escapes Herod's henchman unharmed (Joseph had been warned in a dream to flee to Egypt) many youngsters do not. Herod's murderous act is often referred to as "The Slaughter of the Innocents."

Out of Egypt (Matthew 2:13–23)

Matthew reports that Jesus and his parents remain in Egypt until Herod's death in 4 B.C.E., after which they set out for their home. Yet, while on their way, Joseph receives word that Herod's son, Archelaus, is now ruler in Judea. Fearing that Archelaus may be seeking Jesus' life, Joseph decides to take his family to Nazareth (refer to Figure 18-1). According to Matthew, Jesus' journey

Meeting Herod the Great

Herod the Great (so named due to his long and illustrious reign) and his descendants play an important role throughout the New Testament, so it's important that we introduce you to him.

Herod was appointed King of the Jews by the Romans, who during this period ruled over what was once ancient Israel. Although a convert to Judaism, Herod was an Idumean (descendants of the Edomites, who had been longtime enemies of Israel). Therefore, many Jews did not consider Herod to be a legitimate King of the Jews. Despite not having the right pedigree, Herod was a fairly capable ruler. He was so capable, in fact, that he remained King of the Jews from 37 B.C.E. until his death in 4 B.C.E., and afterward his descendants ruled over parts of Judea until 70 C.E., when the Romans destroyed Jerusalem in response to the Jewish Revolt (66–72 C.E.). Yet, perhaps Herod's greatest achievement was his complete renovation of the Jerusalem Temple, which he transformed into one of the most beautiful structures in the ancient world.

Despite Herod's many accomplishments, his reign also had its share of, let us say, indiscretions. For example, early in his rule, he executed many members of the Jewish Council of Elders (a group known as the *Sanhedrin*) for their support of his rivals: the Hasmoneans, a Jewish family who had long ruled over Israel (see Chapter 16). In an attempt to legitimize his rule in the eyes of the people, Herod eventually married the Hasmonean princess, Mariamme. This did little to win the people's (or Mariamme's) affections, a situation that was only aggravated when he killed Mariamme on suspicion of adultery — a decision he later regretted and one that plagued him for the rest of his life. Herod then killed his mother-in-law (put that thought out of your mind), because she was plotting with Cleopatra of Egypt (yes, *the* Cleopatra of Egypt) to avenge her daughter's death and to appoint one of her own grandsons as the new king. Even after killing his mother-in-law, Herod feared that his two sons might seek revenge for their mother's death and take his throne; so he killed them as well. As the Roman emperor, Caesar Augustus, is reputed to have said, "I would rather be Herod's pig than his son." It is into this political and religious climate that another King of the Jews would be born, and Herod would try to kill him, too.

to Egypt and his subsequent relocation to Nazareth fulfills two prophecies relating to the Messiah:

- ✔ God would call His son "out of Egypt" (Hosea 11:1) — a notice that originally referred to Israel's exodus from Egypt.

- ✔ The Messiah "would be called a Nazarene." It's unclear where this prophecy comes from. Most scholars think it refers to Isaiah 11:1, which predicts the coming of "a sprout (Hebrew: *nezer*) from the stump of Jesse." Because Jesse is David's father, this passage predicts the coming of a Davidic Messiah who would establish a kingdom of everlasting righteousness and peace. Jesus, then, is the promised "little sprout."

Thus, Joseph, Mary, and Jesus settle in Nazareth.

Growing Up with Jesus

The New Testament provides very little information about Jesus' youth, requiring us to fill in the details from what we know about growing up in first-century Palestine.

Living in Nazareth (Luke 2:39–40)

Nazareth, Jesus' hometown, was a small village in the foothills of Galilee (refer to Figure 18-1). With a total population of no more than 500 people, Nazareth was like many small towns both then and now: Everybody knew everybody. If you grew up in a small town, then you know this has both its advantages and its disadvantages. As a demonstration of the latter, when Jesus impresses his hometown with his amazing teaching and miracles, they ask in apparent derision, "Is this not the carpenter's son?" As Jesus later retorts, "A prophet is never welcome in his hometown" (Luke 4:24).

Jesus, like most boys in first-century Palestine, learned his father's trade. Although most translations describe Joseph's trade as "carpenter," the Greek word *tekton* can also mean "mason" or "blacksmith," and may even denote a person skilled in any handyman-like craft. In other words, Joseph & Sons could probably build or fix just about anything you needed for everyday life in a small agriculture town like Nazareth.

Yes, we said Joseph & *Sons* (plural). Jesus is said to have had four brothers and at least two sisters. Later Catholic doctrine, however, would contend that these were not actual brothers and sisters, because Mary remained a virgin even after Jesus' birth — a doctrine known as "The Perpetual Virginity of Mary." Although the New Testament never says that Mary was a perpetual virgin, in defense of this doctrine, the Greek word used for brothers and sisters can also mean close relatives, or even friends or affiliates. Yet, suggesting that these are *actual* siblings (that is, born of Mary and Joseph, and therefore really Jesus' half brothers and sisters) is Matthew's notice that Joseph did not have sexual relations with Mary "*until* Jesus was born." "Until" is a strange word to use if Joseph *never* had relations with Mary.

We are even given the names of Jesus' brothers, one of whom, James, goes on to become the leader of the Christian church in Jerusalem. And not just James but all of Jesus' siblings are said to eventually believe in him as the Messiah, which is remarkable because early in Jesus' ministry the New Testament reports that "they didn't believe in him" (John 7:5), and even thought he was "out of his mind" (Mark 3:21).

Traveling to Jerusalem (Luke 2:41–52)

The gospel of Luke says that when Jesus is 12 years old, his family and relatives go to Jerusalem for their annual celebration of the Passover — a feast commemorating Israel's deliverance from Egyptian slavery (see Chapter 27). After the week-long festivities, Jesus' family packs up their belongings and begins the long journey home. After the first day of travel, Mary and Joseph realize that Jesus isn't with them. Now before you call the ACPS (Ancient Child Protection Service), it is important to keep in mind that Joseph and Mary are traveling with their extended family, and they probably assume that Jesus is with one of his cousins' families.

Mary and Joseph hurry back to Jerusalem and, after three days of searching, they finally find Jesus at the Temple, listening to and questioning the Jewish priests and religious authorities. Jesus shows such insight, in fact, that "everyone was amazed at his great understanding" (Luke 2:47). Mary and Joseph are more annoyed than amazed, and Mary asks, "Why have you done this to us? Your father and I have been anxiously looking for you everywhere!" Unflustered, Jesus responds, "Why were you looking for me? Didn't you know that I had to be in my Father's House?" (Luke 2:49).

Jesus' response that the Temple is his "Father's House" is intended to remind his parents (and the reader) that, although Jesus is "born of a woman," he is ultimately of divine origin, which sets the stage for his miracles and teachings soon to follow.

The "Lost Years" of Jesus

From the time Jesus is 12 to the time he begins his public ministry (about 18 years later) nothing is recorded about Jesus' life except that he "grew in wisdom and in stature, and in favor with God and people" (Luke 2:52). Some scholars call this period the "Lost Years" of Jesus and have proposed all kinds of imaginative activities for Jesus during this time, including studying philosophy in Greece, Buddhism in China, Hinduism in India, and Native American religion in the Americas. Although the intent of these theories is admirable (explaining how someone from the "backwaters" of the Roman Empire could captivate the world with his profound teaching and exemplary life), the theories themselves are, well, quite imaginative.

What really may have happened during Jesus' growing-up years raises far more interesting questions than these theories. For example, when did Jesus come to believe he was the Messiah? Did Jesus perform any miracles during this period? And what would it have been like growing up with Jesus? (You thought you had it bad! This would give the perennial parental question, "Why can't you be more like your brother?" an entirely different meaning!)

As with many figures of antiquity, much of Jesus' early life is lost to us. But what he accomplished in the few short years recorded of his adulthood, was enough to change the world.

Witnessing Jesus' Baptism

When we encounter Jesus again, Luke tells us he is "about 30 years old" and on the verge of undergoing a religious rite known as *baptism* (a ritual washing by immersion in water) at the hands of a man named John the Baptist.

John the Baptist is an interesting character. He hangs out in the wilderness, eats bugs and wild honey, wears camel-hair jackets (okay, actually just camel-hair garments), and tells people to prepare themselves for God's coming kingdom. Then, as an expression of people's readiness, he dunks them in water. So, who is this guy? And why is he doing this?

Getting to know John the Baptist (Luke 1:5–23, 39–80)

John the Baptist belongs to the priestly class of Israel, and, like Jesus, is born under miraculous circumstances. One day, while John's father, Zechariah, is serving at the Jerusalem Temple, Gabriel appears to him and announces that, although Zechariah's wife, Elizabeth, is barren, God is going to give them a son who will prepare the way for the Messiah (God's appointed deliverer for the Jews). Zechariah is dumbfounded — literally. Because he doesn't believe Gabriel, Gabriel makes him "dumb" or mute until John is born.

Six months after Gabriel's announcement to Zechariah, Gabriel goes to Nazareth to tell Mary that she too will bear a son (see the section, "Receiving Jesus' Birth Announcement," earlier in this chapter). As evidence that God will accomplish this miracle, Gabriel tells Mary, "Even now your relative Elizabeth has conceived a son in her old age, and she, who was thought barren, is in her sixth month" (Luke 1:36). That's right. Mary and Elizabeth are related, although their exact relationship is never specified.

When Mary visits Elizabeth after hearing about her pregnancy, John leaps for joy in his mother's womb. At this, Elizabeth realizes that Mary is carrying the promised Messiah in her womb, and exclaims, "Blessed are you among women, and blessed is the child you will bear!" In response, Mary praises God with a psalm of thanksgiving now called the *Magnificat,* after its first word in Latin, which means "to glorify" (*Magnificat anima mea Dominum:* "My soul glorifies the Lord," Luke 2:46b). The Church of the Visitation in the small town of Ein Karem near Jerusalem commemorates this event.

After John's birth narrative, Luke simply reports, "And the child grew and became strong in spirit, and lived in the wilderness until he became manifest to Israel" (Luke 1:80).

Undergoing baptism with Jesus (Matthew 3; Mark 1; Luke 3; John 1)

When the gospels reintroduce you to John the Baptist, he is already an adult and attracting large crowds in the desert with his preaching and baptizing. According to the gospel writers, John's activity fulfills two predictions made long ago by the prophets Malachi and Isaiah (see Chapter 13). Quoting from both prophets (although only mentioning Isaiah), Mark writes,

> *I will send my messenger before you to prepare your way. A voice calling in the wilderness, "Prepare the way for the LORD, make straight His paths."*

—Mark 1:2–3

It is into this context that Jesus approaches John to be baptized.

Many theologians have thought it strange that Jesus would seek to be baptized by John because the stated purpose of John's baptism was for "repentance leading to the forgiveness of sins." According to the New Testament, Jesus was sinless, and therefore had no need for repentance or for forgiveness. Even John is taken aback by Jesus' request, saying to Jesus, "I should be baptized by you!" But Jesus insists, and John complies.

As Jesus comes up from the water, the heavens open and the Spirit of God descends upon him in the form of a dove. Then, as though this isn't remarkable enough, a voice from heaven declares, "This is My beloved Son, in whom I am well pleased." With this affirmation, Jesus is now ready to meet the forces of darkness and begin his ministry.

Experiencing Jesus' Temptation

Following Jesus' baptism, he goes into the desert where he fasts for 40 days.

Jesus' 40-day stint in the desert is reminiscent of Israel's desert wanderings of 40 years (see Chapter 7). In Matthew, this parallel is particularly striking, because this account comes shortly after Jesus' Moses-like escape from the tyrannical Herod, who, like Pharaoh, mercilessly kills Israel's infant boys in order to remove a threat to his kingdom. Jesus' fasting for 40 days is also reminiscent of the great Hebrew Bible prophet, Elijah, who similarly lasts 40 days without food while traveling through the wilderness on his way to Mount Sinai (which itself is intended to point to Israel's wilderness experience). On a number of occasions, in fact, Jesus' activity parallels Elijah's, as well as Elijah's successor, Elisha (see Chapter 9). For example, both Jesus and his Hebrew Bible counterparts miraculously feed large groups of people, and also bring back people from the dead (see Chapter 19). Jesus' ministry so reminds people of Elijah and Elisha that when Jesus asks his disciples who people thought he was, they report, "some say you are Elijah."

While in the wilderness, Satan comes to Jesus in order to tempt him. (In what form Satan comes the Bible, profoundly, doesn't specify.) Satan presents three temptations to Jesus, each of which touches on a universal desire or concern of the human spirit:

- **Provision:** Satan tells Jesus to turn stones into bread.
- **Protection:** Satan tells Jesus to jump off the pinnacle of Jerusalem's Temple because, if he is the Son of God, God will protect him.
- **Power:** Satan tells Jesus to worship him, and he will give Jesus all the kingdoms of the world.

Interestingly, Jesus responds to each of Satan's temptations with a passage from the Bible, which intends to underscore the importance of using the truth in combating evil. Satan, however, can play the Quote the Bible game, too. When he challenges Jesus to jump off the pinnacle of the Temple, for example, Satan notes that God's angels will "bear you up so that you don't strike your foot against a stone" (Psalm 91:11–12).

Satan's (mis)use of the Bible is intended to point out to the reader that God's word can be manipulated to say things it never intended. And such misuse of the Bible, and other holy texts, has been practiced over the centuries to justify some fairly heinous actions, all "in the name of God."

As with the other temptations, Jesus retorts with the proper use of God's word: "You shall not test the LORD your God" (Deuteronomy 6:16). And with this said, Satan departs.

Having successfully repelled the forces of evil, Jesus leaves the wilderness to begin his ministry of preaching and miracle working — a ministry that, although brief, still impacts us today (see Chapter 19).

John the Baptist's latter days

After baptizing Jesus, John's popularity began to wane as more and more people followed Jesus. John's response to this circumstance reveals his humility, as well as the preparatory nature of his ministry of baptizing and teaching: "He must increase, while I must decrease" (John 3:30). Notwithstanding John's humility, Jesus describes John as "the greatest of those born of women" and "more than a prophet."

Eventually John was imprisoned and executed by Herod Antipas, the son of Herod the Great, for confronting him for marrying his own brother's wife (Matthew 14:3-12). Interestingly, the first century C.E. Jewish historian, Josephus, also records these events and, similar to the New Testament, describes John as a "good man, who commanded the Jews to do what's right, both towards one another and towards God" (*Antiquities of the Jews* 18.5.2).

Chapter 19

Jesus Christ, Superstar: Jesus' "Ministry Years" (Matthew, Mark, Luke, and John)

. . . .

In This Chapter

▶ Tracing Jesus' transformation from a carpenter's son to the Son of God

▶ Joining the twelve disciples as they follow Jesus

▶ Understanding the importance of Jesus' miracles to his message

▶ Listening to Jesus' Sermon on the Mount and his parables

▶ Following Jesus through his last meal, betrayal, trial, and crucifixion

▶ Witnessing Jesus' resurrection from the dead

. . . .

*J*esus was raised in a small village by parents of modest means in an area considered the backwaters of the Roman Empire. He had no formal education, never held a political or religious office, never led an army (in fact, he condemned violence), and as an adult never traveled more than 100 miles from his hometown. Yet, because of the impact of Jesus' life and teachings, over 1 billion people today identify themselves as Christians.

In this chapter, you witness Jesus' transformation from a carpenter's son to the Son of God, and you watch as his life and teachings initiate a movement that quite literally changed the world.

The four New Testament gospels — Matthew, Mark, Luke, and John — each approach the life of Jesus from a different perspective (see Chapter 18). These differences in perspective often result in differences of detail, even when recounting the same story or teaching. In addition, these differing viewpoints can affect the order in which the events of Jesus' life are presented. In this chapter, we weave together the accounts of these gospels in order to provide you with a coherent retelling of the life of Jesus. However, we also point out some of the more important and interesting differences among the gospels, so you can compare their different perspectives.

Charting Jesus' Ministry

We don't know the exact duration of Jesus' ministry of teaching and miracle working, though most scholars believe it spanned about three years. Although not corresponding to these three years exactly, Jesus' ministry is usually divided into three general periods:

- ✔ Period of Inauguration
- ✔ Period of Popularity
- ✔ Period of Opposition

This outline is, by necessity, oversimplified, because life — especially a life as complex as Jesus' — rarely fits into neat stages or categories. However, it provides a useful way for understanding the overall development of Jesus' ministry and why he left such an indelible mark on our world.

The Period of Inauguration

The inauguration or beginning of Jesus' ministry seems to have taken place largely in and around his hometown of Nazareth. At the nearby village of Cana, for example, Jesus performs what the Gospel of John calls his "first miracle" — changing water into wine at a wedding celebration (John 2:1–11). Now you may be thinking that providing alcohol at a party is a pretty trivial miracle for starting a worldwide movement. Some have argued, however, that the "trivial" nature of Jesus' first miracle is just the point: God cares about every detail of life (though, if you've ever thrown a wedding reception, you know that these are anything but trivial affairs).

Changing addresses with Jesus

Despite his ability to rescue parties from certain disaster, Jesus eventually falls out of favor with his hometown of Nazareth when he rebukes them for not believing he is the Messiah. As Jesus reminds them, "No prophet is accepted in his hometown" (Luke 4:24). After further rebukes, the people listening become angry, and try to kill him by throwing him off a nearby hillside, but Jesus escapes. After this event, Jesus changes his base of operations to Capernaum, a town on the northern shores of the Sea of Galilee.

Beyond leaving those hometown blues, Jesus' move to Capernaum is strategic — Capernaum is located on the major trade routes going around the Sea of Galilee, and it would be along these thoroughfares that news of Jesus' miracles and teaching would spread far and wide.

Choosing Jesus' twelve closest followers

Another strategic move is Jesus' choice of disciples "to be with him always." The gathering of students or disciples around a master for the impartation of instruction was well known in the ancient world. That the sayings and actions of many great teachers from the past have endured to the present testifies to the effectiveness of choosing disciples.

Jesus' choice of twelve disciples has tremendous symbolic significance as well, because twelve was the traditional number of tribes making up ancient Israel (see Chapter 6). Thus, Jesus' disciples represent the totality of Israel — a fact that Jesus alludes to when he says that the disciples will one day sit in judgment over the twelve tribes of Israel (Matthew 19:28).

The makeup of Jesus' disciples is also significant for understanding the intended scope of Jesus' ministry.

Fishermen

Four of Jesus' disciples, and perhaps more, were fishermen:

- Peter, also called Simon or Cephas (both Peter and Cephas mean "rock" in Greek and Aramaic, respectively; a name given to Simon by Jesus)
- Andrew, Peter's brother
- James and John, brothers whom Jesus affectionately calls "the sons of thunder," in apparent recognition of their explosive temperaments

When Jesus first calls these fishermen, he simply says, "Come, follow me, and I will make you fishers of men" (Mark 1:17). With this call, the disciples "left their nets and followed him."

Why fish ride on the back of cars

The majority presence of fishermen among Jesus' disciples, along with Jesus' call to become "fishers of men," resulted in the figure of the fish becoming a symbol of early Christianity, and was even used as a secret code to escape detection during times of persecution. Also, the Greek letters for the word "fish" became an acronym for "Jesus Christ, Son of God, Savior." Today, many people still use this symbol to identify themselves as Christians, including wearing fish symbols on jewelry and clothing, as well as placing the outline of a fish on the back of their cars.

Jesus' choice of fishermen emphasizes that knowledge of God is not restricted to the learned or priestly classes. As one New Testament writer puts it, "God chose the simple things of this world to confound the wise" (1 Corinthians 1:27). (And, no doubt, Jesus knew that changing the world took patience — so what better choice than fishermen?)

A tax collector

In addition to fishermen, Jesus chooses a tax collector named Levi or, as he is also called, Matthew (the reputed author of the gospel by that name — see Chapter 18). Few professions were more despised in first-century Judea than the ancient version of the IRS. As evidence of the disdain people felt toward tax collectors, when the religious leaders wanted to slur Jesus' character, they would say he spent time with "tax-gatherers and sinners." Now that's low — but it was also true. As Jesus would say in response: "It is not those who are well who need a physician, but those who are sick" (Luke 5:31).

A Zealot

The Jews' growing disdain for foreign rule helps to explain another group represented by Jesus' disciples: the Zealots. As the name suggests, this movement was "zealous" for Israel's ancestral traditions and, by implication, the removal of foreign rule and religion from Israel. For many Zealots, nothing less than the violent overthrow of Rome would do. Thus, Jesus' choice of the Zealot Simon carried with it certain risks. Jesus will condemn violence, but his choice of Simon demonstrates that no one is excluded from God's kingdom merely because of an ideological orientation.

The other disciples

Although the gospels don't specify the professions of the other disciples (most were probably fishermen), here are their names to round out the list:

- **Philip:** Perhaps the brother of Bartholomew (next on the list), if Bartholomew's alternate name is Nathanael.

- **Bartholomew:** Seemingly the same person as Nathanael in John's gospel.

- **Thomas:** Best known as Doubting Thomas, for doubting Jesus' resurrection.

- **James:** Different from James, the brother of John.

- **Thaddaeus:** Also called Judas, though not the same person as Judas Iscariot.

- **Judas Iscariot:** The disciple who would betray Jesus.

Although the twelve disciples are all men, Jesus' wider circle of followers includes women. Women help to support Jesus and the twelve disciples financially (Luke 8:1–4). Moreover, women are present at Jesus' crucifixion, when most of the male disciples have fled for their lives. Finally, women are the first to testify to Jesus' resurrection. In light of a woman's diminished status in the ancient world, Jesus' choice of women among his followers would convey that God's kingdom is intended to be equally enjoyed by all.

The Period of Popularity

Although Jesus' popularity is first localized to the Galilee region, it soon spreads far and wide due primarily to two factors: his miracles and teachings.

Witnessing Jesus' miracles

The word *miracle* comes from the Latin word *mirari,* meaning "to wonder at." And, according to the New Testament, Jesus gives the people of his day plenty to wonder at. Jesus calms tempestuous seas, gives sight to the blind, makes the deaf to hear, enables the lame to walk, and even raises the dead.

Yet many scholars contend that Jesus' miracles are not really important for understanding his life. Some even extract his miracles from the gospel accounts in order to restore the *real* Jesus. One of the best-known examples of this editorial exercise is the work of Thomas Jefferson, who not only removed most of Jesus' miracles but also those teachings he felt "unworthy" of the Son of God. The product of his labors is called *The Thomas Jefferson Bible.*

The New Testament writers, however, clearly believe that Jesus' miracles are essential for understanding his ministry and message.

- Pragmatically, Jesus' miracles serve the purpose of attracting crowds, which, in turn, provide large audiences for his teachings.

- Thematically, Jesus' miracles underscore his message. For example, shortly after miraculously feeding 5,000 people with just a few loaves and fish, Jesus says, "I am the bread of life. Whoever comes to me will never hunger" (John 6:35). And just before raising his good friend, Lazarus, from the dead, Jesus announces, "I am the resurrection and the life. Whoever believes in me will live, even if he dies" (John 11:25).

- Spiritually, Jesus' miracles produce faith in those experiencing them. As John 2:23 reports, "many people believed in Jesus because of the signs he performed." Yet, Jesus' miracles also *require* faith. Although that may sound contradictory, the New Testament writers understand faith to be a dynamic interchange between what you believe and what you experience. This tension is best illustrated in the case of a man who asks Jesus to heal his son. Jesus asks, "Do you believe I can?" The man responds, "I do believe, Lord, but help me with my unbelief" (Mark 9:24). Jesus does help him with his unbelief, and heals his son. Conversely, when those asking for a miracle have no intention of believing in Jesus, he won't indulge them.

Finally, the New Testament writers all agree that one miracle is absolutely essential for understanding Jesus' life: his resurrection. Jesus' resurrection, according to the disciple Peter, proves he is "both Lord and the Messiah" (Acts 2:36). And, according to the apostle Paul, "If Jesus didn't rise from the dead, then our faith is in vain" (1 Corinthians 15:17).

Understanding Jesus' sermons

Even if Jesus never performed a single miracle, his teachings would have secured his place as one of the greatest moral philosophers who ever lived. In fact, Jesus is a moral philosopher in the true sense: He intends that his teachings be not only contemplated but acted upon. As Jesus himself says, "He who hears my words and does not do them is like a foolish man who builds his house on the sand" (Matthew 7:26).

So what did Jesus teach? In short, a lot. It's from Jesus that we get such famous statements as "turn the other cheek" (Matthew 5:39), "go the extra mile" (Matthew 5:41), "love your enemies" (Matthew 5:44), and the so-called Golden Rule, "Do to others what you want them to do to you" (Luke 6:31).

Yet, Jesus' teachings are not entirely new. The Golden Rule, for example, could be found in Greco-Roman and eastern philosophical traditions (though usually posed in the negative), and much of what Jesus says had already been expressed in the Hebrew Bible, as Jesus himself admits (see "The Sermon on the Mount," in this chapter). Still, Jesus' teachings are unrivaled for their penetrating simplicity and enduring appeal.

The Sermon on the Mount (Matthew 5–7; Luke 6:17–49)

Jesus gives lectures, or *sermons,* on a variety of subjects. His most famous, though, is the Sermon on the Mount (so named because, in Matthew, Jesus stands on a mountain when delivering this message). A brief look at this sermon gives us a good idea of what Jesus is all about.

The Sermon on the Mount is, in short, a body of moral teaching characterized by an emphasis on sincere devotion to God, and a corresponding heartfelt benevolence toward others. The emphasis, as this definition suggests, is on the heart. And, therefore, it is to the heart that Jesus directs his teaching.

The *Beatitudes* or Blessings ("Blessed are . . .") make up the first part of Jesus' sermon. Although scholars speculate that the Sermon on the Mount is a compilation of Jesus' teaching, brought together only later into one message, the Beatitudes' emphasis on personal righteousness and patience in affliction serves as a fitting introduction. Among its teachings you find:

✔ Blessed are the poor in spirit, for theirs is the kingdom of heaven.

✔ Blessed are those who mourn, for they shall be comforted.

✔ Blessed are those who hunger and thirst for righteousness sake, for they shall be filled.

✔ Blessed are the merciful, for they shall receive mercy.

✔ Blessed are the peacemakers, for they shall be called children of God.

Following the Beatitudes is a series of teachings that present clarifications, and sometimes reformulations, of earlier teachings found in the Hebrew Bible and later Jewish tradition. Here Jesus uses the recurring formula, "You have heard it said . . . but I say. . . ." However, Jesus' use of this formula doesn't mean he's rejecting the Law of Moses (as some people believe), but rather he's rejecting later interpretations of that Law. As Jesus says in the introduction to his sermon, "I came not to abolish the Law, but to fulfill it."

In the Sermon on the Mount, Jesus attempts to change people's attitude toward Moses' Law from external obedience (that is, "I haven't killed anyone today") to internal obedience (that is, "I have forgiven everyone today").

For example, Jesus says,

> *You have heard it said long ago, "Do not murder". . . But I say that if anyone is angry with his brother, he will be worthy of judgment. And if anyone says to his brother, "Empty-headed," he will be answerable to the Sanhedrin [the Jewish high court]. But if anyone says, "You fool," he will be in danger of the fire of hell.*

> —Matthew 5:21–22

Note the progression of Jesus' teaching.

✔ Don't murder.

✔ Don't even remain angry.

✔ Furthermore, don't devalue others by considering them fools.

According to Jesus, when Moses said, "Do not murder," he didn't only mean, "Try to make it through the day without killing anyone," but he also meant, "Don't devalue others by thinking yourself superior to them or harboring anger toward them." For Jesus, devaluing others is akin to (and ultimately the source of) murder. Now that's deep (and a lot harder to obey by the way).

Jesus goes through the same process with other commands, including adultery ("If you lust over another you've already committed adultery in your heart"), oath taking ("Don't swear oaths," but "Let your yes mean yes, and your no mean no"), retaliation ("If someone strikes you on the right cheek, turn to him the other as well"), and hating your enemies ("Love your enemies" and "pray for those who persecute you"). In case you weren't feeling under the pile already, Jesus concludes this part of his sermon by saying,

> *Be perfect, therefore, just as your heavenly Father is perfect.*

> —Matthew 5:48

Jesus' point in saying "be perfect" is not to make people overachievers or type-A personalities. Rather, Jesus wants people to stop comparing themselves with others, because this leads to a false sense of righteousness. You can always find someone more "morally challenged" than you are, but everyone has room for improvement when compared to God's perfection.

The tendency toward self-righteousness explains why Jesus then moves to a discussion of religious showmanship, which he describes as those who "practice their righteousness before others to be noticed by them." The word Jesus uses to describe this false piety is *hypocrisy*, which was a word used to describe actors in a play. To Jesus, those who practice their piety for public consumption are like actors, pretending to be someone they're not.

The Lord's Prayer (Matthew 6:9–13; Luke 11:2–4)

It is in the context of Jesus' teaching against hypocrisy, and in particular hypocrisy when praying (for example, saying words you don't mean, or saying long prayers just to impress others) that Jesus prays his well-known Lord's Prayer. Although it appears in slightly different forms in the gospels of Matthew and Luke, the overall thrust is the same. It is a prayer of simple devotion to God, expressing the speaker's longing for God's righteous rule on earth, as well as God's daily provision for food, forgiveness, and protection.

> *Our Father, who art in heaven*
> *hallowed be Thy name.*
> *Thy kingdom come,*
> *Thy will be done,*
> *on earth as it is in heaven.*
> *Give us this day our daily bread.*
> *Forgive our trespasses,*
> *as we forgive those who trespass against us.*
> *And lead us not into temptation,*
> *but deliver us from evil,*
> *For Thine is the kingdom, and the power,*
> *and the glory, forever.*
> *Amen.*

Amen comes from a Hebrew word meaning "trustworthy" or "true." Therefore, saying amen means that you agree with what was prayed *and* that God is trustworthy to answer the prayer. Sometimes Jesus even begins his teaching by saying, "Amen, amen," which means, in essence, "You can take what I'm about to say to the bank."

The greatest commandment

Jesus is once asked, "What is the greatest commandment?" Jesus responds, "'Hear, O Israel, the Lord our God is one. Love the Lord your God with all your heart, soul, mind, and strength.' This is the first and greatest commandment. The second is this: 'Love your neighbor as yourself.' All the Law and Prophets hang on these two commandments" (Mark 12:29–31).

For Jesus the "unifying principle" of life is love (the Beatles got it right). If you truly love God and others, then you will obey God and do good to others, which, in essence, is what God commands in the Law of Moses, and reflects the messages He gave to the Hebrew Bible prophets to deliver.

Deciphering Jesus' parables

When Jesus is not delivering sermons, he is speaking in *parables* (stories drawn from everyday life that communicate a theological truth or moral principle). In fact, Jesus uses parable more than he does direct discourse.

The purpose of Jesus' parables: Clarity and understanding (not)

The reason for Jesus' prolific use of parable is twofold: to make his teachings *more* understandable, and to make his teachings *less* understandable. That may sound like a contradiction, but read on for an explanation.

When using parables, Jesus takes things from everyday life and transforms them into a moral or spiritual lesson. By doing so, Jesus paints a picture in his listener's mind, making what he says clearer and more memorable. Yet, when Jesus is asked *why* he teaches in parables, the answer is surprising:

> This is why I speak in parables:
> So that even though they see, they won't really perceive,
> and even though they hear, they won't really listen or understand.
>
> —Matthew 13:13

Say what? Jesus doesn't want people to understand him? Well, yes and no. As in the case of his miracle-working, Jesus doesn't want those who are merely interested in a spectacle to follow him. He wants those who follow him to really want "the truth." So he speaks in parables. If someone doesn't understand, and doesn't care to, then he or she won't go to the trouble of pursuing an answer. But if someone wants to understand Jesus' teachings, then he or she will go to the trouble to ask, just as Jesus' disciples do.

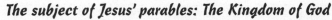

The subject of Jesus' parables: The Kingdom of God

Most of Jesus' parables — actually, most of Jesus' teachings — have to do with what he calls the *Kingdom of God.* So what is the Kingdom of God? A study of Jesus' teachings on the Kingdom of God reveal that it's quite a number of things, but falls under two general categories embodied in the phrase "now, but not yet." That is, Jesus' notion of the Kingdom of God is that it exists both in the present ("the Kingdom of God is in your midst," Luke 17:21) and in the future ("until the Kingdom of God comes," Luke 22:18). Those who know God and obey His commandments can begin experiencing His Kingdom right now on earth through the inner and enduring qualities of righteousness, peace, love, and joy. But God's Kingdom won't be experienced fully until God returns to earth and establishes it.

The following sections include some of Jesus' most famous parables.

The parable of the soils (Matthew 13:3–8, 18–23; Mark 4:3–8, 14–20; Luke 8:5–8, 11–15)

In the parable of the soils, Jesus describes a farmer who sows seed that falls on four different types of soil. The seed, Jesus tells us, is "the word of God." The four different types of soil represent the different "hearts" or receptivity that people have toward God and His word:

- ✔ The first type of seed, which falls on a hardened path and is immediately eaten by birds, corresponds to those who have a hard heart toward God. When they hear God's word, they are unreceptive to the truth and, therefore, Satan (symbolized by the birds) takes the truth away.

- ✔ The second type of seed, which falls on rocky soil, corresponds to those who initially respond positively to God's word, but when the truth "starts to hurt," they abandon it.

- ✔ The third type of seed, which falls among the thorns and weeds, are those who receive God's word, but then the "worries of this world" and the "deceitfulness of wealth" begin to take over the garden of the heart.

- ✔ The fourth type of seed, which falls on good soil, is the individual who hears and understands God's word, and whose heart then brings forth the fruit of a good life.

Thus, the purpose of this parable — in fact, of all Jesus' parables — is to weed out (pardon the pun) those who aren't receptive to the truth from those who are.

The parable of the Good Samaritan (Luke 10:25–37)

Today we use the term *Good Samaritan* to denote someone who does good to others, and, in particular, to strangers. Yet, this understanding doesn't go far enough in defining what Jesus means by this term.

In the parable of the Good Samaritan, Jesus tells the story of a Jewish man who, while traveling a desert road, is attacked and robbed by bandits, and left for dead. Soon a priest passes by and, seeing the man in distress, crosses over to the other side of the road and continues on. Then a Levite (another type of priest) happens upon the dying man and does the same thing. Eventually a Samaritan, traditionally an enemy of the Jews (see the sidebar "Who are the Samaritans?" later in this chapter), comes upon the dying man and feels compassion for him. Thus, rather than leave the man for dead, the Samaritan bandages his wounds and takes him to a nearby village where he pays for the man's expenses until he recovers.

Through this parable, Jesus attempts to expand people's notion of those they should love to include not only those they know (neighbor), or even those they don't know (stranger), but those they've been taught to hate (enemy).

The parable of the prodigal son (Luke 15)

One of Jesus' most famous parables is that of the prodigal son, who insultingly asks his father for his inheritance before his father's death, and then spends it all on loose living in a faraway country. Forced to take a job feeding pigs (a detestable animal to the Jews), the son soon realizes that even his father's servants live better than him. Therefore, deciding to ask for forgiveness from his father and then offer himself as a servant, the son begins the long journey home. As the son approaches his former home, his father sees him in the distance and runs out to meet him. Before the son can fully apologize, the father embraces and kisses him, and then commands his servants to make preparations for a celebration.

Who are the Samaritans?

To understand the revolutionary nature of Jesus' parable of the Good Samaritan, you need to understand a little something about Jewish-Samaritan relations during his day.

According to the Samaritans (who still exist as a people today), they were (and are) Israelites, deriving primarily from the tribes of Manasseh and Ephraim. They also believed that they, not the Jews, maintained the authentic site of worship: the temple on Mount Gerizim. According to Jewish tradition, however, the Samaritans were not descendants of the Israelites. Rather, they were either foreigners transplanted into Israel by the Assyrians (721 B.C.E.), or, worse, they were the product of mixed marriages between Israelites and foreigners. The Jews also believed that Samaritan religion was a mingling of foreign cultic practices and the worship of God (2 Kings 17).

These are hardly the attitudes that lead to good relations, and on several occasions the hatred these two groups felt toward one another expressed itself in real violence. As a result, many Jews avoided Samaritan territory altogether, even if it meant going a significant distance out of their way. So when Jesus says that a Good Samaritan helped a distressed and dying Jew when his fellow Jews (religious leaders at that) passed him by, and when Jesus interacts with a Samaritan woman on Samaritan soil (see John 4), he is undermining the prejudices of his day.

When the prodigal son's older brother hears that a celebration is being held for his wasteful brother, he becomes angry and refuses to attend. The father goes to his son, assuring him that everything he owns will one day be his. "But," the father says, "we had to celebrate and rejoice, since your brother was dead and now is alive; he was lost, but now is found" (Luke 15:32). (**Note:** These words inspired the lyrics to the famous hymn *Amazing Grace*.)

Scholars have offered a number of interpretations for this parable, including equating the younger brother with the gentiles (who, like pigs, were considered ritually unclean by the Jews), and the older son with the Jews (who, like the older son, were destined to inherit the father's [God's] riches). Whatever the exact identity of the sons, one identification is clear: The father of the parable is God, who lovingly embraces anyone who turns back to Him after going astray. As Jesus says just prior to this parable: "There is rejoicing in the presence of God's angels over one sinner who repents" (Luke 15:10).

The Period of Opposition

Despite Jesus' reconciling message (and, perhaps, because of it) Jesus' popularity begins to wane, and opposition begins to grow as more and more people, and especially the religious and political authorities of his day, become nervous about his growing influence and revolutionary ideas.

The most important religious and political movers and shakers among the Jews during Jesus' day, and the ones that give him the most trouble, are the Pharisees and the Sadducees.

Offending the Pharisees with Jesus

The name Pharisees seems to come from the Hebrew word *parash,* meaning "separated one," which refers either to their separation from an earlier movement within Judaism, or their separation as devout followers of the Law of Moses (that is, separating between what is "clean and unclean"). Similar to Jesus, the Pharisees believe that not just the writings of Moses, but the entire Hebrew Bible is authoritative for life and doctrine (for a contrary view, see "Confronting the Sadducees with Jesus" later in this chapter). Therefore, the Pharisees, like Jesus, believe in the resurrection of the dead, angels and demons, and a final judgment where God will assign people to eternal life or eternal contempt.

Despite the many similarities between Jesus and the Pharisees, Jesus publicly renounces them as hypocrites and frauds. In fact, the saying "practice what you preach" comes from Jesus' words directed at the Pharisees (Matthew 23:3). In Jesus' view, the Pharisees place on others religious burdens they themselves are unwilling to bear. Externally they may meticulously keep the law, but internally they are "full of everything that is unclean" and neglect the weightier matters of the law: justice, mercy, and faithfulness.

Confronting the Sadducees with Jesus

The name Sadducees seems to derive either from the Hebrew word _tsaddiq,_ which means "righteous one," or from the name Zadok, the High Priest during King David's reign and whose descendants (the Zadokites) were thought to be the only legitimate High Priests. Whatever their exact origin, the Sadducees during Jesus' day are associated with the priestly upper-class, and therefore hold more formal power than their religious counterparts, the Pharisees. (For example, the High Priests of the Jews are all Sadducees.) Also unlike the Pharisees, the Sadducees believe that only the five books of Moses or _Torah_ (Genesis through Deuteronomy) are authoritative. As a result, they don't believe in an afterlife or final judgment, as they feel these doctrines are not explicitly taught in the books of Moses.

Jesus has less in common with the Sadducees. The Sadducees' contention that there is no resurrection or final judgment makes them, in Jesus' mind, worthy of final judgment. But Jesus' greater difficulty with the Sadducees is how they use their position of power for their own advancement, and not the advancement of God's Kingdom. True authority, according to Jesus, comes from God and from doing what He commands.

Jesus' Final Week and Crucifixion

Jesus' "offenses" against the political and religious powers of his day come to a crescendo during his final week of life (or Passion Week, as it is called, in recognition of the "passion" or suffering Jesus endures during this period). At the beginning of this week, which is just prior to the Jewish feast of Passover, Jesus rides into Jerusalem to the shouts of "Blessed is he who comes in the name of the Lord!" but by week's end he is driven out of Jerusalem to the cries of "Crucify him! Crucify him!" How this transition takes place makes for one of the most moving and dramatic narratives in world literature and world history. Because Jesus' last days are so important for understanding his life and teachings, we walk you through these events in some detail.

The gospel writers' different approaches to the life of Jesus are nowhere more apparent than during Jesus' final week, where the need to interpret his life (and death) becomes a pressing issue. What follows is a merging of these accounts. However, you should keep in mind that the differences among the gospel writers' accounts (several of which we highlight below) are just as important for getting a complete picture of Jesus' life as trying to fit these varying accounts into a coherent story.

Sunday: The triumphal entry

On Sunday of his final week, Jesus makes a dramatic entry into Jerusalem by riding in on a donkey. Jesus' choice of a donkey fulfills a prediction made by the prophet Zechariah that the Messiah would one day ride into Jerusalem on "a colt, the foal of a donkey" (Zechariah 9:9). According to Zechariah, the colt is a sign of peace, in contrast to the "warhorses" present in Jerusalem.

Jesus' victorious reception

As Jesus approaches the city, a large crowd gathers and places their cloaks and freshly cut foliage on the ground before him. Others wave palm branches (hence, the name *Palm Sunday* to denote this celebration in Christian liturgy), as a sign of victory and celebration. In addition to these actions, the people shout "Hosanna! Blessed is he who comes in the name of the LORD!" which comes from Psalm 118, the last of the so-called Hallel or Praise Psalms (Psalms 113–118) typically sung at Passover.

Jesus' cold confrontation

Hearing the people's praise, the religious authorities become angry and confront Jesus, "Teacher, rebuke your disciples!" (Luke 19:29). Jesus, believing their praise is rightly directed, responds, "I tell you the truth, if they kept silent, the stones would cry out."

As Jesus draws closer to Jerusalem, he weeps, saying, "If only you had known on this day what would bring you peace; but now it is hidden from your eyes" (Luke 19:42). Then, upon entering the city, Jesus goes to the Temple courts and looks around. Because it is late, Jesus departs for Bethany, a small village east of Jerusalem that will be his base of operations throughout the week.

Monday: Cleansing the Temple

The next day, according to the Gospel of Mark, Jesus again enters the Temple courts, but this time he immediately goes to work.

Prohibiting the commercialization of religion

The specific area Jesus enters is known as the Court of Gentiles (see Figure 19-1), which was the outermost court surrounding the Temple. It was called the Court of the Gentiles because it was the only place within the Temple precincts where non-Jews were allowed. This was a place of vibrant commercial activity, as people from all over the Roman Empire came to exchange money and purchase animals for the Temple offerings and sacrifices. Jesus, however, perceives this activity as the commercialization of religion. In response, he begins overturning the moneychangers' tables and driving out the animals.

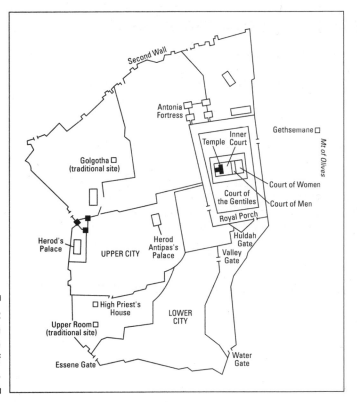

Figure 19-1:
Jerusalem
during the
time of
Jesus.

In defense of his actions, Jesus cites two prophets from the Hebrew Bible:

My house is to be a house of prayer for all nations.

—Isaiah 56:7

But you have made it a robbers' den.

—Jeremiah 7:11

Plotting Jesus' undoing

After Jesus' "cleaning house," many people gather around him, some for healing, others to get a closer look at this "prophet from Nazareth," and others to sing his praises. The religious leaders, however, are not amused. After confronting him, they begin secretly plotting how to get rid of him.

Tuesday: Paying taxes, giving tithes, and predicting the future

When Jesus enters Jerusalem the next day, he is immediately confronted by the religious authorities. They waste no time in getting to their point: "Who gave you the authority to do these things?" (Luke 20:2). Their concern is understandable, because Jesus has no official religious training nor does he hold any official religious office. Yet, he's stirring up the people with his revolutionary ideas and actions. The religious leaders, as the shepherds of the people, are responsible for protecting their sheep from danger of this sort.

Rendering unto Caesar his due

In order to test whether Jesus has any revolutionary intentions, some Pharisees and Herodians (supporters of Roman rule under the Herods) ask Jesus if the Jews should pay taxes to Rome. More than a test, this is a trap. If Jesus says yes, the Jews (represented by the Pharisees) will perceive this as giving tacit approval to their subjection under foreign rule — a condition that the Messiah is supposed to rectify. If Jesus says no, the Romans (represented by the Herodians) will perceive this as supporting a revolt. To answer their question, Jesus asks for a coin. Holding it up, Jesus says, "Whose likeness is this, and whose inscription?" (Luke 20:24). The crowd replies, "Caesar's." Jesus declares, "Then render unto Caesar what is Caesar's, and unto God what is God's!" And we've been paying taxes ever since.

Weighing the widow's mites

During this same day, Jesus points to a widow who is placing her offering into the Temple treasury. The amount of her offering is described as two "mites," which seems to refer to the Greek *lepton,* the smallest coin in circulation at the time. The Temple treasury of Jesus' day was located in the Court of Women (see Figure 19-1), and consisted of large trumpet-shaped receptacles that rattled as people deposited their money. This allowed for the demonstration of one's "piety," because the amount given would be readily discerned by the noise produced. The sound of the widow's two small coins, smaller even than a modern penny, no doubt would have escaped notice. Yet, as she deposits her coins, Jesus turns to his disciples and says, "I tell you the truth, this poor widow has given more than anyone. Others give from their surplus, but she has given out of her poverty all that she had to live on" (Luke 21:3).

Predicting the destruction of the Temple

The disciples, apparently still thinking that external extravagance is an indicator of religious piety, do some pointing of their own. Turning toward the Temple, the disciples call Jesus' attention to its beautifully adorned buildings. Jesus is unimpressed, and says in response, "I tell you the truth, not one stone will be left on another" (Luke 21:6) — a reference to the destruction of the Temple by the Romans some 40 years later.

Describing the end times

As Jesus and his disciples begin to leave Jerusalem, they stop on the western slopes of the Mount of Olives (refer to Figure 19-1). Apparently still thinking about Jesus' comments about the destruction of Jerusalem, the disciples ask, "What will be the sign of your coming and of the end of the age?" (Matthew 24:3). Looking over the city, Jesus begins to describe the events leading up to the end times, including a "desecration" of the Temple similar to that carried out by Antiochus Epiphanes (see Chapter 16). In addition to the devastation awaiting Jerusalem, there will be worldwide famines, natural disasters, and "wars and rumors of war." Despite the dark days ahead, all will end well for the righteous, because the Son of Man will come "on the clouds with power and great glory" and establish God's Kingdom on earth (Matthew 24:30).

Jesus' thoughts, however, seem captured by a more immediate event: his imminent death. Therefore, he concludes his discourse on the end times by saying, "As you know, the Passover is only two days away, and the Son of Man will be handed over to be crucified" (Matthew 26:2).

Wednesday: Jesus' anointing and Judas' desertion

On Wednesday, Jesus and his disciples remain in Bethany. Presumably Jesus' confrontations the day before, along with his prediction of the Temple's destruction, mark the end of his warnings to Jerusalem. He will now stay in Bethany until the Passover, which is less than two days away.

Anointing Jesus for burial

While in Bethany, Jesus and his disciples are entertained at the home of Simon the Leper — apparently someone healed by Jesus, but whose name had stuck. Suddenly, a woman enters the house and anoints Jesus with costly perfume. The disciples are taken aback — not from surprise or from admiration of her devotion, but from the loss of revenue. As the disciples reason, the perfume could have been sold and the money used to feed the poor. Actually, the Gospel of John says this protest came from only one disciple: Judas Iscariot, who, as the treasurer of the group, intended to take the money for himself, just as he had been doing throughout Jesus' ministry. Jesus' response ("The poor you will always have with you, but I will be with you only a little while longer") intends to underscore the importance of his death. Jesus then says, "Wherever the gospel is preached, so will what this woman did be told, in memory of her" (Matthew 26:13).

Deserting Jesus with Judas

After this episode, Judas leaves to inform the religious authorities of his willingness to betray Jesus. What it is about this event that leads Judas to this action — if there is meant to be any connection at all — is unclear. Perhaps

Judas gets what the other disciples seem to miss: Jesus is about to die, which was hardly the expectation of the Messiah, who was supposed to bring "deliverance from our enemies and from the hand of those who hate us" (Luke 1:71). Judas agrees to betray Jesus for 30 pieces of silver, which is about 4 months' wages — a small amount for so infamous a deed.

Thursday: The Last Supper, Judas' betrayal, and Jesus' arrest

Thursday is the Day of Preparation for the Passover. As such, Jesus sends two of his disciples (Peter and John, according to the Gospel of Luke) to Jerusalem to make arrangements for their Passover meal. Jesus says,

> When you enter the city, a man carrying a jug of water will meet you. Follow him to the house he enters and say to the owner, "The Teacher asks, 'Where is the guest room where I may observe the Passover with my disciples?'" He will show you a large upper room. Make preparations there.

—Luke 22:10–12

It's not clear whether this is intended to be another example of Jesus' abilities to predict the future or merely to plan ahead, though Luke's comment "they found it just as he had said" points slightly in favor of the prophetic.

After everything is prepared, Jesus and the other disciples gather in the upper room (see Figure 19-1) to celebrate Jesus' last Passover, or, as later Church tradition would call it, the Last Supper.

Washing the disciples' feet

According to the Gospel of John, as the meal is being served, Jesus unexpectedly gets up and begins washing the disciples' feet. People usually washed their own feet or the washing was done by a servant. Because Jesus is the leader of the disciples, Peter protests: "You will never wash my feet!" Jesus responds, "Unless I wash you, you can have no part with me." For Jesus, this is not about clean feet, but about humility. As Jesus says elsewhere, "the greatest among you will be the least, and the one who rules the one who serves" (Luke 22:26). Yet, this action is also intended to foreshadow Jesus' ultimate act of service: his death. As Jesus says in another context, "The Son of Man came not to be served, but to serve, and to give his life as a ransom for many" (Mark 10:45).

Announcing Jesus' death and betrayal

After everyone is settled around the table, Jesus makes an announcement: "I have eagerly desired to share this Passover with you before I suffer. For I tell you, I will not eat of it again until it finds fulfillment in the Kingdom of God"

(Luke 22:15–16). The impact of these words, however, seems to be overshadowed by Jesus' other announcement that someone sitting at the table will betray him. Amidst the attestations of innocence, Judas asks Jesus straightforwardly, "Surely it is not I, Rabbi?" to which Jesus, equally straightforwardly, replies, "Yes, it is you." Apparently the disciples don't catch this interchange, and Judas stays throughout the meal, including the institution of what later tradition would call Communion or the Eucharist.

Jesus takes the unleavened bread that Moses proscribed for the Passover meal and "gave thanks, broke it, and gave it to his disciples" (Luke 22:19). The Greek word for "gave thanks," *eucharistesas,* has given rise to the name of this meal in Catholic liturgy: the Eucharist. The unleavened bread of the Passover meal was intended to be a reminder of Israel's hurried departure from Egyptian slavery. Jesus, however, takes this central element of the meal and applies it to himself, "This is my body, given for you."

Jesus' equating the bread with his body (and later, the wine with his blood) is taken literally by the Catholic Church, which holds that during the Church's celebration of the Eucharist the bread and wine actually transform into Jesus' body and blood (a doctrine known as Transubstantiation). Most Protestant churches understand the bread and wine to be symbols of Jesus' death.

Establishing a "new" covenant

After the meal, Jesus takes a cup of wine, and in the same way as the bread, "gave thanks" and distributes it among his disciples. That Jesus does this after the meal indicates this is the third cup of the Passover meal, known as the *cup of redemption.* This is particularly fitting because Jesus says of this cup, "This cup is the new covenant in my blood, which is poured out for you."

Jesus' reference to a "new covenant" harkens back to the prophet Jeremiah, who predicted a day when God would make a new covenant with Israel (Jeremiah 31:31). It is from the Latin word for "covenant," *testamentum,* when combined with Jesus' words, that the term "New Testament" derives — a term which has since been applied to the inspired writings of Christianity.

At the conclusion of the meal, Jesus and his disciples sing a hymn, which was probably the second half of the Hallel Psalms (Psalms 115–118) sung at Passover. They then make their way to the Mount of Olives (see Figure 19-1), where they hope to get a good night's sleep before resuming their celebrations the next day. They wouldn't get that good night's sleep.

Going to the Mount of Olives

The choice to stay on the Mount of Olives, besides its proximity to Jerusalem, had tremendous symbolic value for Jesus' messianic mission. According to the prophet Zechariah, God would one day stand on this mount just before delivering Israel from its enemies (Zechariah 14:4–9).

The specific location on the mount where Jesus and his disciples retire is called Gethsemane (see Figure 19-1), which means "oil press" and refers to the olive oil production that took place here, from which the mount gets its name. While here, Jesus warns his disciples that they will soon deny him, at which Peter declares, "Even if all these fall away on account of you, I never will" (Matthew 26:33). Jesus replies, "I tell you the truth, this very night, before the rooster crows, you will disown me three times." Jesus then tells his disciples to keep watch while he prays. Shortly after he withdraws to pray, and as a foreshadowing of their impending denial, the disciples all fall asleep.

While on the Mount of Olives, Jesus prays one of his best known, yet least understood, prayers: "Father, if you are willing, take this cup from me. However, not my will, but yours be done" (Luke 22:42). In what sense Jesus' will could be at cross-purposes with his Father's will has been a point of ongoing theological debate. At minimum, Jesus' words intend to communicate his deep anguish at his approaching death. This anguish is further underscored by Jesus' sweating what appear to be "drops of blood." Whether we are to understand this as actual blood mixed with sweat (a condition occurring under severe duress), or as a symbolic way of expressing Jesus' distress, or even as a foreshadowing of his death, is unclear. Today the Church of All Nations on the Mount of Olives marks the traditional location of this event.

Betraying and arresting Jesus

When Jesus returns to his disciples, they are asleep. Waking them, he tells them to prepare for what is to come. No sooner does Jesus speak these words than a crowd approaches with weapons and torches. Among those present are the temple guards, the religious rulers, and last (and arguably least) Judas.

Judas approaches and, in a scene that, despite its familiarity, still startles, he betrays Jesus "with a kiss." Having identified the leader of the "revolution," the guards seize Jesus.

Peter, in an attempt to deliver his master and friend, takes a sword and cuts off the ear of the high priest's servant. Because cutting off an ear is hardly strategic sword play, some have seen in this maneuver the fisherman's lack of skill (though, in defense of Peter, perhaps he meant this as a warning shot).

To prevent further bloodshed, Jesus rebukes Peter, and with him, all who would rush too hastily into armed conflict: "Those who live by the sword will die by the sword" (Matthew 26:52). Then, reminding his disciples who is in ultimate control of the situation, Jesus says, "Don't you know that I could ask my Father, and He would send more than 12 legions of angels on my behalf? But then how would the scriptures be fulfilled that say it must happen this way?" (Matthew 26:53). As a demonstration of Jesus' control over the situation, and to repair the damage done, Jesus heals the servant's ear.

When the disciples realize that Jesus is resigned to being arrested, they flee the scene. In a detail found only in the Gospel of Mark, we are told that a guard seizes the garment of one of Jesus' followers, who then flees, leaving "his tunic behind" (Mark 14:51–52). Mark says that the tunic was all this person was wearing. Thus, one of Jesus' followers was *streakin' in the night*. Given the anonymity and peculiarity of this notice, some have suggested this is an autobiographical comment by the author of the gospel himself: the young John Mark. (As Popeye is fond of saying, "How embarasskin'.")

Going on trial before the religious leaders

Because it is nighttime, Jesus is taken to the home of the High Priest for questioning (see Figure 19-1). During his "deposition," several "witnesses" are produced, but their reports contradict each other, rendering their testimony useless. At this, the high priest asks Jesus a question that, depending on his answer, would be enough to condemn him: "Are you the Messiah, the Son of the Blessed One?" (Mark 14:61).

The term *Blessed One* is a way to refer to God without mentioning His name. This practice, still used by many Jews, ensures that you don't inadvertently violate the biblical commandment against using God's name "in vain."

In one of the few times Jesus actually speaks during his various trials, he says, "I am. And you will see the Son of Man sitting at the right hand of the Mighty One and coming on the clouds of heaven." (During Jesus' day, the title "Son of Man" referred to the Messiah, based on a prediction by the prophet Daniel.) In response to Jesus' words, the High Priest tears his robe as a sign of extreme repudiation, and those present agree that Jesus is worthy of death and begin to beat him.

Some readers mistakenly interpret the religious leaders' beating of Jesus as a childish expression of frustration or anger. However, the Hebrew Bible teaches that, in cases of blasphemy, the guilty party must be stoned. Because the Jews are unable to administer capital punishment under Roman rule, the act of hitting Jesus is a symbolic way of fulfilling the Mosaic Law without violating Roman law.

Listening in on Peter's denial

As Jesus' trial transpires inside, Peter lingers outside in the courtyard of the High Priest. While Peter warms himself by a fire, a servant girl approaches and says she recognizes him as a follower of Jesus. Peter denies any association. Soon others join in the accusation, saying Peter's Galilean accent and appearance give him away as Jesus' follower. Again Peter denies knowing Jesus. Then someone who had been at Jesus' arrest, and who had seen Peter perform his "ear surgery," says he *knows* Peter is Jesus' disciple. At this, Peter calls curses down upon himself and swears he doesn't know Jesus. With this third denial, a rooster crows, fulfilling Jesus' prediction.

According to Luke, Jesus both hears and sees Peter out in the courtyard. When the rooster crows, Luke records that Jesus "turned and looked straight at Peter" (Luke 22:61). The gaze of his friend and the guilt of what he had just done are too much for him to handle, and he flees the courtyard. Finding a solitary place to hide, the text says that Peter "wept bitterly."

Witnessing Judas' suicide

Perhaps one the most captivating scenes in the musical *Jesus Christ Superstar* is Judas Iscariot's suicide and subsequent torment in hell. Actually, the conflicted soul so skillfully portrayed in this musical is not too far from the gospels' own account of Judas's remorse for having betrayed Jesus, who Judas calls "an innocent man." Interestingly, Matthew places Judas's remorse and suicide immediately after Peter's own remorse and weeping, leaving us to contemplate both their similarities and differences — why one "betrayer" would hang himself, and become the epitome of treachery, and the other would live, and become the "rock" upon which the church would be built.

Friday: Jesus' trials and crucifixion

The next morning, Jesus is brought to Pontius Pilate, the Roman-appointed governor of Judea, for trial. Because blasphemy is not a condemnable crime under Roman Law, the chief priests decide to charge Jesus not only with undermining Jewish law but with stirring up a "rebellion." Pilate could not brush aside this latter accusation. It was the Passover, when the streets of Jerusalem were filled with Jewish pilgrims from all over the Roman Empire celebrating how God delivered them from foreign oppression in the exodus, and who had the expectation that God would do it again in the near future by overthrowing the Romans. Such uprisings were not uncommon at Passover, and often resulted in considerable bloodshed.

So Pilate, faced with the problem of Jesus, does what any leader does when a difficult decision needs to be made — he passes the buck.

Questioning Jesus with Herod

Pilate discovers that Jesus is from Galilee, which is Herod Antipas's (Herod the Great's son; see Chapter 18) jurisdiction. Because Herod happens to be in Jerusalem for the Passover, Pilate sends Jesus to him (see Herod Antipas's palace in Figure 19-1).

Herod is extremely pleased to finally meet this wonderworker from Galilee. In fact, Herod asks to see a miracle. Unfortunately for Herod, he falls under the "I-don't-do-miracles-for-people-who-have-no-intention-of-believing-in-me" clause of Jesus' miracle contract. After all, Herod killed John the Baptist, Jesus' relative and the forerunner of his ministry. In addition, Herod had wanted to kill Jesus earlier in his ministry (Luke 13:32).

Seeing that he is not going to get his miracle, Herod mockingly clothes Jesus in a royal robe and sends him back to Pilate. For this act of deference, Herod and Pilate, who had been enemies, become fast friends (Luke 23:12).

Sentencing Jesus with Pilate

Having received no formal charge from Herod, Pilate decides to punish Jesus, and then let him go. However, the religious leaders agitate the crowds to call for Jesus' crucifixion. Whether to placate his own guilt or to provide one more opportunity for Jesus to be released, Pilate offers to set free "a prisoner whom the people requested" — an offer scholars call the *privilegium paschale* ("Passover privilege").

The religious leaders, however, convince the people to ask for the release of a certain Barabbas, who had committed murder during an uprising (Mark 15:7). Pilate gives the crowd what they want. Yet, as a demonstration of his disapproval, he requests that a water basin and towel be brought to him. Placing his hands in the basin of water, he says, "See, I wash my hands of this man's blood." (The modern saying, "I wash my hands of this" to express one's non-involvement in or disapproval of an action comes from this story.) With this said, Barabbas is released, and Jesus is led off to be crucified.

Understanding Jesus' beatings

Prior to his crucifixion, Jesus is taken into the governor's residence, also called the *Praetorium,* to be whipped and beaten — a common precursor to crucifixion. Mocking his claim to be King of the Jews, the Roman soldiers clothe Jesus in purple and place a crown of thorns on his head. Following this, they strike him on the head with a "royal staff" and spit on him, which, beyond its abusive

Who killed Jesus?

Some scholars have argued that the gospels go out of their way to excuse the Romans and implicate the Jews in Jesus' death. This is not entirely correct. The Synoptic Gospels (Matthew, Mark and Luke) actually go out of their way *not* to blame the Jews, but rather the *religious leaders* of the Jews. (After all, nearly all the New Testament writers and most of the early Christians were Jews.) The prophets of the Hebrew Bible often implicated the political and religious leaders of the Israelite community for leading God's people astray, and the New Testament writers do the same. Only the Gospel of John uses the inexact title "the Jews" when describing those opposed to Jesus' teaching and in support of his crucifixion. This language, though not intended by the author of John's Gospel as anti-Semitic, has been used by later anti-Semites to blame the Jews for Jesus' death. (Of course, hatred seeks justification wherever it can find it, even if it means distorting the words of others.)

What is clear — both from the New Testament and our understanding of Roman rule — is that Jesus' execution required Roman sanction, and there is little doubt that they, too, were interested in removing this threat to the Roman peace — no matter how "innocent."

Crucifixion: The most wretched of deaths

Cicero, the first-century-B.C.E. Roman statesman described crucifixion as "that most cruel and disgusting penalty." And Josephus, a first-century C.E. Jewish historian called it "the most wretched of deaths." Despite its wretched nature, crucifixion was practiced widely in the Roman empire. Although most often crucifixion was used in cases of insurrection, rebellion, or murder, "lesser" crimes, such as robbery, could also qualify. Slaves, who had few rights, could be crucified for even the most minor crimes. Conversely, Roman citizens were, except in rare cases, exempt from crucifixion. As Cicero said, "the very word 'cross' should be far removed not only from the person of a Roman citizen but also from his thoughts, eyes, and ears."

At the place of crucifixion, the condemned was stripped and placed on the cross. To transfix the criminal on the cross, ropes and nails were employed. The nails were driven through the victim's hands (or wrists) and feet. Based on the remains of a crucified man discovered in Jerusalem from about the time of Jesus, the nails used measured about 5 inches long.

Sometimes a list of crimes was nailed to the cross. Though worded differently in each gospel, on Jesus' cross was nailed the accusation "Jesus of Nazareth, King of the Jews" — sometimes rendered on depictions of Jesus' cross with the Latin initials INRI or the Greek INBI, such as in this image of the crucified Christ located above the traditional mount of Jesus' crucifixion in Jerusalem's Church of the Holy Sepulcher. (**Note:** The letters below INRI in the picture are the Hebrew initials for the same title.)

intent, mimicks the coronation and anointing of a king. In addition, the soldiers mockingly kneel down before Jesus.

Yet, what the soldiers do in jest, the gospel writers understand to be ironic — they believed Jesus was God's appointed ruler or Messiah, and that one day he would return to earth (after his death and resurrection) to establish God's kingdom.

Witnessing Jesus' crucifixion

After being whipped and beaten, Jesus is led to a hill called Golgotha, meaning "skull" in Aramaic (which in Latin is *calvary*). The mount is so-named because of its head-like shape, though it could also have referred to its status as a place of executions (place of skulls).

It was customary for those heading off to crucifixion to carry a beam of their own cross. Apparently Jesus begins to do so but can't continue because he is weakened from his many beatings. Therefore, the soldiers enlist the help of a certain Simon of Cyrene. Although it's not entirely clear who this is, evidence from the Gospel of Mark suggests that Simon and his family, if not followers of Jesus already, become so after (and perhaps as a result of) Simon's participation in Jesus' crucifixion.

Jesus is led to Golgotha (see Figure 19-1), where he is crucified between the crosses of two thieves. Interestingly, Matthew and Mark present these thieves as joining in mocking Jesus, while Luke reports that one of the thieves rebukes the other for his impiety: "Don't you fear God! . . . We're being punished justly, getting what we deserve. But this man is innocent" (Luke 23:40–41). Then, turning to Jesus, he says, "Remember me when you come in your kingdom." Jesus replies, "I tell you truly, today you will be with me in paradise" (Luke 23:43).

Luke's mention of the repentant thief fits well with his theme that Jesus is the savior of the world, no matter what your background or criminal record.

According to both Matthew and Mark, as Jesus hangs on the cross he shouts, "My God, My God! Why have you forsaken me?" (Matthew 27:46; Mark 15:34). Theologians have long queried over this statement. What does Jesus mean by saying that God abandons him? At minimum, Jesus' statement is intended to fulfill Psalm 22, which Jesus is quoting, and which the New Testament writers believed was a prediction of the Messiah's suffering. In addition, Jesus' words communicate his deep anguish while on the cross. Finally, some theologians have suggested that Jesus really is "forsaken" by his Father, because, when Jesus dies, he takes upon himself the sins of the world, requiring a holy God to remove Himself or turn away

Perhaps Jesus' most penetrating statement on the cross is his prayer for his executioners, "Forgive them Father, for they know not what they do" (Luke 23:34). Then, just before his death, Jesus cries out, "Father, into Your hands I commit my spirit!" (Luke 23:46). With these words, Jesus "breathed his last."

Joseph of Arimethea and the Holy Grail

According to later Medieval lore, Joseph of Arimethea was also the keeper of the Holy Grail, the name later applied to the cup used by Jesus at the Last Supper. According to these traditions, Joseph caught some of Jesus' blood in this cup, and anyone who drinks from the Holy Grail would live forever. Although scholars once dismissed these stories as useless fairy tales, we now know, thanks to Monty Python's *In Search of the Holy Grail* and *Indiana Jones and The Last Crusade,* that these stories are *not* useless, but rather make for pretty good movie scripts.

Jesus' burial

After Jesus' death, his body is taken off the cross to be buried. Once removed, a man named Joseph of Arimethea comes to Pilate to ask for the body. This is a bold move on Joseph's part, because he is a member of the Jewish Council of Elders (also known as the Sanhedrin), the majority of whom wanted Jesus executed. Joseph's actions publicly identify him as sympathetic to Jesus' cause, if not one of his followers, putting him at odds with his peers.

Joining Joseph in preparing Jesus' body for burial is another member of the Sanhedrin, Nicodemus, who early in Jesus' ministry asked him what one must do to enter the Kingdom of God (John 3). Jesus' answer, that a person must be spiritually "born again," has given us the term *born again Christian.*

After wrapping Jesus in linens and spices (to lessen the inevitable stench of the decaying body), Joseph and Nicodemus place Jesus' body in Joseph's new rock-hewn tomb. That Jesus dies as a common criminal, but is buried in so rich a grave, was understood by the early Christians to fulfill a prediction made by the prophet Isaiah:

> *He was assigned a grave with the wicked, but with the rich in his death.*
>
> —Isaiah 53:9

Jesus' Resurrection

Jesus' death catches the disciples completely off-guard. After all, they were convinced he was the Messiah, the invincible "son of David" and "Son of God," who would deliver Israel from its enemies and establish God's kingdom on earth. Even at the Last Supper the disciples were jockeying for position to see who among them would be "first" in the Kingdom of God. But now their hope for the future, as well as their friend, is lying dead in a tomb.

Three days later, the disciples are still struggling to understand Jesus' death when some women, who had visited the tomb earlier that day, report that Jesus is alive. According to the women, an angel announced Jesus' resurrection:

> *Why do you look for the living among the dead? He is not here. He is risen!*
>
> —Luke 24:5–6

Rather than rejoice at the women's report, the disciples refuse to believe it, not because it comes from the women (as some have suggested), but because "their words seemed like nonsense to them" (Luke 24:11). Despite their disbelief, two of the disciples — Peter and John — quickly set out for the tomb. John even tells us (twice!) that he outran Peter to the tomb (though, he admits Peter entered first). They, like the women, also find the tomb empty, and leave wondering what this all might mean.

The day of Jesus' resurrection is called Easter. However, you won't find this name in the Bible because it belongs to a pagan fertility goddess, whose springtime festivals were eventually displaced by Christian celebrations of Jesus' resurrection. (See Chapter 27 for more on the celebration of Easter.)

Although it is difficult to present a unified chronology of Jesus' "post-resurrection appearances," a general outline emerges in the gospel accounts.

- ✔ **Mary Magdalene (John 20:10–18):** Jesus first appears to Mary Magdalene, from whom he had earlier cast out seven demons. That Jesus would first appear to a woman emphasizes the importance of women to his ministry. Some interpreters have even argued that Jesus' appearance to Mary testifies to the authenticity of this event, since a woman's testimony typically had less value in Jewish or Roman legal contexts.

- ✔ **Two men and the disciples (Luke 24:13–49; 20:19–25):** On the same day, Jesus appears to two men traveling along a road to Emmaus, a village about 7 miles northwest of Jerusalem. The two men quickly return to Jerusalem, where they tell the disciples about what they saw. While they are still speaking, Jesus himself suddenly appears, saying "Peace be with you." Jesus goes on to explain that his death "fulfilled what was written . . . in the Law of Moses, the Prophets and the Psalms." The Messiah had to be killed, according to Jesus, in order to provide for the forgiveness of sins.

- ✔ **Doubting Thomas (John 20:26–31):** According to John, a week later Jesus makes his famed appearance to "Doubting Thomas," who would not believe "unless I see the nail wounds in his hands and put my finger where the nails were and my hand into his side" (John 20:25). With the doors locked, Jesus enters the room and again says, "Peace be with you." Then turning to Thomas, Jesus invites him to place his finger and hands in his wounds. Thomas does, and he is doubting no longer. Jesus then says, "You believe because you have seen me. Blessed are those who have not seen me and yet believe" (John 21:29).

✔ **The disciples in Galilee (John 21:1–23):** Jesus appears to his disciples again in Galilee, where he had spent so much time with them in "the early days." On one occasion, the disciples are fishing, but catch nothing. A stranger on the shore tells them to throw their nets on the other side of the boat. They do and catch so many fish they don't know what to do . . . except for Peter, that is. Realizing that the stranger is Jesus, Peter jumps into the water and swims to shore. This account provides a fitting conclusion to Jesus' interactions with his disciples, because it was in the context of another miraculous catch of fish that Jesus first called his disciples to be fishers of men (Luke 5:1–11).

The Great Commission and Ascension

While still in Galilee, the disciples gather one last time "on the mountain where Jesus told them to go." Though the text does not say explicitly, this seems to be the same mountain upon which Jesus gave his first discourse: The Sermon on the Mount. It is on this mount that Jesus gives another discourse — his last, known as The Great Commission:

> *All authority has been given to me in heaven and on earth. Go, therefore, and make disciples of all nations, baptizing them in the name of the Father, the Son, and the Holy Spirit, and teaching them to obey everything I have commanded you. And, lo, I am with you always, even to the end of the age.*

> —Matthew 28:18–20

The fact that Christian communities could be found throughout much of the Roman Empire by the end of the first century testifies to the seriousness with which the disciples took Jesus' words.

Jesus remains with his disciples for 40 days after his resurrection, appearing, according to one New Testament source, to as many as 500 people. Then, in an event known as the Ascension, Jesus ascends into heaven as his disciples look on — but not before promising them that he will one day return, not as a baby, but "with power" to establish God's Kingdom on earth. At that time, God's will really will be done "on earth as it is in heaven."

Chapter 20

The Early Christian Church (Acts 1–8, 10–12, and 15)

*Y*ou may be old enough to remember the Jesus Freaks. As a product of the hippie culture, this movement was characterized by being "high" on Jesus.

Well, it may surprise you to find out that the Jesus Freaks of the hippie era were not the first Jesus Freaks. Yes, they were the first to be called Jesus Freaks, but nearly 2,000 years before them there was a group who, like them, couldn't stop talking about, praying to, and singing about Jesus. Only this wasn't a mere fad. When the Book of Acts opens, there are a little over 100 followers of *the Way* (as Christianity is first called). By the end of Acts, there are thousands of Christians spanning from Judea, the birthplace of this movement, to Rome, and beyond.

So how is it that this small movement, begun by an itinerant preacher from the "backwaters" of the Roman Empire, could eventually grow into a worldwide movement?

In this chapter, you trace the growth of early Christianity, from its humble beginnings on the Jewish holiday of Pentecost to its inclusion of the first gentile converts — after which it was just a matter of time before it could be found everywhere.

"Mission Impossible": Jesus' Strategy to Change the World

When the Book of Acts opens, Jesus has been with his followers for 40 days since his resurrection. (For details about the resurrection, see Chapter 19.) During this time, Jesus "gave his disciples many convincing proofs that he was alive . . . and spoke to them about the kingdom of heaven" (Acts 1:3). Now it is time for Jesus to ascend to heaven. But before Jesus leaves, he gives his followers a "Mission Impossible."

Jesus tells his disciples to be his witnesses "in Jerusalem, in all Judea and Samaria, and to the uttermost parts of the world" (Acts 1:8). This three-tiered commission provides the structure for the Book of Acts, as well as the outline for the growth of early Christianity.

The word *witness,* similar to the legal definition, means "to testify." Yet, because many early Christians experienced severe persecution for their testimony about Jesus, the Greek word for witness — *martyros* (English "martyr") — has come to denote someone who dies for his or her beliefs.

Witnessing In Jerusalem

The disciples cannot carry out their mission of spreading Jesus' message to the ends of the earth without serious help. Therefore, Jesus instructs his disciples to stay in Jerusalem until they receive "power" from God. This "power" is God's Holy Spirit, whom Jesus says will come "after I go away." In a motif later borrowed by George Lucas for his *Star Wars* films, the early Christians can't experience the full power of "the force" (only here it is "The Force") until the master departs. Thus, after Jesus ascends into heaven, the disciples wait for the promised Holy Spirit.

Pentecost: The birthday of the church

Pentecost is considered the "birthday of the church" in Christian liturgy, and some churches are called "Pentecostal" for their emphasis on the role of the Holy Spirit in the life of a Christian. Yet, many Christians don't realize that Pentecost is a Jewish holiday. Pentecost (or Shavuot, as it is called in Hebrew) is an agricultural festival that occurs 50 days (Pentecost is Greek for 50) after the Passover. Because Pentecost is one of the three pilgrimage feasts incumbent on all Jewish adult males, the streets of Jerusalem in antiquity were full to overflowing with people from all over the Roman Empire — the perfect setting for initiating a new movement.

The coming of the Holy Spirit (Acts 2)

On the first day of *Pentecost* (described in the sidebar "Pentecost: The birthday of the church" in this chapter), the disciples are praying in "an upper room" — the same upper room, it is thought, where Jesus and his disciples celebrated their last Passover together (also called the Last Supper, which is covered in Chapter 19). While the disciples are praying, a noise like a rushing wind fills the house, and flames of fire separate and rest on each of them (Acts 2:2–3). Although you should normally call 911 in such circumstances, in this particular case the fire falling on the disciples is none other than the promised Holy Spirit.

The imagery of fire alighting upon an individual's head, while perhaps seeming strange today, signified divine blessing in the Roman world. Moreover, this particular fire seems to recall the words spoken by John the Baptist, "I baptize you with water, but one will come who is greater than I, and he will baptize you with the Holy Spirit and with fire" (Luke 3:16).

The coming of the Holy Spirit has an amazing effect on the disciples — they begin speaking in a wide variety of languages. When they make their way outside, people gather in amazement. Some, however, are not impressed. They've seen this behavior before. "These people have had too much wine!" they shout. Peter's response seems to be both an answer to their accusation and an attempt at humor:

> *These people are not drunk, as you think. It's only nine in the morning!*
>
> —Acts 2:15

Peter says, in effect, "How can we be drunk? The bars are closed!" He then goes on to explain that what the people are witnessing is the fulfillment of a prophecy made long ago by the prophet Joel:

> *In the last days I will pour out my spirit on all people, declares God. Your sons and your daughters will prophesy, your young men will see visions and your old men will dream dreams.*
>
> —Joel 2:28

Peter continues by explaining that this miracle shows that Jesus was, and is, God's promised Messiah, and that his death on the cross was part of God's preordained plan to deliver Israel — not politically (though that would come), but personally, by providing for the forgiveness of sins. Jesus' resurrection, Peter continues, demonstrates that he is "both Lord and Christ" (Acts 2:36). Many of those listening to Peter's message believe, and "about 3,000 were added to their numbers." A movement is born.

The disciples go to jail (Acts 3–4:31, 5:12–42)

As Christianity grows so does the opposition against it. The first to experience this opposition are Peter and John, two of Jesus' closest disciples. As they approach the Temple to pray, a crippled man at the entrance to the Temple courts asks them for money. Peter's response may sound familiar to you: "I don't have any." But Peter, being a follower of Jesus, is not lying — and for this, the crippled man is extremely glad, as Peter continues, "But what I do have I give to you. In the name of Jesus Christ of Nazareth, walk!" Then, helping the man to his feet, Peter and John enter the Temple courts with their newfound friend.

Peter's polished prose: The fisherman preaches in the Temple

Once in the courts, and in further demonstration of the extent of his healing, the man begins "*jumping* and praising God" (Acts 3:8). Soon a crowd gathers, and Peter begins declaring the "good news" about Jesus. And for an uneducated fisherman, Peter's sermon is a literary masterpiece, marked by clever turns of phrases ("you killed the author of life") and extraordinary irony ("you disowned the holy and righteous one, and asked for a murderer in his place"). Yet, Peter is not allowed to see the impact of his sermon, as the religious authorities enter the Temple courts and arrest him and John.

The religious authorities are understandably concerned about Peter's and John's activities for two reasons:

- ✔ First, Peter and John are followers of a man who had been tried and condemned as a heretic and revolutionary. Continuing to promote his ideas could stir up the masses and was a direct violation of Roman law.

- ✔ Second, Peter and John had no religious authority or training. They were fishermen, and their teaching was viewed as undermining Mosaic Law.

Thus, the religious authorities insist that the disciples stop speaking in the name of Jesus. Peter and John, however, say they obey a higher authority:

> *Whether it is right in God's eyes to obey you rather than God, judge for yourselves. But we cannot help speaking about what we have seen and heard.*

—Acts 4:19–20

Although the New Testament teaches that one should obey governing authorities (Romans 13:1–7), Peter's and John's remarks suggest that "civil disobedience" in matters of conscience is acceptable. Subsequent Christian activists, such as Martin Luther King, Jr., understood the Bible to sanction such disobedience — and they have done remarkable good by their actions.

Religious toleration: The disciples are rescued by a moderate

Because Peter and John had done nothing wrong (quite the contrary, they healed a man) they are released, but they are also given a stern warning not to preach anymore about Jesus. But, as promised, they do, and soon they are rearrested (repeat offenders were a problem in the ancient world as well). As before, Peter insists that they cannot go against their conscience and be silent about Jesus. Incensed at Peter's stubbornness, some of those present want to execute Peter and his associates. But then a more sober voice speaks up:

> *Leave these men alone, and let them go. If what they are doing is of human origin, then it will fail. But if it is of divine origin, then you won't be able to stop them — you will even find yourselves fighting against God!*

> —Acts 5:38–39

According to the Book of Acts, these words come from one of the most esteemed rabbis of the first century, Gamaliel, about whom later Jewish tradition would say: "When Gamaliel died, the glory of the Law also died." Thankfully for the disciples, Gamaliel's moderate views win the day, and the disciples, after being flogged, are allowed to leave on their own recognizance.

Giving it up for God: Life together in the early church (Acts 4:32–6:7)

Despite external threats, "the church" (as Christianity comes to be called) continues to experience amazing growth.

The word *church* comes from the Greek term *ekklesia*, which simply means "an assembly" or "a gathering." (The word *ecclesiastical*, which means "relating to the church," comes from this same Greek word.) Christian gatherings in the first century C.E. met together in homes or public places for encouragement, prayer, instruction in the Scriptures, and shared meals (Acts 2:42). The practice of meeting in an official church building only developed gradually, and did not become widespread until Christianity was made an official religion of the Roman Empire in the fourth century C.E. under Emperor Constantine.

Ancient communism and the early church

Because many of those making up the early church have come from distant lands to celebrate the Pentecost and now unexpectedly find themselves staying over in Jerusalem as part of this new movement, they run out of resources. In response, those who have plenty begin giving what they have in order to help those with little or nothing. Soon everyone is "sharing everything in common" (Acts 2:44) — a sort of "Christian communism," if you will.

Later proponents of communism would appeal to the case of "Christian communism" in Acts 5 as evidence that this is God's intended model for the human community. (Ironically, some of these same proponents had little use for religion, as it was "the opiate of the masses" — a true case of having your cake and eating it, too.)

Lying in the name of religion: Ananias and Saphira lie and die

Several of the more wealthy Christians decide to sell their property to supply for the needs of this growing movement. One such couple, Ananias and Saphira, sell some property, and then Ananias brings the money to Peter for distribution. Instead of saying "Thank you," Peter asks, "Is this all you received from the sale of your property?" Ananias says yes. But it isn't. In response, Peter says, "You have not lied to a human, but to the Holy Spirit." And with this, Ananias falls dead. A few hours later, Saphira, who is unaware of her husband's demise, also comes into the room. Peter asks, "Is this the full amount you received from the sale of your property?" (Don't say yes! Don't say yes!) Saphira replies, "It is." (Uh-oh.) Peter retorts, "Behold, the feet of those who buried your husband are standing at the door to bury you." And with this, Saphira falls dead at Peter's feet.

The passage recounting Ananias's and Saphira's deaths is disturbing and perplexing. But it does follow a pattern seen elsewhere in the Bible: God deals more severely with rebellion and wrongdoing when He is initiating a new movement. For example, when Israel is delivered from slavery under Moses (see Chapter 7), and God's presence is manifest among the Israelites in the pillar of fire and smoke, God deals with the people's wrongdoing immediately. In the case of the early church, God's presence is made visibly manifest through the Holy Spirit, and Peter is God's ordained leader. For Ananias and Saphira to lie to Peter is an affront to his and, by implication, God's authority. And the point is well taken, as "great fear seized the whole church and those who heard about these things" (Acts 5:11).

Learning to share: "The Twelve" delegate to "the Seven"

Another internal problem encountered by the early Christians is the fair distribution of food. Apparently the early church, like many organizations, had its share of discrimination, and in the present case the Jews from Judea are given the lion's share of food, while their fellow Jews from abroad are short-changed. At first, the disciples take care of the problem themselves. However, soon their other duties of preaching and teaching begin to suffer.

To solve the problem, the disciples select seven individuals "full of the Spirit and wisdom" to look after the administrative concerns of the church. These become known as "the Seven" (as compared to "the Twelve," which refers to Jesus' original twelve disciples, who, though losing Judas, are again "Twelve," having replaced Judas with a certain Matthias; see Acts 1). "The Seven" are not merely good administrators; they are gifted speakers. And it is when one of these "Seven" — Stephen — begins to speak that we witness the first martyr of the church in the modern sense of the word.

Witnessing In Judea and Samaria

While defending the claim that Jesus is the fulfillment of the Hebrew Bible's prophecies about the Messiah, Stephen, one of the seven church administrators appointed by the disciples, offends a group belonging to "the Synagogue of the Freedmen."

Freedmen are former slaves, and the "Synagogue" being referred to here is not a physical building, but an association of individuals from throughout the Roman Empire who had the shared experience of being former slaves.

These influential individuals accuse Stephen of "speaking blasphemy against Moses and God" — the same charges brought against Jesus just before his execution. And Stephen would soon meet a similar fate. However, his death would propel Christianity from Jerusalem "to all Judea and Samaria" as Jesus had commissioned.

Winning enemies and influencing people: Stephen on trial (Acts 6:8–8:2)

As a result of Stephen's "blasphemy," the members of the Synagogue of the Freedmen bring him before the religious authorities, where he is given the opportunity to defend his teachings. Stephen's discourse is rather remarkable, giving, in relatively short order, a history of the Jews from Moses to Jesus (Acts 7). The point of Stephen's history lesson is to demonstrate that the religious authorities in his day are no different than their ancestors who similarly rebelled against God. Stephen's primary example is the Israelites of the exodus (see Chapter 7 for information about the exodus), who rebelled against God even though He had delivered them from slavery. Stephen concludes his defense with a statement that was sure to offend:

> *You stiff-necked people with uncircumcised hearts and ears! You are just like your ancestors! You always resist the Holy Spirit. Was there ever a prophet whom your ancestors did not persecute? They even killed those who predicted the coming of the righteous one. And now you have betrayed him and had him killed.*
>
> —Acts 7:51–52

With this said, the religious authorities become enraged and seize Stephen, dragging him outside the city to stone him — the requisite penalty for anyone guilty of blasphemy according to the Law of Moses. As Stephen dies, his final words echo those of Jesus, who also died outside the city, and perhaps in this same location:

Lord, do not hold this sin against them.

—Acts 7:60

With these parting words, Stephen, the church's first martyr, dies.

In the wake of Stephen's death, a massive persecution breaks out against the church, and those initially content to stay in Jerusalem soon find themselves fleeing for their lives. But as they flee, far from being silenced, they take the message of Jesus with them wherever they go. Thus, the death of Stephen has the opposite effect intended by his executioners, as soon this movement, that had been relatively localized to Jerusalem, spreads "throughout Judea and Samaria" (Acts 8:1) — thus fulfilling Jesus' final commission (Acts 1:8).

Breaking down the walls that divide: Philip with foreigners (Acts 8:3–40)

Among those fleeing Jerusalem after Stephen's death is a man named Philip, who, like Stephen, is one of "the Seven." Therefore, it is somewhat fitting that just as Stephen gives the church its first martyr, so Philip gives the church its first non-Jewish converts.

Infiltrating enemy territory: Philip in Samaria

As described in Chapter 19, the Samaritans and Jews had a long history of ethnic and ideological differences that sometimes resulted in actual violence. Despite this problematic history, the early church had the example of Jesus, who not only interacted with Samaritans (something most Jews refused to do) but also incorporated them into his teaching on the Kingdom of God. Most famous among Jesus' teachings was his parable of the "Good Samaritan," who, defying racial and religious barriers, helped a distressed and dying Jew,

---

Corruption in the Church: Simon Magus and the purchase of church offices

Among the Samaritans who believe in Philip's message is a certain Simon Magus, a magician who astonished people with his magical arts. But when Simon Magus sees Peter's ability to impart the Holy Spirit on those whom he touches, Simon wants this power for himself and offers to pay Peter money for the privilege.

Peter is not amused, and declares, "May your silver perish with you, since you thought you could purchase the gift of God with money" (Acts 8:20). From this episode comes the word *simony*, which describes the practice of purchasing church offices.

ultimately saving his life. With Jesus as his model, Philip begins preaching to the Samaritans he encounters while fleeing the persecution in Jerusalem. And, as in the case of Jesus, many Samaritans believe Philip's message. When the leaders of the Jerusalem church hear that the Samaritans have believed, they journey north and enter this former "enemy territory." Upon seeing the Samaritan's faith, the disciples lay their hands on them to give the Samaritans the Holy Spirit.

Running with chariots: Philip and the Ethiopian eunuch

Philip does not end his international outreach with the Samaritans. After leaving Samaria, he encounters the chariot of an Ethiopian royal official. In demonstration of Philip's enthusiasm to spread the gospel, as well as his athletic ability, he begins running alongside the chariot. The Ethiopian, as it turns out, is reading from the scroll of Isaiah, and in particular the Suffering Servant Song of Isaiah 53 (see Chapter 13). Philip asks the Ethiopian if he understands what he is reading. "How can I unless someone teaches me?" With this invitation, Philip climbs onto the chariot, and explains to the Ethiopian "the good news about Jesus." When Philip finishes, the Ethiopian asks if he, too, can become a follower of this Jesus. Requesting that the chariot stop, both the Ethiopian and Philip descend from the chariot and Philip baptizes the Ethiopian as a Christian.

At this, something very peculiar happens — peculiar even for the Bible. The text records that as the Ethiopian came out of the water, "suddenly the Spirit took Philip away . . . and he appeared in Azotus." That's right, Philip is miraculously "transported" from one location to another. (*The X Files* got it right — the truth *is* out there.) Philip then continues northward along the coast to Caesarea, the Roman capital of the region.

Although Philip is not mentioned again until the closing chapters of Acts, he sets in motion the fulfillment of Jesus' commission to declare his message "to the uttermost parts of the world." In fact, the Ethiopian eunuch whom Philip introduces to Christianity would, according to later church tradition, be responsible for the spread of Christianity to Ethiopia and broader Africa.

Witnessing In the Uttermost Parts of the World

As Christianity grows over the next several years, the church leaders in Jerusalem find themselves traveling throughout Judea and Samaria in order to encourage those who are becoming Christians. While on one of these trips, the apostle Peter has an experience that changes the course and character of this new movement forever.

New horizons: The incorporation of gentiles into Christianity (Acts 10–11)

Yes, you read that title correctly. Although it is hard for us to imagine in our current religious climate, at one time nearly all Christians were Jews. In fact, it was with great hesitation and reluctance that the early Jewish Christians allowed gentiles into this movement. Here's the story.

Peter's "foreign assignment"

While checking on the welfare of those who had recently become followers of Jesus in various parts of Judea, Peter finds himself at the coastal city of Joppa (modern-day Jaffa), which was the traditional site of Jonah's attempted escape from God after God told him to preach to Nineveh (see Chapter 13). It is fitting, then, that while here Peter is given a similar "foreign assignment."

While in Joppa, Peter stays at the house of a man named Simon the Tanner (a reference to his profession of tanning and treating leather goods). Just before lunchtime, Peter goes on top of the roof to pray. As he is praying, he falls into a trance (perhaps you've experienced something similar just before lunch). While in this trance, Peter sees a vision: A sheet descending from heaven carrying all kinds of unkosher insects and animals (see Chapter 7 for more information about kosher foods). As he is looking at these creatures, a voice from heaven calls out, "Get up, Peter! Kill and eat!" Peter has eaten only kosher foods all his life, and he is not about to give it up now, even though "he was hungry and wanted something to eat." Not taking "no" for an answer, the voice from heaven declares, "Do not call anything unclean that God has made clean." This happens three times, and each time Peter refuses to eat, and each time the voice declares that what God has made clean is now clean.

Engaging the enemy: Peter associates with gentiles

While Peter is pondering what this midday matinee could mean, he receives word that there are visitors outside waiting to see him. When Peter comes down to meet them, he sees that they are gentiles. He then learns that they have been sent from Caesarea by a Roman centurion named Cornelius. Cornelius wants to see Peter — not to arrest him, but to speak with him. Although under normal circumstances it was against Jewish law "to associate with a gentile or to visit him," (as Peter says, apparently referring to the Jewish prohibition against coming in contact with anything or anyone unclean or ritually impure), these are not "normal" circumstances. First of all, this is not an ordinary gentile, but one who "feared God and was respected by all the Jews." In addition, Peter is no ordinary Jew, but one who had the example of Jesus, who openly accepted and performed miracles for gentiles, including a Roman centurion. Finally, Peter just had a vision that further expanded his definitions of what was "clean" (acceptable for a Jew). So Peter invites these men to stay the night, and agrees to join them on their return journey to Caesarea the next day.

No longer "members only": Gentiles are allowed in the club

The next morning Peter and his companions make the approximately 30-mile journey from Joppa to Caesarea and arrive at Cornelius's house. When Peter enters, he finds a whole entourage of Cornelius's family and friends waiting to hear what Peter has to say. Ironically, Peter doesn't know what to say, and so he asks Cornelius why he has sent for him. Cornelius tells Peter that a few days earlier an angel appeared to him telling him that God has heard his prayers and has taken note of his acts of charity. Therefore, he should call for a man named Peter who is staying in Joppa. Peter, now realizing why he is here, declares, "Now I know that God does not show partiality but accepts people from every nation who fear him and do what is right" (Acts 10:35). Peter goes on to describe the meaning of Jesus' life, death, and resurrection, and how "everyone who believes in Jesus receives forgiveness of sins." Interestingly, Peter had said these very same words earlier to a Jewish audience. Only when he said "everyone," he meant "every Jew." Now when Peter says "everyone," he means *everyone*.

God's seal of approval: The gentiles receive the Holy Spirit

When Peter concludes his message, suddenly the Holy Spirit descends upon Cornelius and his guests, and they begin to speak in various languages as the disciples did on the day of Pentecost. This demonstrates that they, too, are equal participants in the Kingdom of God.

When Peter and his companions return to Jerusalem to inform the church that the gentiles have also believed in the gospel, the church leaders are outraged: "You went into the house of a gentile and ate with him!?!" They apparently cared more about Peter's ritual purity than the gentile's spiritual well-being. Yet, when Peter relays to them his vision and how the gentiles also received the Holy Spirit, their anger turns to joy, as they realize that "God has even granted to the gentiles the repentance that leads to eternal life" (Acts 11:18).

The first church council (Acts 15)

Although the Jewish Christians agreed that gentiles should be accepted as fellow Christians, there is still a serious question that needs to be answered.

The Jews had long considered themselves God's "chosen people." With this privilege came certain responsibilities, including fulfilling the Mosaic Laws (see Chapter 7). So the question was, "Do the gentiles who are coming to faith in Jesus as the Messiah need to fulfill the Mosaic Law?" Many of the Jewish Christians believe that the gentiles do, even saying that it is necessary for them to be circumcised in order to be saved. Others, however, feel that Jesus' death on the cross satisfied all the requirements of the Law, and that faith in Jesus is all that is necessary for salvation. In order to resolve these disagreements, the church calls together its first council.

People speak out on both sides of the issue. After some rather heated debate, Peter stands up and describes how God demonstrated His acceptance of the gentiles apart from their fulfilling the Mosaic Law. Peter concludes, "If God has accepted the gentiles, who are we to place a greater burden on them?" At this, others speak in defense of Peter's point, providing evidence from the Hebrew Bible that gentiles have always been part of God's plan of blessing and salvation.

James, the leader of the Jerusalem church and the "brother" of Jesus himself (see Chapter 18), along with the rest of the council, concludes that the gentiles do not have to fulfill the Mosaic Law in order to be accepted by God, and a letter to this effect is drafted to be distributed to all the churches.

The council's decision that gentiles are now full and equal members in God's plan of salvation changes the character of Christianity forever. No longer is Christianity only a sect within Judaism, but it is an inclusive movement where, as one New Testament writer puts it, "there is neither Jew nor gentile, slave nor free, male nor female" (Galatians 3:28). This inclusiveness helps ensure that Christianity will one day displace the religions of Rome.

Peter's narrow escape and disappearance

Peter's last appearance in the Book of Acts (aside from the church council mentioned in Acts 15) occurs in Acts 12, where he and James (one of Jesus' twelve disciples and *not* the James who is Jesus' "brother" and the leader of the Jerusalem church) are arrested and thrown into jail by Herod Agrippa I (Herod the Great's grandson). James is executed, making him the first of Jesus' disciples to be martyred.

Seeing that James' death pleased those opposed to Christianity, Herod determines to kill Peter as well. However, an angel appears to Peter the night before his execution and helps him escape from jail. After Peter presents himself to the Christians praying for his release, the text reports that Peter "left for another place"

(Acts 12:17). And that's it. So what happened to Peter? Beyond the two letters in the New Testament bearing Peter's name, he is mentioned only a few other times in the New Testament (see, for example, Galatians 2:11–21, where the apostle Paul confronts Peter for being a hypocrite!). According to church tradition, Peter plays an important part in spreading the gospel throughout the Roman Empire, and then eventually ends up in Rome, where he is martyred by the Emperor Nero (around 64 to 68 C.E.). According to these same traditions, Peter was crucified upside-down, because he did not feel himself worthy to die in the same manner as his Lord, Jesus.

Chapter 21

The Traveling Salesman of Tarsus: Paul's Life and Letters

In This Chapter

▶ Witnessing Paul's transformation from Christian persecutor to persecuted Christian

▶ Traveling with Paul around the Mediterranean on his missionary journeys

▶ Reading (and understanding) Paul's letters

C hristianity's spread "to the uttermost parts of the world" was due in large part to a man named Paul. This is extraordinary since when we first meet Paul he is vigorously persecuting Christians in order to stop this "heresy" from spreading. Then, unexpectedly, he changes from the movement's chief persecutor to its chief proponent, and through his influential missionary journeys and letter writing Christianity is transformed from a Jewish sect into a worldwide movement. In this chapter, you explore Paul's life and writings to see what about him made such an impact on his world . . . and ours.

From Persecutor to Persecuted: Paul's Transformation

When we first encounter Paul (or "Saul," as he is first called; see "Paul's First Missionary Journey" later in this chapter for why his name is changed), he's at the execution of Christianity's first martyr, Stephen:

> *[Stephen's accusers] rushed at him and dragged him out of the city, where they began to stone him. Those present laid their garments at the feet of a young man named Saul . . . and Saul was giving approval to Stephen's death.*
>
> —Acts 7:57-58; 8:1

Paul's life before his conversion

Paul was born in Tarsus, a city in eastern Asia Minor (modern-day Turkey) and one of the intellectual centers of the Roman Empire. Though Jewish, Paul was also a Roman citizen, a status that afforded him tremendous rights and privileges, including the right to trial before being tortured or imprisoned, as well as the right to appeal "lower court" decisions to the highest court in the Empire: the emperor himself.

Although born in Tarsus, Paul was raised and educated in Jerusalem, where he studied under the leading rabbi of his day: Gamaliel. As an indication of Gamaliel's influence, in the book of Acts he talks his colleagues out of executing Christians. Paul, however, didn't share his teacher's moderate views. As Paul describes it: "I put many [Christians] in prison, and when they were put to death, I cast my vote against them" (Acts 26:10). With similar zeal, Paul gained the respect of his contemporaries. Yet, while climbing this ladder of success, the ladder toppled, and Paul was never the same.

The act of laying garments at another's feet is a sign of honor and indicates that Paul is overseeing not the coatroom but Stephen's execution. Confirming this are Paul's actions following Stephen's death:

> *Saul set out to destroy the church, going from house to house, where he dragged men and women off to prison.*

—Acts 8:3

Eventually Paul heads toward Damascus, a leading city of the eastern Roman Empire, to arrest the followers of "this Way," as Christianity is first called (its followers aren't called Christians until around 40 C.E. — see Acts 11:26). On the way, he has a life-changing experience.

A Damascus Road experience: Paul's conversion and commission (Acts 9:1–19)

We say someone has had a "Damascus Road experience" when an event completely changes his or her perspective on life. Paul has one of these. In fact, he has the first and most dramatic of all Damascus Road experiences.

As Paul and his companions approach Damascus to apprehend Christians, a blinding light surrounds them and Paul falls to the ground. He then hears a voice: "Saul, Saul, why are you persecuting me?" (Acts 9:4). "Who are you, Lord?" Paul asks. The voice replies, "I am Jesus, whom you are persecuting." This answer would have been more shocking than the phenomena surrounding it, since Paul believed he was defending God in his efforts to stamp out the movement founded on Jesus' life and teachings. Here Jesus says that his efforts are accomplishing the exact opposite. When the light departs, Paul, now blind, is led by his companions into Damascus.

In Damascus, Paul has a vision that a man named Ananias will heal him of his blindness and tell him what to do next. Meanwhile, in another part of town, Ananias receives a similar vision in which God tells him to find Paul and lay his hands on him to restore his sight. Ananias, a Christian, protests, saying he has heard about Paul and his efforts to arrest Christians. God's response both allays Ananias' fears and informs him (and the reader) of Paul's future:

> Go! This man is My chosen instrument to bear My name to the Gentiles and their kings, and the people of Israel. I will show him how much he must suffer for My name.

> —Acts 9:15–16

Ananias does as God commands, healing Paul "in the name of Jesus." Paul is then baptized as a sign of his identification with this new movement.

Man on the run: Paul escapes Damascus and Jerusalem (Acts 9:20–31)

Paul soon begins preaching in the synagogues of Damascus that "Jesus is the Son of God." The people are shocked: "Was this not the man who raised trouble in Jerusalem for those who called on this name?" Shock soon turns to anger, as many believe Paul is committing blasphemy (speaking falsehoods about God). Some even conspire to kill Paul, and a 24-hour watch is posted at the city gates to ensure that he doesn't escape the city. With his life in danger, some Christians lower Paul in a basket from the city wall at night.

Paul eventually makes his way to Jerusalem, where he presents himself to the church leaders as a recent convert. However, they think Paul's supposed conversion is a trick to gain information in his efforts to destroy the church. One disciple, though, is willing to take a chance on Paul. His name is Barnabas, a name that, appropriately enough, means "son of encouragement." Barnabas eventually convinces the apostles that Paul's conversion is genuine, and Paul, the one-time persecutor of the church, is now accepted as a member.

Once word gets out that Paul has become a follower of "this Way," his former allies become his enemies and he is forced to flee Jerusalem. This is only the beginning of Paul's troubles. Throughout his three-decades- long adventure as a representative of Christianity, he experiences many other close calls. In one of his letters, he tells of the many trials he has endured:

> *Five times I received from the Jews the forty lashes minus one. Three times I was beaten with rods. Once I received a stoning. Three times I was shipwrecked; for a night and a day I was adrift at sea; on frequent journeys, in danger from rivers, from bandits, from my own people, from Gentiles, in the city, in the wilderness, at sea, from false brothers and sisters; in toil and hardship, through many a sleepless night, hungry and thirsty, often without food, cold and naked. And, besides other things, I am under daily pressure because of my anxiety for all the churches.*
>
> —2 Corinthians 11:24–28

Paul certainly did learn how much he must suffer for the sake of Christianity.

1 Get Around: Paul's Missionary Journeys

The context for much of Paul's suffering is his several missionary journeys. On these journeys, Paul travels extensively throughout the Mediterranean region, including Syria-Palestine (modern-day Syria, Lebanon, Israel, Palestine, and parts of Jordan), Asia Minor (modern-day Turkey), Macedonia (modern-day Bulgaria and Yugoslavia), Greece, Italy, and perhaps as far as Spain (see Figure 21-1). As he travels, Paul preaches to both Jews and Gentiles, starts new churches, visits existing churches, and writes numerous letters that now make up nearly half of the New Testament.

To help you understand the impact of Paul's journeys on what was still a fledgling movement at his conversion, we follow his travels in this section, highlighting a few of the episodes that characterize Paul's energy and sincerity in his efforts to spread the "good news" of Christianity.

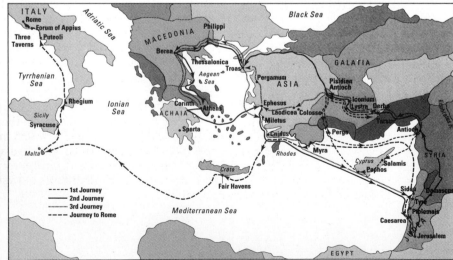

Figure 21-1: A map of Paul's travels throughout the Mediterranean to spread Christianity.

Paul's first missionary journey (46–49 C.E.)

Paul's first missionary journey, recorded in Acts 13 and 14, takes place about 10 to 12 years after his conversion. Between his conversion and his first journey, Paul spends time in a number of places, including Arabia (not Saudi Arabia, but an area roughly corresponding to southwestern Jordan and southern Israel), Jerusalem, Tarsus (Paul's hometown), and Syrian Antioch, the third largest city of the Roman Empire (after Rome and Alexandria). While in Antioch, Paul, Barnabas, and Barnabas' nephew, John Mark (the person credited with writing the second gospel) are "called apart by the Holy Spirit" to preach the gospel. This begins Paul's first missionary journey.

Paul's name change: Paul and company go to Cyprus (Acts 13)

On this journey, Paul and his companions sail first to the island of Cyprus (reputedly Barnabas' home), where Paul meets his first gentile (non-Jewish) convert, who is named Paulus. Interestingly, prior to this event, the book of Acts refers to Paul by his Semitic name: Saul. After this event, Acts begins calling him Paul — in apparent recognition of Paul's initiation into the gentile ministry that would characterize his life. From Cyprus, Paul, Barnabas, and Mark sail on to the southern coast of Asia Minor, where Mark is said to have left them for home. Paul and Barnabas then continue on to central Asia Minor, where, in the city of Lystra, they have a very strange experience.

The gods must be crazy: Paul and Barnabas in Lystra (Acts 14)

Lystra was a Roman colony founded in 26 B.C.E. by Caesar Augustus, who settled it with veterans of the Roman army. In other words, Lystra had a largely gentile population who worshiped the full entourage of Greco-Roman gods. Thus, when Paul heals a crippled man there, the people mistake him and Barnabas for gods. Because Paul is the chief spokesperson of the two, the people think he is Hermes, the messenger god of the Greek pantheon, and identify Barnabas, the strong, silent type, with Zeus. Before Paul and Barnabas realize what is going on, the town priest is offering them sacrifices. Only with great difficulty do Paul and Barnabas persuade the city's inhabitants that they are not gods, but mere mortals.

Although this scene may strike you as peculiar, the belief that gods periodically visited communities to test their virtue was widespread in the ancient world and is even evident in the Hebrew Bible's account of Abraham's three divine visitors (Genesis 18). In addition, Lystra seems to have had a tradition that it was once visited by gods who went unrecognized, except by an elderly couple who were blessed for their alertness. The inhabitants of Lystra were not going to make that mistake again.

Paul and Barnabas' near-deification experience soon turns into a near-death experience as certain individuals opposed to their message stir up the crowds, who in turn stone Paul and drag him outside of the city, leaving him for dead. Paul's companions also fear the worst, as he lay motionless for a long time. Suddenly, however, Paul stands up (whether by miracle or might, the Bible does not say). In keeping with his character, Paul boldly reenters the city. Eventually, Paul and Barnabas make their way back to Antioch and report to the church all that they experienced. They then continue to Jerusalem, where they participate in the church's first council (Acts 15; see Chapter 20).

Paul's second missionary journey (50–52 C.E.)

Paul's second missionary journey, recorded in Acts 15:36 through 18:22, takes place shortly after the council in Jerusalem. The stated purpose of this journey is to "visit the communities of believers in all the towns where we preached the word of the Lord to see how they're doing" (Acts 15:36). Yet Barnabas does not join Paul because they have a disagreement over whether Mark, who left them during their first journey, should come along. Paul views Mark's departure as desertion. Barnabas, Mark's uncle and one who takes chances on risky propositions (such as Paul earlier), wants to give Mark another chance. So sharp is their disagreement that these two friends, who had experienced so much together, part ways. Barnabas and Mark go to Cyprus, while Paul and Silas, a prophet from Jerusalem, take the inland route to revisit the churches that Paul and Barnabas founded on their first journey.

Paul picks up Timothy and Luke (Acts 16)

Paul and Silas's inland route takes them to Paul's hometown of Tarsus, and then on to Lystra, where Paul had his earlier near-death experience (see "Paul's first missionary journey" earlier in this chapter). While in Lystra, Paul and Silas pick up a young man named Timothy, whose father is a Greek, but whose mother and grandmother are Jews and followers of Christianity. As Timothy is uncircumcised, Paul has him circumcised so he won't offend his fellow Jews when they preach the gospel to them. Although Paul may not have realized it at the time, Timothy would remain one of Paul's closest and most loyal friends throughout his ministry (despite the surgery).

Eventually, Paul, Silas, and Timothy make their way to Troas, named after Troy of Homeric fame (but situated some 10 miles from the ancient city). While they are in Troas, the so-called "we" passages of Acts begin (Acts 16:11), suggesting that the author of Acts — traditionally Luke, who is also the author of the third gospel — joins Paul at this point. Like Timothy, Luke, whom Paul elsewhere calls "the beloved physician," is mentioned in several of Paul's letters as being with him when others had deserted him. (Paul also mentions John Mark in these letters. Apparently Mark proved a faithful friend to Paul after all!)

When in Greece . . . : Paul goes to Athens (Acts 17)

Paul eventually arrives at Athens, once the intellectual and cultural center of Greece. In Paul's day, however, it is little more than a symbolic center of Greece's great past. For Paul, a monotheist, Athens is anything but admirable. Noticing the innumerable idols and altars to various gods, Paul becomes agitated and begins preaching in the marketplace. Among the crowd is a respected group of philosophers, who invite Paul to be a guest lecturer at the preeminent "university" of Athens: the Areopagus.

The Areopagus, or "Hill of Ares," is named after Ares, the Greek god of war (Roman Mars, and thus sometimes called "Mar's Hill"). The Areopagus was once the great legal and administrative center of Athens. Under Roman rule, however, its authority was largely formal in character, and its pursuits had, in the opinion of some, become trivial. As the author of Acts puts it, "All the Athenians and the foreigners living there spent their time doing nothing except talking about and listening to the latest ideas" (Acts 17:21).

Paul doesn't cite the Hebrew Bible during his lecture, because doing so would have meant little to his Greek audience. Instead, he puts a positive spin on the plethora of altars that earlier provoked him to speak in the marketplace. In particular, Paul refers to an altar he saw with the inscription: "To an Unknown God." Paul informs the crowd that the god they desire to appease by this altar is none other than "the God who made the world and everything in it" (Acts 17:24). Paul then quotes from their own philosophers who had monotheistic inclinations, including Epimenides (around 600 B.C.E.), who in his *Cretica* wrote, "in him (the one god) we live and move and have our being," as well as Cleanthes (331–233 B.C.E.) and Aratus (315–240 B.C.E.), who in their *Hymn to Zeus* and *Phaenomena,* respectively, state, "we are his (the one God's) offspring." Paul explains that this one God intends to judge the world which He will accomplish through a man He raised from the dead.

At the mention of the resurrection, some balk (most likely the Epicureans; see the sidebar "Epicureans and Stoics" later in this chapter). Others want to hear more (most likely the Stoics). Still others believe, including Dionysius, who is a member of the Areopagus and who, according to later church tradition, would become the bishop of Athens.

After traveling through Greece, Paul and his companions eventually make their way back to Antioch, where they report the amazing things that are happening among the gentiles who are coming to faith.

Epicureans and Stoics

Among those present at Paul's lecture on the Areopagus are representatives from two of the most influential philosophical schools of the Greco-Roman Period: Epicureanism and Stoicism.

Epicureanism was founded on the teachings of the Greek philosopher Epicurus (fourth through third centuries B.C.E.), who argued that everything was made of matter and that upon death the individual ceased to exist. The chief aim of life, then, was to avoid pain and pursue pleasure. For Epicurus, pursuing pleasure meant seeking truth through philosophical discourse and reflection. By Paul's day, however, Epicureanism had become, at least by reputation, a philosophical front for hedonism. "Eat, drink, and be merry, for tomorrow we die," captures the essence of their worldview.

Stoicism was founded on the teachings of Zeno, a contemporary of Epicurus who had been influenced by the teachings of Socrates. Stoics held to the existence of the eternal soul. As a consequence, Stoics believed in an afterlife and that your actions in this life would determine your eternal state. A Stoic's central aim was to seek *pietas* (from which we get the word *piety*), which meant living a life of devotion and dedication to the gods, your country, and your family. Carnal desires, especially if allowed to override the rational mind, were the enemies of *pietas* and therefore stringently held in check.

Paul's third missionary journey (54–58 C.E.)

Paul stays in Antioch less than a year before setting out on his third missionary journey. As with his second, Paul takes the land route and revisits churches throughout Asia Minor, eventually arriving at the city of Ephesus, where he, in keeping with his track record, causes trouble.

Raising a ruckus in Ephesus (Acts 19)

Paul stays in Ephesus for almost three years, speaking in its synagogues, writing letters to churches he had visited or intended to visit, and teaching in the lecture hall of a certain Tyrannus. Paul also performs numerous miracles, including healing diseases and casting out demons. Despite the positive impact of Paul's activities on the local population, they have a negative impact on the local economy. Ephesus was a center for Artemis (Roman Diana) worship, and Paul's preaching lessens the demand for her idols as people begin worshiping the invisible God of the Jews and Christians. In response to the idle idol economy, a silversmith named Demetrius, who "brought in no little business for the craftsmen," instigates a riot. Soon Demetrius and his fellow craftsmen have the whole city shouting, "Great is Artemis of the Ephesians!" in the Greek theater at Ephesus (which is still standing today).

Although the rioting eventually dies down, Paul realizes that he's probably overstayed his welcome and leaves. After visiting other churches in Asia Minor, Macedonia, and Greece, Paul heads back to Jerusalem to attend the Feast of Pentecost. This seems to have been the last feast Paul attends in Jerusalem. As Paul would say to the church leaders at Ephesus, "Everywhere I go the Holy Spirit warns me that imprisonment and hardships lay ahead of me" (Acts 20:23). And they do.

Paul's arrest in Jerusalem (Acts 21–22)

Soon after arriving in Jerusalem and reporting to the apostles all that happened on his last journey, Paul is spotted in the Temple courts by men from Asia Minor who had opposed him there. Accusing Paul of blasphemy, a crowd soon gathers and tries to kill him. Paul's life is saved only when the Roman commander in charge of controlling riots intervenes and takes Paul to the Antonia fortress adjacent the Temple for "questioning." Paul is about to be beaten for instigating a riot when he asks, "Is it lawful to flog a Roman citizen without a trial?" It isn't, so the Roman commander arranges a trial in which Paul's accusers bring formal charges against him. As their accusations fall outside Roman concerns, the commander decides to send Paul to the Jewish legal authorities to be tried. However, he finds out from Paul's nephew (the son of Paul's sister, who lives in Jerusalem) that Paul's opponents are planning to kill Paul by ambush. The commander can't allow this to happen to a Roman citizen, so he sends Paul to Caesarea, the residence of the Roman governor, where his case could get the attention it deserved.

Paul's imprisonment in Caesarea (Acts 23–26)

Paul stays in prison in Caesarea for two years, during which time he is required to defend himself on several occasions. Although Paul is not found guilty by the two Roman governors whose tenures overlap his imprisonment — Antonius Felix (52–60 C.E.) and Porcius Festus (60–62 C.E.) — they keep him in custody to appease his accusers and to keep him out of trouble. Moreover, both governors find Paul's ideas and sincerity fascinating, even if peculiar. Felix, for example, whose wife Drusilla is a Jew, often speaks with Paul about matters of faith and piety. Then, when Felix is recalled to Rome, Festus asks Paul to present his case before a special visitor who has come to pay his respects to Festus on his new governorship: Herod Agrippa II.

Herod Agrippa II is the son of Herod Agrippa I, who had killed James, the first of the twelve disciples to be martyred (Acts 12). He is also the great grandson of Herod the Great, under whose reign Jesus was born and who, according to the Gospel of Matthew, tried to kill the newborn "King of the Jews." Despite his ancestral history of opposition to Christianity, Agrippa II is impressed by Paul's preaching, though not enough to become an adherent. In response to Paul's invitation to believe in Jesus, Agrippa says, "Do you think in so short a time you can convince me to become a Christian?" Paul's retort underscores his sincerity, even in the face of a rhetorical question:

> *Whether in a short time or long, I pray to God that not only you but all those listening to me today would become as I — except for these chains.*

> —Acts 26:29

Agrippa agrees that Paul has done nothing to deserve imprisonment or death. However, in an earlier trial, Paul had appealed to Caesar, the Supreme Court of his day, and so Agrippa and Festus are obliged to send him on to Rome.

Paul's journey to Rome (Acts 27–28)

Paul's trip to Rome is an adventure. The large ship on which he and his companions make their journey encounters a severe storm known as the Northeaster, which pushes the ship out into the open seas. After more than two weeks of rough sailing, and with food in short supply, Paul receives a visit from an angel who tells him that all the passengers will survive and that he and his companions will make it safely to Rome. It's a good thing Paul has this assurance, since the next day the ship wrecks and sinks, but not before everyone gets off safely.

Eventually arriving in Italy, Paul is greeted by the Christians there, who, along with the armed guard, escort him to Rome, where he is placed under house arrest. Paul remains under house arrest for at least two years, where he preaches to his fellow Jews and his Roman captors and writes letters to various churches (discussed later in this chapter). Acts ends with the following report:

> *For two years Paul remained in his own rented house and welcomed any who came to him. He preached about the Kingdom of God boldly and without hindrance and taught about the Lord Jesus Christ.*

> —Acts 28:30–31

What happened after this is not entirely clear. Some think Paul remained in Rome and was martyred under Nero's persecution of 64 C.E. Yet, evidence from later church tradition and Paul's own writings suggest that he was eventually released and went on a fourth missionary journey, where he ventured as far as Spain. By this account, Paul was later arrested again and beheaded around 67 CE. Whatever the exact circumstances of his death, Paul left quite a legacy.

Say It in a Letter: Paul's Letters

Whereas Jesus' life and teachings provide Christianity with its foundation (or "corner stone" as the New Testament puts it), Paul's letters build the structure. His insights into human nature, faith, and the meaning of Jesus' life, death, and resurrection give Christianity some of its most important doctrines.

Paul's letters fall into two categories:

- ✔ **Church epistles:** Letters to communities of Christians ("churches")
- ✔ **Pastoral epistles:** Letters addressed to individual church leaders

Scholars debate whether Paul wrote all the letters ascribed to him. These debated letters, which are called the Deutero-Pauline epistles, include 2 Thessalonians, Ephesians, Colossians, 1 and 2 Timothy, and Titus. In the following survey, however, we treat these letters as Paul's, because this understanding has shaped Christianity over the past two millennia — and, in the end, this understanding may be correct.

Paul's church epistles

Paul's main purposes in writing his church epistles are to (1) instruct churches about the central tenets of Christianity and (2) encourage Christians to live righteously in a world that doesn't share their values or beliefs. Here's a brief survey of Paul's church epistles.

Romans

Paul wrote Romans near the end of his third missionary journey (around 57 C.E.). Although he hadn't been to Rome at the time of his writing, he was well acquainted with the church there, mentioning numerous people by name in the letter. Romans is arguably Paul's most complex theological work and has contributed to the development of many important doctrines over the centuries, including Augustine's notion of Original Sin (Romans 5), Martin Luther's ideas about justification by faith alone (Romans 3–4) and John Calvin's doctrine of predestination (Romans 9). In fact, Luther's study of Romans, in combination with his work on Galatians (discussed later in this section), provided the theological impetus for the Reformation (16th century).

Despite its complexity, the central thesis of Romans is quite straightforward. Paul himself summarizes it near the beginning of his letter:

> *For I am not ashamed of the gospel for it is the power of God for salvation to everyone who believes — first to the Jews and then to the Gentiles.*

> —Romans 1:16

In the remainder of the letter, Paul develops this thought, explaining (1) how the gospel provides all that's necessary for salvation, (2) why salvation can be achieved only by faith, and (3) how God's inclusion of the Gentiles among His "chosen" fits in with His earlier choice of the Jews.

Concerning his first point, Paul argues that everyone, Jew or Gentile, "has sinned and falls short of God's glory, and is justified freely by His grace through the redemption that comes by Christ Jesus" (Romans 3:23–24).

This leads to Paul's second point: that everyone, Jew or Gentile, is ultimately made right (or "justified") before God through faith in Jesus' payment for sin "apart from works of the law" (Romans 3:28). This salvation "apart from works of the law" doesn't mean that God has abandoned the law previously given to Moses in the Hebrew Bible. Quite the contrary, Paul argues that Jesus' death underscores the importance of the law — whether the Mosaic Law (Jews) or the "law of conscience" (gentiles) — because violations against God's law required that He sacrifice His own Son. Moreover, Paul reminds his readers that even Abraham, the ancestor of the Jews, was made righteous by faith (Genesis 15:6).

This leads to Paul's final point: God's promises to the Jews are still valid, and one day "all Israel will be saved" (Romans 11:26). Until then, God has opened the door of faith to the gentiles to allow them to be co-heirs of His promises. Given their status as God's chosen, Christians are to live together in unity and love. In this context, Paul gives some of his most profound moral teachings — teachings that he reiterates in many of his other letters:

- ✔ Love one another with a brotherly love.
- ✔ Honor others above yourself.
- ✔ Share with those in need, even your enemy.
- ✔ Bless those who persecute you.
- ✔ Live in peace with everyone.
- ✔ Don't be too proud to associate with people of low social standing.
- ✔ Don't take revenge.
- ✔ Overcome evil with good.

1 and 2 Corinthians

Paul wrote several letters to the church at Corinth, two of which are preserved in the New Testament. (Paul mentions a third letter in 1 Corinthians 5:9, but most scholars believe that its content is preserved in the surviving letters.) Paul wrote both 1 and 2 Corinthians during his third missionary journey, the first probably while in Ephesus (around 56 C.E.) and the second while in Macedonia (around 57 C.E.). Unlike the church at Rome, Paul had been to Corinth and was even considered the church's founder. His personal relationship with the Corinthian church is evident throughout his letters.

Corinth was an ancient Greek city with a rich historical and cultural legacy. Part of this legacy was numerous temples to the various Greek gods, the most dominant being the temples to Apollo, the god of wisdom, and to Aphrodite, the goddess of love. These two temples seem to have captured the spirit of Corinth, because, like Apollo, the Corinthians placed a high priority on the pursuit of wisdom, and, like Aphrodite, they placed a high priority on the pursuit of "love." In fact, Corinth had become so intimately connected with ritual prostitution that the Greek verb "to corinthianize" meant "to engage in sexual relations." The Corinthians' love of learning and loving helps explain Paul's focus in his letters on what constitutes true wisdom and love.

1 Corinthians

In 1 Corinthians, Paul begins by arguing that true wisdom comes not from studying philosophy or religion but from knowing God. Moreover, true wisdom finds its ultimate expression in Jesus' death on the cross. As a result, God's wisdom appears foolish to those who think themselves wise (1 Corinthians 1:18–31). Paul then writes his now-famous definition of love (you've probably heard this passage read at a wedding — even your own!):

> *Love is patient, love is kind. Love is not envious, boastful, proud or rude. Love is not selfish, is not easily angered, and keeps no record of wrongs. Love does not rejoice in wrong, but rejoices in the truth. Love always protects, always believes, always hopes, always endures. Love never fails.*

> —1 Corinthians 13:4–8

Related to his teachings on love, Paul addresses issues such as marriage and celibacy (see the sidebar "Paul on the celibacy of the clergy"), the role of women in the church (see the sidebar "Paul on women"), and the importance and place of the "gifts of the Spirit" (see the sidebar "Paul on 'the gifts of the Spirit'") — themes that he expresses in several of his other letters. Paul concludes this letter by answering the Corinthians' questions about Jesus' resurrection, which he says was witnessed not only by the disciples but also by "more than 500 people." To Paul, the resurrection is the central hope of Christianity:

> *If Christ has not been raised from the dead, then your faith is futile, and you are still in your sins . . . but Christ has indeed been raised from the dead.*

> —1 Corinthians 15:17, 20

Paul on the celibacy of the clergy

As part of Paul's solution to the problem of sexual immorality, he recommends marriage. As he puts it, "It's better to marry than to burn [with passion]" (1 Corinthians 7:9). For those not "burning," Paul recommends remaining unmarried so that they can be undistracted in their service to God. Paul admits, though, that most people don't have this "gift," and that other apostles, such as Peter, have wives and serve God just fine. Over the next thousand years, many men and women took Paul's advice on celibacy to heart, and celibacy gradually became the ideal for those wanting to devote themselves fully to God's service. Then, in the 11th century C.E., what Paul put forth as a *recommendation* Pope Gregory VII made a *requirement* for all those wanting to serve as clergy in the Catholic Church. When the Protestant Reformation took place in the 16th century, the celibacy of the clergy was one of the first things to "go out the window" — literally, as Martin Luther, a (former) Catholic monk, married a (former) Catholic nun after helping her escape from her convent through a window.

2 Corinthians

Paul's second letter to the Corinthians touches on some of the same themes as his first letter, but he finds himself needing to correct their "over-correction." For example, in his first letter Paul admonishes the Corinthians to distance themselves from sexual immorality, including a member of their church who was sleeping with his own father's wife. Not only did the church do what Paul had asked, but they refused to allow that man back into the Christian community even after he repented of his sin (2 Corinthians 2:5–11). Instead, Paul says, "you should forgive and comfort him so he won't be overwhelmed with excessive sorrow" (2 Corinthians 2:7).

In the majority of the letter, however, Paul defends why he hasn't visited the Corinthians as he said he would. Some understood this as Paul going back on his word, which undermined his authority (2 Corinthians 1:12–24). Paul tells them that his change in itinerary was for their own good, giving them a chance to clean house (2 Corinthians 2:1–4, 12:14–21). Moreover, he assures them that he'll visit them soon to collect their promised offering for the poverty-stricken Christians in Jerusalem, as well as encourage those who have remained faithful to his message and to deal severely with those who have spread falsehoods about him in his absence.

Galatians

Paul probably wrote Galatians while in Ephesus during his third missionary journey (around 55 C.E.). "Galatia," whether referring to the Roman province by that name or to the ethnic region where Celtic tribes had settled (yes, related to the ancestors of the good ol' Irish), was located in northern Asia Minor. Whatever the exact *geographical* locale of these Christians, they were, according to Paul, in real *spiritual* peril. After Paul's departure, certain "Judaizers" (Jewish Christians who believed that the Mosaic Law, and especially circumcision, was incumbent on all Christians) came in and started preaching a different gospel. Paul adamantly opposes this new gospel, saying that to add to what Jesus has already accomplished on the cross "is to say Christ died needlessly" (Galatians 2:21). For Paul, "a person is not justified by the works of the law but through faith in Jesus Christ" (Galatians 2:15).

Paul goes on to say that he even had to confront the apostle Peter on this matter because Peter distanced himself from gentile Christians when certain Jewish Christians were present, which implied that there was a distinction between Jewish and gentile Christians. Paul explains that in God's eyes, "there is neither Jew nor Gentile, slave nor free, male nor female, for you are all one in Christ Jesus" (Galatians 3:28). However, he is careful to add that this newfound freedom does not mean that you can do whatever you want. As he puts it, "We were called to freedom, but do not use your freedom to indulge the flesh, but rather serve one another in love — for the entire Law is embodied in the single command: 'Love your neighbor as yourself'" (Galatians 5:13–14). According to Paul, the ability to live the life of love comes from God's Spirit, the fruit of which is "love, joy, peace, patience, kindness, goodness, faithfulness, gentleness and self-control" (Galatians 5:22–23). As Paul says, "against such things there is no law."

Ephesians

Paul made Ephesus his "base of operations" for several years during his third missionary journey, and he is thought to have written several of his church epistles from there. Yet, when Paul writes to the church at Ephesus, he is not traveling, but rather in prison, probably in Rome (around 60 C.E.). Perhaps as a result of the time Paul spent in Ephesus, the Ephesian church doesn't seem to have any major problems requiring Paul's attention. This allows him to focus on the benefits of being "in Christ," which Paul says gives them "every spiritual blessing in the heavenly realms," including "being adopted" as God's children, receiving "forgiveness of sins," and having access to "all wisdom and understanding" (Ephesians 1–2).

In keeping with this positive tone, Paul tells the Ephesians not to be distraught over his imprisonment, but to use the example of his suffering to motivate themselves in their own service to God and one another (Ephesians 3). For Paul this means treating one another with gentleness and love in order to maintain unity, because Jesus destroyed "the dividing wall of hostility" that separated people of diverse backgrounds and cultures (Ephesians 4).

Part of maintaining unity requires that the Ephesians "submit to one another" (Ephesians 5:21). In this context, Paul outlines the various roles of different members of the Christian community, including husbands and wives, parents and children, and slaves and masters. Wives should submit to their husbands, while husbands should love their wives "even as Christ loved the Church and gave himself up for her" (Ephesians 5:25). That is, although Paul believes that everyone should "submit to one another," he still maintains a distinction of roles and authority within the home (see the sidebar "Paul on women"). Paul continues by saying that children should obey their parents and slaves should obey their masters (see the sidebar "Paul on slavery"). Again, this is a two-way street, as Paul tells fathers (interestingly, not mothers) not to exasperate their children and masters not to mistreat their slaves. As Paul says, "for with God there is no favoritism" (Ephesians 6:9).

Paul concludes Ephesians by telling his readers to remain "strong in the Lord" by putting on "the full armor of God," which he describes by equating Roman armor with a Christian's "spiritual" armor. For example, Paul calls the scriptures a sword, and faith a shield. Apparently, Paul learned a little something about Roman armor during his imprisonment!

Philippians

Paul not only spent time in Philippi, he did time in Philippi, having been put in jail for "teaching customs unlawful for Romans" (see Acts 16). It's ironic, then, that Paul is again in prison when writing this letter (probably in Rome around 61 C.E.). Far from being disheartened, Paul considers his imprisonment an advantage because it has resulted in the spread of the gospel "throughout the whole palace guard" (Philippians 1:13), and it has encouraged others to preach "more boldly and fearlessly" (Philippians 1:14). Also striking in this letter is Paul's emphasis on being "joyful" or "rejoicing" — words he uses some 16 times, such as in the admonition, "Rejoice in the Lord always! Again, I say rejoice!" (Philippians 4:4).

Paul on "the gifts of the Spirit"

In several of Paul's letters, he refers to certain "gifts" that all Christians receive upon believing in Jesus and receiving the Holy Spirit. These gifts include wisdom, knowledge, faith, healing, miraculous powers, prophecy, discernment, and speaking in various languages or "tongues" (see 1 Corinthians 12). At Corinth, however, these gifts became another point of pride, with those having the more "visible" gifts (speaking in tongues, prophecy, and so on) feeling superior to those with less noticeable gifts. In response to this problem, Paul uses the analogy of the body, asking rhetorically, "If the whole body was an eye, where would the sense of hearing be? And if the whole body was an ear, where would the sense of smell be?" (1 Corinthians 12:17). For Paul, "there are many parts but one body." In the context of Paul's discussion of gifts, he gives his famous treatise on love (1 Corinthians 13) — because there is no greater gift one can possess or give.

Yet things are not all joy and rejoicing in Philippi. Whether due to their pride in being Roman citizens or in having retired military in their midst (or both), the church at Philippi was struggling to remain humble, which was causing divisions. Paul combats the Philippians' pride by reminding them that their true citizenship is not Roman but "in heaven" (Philippians 3:20). Moreover, Paul gives them the ultimate example of humility — Jesus:

> *Who though existing in the form of God did not consider equality with God a thing to be grasped, but emptied himself by taking the form of a servant, and being found in the likeness of humankind and in the appearance of a man, he humbled himself by becoming obedient to death, even death on the cross.*

> —Philippians 2:6–8

Because a Christian's confidence should not be in his or her accomplishments, Paul warns the Philippians about those who say circumcision is necessary for salvation. Using words that would one day adorn fences all over the world, Paul says, "Beware of the dogs!" (Philippians 3:2). Only these are not canine predators but humans "who mutilate the flesh [circumcision]." For those wanting to boast, Paul reluctantly gives his life as an example, having been raised "a Hebrew of Hebrews," trained as "a Pharisee," and demonstrating his zeal for God by "persecuting the church." Paul now considers all this "loss in comparison to the surpassing value of knowing Christ Jesus my LORD" (Philippians 3:8). In fact, when describing the relative value of his former life to his life in Christ, Paul calls his former life *skubalon*, a Greek word meaning "dung." Now that's quite a contrast!

Colossians

Although Paul had not been to Colosse, one of his converts, Epaphras, whom Paul met during his three-year stay at Ephesus, founded the Colossian church. Some date the letter of Colossians to Paul's stay at Ephesus (around 55 C.E.), but he probably wrote it during his Roman imprisonment (around 60 C.E.). Paul's letter addresses what's been called the "Colossian Heresy," which, as its name implies, means that we have no idea what it was. Some identify this heresy with an early form of *gnosticism,* a belief system that emphasized the importance of "secret knowledge" in attaining salvation. The central tenet of this secret knowledge was that all matter, including the body, is evil, and that only the spirit has any value. This belief system resulted in a diminishing of Jesus' stature, (because Jesus "became flesh" when he came to earth) and an overemphasis on legalism (to combat the sinful desires of the flesh).

Paul deals with the diminishing of Jesus' stature and the premise of this heresy together by describing Jesus as "the image of the invisible God" (which underscores Jesus' divine nature), who created "all things," both "in heaven and earth" (which affirms the basic goodness of both the spiritual and material world). Moreover, Paul says that "in Jesus all the *fullness of God* [exaltation of Jesus] dwells in *bodily form* [importance of physical matter]" (Colossians 2:9). Paul addresses the problem of legalism head on, saying, "Don't let anyone judge you by what you eat or drink, by a religious festival, a new moon or Sabbath day. These are merely shadows of things to come, the reality, however, is in Christ" (Colossians 2:16–17). This leads Paul to his main point concerning this heresy's pretended "knowledge": that all *true* knowledge is found in Jesus. As Paul puts it:

> *My hope is that they are encouraged in heart and united in love, so that they may have all the riches of complete understanding, in order that they may have the knowledge of God's mystery: namely, Christ, in whom are hidden all the treasures of wisdom and knowledge.*

> —Colossians 2:2–3

1 Thessalonians

First Thessalonians is believed to be Paul's earliest letter, and perhaps the earliest letter of those preserved in the New Testament. Usually dated to about 50 C.E., 1 Thessalonians was most likely written during Paul's second missionary journey shortly after he preached in Thessalonica (Acts 17). According to Acts, Paul had to leave Thessalonica quickly due to opposition that arose there against his preaching. Thus one of Paul's main concerns in this letter is to instruct and encourage the Thessalonians in their newfound faith, especially in light of the persecution they, too, were facing.

The Thessalonians seemed to be under the impression that all those who believed Paul's message would live until Jesus returned to take them to heaven. But because some had already died (whether due to persecution or to another cause is unclear), the Thessalonians wanted to know what would happen to them. This provides Paul the opportunity to explain the doctrine popularly known as "the Second Coming of Christ." Paul writes:

> *The Lord himself will come down from heaven with a loud shout, with the voice of the archangel and the trumpet call of God, and the dead in Christ will rise first. After that, we who are still alive and are left will be caught up together with them in the clouds to meet the Lord in the air — and so we will be with the Lord forever.*

> —1 Thessalonians 4:16–17

The event Paul describes — where Christians both dead and alive are taken from earth into heaven, is called the Rapture by theologians. Paul is quick to point out, however, that no one really knows when this event will happen, since Jesus' coming will be "like a thief in the night" (1 Thessalonians 5:2). Therefore, Christians should live as though Christ could come at any time.

2 Thessalonians

Paul's reasons for writing 2 Thessalonians are similar to those prompting his first letter, namely

- ✔ To encourage the Thessalonians to continue in their faith despite being persecuted

- ✔ To admonish them to be diligent in their work, since many thought Jesus' imminent return made working useless

- ✔ To clarify his teachings on Jesus' return

On the first point, Paul assures the Thessalonians that those who suffer in this world will be rewarded in God's kingdom, and those who are persecuting them will pay for their wrongdoing (2 Thessalonians 1:8–10). Concerning the need to work diligently, Paul states plainly: "If a person does not work, he should not eat" (2 Thessalonians 3:10). Paul also warns the Thessalonians that before Jesus returns, "the man of lawlessness," who will oppose God, will arise and even proclaim himself to be God. This lawless one will come from Satan and will be able to perform miracles and signs in order to deceive people into believing in him (2 Thessalonians 2:1–7). But Paul encourages the Thessalonians not to fear since God loves them and has chosen them. Moreover, the Lord will "overthrow [the lawless one] with the breath of his mouth and destroy him by the splendor of his coming" (2 Thessalonians 2:8). Until then, Christians are to work hard, keep the faith, and do what's right.

Pastoral epistles

Paul's pastoral epistles, which include 1 and 2 Timothy, Titus, and Philemon, are addressed to leaders (or "pastors") responsible for "shepherding" the church. Timothy and Titus were Paul's traveling companions whom he sent to churches to provide leadership and instruction in the Christian faith. Paul's letter to Philemon is unique in that it has more to do with a personal concern between the two of them than about the administration of the church. However, the content of that letter was thought important enough to be included in the New Testament and has subsequently played an important role in debates over the Bible's perspective on slavery.

1 and 2 Timothy

Timothy was a traveling companion of Paul, joining him on his second journey and staying with him on and off until Paul's death. As further indication of their close relationship and work together, six of Paul's letters (2 Corinthians,

Philippians, Colossians, 1 and 2 Thessalonians, and Philemon) mention Timothy as a co-author. Moreover, Paul requested that Timothy be with him during his imprisonment in Rome near the end of his life.

1 Timothy

Although the date of Paul's first letter to Timothy is uncertain, he most likely wrote it during his first imprisonment in Rome (around 60 to 62 C.E.) or, if he was subsequently released, during his fourth missionary journey (around 62 to 67 C.E.). After a brief reminder of why he sent Timothy to the Ephesian church, Paul recalls how God graciously saved him even though he once persecuted the church. For Paul, this proves one thing:

> *Christ Jesus came into the world to save sinners of whom I am the foremost. Yet this is the very reason I was shown mercy: so that in me, the worst of sinners, Christ Jesus might show his unlimited patience as an example for those who would believe on him for eternal life.*

> —1 Timothy 1:15–16

In other words, if God could love someone like Paul, He could love anyone.

Paul then moves on to talk about various issues relating to the administration of the church, in particular church worship and leadership. Regarding worship in the church, he writes on everything from prayer to women's dress and behavior. Concerning prayer, he emphasizes the importance of praying for everyone, including governmental authorities, "so that we might live in peace and quiet, in all godliness and holiness" (1 Timothy 2:2). He encourages women not to be preoccupied with external beauty, such as "braided hair, gold or pearls or expensive clothes," but to focus on the internal qualities of "faith, love and holiness" (see the sidebar "Paul on women"). Regarding church leadership, Paul describes the qualifications necessary for leaders, including being "the husband of one wife, temperate, self-controlled, respected, hospitable, able to teach, not a drunkard, not violent but gentle, not argumentative, not a lover of money" (1 Timothy 3:2–3).

In this context, we begin to see the manifestation of what you might call a primitive hierarchy in the church. Paul refers to two "offices":

- **Overseers** (also "elders"), which comes from the Greek word *episkopos* (from which we get the words *bishop* and *Episcopal*)
- **Deacons,** which comes from the Greek *diakonos,* meaning "to serve"

The primary duties of an overseer include teaching and preaching, administrating the church's affairs, and protecting the church from error. The primary duty of a deacon, as the word suggests, is to "serve" or assist the elders in their duties, especially by freeing them up to teach and preach (see Acts 6:1–6). Paul says that those who serve the church well will be rewarded by God (1 Timothy 3:13) and should be rewarded by the church (1 Timothy 5:17). Paul then warns Timothy to beware of those who seek to lead others astray, especially those who "forbid marriage and order people to abstain from certain foods, which God has created to be received gratefully by those who believe and know the truth" (1 Timothy 4:3).

While on the subject of church administration, Paul gives advice on the various relationships within the church. For example, he says that the church must take care of widows if they have no family and are over 60 or can't take care of themselves. Moreover, he says that slaves should show respect to their masters and, if they have a believing master, should show them no less respect simply because they are brothers (see the sidebar "Paul on slavery" later in this chapter). He concludes by warning Timothy of the snare of riches, saying that "the love of money is the root of all evil" (1 Timothy 6:10). Paul encourages those who are wealthy in this life to be "rich in good deeds, being generous and willing to share" (1 Timothy 6:18). "In this way," he says, "they will lay up treasure for themselves [in heaven]."

2 Timothy

In 2 Timothy, you read the parting words of a man who has given his life for the gospel. Paul begins by encouraging Timothy to remain faithful to the gospel, reminding him that "God has not given us a Spirit of timidity, but of power, love and discipline" (2 Timothy 1:7). These words are particularly apropos because Paul himself sits in prison, awaiting his own imminent death under the Roman Emperor Nero (around 64 or 67 C.E.). Making matters worse, many of Paul's closest companions have deserted him. Thus Paul turns to the subject of remaining faithful, telling Timothy that "in the last days" people's hearts will grow increasingly cold and therefore "everyone who wants to live a godly life in Christ Jesus will be persecuted, while evil men and impostors will go from bad to worse, deceiving and being deceived" (2 Timothy 3:12–13). But because God will ultimately vindicate those who "keep the faith" and judge those who oppose it, Paul encourages Timothy to endure his present hardship and continue in his work of leading the church.

Before his closing remarks, Paul gives a moving epitaph on his life:

> *For I am already being poured out like a drink offering, and the time has come for my departure. I have fought the good fight. I have finished the race. I have kept the faith. Now there is stored up for me the crown of righteousness, which the Lord, the righteous judge, will award me on that day — and not only me but all those who have longed for his appearing.*
>
> —2 Timothy 4:6–8

Titus

Based on evidence within the letter of Titus, Titus was introduced to Christianity by Paul and subsequently joined Paul on his third missionary journey. Assuming that Paul was released after his so-called "first" Roman imprisonment (60–62 C.E.), this letter suggests that they joined up again, working on the island of Crete and then on the western coast of Greece.

Paul on women

Few issues in New Testament studies are more controversial than Paul's views on women. Part of the controversy stems from passages like those found in 1 Corinthians 14 and 1 Timothy 2, in which Paul says that he doesn't allow women to speak in church. The exact intent of these passages has been the subject of considerable debate. Given Paul's earlier acknowledgment that women prophesy in public gatherings (1 Corinthians 11:5), many scholars think that Paul's teaching refers to disruptions by particular women during church meetings. Others suggest that Paul didn't want to cause unnecessary offense to those accustomed to male leadership in public religious life. Still others argue that, although Paul held to the basic equality of men and women (Galatians 3:28), he believed that God ordained male leadership in the home and church. Whatever Paul's exact intent in these particular passages, Paul elsewhere acknowledges and even praises women for their leadership in the church (see, for example, Romans 16).

According to 2 Timothy 4:10, Titus eventually went to Dalmatia (modern-day Yugoslavia) to preach the gospel. At the time of Paul's writing, Titus is on the island of Crete, where Paul had left him to provide leadership to the church there. As a result, Paul writes to give Titus advice on the administration of the church as well as on how to handle false teachers. Paul's advice on the qualifications of leaders mirrors that of 1 Timothy 3, although Paul places special emphasis on an elder's ability to teach, probably due to the false doctrines being promoted on Crete. Paul mentions specifically what he calls the "circumcision party," who demanded that Christians be circumcised. According to Paul, "They claim to know God, but by their actions they deny Him" (Titus 1:16). Paul quotes from a famous sixth-century B.C.E. Cretan poet, Epimenides, who said, "Cretans are always lying" (Titus 1:12) — the irony being that the speaker was a Cretan.

Paul then gives instruction to various members of the church, including the elderly, husbands and wives, and slaves and masters. He enjoins them all to

> . . . *live self-controlled, upright and godly lives in this present age, while we await the blessed hope of the glorious appearing of our great God and Savior, Jesus Christ, who gave himself for us to redeem us from all evil and to purify for himself a people of his very own, who are eager to do what is right.*

> —Titus 2:12–14

Philemon

Paul likely wrote Philemon at about the same time he wrote Colossians (around 60 CE), because Philemon was a member of the Colossian church and Paul probably sent both letters at the same time. Although Paul addresses the letter to three people, it becomes clear that he's really writing to Philemon about a personal issue: Philemon's slave, Onesimus. For reasons that are not entirely clear, Onesimus had been with Paul for some time, during which time he had become a Christian. The traditional view that Onesimus had stolen something from Philemon and then, having regrets, asked Paul to represent him before his master is possible. A more likely scenario, however, is that Philemon sent Onesimus with a gift to Paul, and Paul asked him to stay, both out of a desire to see him become a follower of Jesus and to use his services. In this regard, Paul even makes a wordplay on the name Onesimus, which means "useful": "Formerly he was useless to you, but now he has become useful both to you and to me" (Philemon 11).

Thus, what was probably stolen from Philemon was Onesimus' time, and Paul was the one responsible. But Paul is careful to remind Philemon that he owes Paul much more than the wages lost by Onesimus' absence: namely his eternal life, since Paul introduced Philemon to Christianity. Now that Onesimus is also a Christian, Paul tells Philemon to treat Onesimus "no longer as a slave, but better than a slave — as a dear brother" (Philemon 16). Paul then asks Philemon to prepare a room for him, because he expects to be released from prison soon. Finally, Paul sends greetings to Philemon from several people who are with Paul in prison, including Mark, the believed author of the Gospel of Mark, and Luke, the reputed author of the Gospel of Luke and the Book of Acts. (Paul hung out in quite a literary circle.)

Paul on slavery

Paul never explicitly condemns slavery, a fact that later supporters of slavery used to defend their "right" to own slaves. Yet Paul clearly states that slavery is not God's ideal and that it is even an appalling practice to God. For example, in 1 Timothy 1:10, Paul includes slave traders among those who are unworthy of the Kingdom of God, even calling them "godless and sinners." Moreover, on a number of occasions Paul underscores the basic equality of humankind, saying explicitly that with God there is neither "slave nor free" (Galatians 3:28). Paul's own attitude about slaves comes out quite clearly in his correspondence with Philemon, in which he instructs him to treat Onesimus "no longer as a slave, but . . . as a dear brother" (Philemon 16).

So why didn't Paul explicitly condemn slavery? Some have suggested that Paul was convinced Jesus would return soon, and therefore his first priority was to see individuals believe in the gospel. For the same reason, Paul never explicitly condemned any institution, even the corrupt imperial rule of Rome that was responsible for the deaths of many Christians, including, eventually, his own. Others have argued that Paul, realizing that he had no power to abolish slavery himself, spent his time instructing Christians how to make the best of a bad situation. Still others have argued that Paul realized that real change comes from within, and that the inevitable outcome of his teaching on the basic equality of humankind — regardless of ethnicity, gender, or social standing — if embraced, would eventually transform society and topple corrupt institutions like slavery. Certainly those opposed to slavery, like the abolitionist William Wilberforce of England, found a ready defender for their cause in Paul.

Chapter 22

Wait a Minute, Mr. Postman: The New Testament's General Letters

*E*ven in our age of e-mail, pagers, and cell phones, few things are more exciting than receiving a letter in the mail. The thought that someone cares enough to write words on a page and then lick those awful-tasting envelopes . . . it's enough to bring tears to your eyes (both the licking and the receiving).

Now imagine the excitement of receiving a letter in the first century C.E., which was a far more momentous occasion. True, they didn't have to lick those awful-tasting envelopes (they usually sealed letters with wax or clay — see Chapter 23). And true, the Roman road system revolutionized travel in the ancient world, making correspondence easier than ever before. But still, they had to compose letters with inferior writing implements (quills or reeds dipped in ink), and then they had to find someone to deliver the letter — and always for a price. Letters were a precious commodity in the ancient world, especially when they came from a good friend during a difficult time with the encouragement to "keep the faith."

In this chapter, you explore the general or *catholic* epistles — letters that have remained precious commodities to many throughout the centuries.

Catholic means "general" or "universal." When used in the context of the New Testament, this term refers to the letters not written by the apostle Paul (see Chapter 21 for more information on Paul) and written for a general audience. Only later did the term catholic become applied to the Catholic Church, in recognition of its claim to be the general or universal church of Christians.

The Bible "Hall of Faith": Hebrews

The letter to the Hebrews is anonymous, which has resulted in its being ascribed to various leaders of the early church, including the apostle Paul (an early opponent of Christianity who later converted and wrote many of the letters now in the New Testament), Barnabas (Paul's friend and traveling companion — see Chapter 21), and Apollos (an Alexandrian Jewish Christian who provided leadership for the church at Corinth — see 1 Corinthians 1). The name *Hebrews* derives from its recipients: Jewish Christians, who are being pressured to return to the ritual requirements of the Law of Moses (see Chapter 7 for more on Moses and the Law). The author of Hebrews is well informed about the rituals performed at the Jewish Temple in Jerusalem, which has led some to identify him as a Jerusalem priest who had become a Christian (see Acts 6:7). In addition, Hebrews contains numerous references to great figures from the Hebrew Bible — especially in Hebrews 11, a passage that is sometimes called the Bible's "Hall of Faith."

Although written in the first century C.E., the exact date of Hebrews is uncertain. The author's use of the present tense to describe the Temple services has suggested to some scholars that the Temple is still standing at the writing of this letter (before 70 C.E., when the Romans destroyed the Temple). Other scholars, however, have observed that even after the Temple's destruction ancient authors use the present tense when referring to the Temple services — perhaps in recognition of their eternal significance.

Yet, it is precisely the issue of the Temple's eternal significance that the author of Hebrews wants to address. According to him, the new covenant initiated by Jesus, where his death on the cross pays for the sins of humankind, brings to completion all previous covenants, and is itself the last and most important covenant. As the opening verse puts it,

> *In the past God spoke to our ancestors through the prophets at various times and in various ways, but in these last days He has spoken to us by His Son.*

> —Hebrews 1:1

Thus, the author of Hebrews seeks to demonstrate that Jesus surpasses all previous covenant mediators, including the angels (Hebrews 1–2), Moses (Hebrews 3), Joshua (Hebrews 4:1–13), and, most importantly for his priestly audience, Aaron, Israel's first High Priest (Hebrews 4:14–10:18).

Concerning Aaron's priesthood, the author notes that earthly priests must repeatedly offer sacrifices "first for their own sins and then for the sins of others" (Hebrews 7:27). Jesus, by contrast, was "without sin" (Hebrews 4:15) and only needed to offer one sacrifice: himself. By dying on the cross, "our Great High Priest" (as Hebrews calls Jesus) covered sins "for all time." Further underscoring the importance of Jesus' sacrifice — and using language that mirrors the Greek philosopher Plato's discussion of the "ideal" forms — the author of Hebrews says that when Jesus offered himself as a sacrifice, he entered the "true" and "perfect" Tabernacle made by God; namely, heaven. In contrast, the priests on earth enter a Temple made by human hands, which is merely a "copy" or "shadow" of the ideal.

The author of Hebrews is careful to point out that this new priesthood and covenant are anything but "new." Quite the contrary, Jesus' eternal priesthood was present during the time of Abraham, whose dealings with the mysterious priest-king, Melchizedek (see Genesis 14, Psalm 110:4, and Chapter 4 of this book), foreshadowed Jesus. Moreover, Jesus' new covenant was prophesied by Jeremiah (Jeremiah 31:31–34). Because Jesus' new covenant is the fulfillment of ancient prophecies, the writer of Hebrews instructs his audience to persevere in the face of persecution. As encouragement, he gives examples, appropriately enough, from the Hebrew Bible of those who endured hardship for their faith, including Noah, Abraham, Sarah, and Moses. According to the author, those making up this Hebrew Bible "Hall of Faith" form "a great cloud of witnesses" who surround these beleaguered Jewish Christians, beckoning them to "keep the faith" (Hebrews 12:1–3).

Working Out Your Faith: James

James was Jesus' "brother" (see Chapter 18), and the leader of the Jerusalem church (see Chapter 20). As the head of the church in Jerusalem, James's activity on behalf of Christianity involved mostly Jewish Christians, which is further evidenced by the recipients of his letter: "to the twelve tribes scattered among the nations" — likely a reference to the Jewish Diaspora (Jews not living in Israel). James' letter, though directed to Jewish Christians, is a practical guide for anyone seeking to live a life of faith and good works. James writes to those who are experiencing both external and internal trials:

- ✔ Externally, they are facing persecution. James tells his readers to consider their difficulties "pure joy," because from the crucible of trials comes the refinement of character (James 1:2–4). Moreover, those who persevere through trials will ultimately receive "the crown of life" (James 1:12) — a reference to eternal life.

- ✔ Internally, there are those among James's recipients who are being despised by their fellow Christians because they are poor. James reminds those who are treating the poor in this way that there is "no favoritism with God," and so there should be none with them (James 2:1–15).

Related to wealth, there are those who have been boasting about their money as though it made them impervious to harm (James 4:13–17). In addition, there are those who are inflicting harm with their wealth by exploiting poor workers (James 5:1–6). To the first issue, James says, "You don't even know what will happen tomorrow. What is your life but a mist that is here for a little while and then vanishes" (James 4:14). Instead of boasting about their business ventures, they should humbly say, "If the Lord wills, then we will live to do such and such" (James 4:15). To those who exploit the poor, James has many choice words, concluding with:

> *Listen! The wages you failed to pay to the workmen who mowed your fields are crying out against you, and their cries have reached the ears of the Lord Almighty. You have lived a life of luxury and self-indulgence. You have fattened yourself for the day of slaughter.*

> —James 5:4–5

In other words, James is writing to people who have a lot of serious problems. Yet, despite the complexity of their problems, James believes there is a simple solution: "Do not merely listen to the word and thereby deceive yourselves. Do what it says" (James 1:22). For those who feel it's okay to do whatever they want because they "believe" in God, James reminds them that "even the demons believe, and they shudder." True faith, according to James, shows itself in a changed life. As James says,

> *What good is it, my brothers, if someone claims to have faith but has no deeds? . . . faith by itself, if not accompanied by deeds, is dead.*

> —James 2:14, 17

James's and Paul's "disagreement"

In James 2:24, James writes, "a person is justified by what he does and not by faith alone." Yet, in Romans 3:28, Paul writes, "a person is justified by faith apart from works of the law." These seem contradictory, no? Some have suggested that these passages reveal what were real differences between James's and Paul's ideas on what was necessary for salvation. For James, salvation was achieved by a combination of faith and works, while for Paul it was only by faith. However, others have noticed that in both Acts (21:17–26) and in Paul's own writing (Galatians 2:6–10), Paul and James are presented as being in agreement on what is necessary to achieve eternal life. Their differences, according to this view, are differences of emphasis due to their differing audiences. James is writing to those who feel that "believing" in God meant they didn't have to do good works, or that they could pick and choose which ones they wanted to do. Conversely, Paul is writing to those who claim that both faith and works justify someone before God, as though Jesus' death provided some or most of what was needed to gain eternal life, but that individuals need to make up the difference. Paul is adamant that works play no part in *attaining* or in *maintaining* one's salvation (Romans 4:1–8). Yet, Paul, like James, is also adamant that those who don't do good works reveal that they don't have genuine faith. As Paul says in response to those who, like James's audience, say they can do whatever they want because they "believe" in Jesus: "Their condemnation is deserved" (Romans 3:8).

No Pain, No Gain: 1 and 2 Peter

Peter was one of Jesus' original twelve disciples, and part of Jesus' "inner circle" of three disciples (the others were James and John) whom he brought along to observe some of his most important miracles, including raising a girl back to life and his so-called "Transfiguration" (which Peter refers to in his second letter). Peter was also a leader in the Jerusalem church, being its chief spokesperson during the "early years," and later introducing the first *gentiles* (non-Jews) to Christianity. Yet, Peter disappears about halfway through the Book of Acts, which records the history of the early church. So it's good to finally get a letter from him.

Church tradition places Peter in Rome at the writing of these letters, perhaps penning both from prison while awaiting execution under the Emperor Nero (around 64–68 C.E.).

1 Peter

The recipients of 1 Peter are described as "strangers in the world," which prepares the reader for this letter's main themes:

- ✔ How to live as "strangers in the world" by not participating in this world's corrupt behavior.
- ✔ How to endure persecution as "strangers in the world" whose real home is heaven.

Concerning the first theme of living morally upright lives "as strangers in the world," Peter tells his readers to "be holy in all you do," which includes being "self-controlled," "loving with a sincere love," and getting rid of "all malice and deceit, hypocrisy, envy and slander" (1 Peter 2:1).

Peter begins and ends his letter with the second theme, telling his readers that they have "an inheritance that can never perish, spoil, or fade — reserved for you in heaven," and that they and this inheritance are "protected by God's power" (1 Peter 1:4–5). This protection, however, does not mean they won't experience persecution in this life. Quite the contrary, at the writing of Peter's letter they have already suffered "all kinds of trials." But these trials have turned out for their benefit, because they have proven their faith to be genuine (1 Peter 1:6–9).

Remarkably, for all the world's corruption Peter admonishes his recipients to submit to "every human authority" (1 Peter 2:13). This attitude comes from Peter's conviction that governmental authority ultimately comes from God.

While on the subject of submission, Peter tells

✔ Slaves to submit to their masters, even enduring mistreatment as Jesus endured mistreatment in order to pay for sins (1 Peter 2:18–25). (For the Bible's views on slavery, see Chapters 7 and 21 of this book.)

✔ Wives to submit to their husbands, seeking a beauty that comes not from external adornment such as "braided hair, golden jewelry, and expensive garments," but the internal beauty of a good character (1 Peter 3:1–6).

✔ Husbands to be considerate toward their wives, treating them as co-heirs of God's grace and giving them what Aretha Franklin wanted: R-E-S-P-E-C-T (1 Peter 3:7).

✔ Those responsible for leading the church during this difficult time to be good "shepherds of God's flock" so that "when the Chief Shepherd appears you will receive the crown of glory that will never fade" (1 Peter 5:1–4).

Peter then offers some final words of encouragement for those who will continue to suffer for God's sake: "Cast all your cares upon God, because He cares for you" (1 Peter 5:7).

2 Peter

Peter's second letter, like his first, provides encouragement to those who are undergoing difficulties. However, unlike in 1 Peter, the primary source of these difficulties is not external persecution, but internal deception caused by false teachers who have infiltrated the church. Thus, Peter begins his letter by reasserting his own authority as a teacher of the truth, saying,

> *We did not follow cleverly devised tales when we told you about the power and coming of our Lord Jesus Christ, for we were witnesses of his majesty.*

> —2 Peter 1:16

The "majesty" Peter refers to here is Jesus' so-called "Transfiguration." According to the gospels, Jesus brought Peter, James, and John to a high mountain where they saw him literally "in all his glory," as Jesus' appearance became dazzlingly radiant. Suddenly Moses and Elijah appeared and began discussing with Jesus his impending death on the cross. According to Peter, this miraculous event, along with the testimony of the Hebrew Bible prophets, testifies that what he has taught them is true.

Turning to the subject of false teachers, Peter says they are easy to identify because they are both immoral and arrogant. Concerning their immorality, Peter says, "They promise freedom, but they themselves are slaves of depravity" (2 Peter 2:19). Concerning their arrogance, Peter says they mock the idea that Jesus will one day return to judge the world. Peter assures them that Jesus will return, and that his seeming delay is the result of God's patience because God "does not want anyone to perish, but everyone to come to repentance" (2 Peter 3:9). Given the certainty of Jesus' return, Peter concludes:

> *Be on your guard so that you are not carried away by the error of immoral individuals and fall from your secure position. Rather grow in the grace and knowledge of our Lord and Savior, Jesus Christ, to whom be the glory both now and forever. Amen.*

—2 Peter 3:17–18

Dear John Letters: 1, 2, and 3 John

John was one of Jesus' twelve disciples and, along with Peter and John's brother, James, was considered one of Jesus' closest followers. As an indication of John's special relationship with Jesus, he refers to himself as "the disciple whom Jesus loved." Also similar to Peter, John "disappears" about midway through the Bible's account of the early church in Acts.

Putting the pieces together, John seems to have remained in Jerusalem as a church leader until the Jewish Revolt (66–72 C.E.), which resulted in the destruction of the Temple (70 C.E.). By then, many of the original disciples, including Peter and James, had been martyred. (According to church tradition, John was the only one of Jesus' original twelve disciples who was not martyred — though not for lack of others' trying!) John seems to have spent his latter years (around 70–100 C.E.) in the region of western Asia Minor (modern-day Turkey), with a brief period of exile on the island of Patmos (around 90 C.E.), where he received the vision that now makes up the Book of Revelation (see Chapter 23). According to these same traditions, John wrote his three letters while in western Asia Minor, most likely at Ephesus (around 85–95 C.E.).

1 John

The recipients of 1 John are Christians, but beyond this we don't know who these recipients are or where they lived. In fact, 1 John doesn't even specify the author! The letter's attribution to the disciple John comes from early church tradition, as well as common themes found in this letter and the Gospel of John (which is also attributed to the disciple by that name). In particular, both the Gospel of John and 1 John emphasize love. This emphasis is not surprising, given that John is referred to as the "disciple whom Jesus loved." Yet, what *is* surprising is why 1 John emphasizes love.

Knowing too much: Understanding Gnosticism

According to 1 John, false teachers infiltrated the church whose falsehood was evident in their immoral and unloving behavior. Scholars have identified this false teaching as an early form of *Gnosticism,* which was a belief system that emphasized the importance of "special knowledge" as a means of attaining salvation (the word *Gnosticism* comes from the Greek word *gnosis,* meaning "knowledge"). Although eventually a complex system of doctrines, the central tenet of Gnosticism was that matter was evil, and spirit was good (see Chapter 21). Because Jesus was good, some Gnostics argued he only seemed to have a physical body, but was actually entirely spirit (a view known as *Docetism* from the Greek word *dokeo,* meaning "to seem"). Others argued that, though Jesus had a body, he was made good when the divine spirit of "Christ" entered him at his baptism.

Confronting Gnosticism head-on

In actuality, John's letter addresses both expressions of Gnosticism quite well. He begins by going after Gnosticism's radical "matter/spirit" dualism by emphasizing Jesus' physical nature:

> *We declare to you that which was from the beginning [that is, Jesus], what we have heard, what we have seen with our own eyes, what we have looked at and have touched with our own hands — the Word of Life.*

> —1 John 1:1

Although some forms of Gnosticism promoted abstinence from physical indulgences (because the bodily appetites were thought to inhibit spiritual development), the particular variety of Gnosticism addressed by John seems to have held that you could indulge in any carnal desire because the physical world had no real affect on your spiritual health. John begs to differ:

> *Beloved children, do not let anyone lead you astray. The one who does what is right is righteous, just as He is righteous. The one who does what is evil is from the Devil, just as the Devil has been sinning from the beginning.*

> —1 John 3:7–8

Putting knowing before loving: Gnosticism's wrong priorities

Another negative consequence of Gnostic teaching was that, because the physical world was unimportant to your spiritual development, the physical needs of others were also unimportant. As they say on the *Family Feud* game show, "Survey says . . . "! John puts it a little differently:

> *If anyone has enough material possessions and yet sees his brother in need and has no pity on him, then how can the love of God dwell in him?*

> —1 John 3:17

According to John, "God is love." Therefore, "whoever doesn't love doesn't know God" (1 John 4:8). For John the ultimate source and example of love is God, who demonstrated His love in giving His Son:

> *This is love: not that we first loved God, but that He first loved us and gave His Son as an atoning sacrifice for our sins. Beloved, since God so loved us, we ought to love one another.*

> —1 John 4:10–11

2 John

The author of 2 John identifies himself only as "The elder" — its attribution to John, the disciple of Jesus, comes from later tradition. This tradition may go back to the time of the letter's writing, but it's certainly informed by the many similarities between this letter and 1 John — particularly in its emphasis on love.

The letter itself is quite short, a mere 13 verses by modern reckoning. The letter is addressed to "the chosen lady and her children," which some have taken to mean an actual Christian woman and her children. However, most likely this refers to a church and its members (though which church or group of churches is not known).

The purpose of the letter is to encourage Christians to stay faithful to the truth and to avoid false teachers. In order to avoid these teachers, who deny that "Jesus came in the flesh" (that is, Gnostics), John instructs his readers not to extend hospitality to any itinerant preacher who won't reveal what he teaches, because anyone who welcomes a false teacher, even inadvertently, "shares in his evil work" (2 John 11).

3 John

John's third letter is addressed to a certain "Gaius," who is otherwise unknown, but who is likely a leader of a Christian community. Like 2 John, 3 John addresses the issue of hospitality toward itinerant preachers. However, unlike 2 John, 3 John commends its recipient for showing hospitality to strangers who teach the truth. As a counter example, John informs Gaius of a certain Diotrephes, who, as a leader of another church, turns away those who teach the truth, since he "loves to be first" (3 John 9). As in 2 John, John explains the reason for his brevity:

> *I have a lot to write to you, but I don't want to do so with pen and ink. Rather, I hope to see you soon, and we will talk face to face.*

> —3 John 13–14

Hey, Jude: The Letter of Jude

The author of Jude describes himself as the "brother of James," who has been traditionally identified with James, the leader of the Jerusalem church and "brother" of Jesus (see "Working Out Your Faith: James" earlier in this chapter). In further support of this identification, the accounts of Jesus' life (Matthew 13:55 and Mark 6:3) mention a brother named Jude (short for *Judah*, Greek *Judas*, a common name in early Judaism, because it was the name of one of the twelve tribes of Israel, from which the word *Jew* arose, and the name of the great liberator of the Jews, Judah Maccabee — see Chapter 16).

Although the original recipients of Jude's letter are unknown, the designation "to those who have been called and are loved by God the Father, and who are preserved by Jesus Christ" suggests the letter was intended for wide distribution. The author explains that he wanted to write a more positive letter about God's gift of salvation. However, he feels he must warn his readers about certain teachers who are speaking falsehoods about Jesus, and who encourage people to participate in wrongdoing (Gnostics; see the section "1 John" earlier in this chapter). Jude equates these false teachers with less-than-admirable individuals from the Hebrew Bible, including the rebellious Israelites under Moses (see Chapter 7) and the inhabitants of Sodom and Gomorrah (see Chapter 5).

Perhaps most interesting, however, is Jude's use of Jewish traditions *outside of* the Hebrew Bible. For example, he mentions an episode from a work called "The Assumption of Moses," where the archangel Michael and the Devil dispute who has the right to Moses' body. According to this story, after Moses' death, the Devil came to claim his body because he had murdered an Egyptian. Michael, rather than revile the Devil directly, rebuked him "in the name of the LORD." With this, the Devil departed. Jude's reason for mentioning this story is to demonstrate that even a powerful angel like Michael respects his fellow angels, even if they are "fallen" or evil. In contrast, the false teachers described by Jude are so proud that they don't think twice about "slandering celestial beings."

Jude also makes use of prophecies from a work known as "The Book of Enoch," which claims to be the visions of Enoch (Genesis 4), whom God seems to have transported to heaven due to his exceptional righteousness (see Chapter 4). Jude quotes from Enoch's prophecies in defense of his point that God will severely judge those who do wrong.

Yet, Jude is finally able to get to the upbeat material he had hoped to write, which, similar to the Beatles' song, is basically "don't be afraid." Jude ends his letter with a blessing that has been repeated throughout the centuries:

> *Now to Him who is able to keep you from falling, and enable you to stand before His glorious presence without fault and with exceeding joy — to the only God our Savior be glory, majesty, power and authority through Jesus Christ our Lord throughout all time, both now and forever. Amen.*

—Jude 24–25

Chapter 23

The Beginning of the End:
The Revelation of John

The Book of Revelation describes the events leading up to the end of the world, when the earth will undergo cataclysmic disasters never before seen or imagined. Earthquakes will rock the planet to its very core. Meteors will cut huge swaths out of the earth. International and supernatural powers will meet in a final battle to determine the fate of the world. How will it all end? When will it all end? *Why* will it all end!?! The Book of Revelation gives the answers to all these questions and more. The only problem is, no one really understands all the answers Revelation gives since it is a highly symbolic and enigmatic work. In this chapter, we help you to decipher this cryptic book and marvel at its magnificent imagery.

Seeing the Future (Revelation 1–3)

The Book of Revelation (also known as The Apocalypse of John) derives its name(s) from the Greek word *apokalypsis,* which means to "uncover" or "reveal." Thus, Revelation is an unveiling or "revealing" of the future. The one to whom God reveals the future is called "John," who has traditionally been identified with Jesus' disciple by that name, and the author of the fourth gospel (see Chapter 18) and 1, 2 and 3 John (see Chapter 22).

Scholars usually place the writing of Revelation around 95 C.E., a time of intense persecution for Christians under the emperor Domitian (81–96 C.E.). John, himself, is the victim of persecution, and now lives in exile on the small island of Patmos in the Aegean Sea. And it is while wastin' away in Potmosianville that John has a most amazing revelation.

John has a revelation

John says that on "the LORD's day" (Sunday) he heard a voice commanding him to write down what he was about to see, and to send his vision to seven churches located in Asia Minor (modern Turkey). Here's what he saw:

> Then I turned to see the voice that spoke to me, and turning, I saw seven golden lamp stands, and in the midst of the seven lamp stands, I saw one "like a son of man," clothed in a robe reaching down to his feet and having a golden sash across his chest. And the hairs of his head were as white as white wool, as snow. And his eyes were like a flaming fire. And his feet were like burnished metal as in a furnace having been fired. And his voice was like the sound of many waters. And he had in his right hand seven stars, and out of his mouth came a sharp two-edge sword. And his face was shining like the sun in all its power. And when I saw him, I fell at his feet, as a dead man. And he put his right hand on me, saying, "Do not fear. I am the First and the Last, and the Living One. I was dead, and now behold, I am living forever and ever. Amen. And I have the keys to Hades and death. Write what you have seen, and what is now, and what is about to occur after these things.

> —Revelation 1:12–19

That's quite a vision! So what does it all mean? And what's going on here?

Reading Apocalyptic literature can be a complicated undertaking. Here are a few points of clarification for this particular passage, which can help you interpret similar passages.

- ✔ The term "son of man" comes from the book of the prophet Daniel (see Chapter 11), and in John's time was a common expression for the Messiah, who in John's view was Jesus.

- ✔ The long robe symbolizes priestly garments, and represents Jesus' status as the ultimate High Priest — having offered the final sacrifice for sins: himself (see Chapter 22).

- ✔ Jesus' white hair and fiery appearance recall the description of God in the Book of Daniel (Daniel 7) and reflect John's view that Jesus shares in God's divine status.

- ✔ The seven stars in Jesus' hand represent the angels of the seven churches in western Asia Minor (apparently guardian angels assigned to each church), while the seven lamp stands represent the seven churches.

John's revelation borrows heavily from the prophet Daniel's own revelations. Therefore, if you find yourself stumped on what something means, turn to the Book of Daniel, especially chapter 7, for possible clues. If this doesn't work, then read the rest of this chapter, because we do a lot of the work for you.

John addresses the seven churches

Jesus asks John to relay messages to each of the seven churches in western Asia Minor, evaluating their condition, recommending certain actions, and encouraging them to persevere during these trying times.

Each of Jesus' messages to the seven churches begins with a description of him that addresses that church's present situation. For example, to the church of Smyrna, Jesus introduces himself as "the First and the Last, who died and who was raised to life"(Revelation 2:8). Why is this important for Smyrna? This church is enduring severe persecution, and some of its members have even died for their faith. So Jesus instructs them, "Keep the faith, even to the point of death, and I will give you the Crown of Life" (Revelation 2:10). As one who died and came to life again, he can make that kind of promise!

Here's a brief summary of what Jesus says to each church:

- **Ephesus:** Jesus empathizes with their recent struggles against false apostles, but warns them not to abandon "their first love" (Jesus), and to maintain the zeal for God that they originally possessed. Additionally, Jesus tells the church at Ephesus to continue to "hate the works of the Nicolaitans."

    Although little is known about the *Nicolaitans,* Revelation associates them with the false prophet Balaam from the Hebrew Bible, who led Israel into idol worship and sexual immorality (Numbers 25:1–2). The Nicolaitans seem also to have mingled their newfound Christian faith with the idolatrous and sexual practices of pagan religion.

- **Smyrna:** Jesus commends this community for their bravery and perseverance against harsh tests and poverty. Jesus encourages them to face their difficulties and, in some cases, impending deaths with courage.

- **Pergamum:** Jesus praises them for their steadfastness in the face of oppression. However, like the church at Ephesus, they are warned about the immorality of the Nicolaitans.

- **Thyatira:** This church is commended for their love, faith, service, and patient endurance in adversity. Yet, they are condemned for tolerating an immoral prophetess equated with Jezebel, the Phoenician princess who was married to King Ahab and who promoted the worship of other gods and goddesses within Israel (see 1 Kings 16:31, 1 Kings 18, and Chapter 10 of this book).

- **Sardis:** Times are hard for the church at Sardis, as they appear spiritually "dead." Yet, Jesus offers hope to those among them who have remained true to him, and warns the others to "obey and repent."

- **Philadelphia:** Jesus commends the Philadelphia church for remaining loyal to him while they hold such little power. They are encouraged to patiently hold out during persecution because Jesus is coming soon.

✔ **Laodicea:** This community, consisting of proud, wealthy, and influential members, is simply going through the motions of devotion to God. Jesus warns them that "because you are lukewarm, neither cold nor hot, I will vomit you out of my mouth" (Revelation 3:16).

Some scholars have suggested that the image of Jesus spewing lukewarm water out of his mouth alludes to the water from nearby hot springs, which was lukewarm (and therefore useless) when it arrived at Laodicea.

Following these messages to the seven churches, John retells his fantastic vision of future events, which is intended to encourage (or frighten — depending on one's allegiances) Christians to remain faithful to God no matter how difficult persecution gets.

Unraveling the Future: Jesus Opens the Seven Seals (Revelation 4–11)

The events in Revelation unfold simultaneously on two stages: heaven and earth. First, John is given the "heavenly" perspective, where he witnesses God majestically enthroned and surrounded by His heavenly court. John is then given the "earthly" perspective, where he witnesses the devastation that takes place on earth. The priority of showing heaven first seeks to remind John's readers that no matter how bad things get on earth, God is still in control — an important message for those undergoing persecution.

In the case of Revelation 4–11, John's heavenly vision is of God holding up a scroll on which is written the apocalyptic events soon to unfold on earth. However, in order to read the scroll, the seven seals first must be opened.

Seals were dabs of clay placed upon strings around a scroll. The clay would be impressed with an individual's stamp, which informed the recipient who was sending the letter and which guaranteed that no one else had opened it.

God asks, "Who is worthy to open the scroll and break its seals?" (Revelation 5:2). Sadly, no one is found who is worthy to fulfill God's request — that is, no one until a slain Lamb, symbolizing Jesus and his sacrificial death, approaches, takes the scroll, and begins opening the seals.

Seals 1–6: The four horsemen of the Apocalypse and the day of wrath

The opening of each seal on the scroll introduces a new stage of God's judgment on earth. Although the judgments are written down on the scroll, John gets to see the action live — the ultimate pop-up book.

- ✔ **The first seal** releases a rider armed with a bow and seated upon a white horse (symbolizing war). The rider is given a crown and sets out to conquer.

- ✔ **The second seal** brings forth the second horseman, mounted on a bright red horse (symbolizing bloodshed). This rider wields a giant sword, and removes peace from the earth so that people begin to kill each other.

- ✔ **The third seal** ushers in the third horseman, who carries a scale to judge people. This rider's horse is black (symbolizing famine), representing the lack of food and intense hunger that inevitably followed war in the ancient Near East. The extent of the people's hunger can be seen in the exorbitant prices for wheat and barley.

- ✔ **The fourth seal** releases the fourth horseman: "Death." He rides a pale green horse (symbolizing the color of death), and he is given power over a quarter of the earth to kill with a variety of weapons: sword, famine, pestilence, and wild beasts.

- ✔ **The fifth seal** reveals the souls of the martyrs, who ask Jesus, "How long before you will judge and avenge our blood on those who dwell on the earth?" They are told it won't be long until they receive their desired justice.

- ✔ **The sixth seal** brings with it the "great day of God's wrath," a day foretold by the prophets of the Hebrew Bible. In preparation for God's judgment, the earth quakes, the sun turns black, the moon turns blood red, the stars fall, and the islands and mountains disappear.

Between the opening of the sixth and the seventh seals, four angels are placed at the four corners of the world, poised to destroy the earth and all its inhabitants. However, one angel is given a seal of protection to be placed upon the foreheads of 144,000 people, 12,000 from each of the twelve tribes of Israel. (We discuss the tribes of Israel in Chapters 6 and 8.) This symbolic number represents Jewish Christians who will escape God's final judgment.

The seventh seal: The beginning of the end

The opening of the seventh seal ushers in a period of silence lasting half an hour. Then, breaking the silence, seven angels sound seven trumpets. A disaster strikes the earth with each blast. For example, hail and fire mixes with blood destroying one-third of the earth's vegetation. A fiery rock the size of a mountain falls from the sky into the sea, destroying one-third of the marine life and ships in the sea. Then a star named *wormwood* (a bitter plant) falls into the earth's rivers and springs, contaminating the water and killing many people. (Many interpreters believe that the descriptions of the fiery mountain and falling star refer to meteors hitting the earth.) Then the sun turns dark, locusts are released on the earth, and 200 million mounted troops kill one-third of the earth's population. The sounding of the seventh trumpet signifies that it is time for God to judge the earth.

Between the sounding of the sixth and seventh trumpets, John sees "two witnesses," who prophesy in Jerusalem against humankind's sins (Revelation 11:3–12). They are eventually killed by those tormented by their prophecies, but three and a half days later they come back to life and ascend into heaven. So who are these two witnesses? Although they are not named, they are described in ways that recall Moses and Elijah, two of the Hebrew Bible's greatest prophets, and who many people thought would return to earth before the coming day of God's wrath.

A Pregnant Woman, a Dragon, and Two Beasts (Revelation 12–13)

Revelation 12 and 13 describe the activity of a woman, a dragon, and two beasts. No, this isn't a kung-fu action flick (at least, not yet). John is speaking metaphorically: The woman is a great people, the dragon is the archenemy of the righteous, and the two beasts represent a great empire. And when these figures collide, it's not a pretty sight.

A star is born: The coming of the Messiah

John has a vision of a pregnant woman. She is clothed with the sun, stands on the moon, and wears a crown of 12 stars. This seems to be an allusion to Joseph's dream in Genesis 37, where Joseph's father (Jacob) and mother are equated with the sun and moon, and he and his 11 brothers with 12 stars. That is, this woman symbolizes Israel, and she is about to give birth to something — or, rather, someone — very important (the Messiah).

In John's vision, the pregnant woman endures a very painful labor, but she eventually gives birth to a son (Jesus, the Messiah). Suddenly, a great red dragon (Satan, or the Devil) appears with seven heads (perhaps the seven hills of Rome) and ten horns (most likely the ten Roman emperors from Augustus to Domitian) and seven *diadems* (or crowns) on his heads (apparently the seven provinces of the Roman empire).

Rome was often described as "the city set on seven hills" in antiquity. Therefore, people reading Revelation during John's day would not miss his allusions to Rome when describing a dragon with seven heads or a woman sitting on seven hills (see Revelation 17:9). Moreover, those familiar with the prophecies of Daniel from the Hebrew Bible would know that horns represent rulers. Thus, the tenth horn or ruler of the Roman Empire was Domitian, the emperor likely in power during the writing of Revelation.

The dragon approaches the woman in order to destroy her child, but God takes him away to His throne (symbolizing Jesus' ascension to heaven), and the woman flees to the wilderness, where she is cared for by God.

The notice that God protected the woman (symbolizing Israel) seems to refer to the Jew's immunity from participating in the imperial cult (worshiping the Roman emperor as a god). This immunity was granted due to the antiquity of the Jewish religion. Christianity by this period was no longer perceived as part of Judaism, but as an upstart religion. Therefore, Christians were compelled to worship the emperor, and many were killed if they refused.

War of the other worlds: Michael battles beasts and the dragon

The dragon's arrival on the world scene ushers in a cosmic war between the forces of good and the forces of evil. Michael (God's warrior angel and Israel's protector) and his forces meet in pitched battle against Satan and his dominions in the heavenly realm. This is actually a "rigged" fight, because Jesus' death and resurrection have rendered Satan ultimately powerless against the forces of good. Therefore, in short order, Michael and his angelic host defeat the great dragon, who is then cast down to earth.

Once on earth, the dragon (Satan) tries in vain to kill "the woman" (Israel), but has to settle on battling her children who "bear testimony to Jesus" (Christians). Two more beasts show up to assist the dragon in his quest: the Beast from the Sea and the Beast from the Earth. The Beast from the Sea receives his power from the dragon, while the Beast from the Earth speaks for and exercises authority on behalf of the Beast from the Sea. In addition, the Beast from the Earth forces others to worship the Beast from the Sea. Finally, the Beast from the Earth makes everyone receive a mark on their right hand or forehead, allowing them to buy and sell. (For more information on what this mark may have been, see the sidebar "The mark of the Beast: 666" later in this chapter.)

In the context of John's day, the Beast from the Sea most likely represents imperial Rome, and in particular the Roman emperor, who demanded that his subjects worship him as a god. The statement that the dragon gave his power to this Beast means that John believed Satan controlled Rome (as evidenced by its persecution of Christians). The Beast from the Earth most likely represents Roman provincial power, since the governors of the provinces enforced the worship of the emperor, and executed those who refused. In addition, they oversaw the right to participate in Roman commerce.

The mark of the Beast: 666

In one of the most famous mysteries of Revelation, John says that the Beast of the Earth will force everyone to be marked on the hand or forehead with the number 666. Those who do not receive the mark will be unable to buy or sell food or other necessities (Revelation 13:16–18). Because seven is the number of perfection in the Bible, the three-fold repetition of six symbolizes complete imperfection or evil. So who is this Beast, and what is the mark? The answers to these questions depend on whether you think Revelation refers to past or future events or both.

✔ Those who think that Revelation refers to past events usually identify the Beast with the emperor Nero, who intensely persecuted Christians, and who many in antiquity thought would come back from the dead to do more of the same. The evidence for this identification derives from a practice known as *gematria*, where letters are assigned numerical values. Nero's name in Aramaic (the common language of first-century Palestine) adds up to 666. Also suggesting that gematria is at work is that in some early manuscripts of Revelation the number of the Beast is 616, which corresponds to the second most common way to write Nero's name.

✔ Those who think that Revelation refers to future events usually argue that anyone is "open game" as a candidate for the Beast. For example, during the Protestant Reformation, many Protestants accused the Catholic Church or Pope of being the Beast. The Catholic Church, in turn, thought this "honor" was more befitting of Martin Luther and the Reformers. Since then just about everyone important in politics or religion has been accused of being the Beast. Similarly, the mark has been identified with everything from ancient monetary systems or tattoos to modern credit cards or the World Wide Web. (**Note:** The Hebrew letter corresponding roughly to English "w" is the sixth letter of the Hebrew alphabet, making www equivalent to 666!)

✔ Those who think that Revelation refers to past *and* future events usually argue that John didn't really think that Nero was going to come back from the dead, persecute Christians, and fight a cataclysmic battle against God. Rather, John is arguing that Nero has already been "resurrected" — not literally, but figuratively in the actions of the emperor Domitian. Moreover, anyone — whether during John's time or in the future — who persecutes God's people and who opposes the truth participates in the "nature of Nero." But this is not to say that John intended his book to be read only figuratively or even "ahistorically." Although many throughout history may embody Nero's attitude toward God and His people, John also believes that there will be an actual final showdown between good and evil, where God's truth will prevail, the righteous will be rewarded, and the wicked will be punished. This "past-future" understanding of Revelation explains why people throughout the centuries have found reflections of their own time in its pages.

Armageddon and Judgment Day (Revelation 14–20)

Armageddon is a Greek pronunciation of the Hebrew words *har megiddo,* or "mountain of Megiddo," a location in the Jezreel Valley of northern Israel. In antiquity, all roads connecting Africa with Asia and Europe passed near Megiddo, and its strategic position ensured that many important battles would be fought here, including, according to Revelation 16, the "final battle" between the forces of good and evil.

Reaping your reward: God's final harvest

Before the climactic battle between good and evil, "one like a son of man" harvests the earth, and then an angel prepares some grapes to make wine (Revelation 14:14–20). These activities are not preparations for a party, but they are metaphors for preparations made just before God's final judgment.

- ✔ The one like a son of man is Jesus, who gathers a harvest of righteous people still on earth in order to spare them from the disasters about to come.

- ✔ The harvest of grapes, which are trampled and made into wine, symbolizes God's wrath, which He is about to pour out on the earth in judgment.

It is from Revelation 14:14–20, along with similar passages in the Hebrew Bible, that *The Battle Hymn of the Republic* gets its famous opening lines: "Mine eyes have seen the glory of the coming of the LORD. He is trampling out the vintage where the grapes of wrath are stored." (Sing it with us now!)

God serves up seven bowls of judgment

With the grapes of wrath fully trampled, God unleashes His wrath in the form of seven plague-wielding angels who pour out their bowls upon the earth:

- ✔ **The first bowl** inflicts sores upon those who bear the mark of the beast and worship its image.

- ✔ **The second bowl** is poured into the sea, turning it to blood and killing all of the sea creatures.

- ✔ **The third bowl** similarly turns all of the world's rivers into blood.

✔ **The fourth bowl** is emptied on the sun creating intense heat that scorches people.

✔ **The fifth bowl** is poured upon the beast signifying Rome, and it turns his kingdom dark.

✔ **The sixth bowl** is dropped on the Euphrates River, causing it to dry up. This allows kings from the east and their armies to cross this great natural barrier. Three demonic spirits issue forth from the dragon, the Beast from the Sea, and the False Prophet (the Beast from the Earth), and they amass a great army for battle at Armageddon.

The dragon, the Beast from the Sea, and the Beast from the Earth represent a type of false or evil trinity, corresponding to the true and righteous Trinity of God the Father, Son, and Holy Spirit.

✔ **The seventh bowl** is poured into the air, causing lightning, earthquakes, and resulting in the total destruction of Rome, here symbolized as "Babylon."

The destruction of the great whore

In Revelation 17, John sees a "great whore" who has committed "adultery" with all the kings of the earth. She rides a seven-headed beast, she is elaborately dressed, and she is drunk from "the blood of the righteous ones." So who is this whore? John tells us that the woman "is the great city that rules over the kings of the earth" (Revelation 17:18). During John's day, this could be none other than Rome, which is further confirmed by the angel telling him that the seven heads of the beast represent seven hills, a common way to refer to Rome during John's day. But these seven heads also represent "seven kings — five who have fallen, one who is, and one who is yet to come" (Revelation 17:10). If applied to John's day, the five "kings" could refer to the five emperors leading up to Nero, who is the sixth (if we count Julius Caesar) or the five emperors since Jesus' life, which would make Domitian "the one who is." Whatever the case, the great whore or Rome (also called "Babylon the Great"), who gets drunk on the blood of the righteous, soon meets a catastrophic end as God destroys the city in judgment.

The final battle between good and evil

Once Rome is destroyed, God turns His attention toward the final defeat of Satan, which occurs in two stages.

The first great battle against Satan and his evil forces (both human and angelic) begins as the heavens open and a white horse bearing a rider named "Faithful and True" descends with the armies of heaven in his trail. The rider is Jesus, whose robe is "dipped in blood" (symbolizing Jesus' death on the cross for sin), and from whose mouth "a sword" protrudes (symbolizing God's truth or the Scriptures, with which Jesus earlier defeated Satan when tempted by him in the wilderness; see Chapter 18 of this book).

The earthly kings, under the leadership of Satan, gather to do battle against the white horse and its rider, as an angel in the sun calls the birds to prepare to eat the flesh of the evil armies (not a good sign if you're one of the earthly kings). Because of the potency of Jesus' death on the cross and the truth of the Scriptures, Jesus quickly defeats Satan's forces, and casts the Beasts from the Sea and Earth into the "lake of fire" (symbolizing God's eternal judgment). Satan is also captured, and he is bound in chains for 1,000 years.

During this 1,000-year period, all those who had been killed "because of their testimony for Jesus and because of the word of God" are resurrected, and rule with Jesus over an earth devoid of the influence of the evil one. God's will is now done on earth as it is in heaven.

After this 1,000-year period of heaven on earth, Satan is released from his chains and once more allowed to deceive the nations into doing battle against God. Surprisingly, and despite the thousand years of righteous rule, many follow Satan. Once gathered for battle, however, fire descends from heaven and destroys Satan's evil army and finally, Satan himself is thrown into the "lake of fire" for eternity. With Satan's removal, death is also destroyed.

The final judgment

With Satan defeated, all those who have ever lived are brought back to life to stand before God's throne for the final judgment. During the proceedings, various books are opened that record everything anyone has ever done, and the world's population is judged based on what is written in these books. Another book is opened, which is called the "Book of Life." Anyone whose name is not found in this book is thrown into the lake of fire for eternity.

According to the New Testament, no one is righteous enough to go to heaven. Therefore, when God judges humankind based on what is written in the books recording everyone's life, the assumption is that everyone is going to eternal judgment (what Revelation calls the lake of fire). The only exceptions to this rule are those who have received God's provision for human wrongdoing — Jesus' death on the cross. For those who have accepted Jesus' payment for sin on their behalf, their names are written in the Book of Life, and they will live forever with God in heaven.

Somewhere Over the Rainbow: Paradise Regained (Revelation 21–22)

God's creation, which had its beginning in the opening chapters of Genesis, now culminates in the last two chapters of Revelation. In fact, the closing chapters of Revelation contain numerous allusions to the opening chapters of Genesis, providing a fitting ending to the Christian Bible.

Here are some of the similarities between the beginning of Genesis and the end of Revelation:

- With Satan and evil defeated, God creates a new heaven and a new earth, which recalls the opening line of the Hebrew Bible: "In the beginning God created the heavens and earth."

- A "new Jerusalem" descends from heaven and becomes God's dwelling place on earth among humans, which harkens back to the "old" Jerusalem, where God figuratively dwelt with Israel in the Temple, and which ultimately pictures the Garden of Eden, where God walked and talked with humans before they ate from the Tree of the Knowledge of Good and Evil.

- Related to the Tree of the Knowledge of Good and Evil, in this new Jerusalem there is no such tree. There is only a Tree of Life (or, more accurately, *Trees* of Life), which bring "healing to the nations" (Revelation 22:2).

At the end of Revelation, humans now live as God intended "in the beginning": free from evil, pain, and death, and in perfect relationship with God, their fellow humans, and creation. Only unlike the Garden of Eden, there is no longer any *potential* for evil or the curse of pain and death it brings. Quite the contrary, John says of this new Jerusalem,

> *God will wipe away every tear from their eyes. There will be no more death or mourning or crying or pain, for the former condition has passed away.*

—Revelation 21:4

Thus, just like Dorothy returning to Kansas after her amazing adventure, humankind has come full circle, winding up right back where we started, right where we belong. And this is the happiest ending of all, because there's no place like home.

Part V

That Was Then, This Is Now: Discovering the Bible's Enduring Influence

The 5th Wave   By Rich Tennant

That one was reeeally close! A little lower and to the left!

In this part . . .

You discover how the traditions surrounding Abraham have contributed to three of the world's major religions: Judaism, Christianity, and Islam. You also see the many ways the Bible has impacted popular culture, from Renaissance paintings and sculptures, to great works of literature, to the height of humankind's artistic expression — Hollywood movies! Okay, we realize that last statement may not resonate with everyone, but we do give you a brief rundown of some of the best (and worst) movies about the Bible.

Chapter 24

The Bible and the Abrahamic Faiths: Judaism, Christianity, and Islam

***

In This Chapter

▶ Engendering Judaism, Christianity, and Islam with Abraham

▶ Visiting Jerusalem, the sacred City of Peace

***

*T*he extent to which your life impacts others cannot be entirely known. Yet, despite what you may recall from *A Christmas Carol, It's a Wonderful Life,* and about every other *Star Trek* episode, individuals rarely alter the world's general flow. However, once in a great while, a person comes along who actually changes the course of history. Perhaps nowhere is this more evident than in the story of Abraham, who laid the foundation for three distinct, though intimately related, religions: Judaism, Christianity, and Islam.

In this chapter, you discover the shared heritage of Judaism, Christianity, and Islam through their common bond in Abraham and Jerusalem.

Abraham: Father of Many Nations and Faiths

Abraham first appears in the Book of Genesis — a book full of beginnings, as the name implies (see Chapter 3). When we meet Abraham, however, his name is not Abraham, but Abram, meaning "exalted father." Yet, as happens often in the Bible, God gives Abram a new name, marking a new beginning for him and those coming after him (see Chapter 5). Abraham means "father of many," which is ironic because at the time of his name change, Abraham and his wife, Sarah, are childless. Moreover, they are 99 and 89 years old, respectively. But God has a new beginning for them, and He guarantees this with a contract, or *covenant* (see Chapters 2 and 4):

No longer will your name be Abram, but Abraham, for I have made you the father of many nations. I will make you very fruitful; and I will make nations from you, and kings will come from you. And I will establish My covenant between Me and you and your descendants for generations after you for an everlasting covenant: to be God to you, and to your descendants after you.

—Genesis 17:5–7

God further tells Abraham that one day his descendants will be as numerous as the sand on the seashore and the stars visible in the sky. Unfortunately, we're too busy to count sand, but an astronomer friend of ours estimates that there are about 6,000 stars visible to the naked eye. Now that's a lot of descendants, but not even close to the incredible impact that Abraham's offspring will have on the world. From Abraham's physical and spiritual children come three of the world's major religions — Judaism, Christianity, and Islam — accounting for about half of the world's population.

Abraham and Judaism

All Jews trace their lineage through Abraham by way of his son Isaac and grandson Jacob, who later took the name Israel. For thousands of years, Jews have looked to Abraham's life as the source of and inspiration for their own. For example, Jews circumcise their male sons on the eighth day, a practice begun when Abraham circumcised Isaac at 8 days old in obedience to God's command and as a sign of God's covenant with Abraham.

Beyond being Abraham's physical descendants, and the inheritors of God's promises to Abraham, the Jews consider Abraham to be an example of faith. Abraham believed in God enough to leave his homeland and his extended family in Mesopotamia to go to a land he had never seen. God simply said, "Go to the land I will show you." (Genesis 12:1) No road map, no tour book, no GPS system, just "I will show you." Abraham also trusted God enough to give back to God that for which he had waited all his life: his son, Isaac. Just as God had initially called Abraham simply to go to a land He would show him, so God commanded Abraham to go and sacrifice Isaac "on the mountain I tell you" (Genesis 22:2). Although God would stop Abraham short, Abraham's willingness to sacrifice what was dearest to him has served as an inspiration to many throughout the centuries.

Abraham and Christianity

Though it often comes as a surprise to people, Jesus was Jewish. Jesus, like his fellow Jews, was circumcised on the eighth day, dedicated to God on the fortieth day, made pilgrimages to Jerusalem for the major feasts, and traced his lineage back to Abraham. In fact, Abraham's life and faith directly impact the New Testament's presentation of Jesus' life and ministry. Not only is Jesus presented as a fulfillment of the promises made long ago to Abraham that his descendants will be a blessing to the nations, but Jesus' own death on the cross mirrors the near sacrifice of Isaac. For example, just as Isaac carries the wood to be used in his sacrifice, so Jesus carries the wooden beam of his own cross. Some Christians even believe that Golgotha, the place where Jesus is crucified, is the same location where Isaac is nearly killed (though many place Isaac's near-death experience on the Temple Mount; see "Jerusalem: City of Peace — And of Conflict" later in this chapter). And although in the end Isaac isn't sacrificed, both Genesis 22 and the crucifixion share the idea of a father sacrificing his son. Finally, Abraham is held out as a model of faith that transcends ethnic, social or gender barriers. As the apostle Paul writes:

> *For there is neither Jew nor Greek, slave nor free, male nor female — for you are all one in Jesus Christ. And if you are Christ's, then you are Abraham's children, heirs according to the covenant.*

> —Galatians 3:28–29

Ibrahim and Islam

Abraham is considered by many to be the first Muslim, and for good reason: The very word Muslim means "one who submits [to God's will]." Abraham, or Ibrahim as he is called in the *Koran* (Islam's sacred text), is the model of one who submits to God, and therefore much of the Islamic religion focuses on Ibrahim. For example, one of Islam's five daily prayers asks God to bless the prophet Ibrahim. Moreover, the direction of prayer, Mecca, is because of Ibrahim. According to the Koran, after Adam and Eve are expelled from Paradise, they build a shrine to God at Mount Arafat in Mecca. This place of worship, however, is eventually destroyed during the Flood. In its absence, religion becomes corrupted, until Ibrahim accompanies the expelled Hagar and Ibrahim's son, Ishmael, to rebuild the shrine. This structure is what is now known as the *Ka'aba* (Ka'aba means "cube," because of its shape, as shown in Figure 24-1). Today some 2 million people annually make the pilgrimage to the Ka'aba in Mecca, a practice known as the *Hajj*.

Islam's founder, the prophet Muhammad, traces his descent through Ibrahim's son Ishmael. Also, according to the Hebrew Bible, both the descendants of Isaac and Ishmael are the Chosen People, because God makes a covenant with both groups. And like Isaac, God promises that Ishmael's offspring will become a "great nation" (Genesis 21:13, 18).

According to a story found in both the Jewish Mishnah (a third century C.E. legal text) and the Muslim Koran (Islam's sacred text), Abraham's father makes a living by constructing idols used in pagan religion. One day, while his father is absent, Abraham smashes all the idols except the largest one, and places a hammer in its hand. When his father returns, he is furious and asks how this happened. Abraham blames the largest idol, and when his father refuses to believe him, he magnificently illustrates to his father the folly of idolatry.

Figure 24-1:
The Ka'aba
at Mecca.

Jerusalem: City of Peace — And of Conflict

Jerusalem means "City of Peace," but it is hard to imagine a place that has experienced more conflict over the centuries. Even today Jerusalem dominates the news more than any city in the world. Part of the reason for this is that Jerusalem lies in the middle of Israel and Palestine, a land bridge linking three continents. Thus, Jerusalem was destined to become the meeting place of different cultures. At times this cultural contact has produced violent conflict; at other times it has produced positive exchange that has greatly benefited humanity.

Jerusalem in Judaism

For Jews, Jerusalem is the most sacred city on earth, because this is where God's home, the Temple, was located until its destruction by the Romans in 70 C.E. For many religious Jews, it is taboo to walk upon the Temple Mount until it is ritually purified. In addition, some Jews fear that by walking on the Temple Mount they may unintentionally step on the plot of ground where the Temple's most sacred place (called the *Holy of Holies*) once stood. Although we can't be certain about its exact location, many people feel that the Holy of Holies was situated under what is today the Dome of the Rock, one of Islam's most important holy sites (see "Jerusalem in Islam" later in this chapter). Therefore, Jews today pray at the Western Wall (also known as the Wailing Wall), which is part of the foundation for the Temple built by Herod the Great (see Figure 24-2). This allows Jews to pray to God in close proximity to and facing where the Temple once stood without having to set foot on the platform.

Jerusalem in Christianity

For Christians, Jerusalem is sacred not only for its roots in the Hebrew Bible but also as the place where many events from Jesus' life took place. Most notably, Jesus' crucifixion, burial, and resurrection occurred in Jerusalem, which are now commemorated within the Church of the Holy Sepulcher, the traditional location of these events (see Figure 24-3). Although the structure has covered over the original topography of where these events are believed to have taken place, the church's architecture and ambience is awe-inspiring, as is the devotion of the millions of pilgrims who pass through its doors to pay homage to Christianity's founder.

Figure 24-2:
The Dome of the Rock and the Western Wall.

Figure 24-3: The holiest site in Christianity, Jesus' empty tomb is commemorated within this stone monument located in the Church of the Holy Sepulcher.

Jerusalem in Islam

For Muslims, Jerusalem is known as *al-Quds,* Arabic for "the holy," and is the third holiest city in Islam behind Mecca (the location of the Ka'aba) and Medina (Muhammad's childhood home and burial site). Originally, Muhammad instructed Muslims to pray in the direction of Jerusalem, though later he changed this to Mecca. Jerusalem is important to Muslims because of its religious heritage. For example, Muslims believe that Ibrahim was ordered to sacrifice Ishmael, not Isaac. The location of this event is identified with a large stone now encased within the Dome of the Rock in Jerusalem. Moreover, Jerusalem is remembered as al-Aqsa, which means "the furthest place," because here Muhammad began his night journey touring heaven. Today the al-Aqsa mosque stands on the Temple Mount in Jerusalem as a memorial to this event.

Thus, both Abraham and Jerusalem are central to Judaism, Christianity, and Islam. One can only hope that these common bonds will help make Jerusalem a true City of Peace.

Chapter 25

Michelangelo, Milton, and Movies: Art, Literature, Life, and the Bible

In This Chapter

▶ Examining the Bible's influence on the arts and civilization

▶ Exploring the arts' impact on the living text of the Bible

▶ Looking at some interesting Bible movies

*A*bout midway into the semester of an art history course, a student asked, "So who's the lady with the baby we keep seeing?" The stunned instructor had assumed that everyone was familiar with the biblical characters of Jesus and Mary. But we all know what happens when you and I *ass-u-me*.

Actually, assumptions, the arts, and the Bible have long gone together. For example, Renaissance paintings of biblical stories often reveal more about the dress, manners, and values of European nobility than anything found in the Bible. Nevertheless, artists' interpretations of the Bible, even when wrong, have done much to bring the Good Book to life, and in this way they have contributed to the Bible's enduring appeal.

In this chapter you look at the Bible's impact on the arts and, conversely, the impact of the arts on how you understand the Bible.

The Bible in Art

Some of the most influential works of art depicting scenes from the Bible were created in Renaissance Europe. The five discussed here are among the best known, and exemplify how artists not only bring the biblical narrative to life but also transform that narrative to reflect their own world.

Creation of Adam (Genesis 2)

The Bible's influence on culture is perhaps best embodied in the Vatican's Sistine Chapel, painted by Michelangelo Buonarroti in the sixteenth century. Of the over 3,000 figures depicting biblical events and persons on its walls and ceilings, the most famous is the one in the center of the ceiling: *Creation of Adam* (see Figure 25-1), seen by many to be the pinnacle of Renaissance art. Here Michelangelo, instead of painting God creating the universe with words as recorded in Genesis 1, depicts a very human (though admittedly buffed!) God, more like that encountered in Genesis 2 (see Chapter 3 of this book).

Figure 25-1: Michelangelo's *Creation of Adam* in the Sistine Chapel.

©Bettmann/CORBIS

The moment captured in the painting isn't the physical creation of Adam, as he already exists, but rather the moment at which God imparts His divine life or spirit into Adam, making Adam a "living" being. In the painting God is accompanied by a retinue of other creatures and persons. Most notably, God's left arm is draped around a woman, who is Eve, and His left hand rests upon the Christ child, whose preexistence and presence with God at creation is a central Christian doctrine.

Thus, in this single image, Michelangelo captures the entire Christian story of humanity's relationship to God. Adam is given a soul, while at the same time God foresees humanity's failure and anticipates the redemption of Christ.

Moses with horns (Exodus 34)

After speaking at length with God on Mount Sinai, Moses descends carrying the Ten Commandments. The text then reports, "Moses did not know that the skin of his face was *qaran*." The Hebrew word used here most often means "horns," which is how the Latin Bible (Vulgate) that Michelangelo read translates it. Thus, Michelangelo's statue of Moses, created around 1515 C.E., portrays him with horns (as shown in Figure 25-2). But *qaran* can also mean "rays of light" and "radiant," which is how many modern translations of the

Bible render this word. Whatever the exact meaning of this word, Moses' appearance is enough to frighten the people, and they ask him to wear a veil.

Figure 25-2: Michelangelo's *Moses* with horns.

©Gianni Dagli Orti/CORBIS

The issue of David's tissue (1 Samuel 17)

When Republican Florence needed an image to symbolize their determination to keep the usurped Medicis at bay, they commissioned Michelangelo to carve this imposing statue of David in 1501 C.E. Although most artists carved David holding the severed head of Goliath, Michelangelo portrays the boy immediately before the battle (see Figure 25-3). David's face, and especially his eyes, masterfully capture David's determination and confidence — what Rocky calls the "eye of the tiger."

But some things in the statue are noticeably wrong. For example, David is, well, exposed. David would certainly have worn clothes in his confrontation with Goliath (though nakedness could be an interesting battle strategy). Yet, more controversial is that Michelangelo seems to present the Israelite hero as uncircumcised. Of course, Michelangelo never met David; he used male models to carve the statue. These models, being Italian Christians in the fifteenth century, would not have been circumcised. Nevertheless, others have argued that Michelangelo's David in the statue is, in fact, circumcised exactly as they did it in biblical times. In these early years, the operator (known as a Mohel) only cut off the preputial tissue that extends beyond the penis glans (sorry, no diagrams). This is known as a Bris Milah. Later, in the second century C.E., circumcision changed, as rabbis began to prescribe that all of the foreskin be removed. This practice arose because Jewish youths wanting to assimilate into Greek culture stretched their remaining foreskins to resemble uncircumcised penises. So in the end, does Michelangelo depict David as anatomically accurate? You'll have to be the judge.

Figure 25-3:
Michelangelo's imposing statue of David.

©World Films Enterprise/CORBIS

What's wrong with this picture? The birth of Jesus (Matthew 1–2, Luke 2)

Jesus was most likely born in the spring, a time when shepherds would have been outside at night watching their flocks (see Chapter 27 for the choice of December 25). And the only thing even remotely close to Christmas trees in the Bible are pagan shrines dedicated to the Canaanite fertility goddess Asherah, which the Bible says to cut down and demolish (not decorate).

Moreover, re-creations of Jesus' birth, whether in children's plays, nativity lawn ornaments, or even Hieronymous Bosch's painting *The Adoration of the Magi* from the fifteenth century (see Figure 25-4), tend to get several things wrong. For example, nativity scenes routinely depict the wise men (or *magi*) at the manger simultaneously with the shepherds. Although the Bible affirms that the shepherds (pictured in Bosch's painting as peeking into the house from the roof and through a hole in the wall) arrive soon after Jesus' birth, the magi seem to visit Jesus as many as two years later (see Chapter 18). In addition, the text doesn't specify the number of magi, only that they bring three types of gifts: gold, frankincense, and myrrh. Finally, the so-called *manger,* meaning "feeding trough," in which Jesus is placed after his birth does not imply that he is born in a stable. Homes during Jesus' day often were multileveled, with people sleeping on the upper floors and animals on the ground floor. Mary, seeking privacy, likely gives birth on the ground floor of such a house, perhaps even in the home of a relative (see Chapter 18).

Figure 25-4:
Bosch's *The Adoration of the Magi.*

©Erich Lessing/Art Resource, N.Y.

The Last Supper (Matthew 26, Mark 14, Luke 22, and John 13)

The Last Supper, painted by Leonardo da Vinci (shown in Figure 25-5), was commissioned in the fifteenth century to decorate a monastery in Milan, Italy. It is justifiably the world's most famous piece of art, but with this prestigious title comes some unfortunate baggage. Its fame has transferred to the more mundane: Today there are Last Supper clocks, wallpapers, mouse pads, paint-by-number sets, pens, and even replicas in wax museums.

Furthermore, much of the painting is historically inaccurate. The characters look and dress like fifteenth-century Italian nobility, and the utensils and dinnerware are identical to those used by the monks who ate in the monastery. Jesus' disciples at this Passover meal would have been wearing less ornate garments, and eaten using their hands while reclining on the floor.

But two attributes elevate this painting to its artistic heights. First, its unprecedented use of perspective makes it actually seem to be part of the refectory — monks would seem to be eating with Jesus and the disciples. Second, the astonished expressions and chaos that follow Jesus' announcement that one of his disciples would betray him is masterfully captured. (From left to right on the painting, the disciples are Bartholomew, Jacob, Andrew, Judas, Peter, John, Jesus, Thomas, Jacob or James the Elder, Philip, Matthew, and Thaddeus.) The only one not surprised by Jesus' announcement is Judas, whose shadowed face symbolizes his dark purposes and guilt. Also, Peter holds a knife at Judas's back, symbolizing not only Judas's back-stabbing nature, but also Judas's inevitable death. Additionally, the knife foreshadows Peter's cutting off the ear of a soldier later that night.

What color was Jesus' skin?

Jesus' skin color has been the subject of a lot of media attention and controversy. So we should say a word about it.

Although we have no descriptions or portraits of Jesus from the first century C.E., those artistic representations of Jesus portraying him with fair skin, light hair, and sometimes even blue eyes are certainly wrong, and reflect the cultural influences of European Christians. Moreover, people in antiquity didn't really think in terms of race, but rather identified themselves with their cultural group. Thus, Jesus wouldn't think of himself as black or white, but as a Jew living in Palestine. And because this area was a land bridge between Europe, Africa, and Asia, it created a population of amalgamated ethnic groups. Jesus' complexion was neither that of a northern European nor a sub-Saharan African, but it would have been somewhere between these two ends of the spectrum, just as today in that part of the world people have a variety of skin colors.

Figure 25-5: da Vinci's *The Last Supper*.

©Bettmann/CORBIS

The Bible in Literature

Like the masterpieces of the applied arts, writers have crafted countless poems and works of prose that directly and indirectly use the Bible for inspiration. Also, much of what people commonly believe to be biblical stems from such writings. In the following sections, we cover three examples.

What's so funny about hell?
Dante's The Divine Comedy

Much of what people believe about heaven and hell comes from Dante Alighieri's *The Divine Comedy,* thus named not because it is funny, but rather because it has a happy ending. In this three-part epic, Dante at midlife finds himself spiritually and metaphorically lost. To regain his way, and reclaim his salvation, he must travel through hell and purgatory, guided by the poet Virgil. He then ascends through the layers of heaven, pictured as a rose, guided by a woman, Beatrice, whom Dante loved, but who had since died.

Dante includes many biblical characters in his story. Most memorable is Judas, who, along with the Romans Brutus and Cassius (who betrayed Julius Caesar), is forever chewed upon in one of Satan's three mouths at the bottom of hell. Hell for Dante is the complete absence of good and warmth, and thus it is a frozen lake of ice (which gives hope to those of us who were told that we'll be called "when hell freezes over"). Dante's levels of hell, purgatory, and heaven are filled with biblical allusion, but you'll search in vain in the Bible for these so-called "circles." Also, the notion that Saint Peter guards the gates to heaven, though predating Dante, is popularized by him in *The Divine Comedy*, but is not in the Bible.

A tempting proposition:
Milton's Paradise Lost

John Milton's *Paradise Lost* is a masterful retelling of the story of Adam and Eve, where Satan tempts Eve into eating the forbidden fruit, thereby introducing sin and death into the world. The poem begins:

> *Of Man's first disobedience, and the fruit*
> *Of that forbidden tree whose mortal taste*
> *Brought death into the world, and all our woe,*
> *With loss of Eden, til one greater Man*
> *Restore us, and regain the blessed seat*

Many people don't read Milton anymore, partly because many find his views on women less than attractive. But *Paradise Lost* is well worth the read. Milton masterfully weaves the theological learning of his day into a poem that rivals the other great epic poems of history. Satan's fall, his creation of *Pandemonium* (the home of the demons and meaning, literally, "all the demons"), and his "incarnation" as a serpent in order to tempt Eve (which purposefully parallels Jesus' own incarnation as a man to redeem humankind) are powerfully and vividly portrayed by Milton. Commonly held ideas about Satan as a jealous angel kicked out of heaven before the creation of humans, as well as a fork-tailed serpent with legs, although being around long before Milton, were popularized because of the influence of his poem.

Pallid baleens and biblical Baals: Melville's Moby Dick

As do many classics, Herman Melville's *Moby Dick* relies heavily upon biblical allegory. The narrator is named Ishmael after Abraham and Hagar's son, while the captain is named Ahab. Like the Bible's King Ahab, Melville's Ahab is a megalomaniac, worships and chases after false gods (King Ahab worships Baal, and Melville's Ahab chases after, and in some ways worships, the white whale), and owns a connection to ivory (King Ahab adorns his palace with inlaid ivory, and Ahab the mariner walks on an ivory leg). Their obsessions with power and revenge cost not only their own lives, but many others' as well.

Totally Epic!: Good and Bad Bible Movies

Most Bible movies are unwatchable, even for Bible scholars. Writers, directors, and actors seem restrained from being creative, and the result is hundreds of films with Moses and Jesus walking around like zombies. They're trying to portray people as holy, but instead, they wind up making them something very forbidden in biblical law — ham. Also, in an effort not to offend anyone, these characters typically wind up caricatures with at most one dimension. But, once in a while, some real gems come along. What follows are seven (a good biblical number) films, some marvelously entertaining, others less so, but all having quite a bit to do with the Bible.

The Ten Commandments (Lasky, 1923)

This movie, though one of our favorites, is not for everyone. It is silent and the plot is pretty simple, though it actually tells two stories. Half the film involves the biblical Moses, a stern lawgiver who condemns dancing and any type of humor. The other tale, set in the 1920s, is thoroughly entertaining though not for the reasons Cecil B. de Mille intended.

At the heart of the story are two sons: one a carpenter named John, the other a manufacturer of large buildings named Dan. When their mom reads them the Ten Commandments, John listens intently, and Dan laughs, saying those laws died with Queen Victoria (can you guess where this is going?). Dan bribes a building inspector to look the other way when he uses lean cement in building a church, and in a scene about as subtle as the rock that fell Goliath, the mom is killed when the church collapses, and a copy of the tablets of the Ten Commandments strikes her on the head. Dan drowns on his way to Mexico in a boat called *Defiance*, while John reads the Bible to a girl who used to like dancing. As a further example of how the times in which you live affect your understanding of the Bible, the film even blames World War I on society's violation of the Ten Commandments (certainly people were violating a few of the commandments during the War).

Cecil B. de Mille's early films were considered pornography by standards in the 1920s. He showed the first bathroom in film, and even portrayed prehistoric people wearing animal skins, which critics felt set a bad example for children. Seeking to turn over a new leaf, de Mille ran a contest in the *Los Angeles Times* to find out what religious theme the public preferred. A manufacturer of lubricants wrote, "You cannot break the Ten Commandments — they will break you." And with this pithy letter, film history (and television at Easter) was forever changed.

The Ten Commandments (Paramount, 1956)

This film has a blockbuster cast, state-of-the-art (for the 1950s) special effects, and one of the Bible's greatest stories as a plot. Although certainly inspiring at parts, it also has its share of humorous and even corny moments. Amazingly, they spent three years writing this script. That means that such timeless lines as "Moses, Moses, you splendid, stubborn, adorable fool" took about three weeks to create, as did "Dance, you mud turtles."

Charlton Heston as Moses is unforgettable, though at times laughable (especially his hairdo after seeing God on Mount Sinai). Moreover, John Derek as Joshua is so peppy and glassy eyed, that you wonder what they were serving for lunch on the set. Another peculiarity of this movie is that few of the actors really interact. The film is more a collection of monologues, most memorable by Edward G. Robinson's gangster-like portrayal of Dathan, the leader of those seeking to undermine Moses' authority in the wilderness.

This movie, like its silent predecessor, is truly a product of its time. Although the original *Ten Commandments* was about society's moral decay during the Roaring '20s, here the same biblical topic is about Civil Rights. In fact, Martin Luther King, Jr., watched this film the night before writing his famous speech "The Birth of a New Nation," which is about Ghana's attempts to end colonization. However, the Bible's version of the exodus is not really about ending slavery — even some of the Israelites owned slaves. Yet, the story does touch on the themes of freedom and the tyranny of oppressive regimes.

The movie is famous for its special effects, but why? The burning bush was inspired by (and even resembles) an electric fireplace with a glowing pink log, and the parting of the Red Sea is simply shot backwards. *Time* magazine in 1956 said it best: "Something roughly equivalent to an 8-foot chorus girl — pretty well put together, but much too big and much too flashy."

Charlton Heston was cast as Moses partially because the actor's face resembled Michelangelo's famous statue of Moses. Heston later portrayed Michelangelo himself in *The Agony and the Ecstasy* (1965).

The Green Pastures (Warner Bros., 1936)

This film is rarely seen, which is simultaneously fortunate and tragic. The film is based on a Pulitzer Prize-winning theatrical version of Roark Bradford's book *Ol' Man Adam an' his Chillun* (1928). The story is a white author's interpretation of black folk versions of God's relationship to humanity in the Torah (try saying that ten times fast). It was controversial (and often banned) when it opened, because God and the angels are played by black actors. It is controversial today because of its stereotypical and offensive portrayal of southern rural blacks. But with these warnings, the movie is amazingly inventive and provides an entertaining and imaginative retelling of some famous Bible stories. It works partly because it isn't wed to the biblical text and has great acting (especially Rex Reed as De Lawd). The singing by the Hall Johnson Choir is inspiring, to say the least.

Ben Hur (MGM, 1959)

This film is a remake by director William Wyler of a 1926 silent film, based on General Lew Wallace's best-selling novel by the same name. *Ben Hur* is often called the best Bible movie of all time, which may have something to do with the fact that the engaging plot has little to do with the Bible. Instead of watching an actor portray the almost unplayable role of Jesus, the movie is set during the time of Jesus, beginning with Jesus' birth and ending with his death. Yet, Jesus only makes brief cameos, and the camera never shows his face; only the faces of those looking at him (a technique that's used very well). As a result, the movie is free to tell another story while displaying the suffering of Jews at the hands of the Romans. For example, when Ben Hur (Charlton Heston) comes face to face with Jesus, he realizes from Jesus' expression and kindness that he is not there to violently overthrow the Romans but to bring love and healing to humanity. Here, unlike other Bible epics, there is action and drama worthy of the huge production. The most famous scene, the chariot race, is a neck-and-neck battle between two equals, and at times this spectacle dwarfs the massive set. (Despite a popular urban legend, nobody died in the filming of *Ben Hur*. However, a stunt man did die in the filming of the silent *Ten Commandments* racing scene.)

Jesus Christ Superstar (Universal, 1973)

You can discover more about the early 1970s by watching this movie than you can about the Bible. Nevertheless, this rock opera by Andrew Lloyd

Webber and Tim Rice is imaginative, and it's the most memorable of all the films produced in the heyday of Jesus movies, including *The Greatest Story Ever Told* (1965) and *Jesus of Nazareth* (1977).

Jesus in *Jesus Christ Superstar* smiles and is happy, as opposed to other portrayals of a stern otherworldly Jesus. That is, the film emphasizes the human nature of Christ, much like other intriguing films including *Jesus of Montreal* (1989). In *Jesus Christ Superstar,* there is no dialogue; everything is sung. This lack of dialogue gives the actors freedom and leaves much to the audience's imagination, not too unlike the Bible itself.

The film focuses on the conflict between Jesus and Judas, played by Carl Anderson, who gives the best performance of the film. However, it is hard not to notice that in this movie and nearly all works of art, Judas is portrayed as a black man, contrasted to Jesus' milk-white skin. Nevertheless, the story is told from Judas's perspective, and chronicles the last seven days in Jesus' life. Judas is determined that Jesus is out of his mind and dangerous. Judas leads soldiers to Gethsemane, but he discovers he has been tricked by God to be an instrument in Jesus' martyrdom.

Raiders of the Lost Ark (Paramount, 1981)

This is a great movie, though it's based only loosely on the Bible. In the movie, Dr. Jones (Harrison Ford), a professor at the Oriental Institute in Chicago, is approached by the curator of the National Museum and two U.S. intelligence officers to prevent Hitler from obtaining the Bible's version of the atomic bomb — the Ark of the Covenant. It turns out that the Ark is buried in "The City of Lost Souls" in Tanis, Egypt, which actually reflects one theory on the Ark's whereabouts. (For more on what happened to the Ark, see Chapter 9.) The replica of the Ark is quite good, as is the high priestly garb worn by the Nazi scholar who opens the Ark. However, the destruction caused by the spirits released when the Ark is opened does not capture the essence of the biblical story where something similar occurs (see 1 Samuel 6:19–20). Of course, Harrison Ford makes an excellent Indy, a role that Tom Selleck declined in order to make the hit television series *Magnum, P.I.*

The Matrix (Warner Bros., 1999)

The Matrix is a big-budget, science-fiction, kung-fu-action, edge-of-your-seat, futuristic thriller in which startling revelations convince a computer hacker to save the world. It is one of the cleverest movies to come out of Hollywood in some time, though most fans are unaware of its heavy reliance on the Bible. The name of the movie's hero, Thomas Anderson, connects him with two biblical figures. The name Thomas is an allusion to Doubting Thomas of John's gospel, because, in the movie Keanu Reeves (who plays Anderson) doubts his role as savior. Anderson literally means "Son of Man," a title that the Bible uses to describe God's coming deliverer or Messiah, and a name applied to Jesus. Thomas Anderson's other name, Neo, means "new," and is an allusion to the New Testament. He dies, and is resurrected with love from a girl named Trinity, defeats the evil system, and then ascends into "heaven" in order to return and bring ultimate deliverance from the Matrix. Perhaps the most obvious reference to Anderson's role as a Jesus figure occurs at the beginning of the movie, when someone says to him: "Hallelujah! You're my savior, man. My own personal Jesus Christ." If that isn't enough, the movie was released Easter weekend!

Other aspects of the movie own biblical themes. The rebel base is known as Zion, which in the Bible refers to the mountain on which Jerusalem is built, and their ship is named Nebuchadnezzar, after the biblical king who exiled the Jews from their land. In addition, the film's Judas character is named Cypher, in reference to the name LuCIPHER (another name for Satan; see Chapter 14). Finally, Morpheus represents John the Baptist, as the figure prophesying the coming of the savior.

And for the kids

There are other Bible movies worth watching, especially for children, including Dreamworks's animated film *The Prince of Egypt,* with Val Kilmer as Moses, Jeff Goldblum as Moses' brother, Aaron, and Sandra Bullock as Moses' sister, Miriam (to name just a few of the stars). Less well known, but just as good, is Dreamworks's "prequel" to *The Prince of Egypt,* called *Joseph, King of Dreams,* with Ben Affleck as Joseph. And if you haven't watched the computer-animated *VeggieTales* series, where vegetables act out biblical stories, then you haven't really lived.

Part VI
The Part of Tens

"Today we celebrate Sukkot, a feast of pilgrimage, which considering how far I had to go to get a decent loin of veal seems most appropriate."

In this part . . .

You meet the ten (well, maybe a few more than ten) most important people in the Bible. Plus, you discover what those holidays are on your calendar, why they're significant, and, most importantly, whether the boss will let you have the day off.

Chapter 26

Ten+ People You Should Know from the Bible

*I*n this chapter, you meet (in order of appearance) ten (or so) of the Bible's most important people. Of course, limiting the Bible's cast of thousands to ten is nearly impossible, so we fudge a little. In addition, the most important character in the Bible is God, but because God isn't a "people," and because we discuss God's nature and role throughout this book, He didn't make the list. However, with this list you'll be sure to impress your friends at dinner parties and improve your score on the TV quiz show, *Jeopardy!*

Adam and Eve

Look, we know that Adam and Eve are two people, and we shouldn't cheat — especially in a book about the Bible. But Adam and Eve really are inseparable. And after all, even the Bible refers to them as "one flesh" in recognition of their coming from the same flesh (Adam's) and being joined together again in marital/sexual union.

Adam and Eve are important because, according to the Bible, they're the first two people in the world, and from them comes everyone who has ever lived — whether Shaquille O'Neal or the Munchkin actors in the *Wizard of Oz*.

The human drama begins when God forms Adam from the ground and breathes life into him. God then performs the first surgery, creating Eve from Adam's side (a more literal translation than "rib"). Adam and Eve live together in Paradise (or what the Bible calls the Garden of Eden) until they disobey God by eating fruit from the Tree of the Knowledge of Good and Evil. This act of defiance, called "The Fall" by many theologians, is a real bummer because from it comes painful childbirth, weeds in your garden, and, ultimately, death. Moreover, Adam and Eve's disobedience introduce fear and alienation into humankind's formerly perfect relationships with God and one another. As evidence of this alienation, Adam and Eve's son, Cain, murders his brother, Abel. To read more about Adam and Eve and their family, turn to Chapters 4 and 5 of this book, and open a Bible to Genesis 2–5.

Noah

Noah is most famous for building an ark — a giant three-decked wooden box in which he, his family, and a whole bunch of animals ride out a massive flood that God sends to destroy humankind for its disobedience. God chooses Noah and his family to survive the deluge because Noah is "the most righteous in his generation." Noah is important not only because his ark decorates most nurseries in North America but also because, according to the Bible, if Noah hadn't been righteous, you and I wouldn't be here right now. To find out more about Noah, see Chapter 4 in this book and read Genesis 6–9.

Abraham

The Bible is filled with stories about people disobeying God. One notable exception is Abraham, a man who, though not perfect, obeys God's command to leave his homeland in Mesopotamia and venture to an unknown Promised Land (ancient Canaan; later Israel). God promises Abraham that his descendants will become a great nation, through which all the people of the earth will be blessed.

The tales of Abraham and his wife Sarah are a roller coaster of dramatic events that repeatedly jeopardize God's promise. Ironically, the biggest threat to God's promise is when God Himself commands Abraham to sacrifice his son Isaac (see Chapter 5). Abraham sets out to do just as God orders, but right before Abraham delivers the fatal blow to his own child, God stops the sacrifice. As a reward for Abraham's faith, God fulfills His promise to make Abraham's descendants a great nation, as Isaac's son Jacob eventually has 12 sons, whose descendants become the nation of Israel.

Today, three of the world's major religions — Judaism, Christianity, and Islam — trace their roots to Abraham. To discover more about these three Abrahamic faiths, see Chapter 24.

Moses

The Hebrew Bible describes Moses as the greatest prophet who ever lived, and for good reason. Moses is born during hard times for ancient Israel. They're enslaved in Egypt, and their growing population so alarms the Egyptians that the Egyptian king orders all newborn Israelite males drowned in the Nile River. Moses' mother saves her son's life by placing him in the Nile in a reed basket, where he is soon discovered by Pharaoh's daughter, who ironically raises Moses in the royal palace. After he's grown, Moses must flee Egypt for killing an Egyptian who was beating an Israelite slave. Eventually, God appears to Moses in a burning bush and tells him that he must return to Egypt to deliver the Israelites from their slavery. With God's help, Moses succeeds in his mission, bringing the Israelites to Mount Sinai, where God first appeared to Moses. At Mount Sinai, God gives Moses the Law, including the Ten Commandments. Moses eventually leads the Israelites to the edge of their Promised Land (ancient Canaan; later Israel), where he dies at the ripe old age of 120. To read more about Moses, see Chapter 7.

David

David is Israel's second and arguably greatest king. As a boy, David courageously defeats a mighty enemy warrior named Goliath with only a sling and a stone. As a man, David conquers all Israel's enemies and begins a dynasty that would rule Jerusalem for nearly 400 years. But not all the news surrounding David is good. David perpetrates one of the Bible's most heinous crimes: He commits adultery with a woman named Bathsheba, who's the wife of one of David's most loyal soldiers, Uriah. Then, to cover up the crime, David has Uriah killed. In David's favor, when the prophet Nathan confronts David with his sin, David repents. Moreover, in God's favor, God forgives David for his sin, but not without punishing David for his crime.

Beyond David's royal exploits (and indiscretions), he's credited with writing many of ancient Israel's worship songs, which you can read in the Book of Psalms. To find out more about David's incredible life, see Chapters 10 and 11 of this book along with 1 Samuel 16–1 Kings 2 and 1 Chronicles 10–29 of the Bible.

Elijah

Elijah is one of Israel's greatest prophets, as well as God's heavyweight champ in an epic bout against a deity named Baal (the Canaanite storm god).

In order to prove to the Israelites that God is the only true God, Elijah gathers the prophets of Baal at Mount Carmel, where for the main event each deity is given a pile of wood with a bull on it. The god who can produce fire and consume the sacrifice wins. Baal goes first, and for half the day his prophets dance, shout, sing, and even cut themselves in order to convince their god to answer Elijah's challenge. When their efforts fail, Elijah prays to God, who immediately sends fire down from the sky and consumes the sacrifice. The Israelites rededicate themselves to God, and they kill the prophets who deceived them into worshiping Baal.

Later, near the Jordan River, a fiery horse-drawn chariot descends from the sky and takes Elijah to heaven, but not before he appoints a successor named Elisha. Elijah's atypical departure influenced later biblical prophets, who predicted that Elijah would return as a precursor to the coming of the Messiah. Because of these prophecies, Jews invite Elijah every Passover to usher in the age of the Messiah (see Chapter 27), and the New Testament writers associate John the Baptist, the forerunner of Jesus' ministry, with Elijah (see Chapter 18). To find out more about Elijah, see Chapter 10 in this book, and read about him in the Bible in 1 Kings 17–21 and 2 Kings 1–2.

Isaiah

Isaiah is one of the most influential prophets in the Hebrew Bible. During his career, Isaiah advises several kings of Judah, helping them to avoid being destroyed by the mighty Assyrian Empire (around 700 B.C.E.).

Beyond Isaiah's political influence, he is a masterful poet, with many of his prophecies inspiring hope for eventual peace and righteousness on earth. Several of these prophecies were later understood by Christians to be predictions of Jesus, including the birth of Immanuel (Isaiah 7); the coming of the Prince of Peace, as quoted in Handel's *Messiah* (Isaiah 9); and the suffering of God's "Servant" for the sins of His people (Isaiah 53). You can read more about Isaiah in Chapter 13 of this book and in the Bible in 2 Kings 19–20, 2 Chronicles 26, 32, and the book that bears his name.

Judah Maccabee

"It's all Greek to me" certainly wasn't a personal motto for Judah Maccabee. Judah spearheads a revolt against the Greek king, Antiochus Epiphanes, who prohibits the Jews from following the Law of Moses, and who offered sacrifices to foreign gods in Jerusalem's Temple.

Judah (nicknamed Maccabee, meaning "hammer") eventually regains control of Jerusalem and cleanses the Temple (165/164 B.C.E.) — an event commemorated by the Jewish holiday of Hanukkah (see Chapters 17 and 28). Although

Judah would eventually die in battle in 160 B.C.E., his efforts ultimately lead to the political and religious autonomy of the Jews, initiating a dynasty known as the Hasmoneans (or the Maccabees, after Judah's nickname). The Hasmoneans would rule the Jews until the Romans overthrew them almost a century later.

So the next time your hammer misses its target and you smash your thumb, try screaming "Judah Maccabee!" You'll feel better knowing your expletive is historically correct. To discover more about Judah and the Maccabees, read Chapter 16 of this book, and 1 and 2 Maccabees of the Apocrypha.

Mary

Being Jesus' mom, as you might imagine, is bound to put you in the theological limelight, and Mary holds this office with dignity and grace.

Betrothed to a man named Joseph at a young age, Mary becomes pregnant under mysterious circumstances. Two of the four gospels say that God is the father, but because of the relative silence of the other two gospels, as well as the lack of this being explicitly mentioned by Peter and Paul, it seems the doctrine of Jesus' virgin birth wasn't emphasized in the early Church — though it certainly did dominate later. The picture of Mary in the gospels is one of a concerned and loving mother, who doesn't fully understand her son at times, but supports him to the end, even painfully witnessing his execution at the foot of the cross.

Much of what Christians believe about Mary arose after her lifetime and highlights theological differences between Catholics and Protestants. For Catholics, Mary maintained her virginity throughout her life. Thus, Jesus' "brothers" and "sisters" were either children fathered by Joseph from previous marriages, or cousins. But for most Protestant groups, Jesus' siblings are just that: his brothers and sisters (though technically they are his half-siblings, since God is Jesus' father). Also in death, Catholics believe that Mary's assumption to heaven involved not only her soul, but her body as well. For all Christians, Mary becomes venerated more than any other woman in the Bible.

Jesus

The New Testament's story of Jesus is as fascinating as it is inspiring. Born and raised in the "backwaters" of the Roman Empire, Jesus begins a religious movement that eventually overtakes the Empire. According to the New Testament, Jesus is the Messiah ("anointed one," Greek "Christos"), the promised deliverer of Israel, whose death on the cross brings deliverance from sin, and whose eventual return to earth will bring deliverance from oppression by ushering in God's kingdom. Jesus' message of caring for the downtrodden, extending kindness to strangers, and loving one's enemies is still unrivaled for its profound insight and penetrating simplicity.

To find out more about Jesus, read Chapters 19 and 20 of this book, and the New Testament gospels of Matthew, Mark, Luke, and John.

Peter

Jesus affectionately gives his closest friend, Simon, the nickname "Rock," though the Greek form of the name is "Peter." Peter is a fisherman until Jesus calls him to be a disciple or "a fisher of men." Peter soon becomes the "rock" on which Jesus builds his church, even giving him the keys to the kingdom of heaven (Matthew 16:18–19) — an action that suggests Peter's privileged position among the disciples. Therefore, according to Catholic doctrine, Peter is the first Pope, the *vicar* (or substitute) of Christ on earth. But even Jesus' closest confidant betrays him, as on the eve of the crucifixion, Peter denies knowing Jesus three times. Following Jesus' death, Peter is restored and helps spread Christianity abroad, even inducting the first gentile or non-Jewish members into this movement. Tradition holds that around 64 C.E., the Roman Emperor Nero executed Peter by crucifying him upside-down — a method Peter requested because he didn't feel worthy to die in the same manner as Jesus. His tomb is now encased within *St. Peter's Basilica* in Rome.

To find out more about Peter, read Chapter 19 in this book, as well as the gospels and the letters ascribed to Peter in 1 and 2 Peter of the Bible.

Paul

Paul (or Saul, as he is first called) is arguably the person most responsible for spreading Christianity throughout the Mediterranean region, on its way to becoming the religion of the Roman Empire. Paul's efforts to convert people to Christianity are all the more remarkable since, when we first meet Paul, he is vigorously attempting to stamp out this movement because he believes that its message contradicts the teachings of the Hebrew Bible. Then, one day, while Paul is traveling to Damascus to arrest Christians, Jesus appears to him in a blinding flash of light and tells Paul his efforts against Christianity are what contradict the teachings of the Hebrew Bible, because Jesus is God's promised Messiah.

Paul spends the rest of his life spreading the "good news" about Jesus' life and teachings throughout the Roman world, suffering intensely for a movement he was once bent on destroying. To find out more about Paul, check out Chapter 20 of this book, the biblical Book of Acts, and Paul's many letters in the New Testament.

Chapter 27

Ten Holidays You Can Take
Thanks to the Bible

In This Chapter

▶ Working for the weekend

▶ Understanding the holidays in your calendar book

▶ Maximizing the number of vacation days you can take (without raising suspicions)

*P*erhaps you've found yourself flipping through a calendar book to plan a family vacation or schedule some sick days, when all of a sudden you noticed a holiday that you'd never seen before. "I wonder if I can get that day off?" you mused. Well, in this chapter, you discover what those holidays are all about, enabling you to look your boss straight in the eye and say, "I won't be in tomorrow — it's Boxing Day, and I'll be observing it with my family by watching the Lewis-Tyson fight." Actually, we don't discuss Boxing Day in this chapter, but we do discuss those holidays that come from the Bible. (Whether you can get them off is between you and your boss.)

Weekends

That's right. The original idea for taking time off each week comes from the Bible (see Chapter 3). Although the modern two-day weekend arose out of a combination of religious tradition and labor laws, the Bible commands that both humans *and* animals take at least one day off each week to rest (okay, okay, if we have to). The word for this day of rest is *Sabbath,* from a Hebrew word meaning "to stop" or "to cease" (that is, from work). Judaism observes the Sabbath from sunset on Friday to sunset on Saturday. Christianity, though originally following this Jewish practice (because Christianity was born out of Judaism, and many early Christians were Jews), eventually moved its day of rest and worship to Sunday in recognition of the day on which Jesus was resurrected (and perhaps to distinguish itself from Judaism; see Chapter 7). So next time someone at the office says, "Thank God it's Friday!" you'll know to respond, "Amen!"

Passover

Passover, which begins on the 15th day of the Jewish month of Aviv (falling sometime within March or April; see the sidebar "Understanding ancient Israel's calendar" in this chapter), commemorates Israel's deliverance from its Egyptian slavery (see Chapter 7).

As part of the first Passover, God, via Moses, instructed the Israelites to apply the blood of a sacrificed lamb to their doorposts so that God's destroying angel would "pass over" their homes on his way to killing the firstborn sons of Egypt. In addition to eating the meat of the sacrificed lamb, the Israelites ate unleavened bread, because their hurried departure from Egypt did not allow them to leaven their bread. As a result, the Passover is immediately followed by the Feast of Unleavened Bread, a week-long celebration where participants refrain from eating anything containing leaven, even removing any trace of leaven from their homes. The Bible also prescribes the eating of bitter herbs during the Passover as a reminder of Israel's bitter life as slaves.

Over time, other elements were added to the Passover, including the recitation of particular prayers and blessings, the presence of other items of food reflecting Israel's life as slaves, and the consumption of several glasses of wine, one of which is set aside for the prophet Elijah, inviting him to return and usher in the coming of the Messiah. (For more detailed information on the various traditions surrounding the Passover and other Jewish holidays, pick up a copy of *Judaism For Dummies,* by Rabbi Ted Falcon, PhD, and David Blatner, published by Wiley.)

The Jerusalem Temple was destroyed by the Romans in 70 C.E., and has not been rebuilt since (most scholars believe the Dome of the Rock now stands where the Temple once stood; see Chapter 24). Therefore, the Jewish holidays requiring pilgrimage to the Temple (Passover, Shavuot, and Sukkot) or sacrifice at the Temple (all the holidays) have undergone some adjustments. Because the first Passover was observed by families in individual homes (see Exodus 12), the adjustments to the Passover weren't that difficult, as families simply returned to the practice of celebrating this meal at home. The other holidays, however, have been more significantly affected.

Shavuot ("Weeks," "First Fruits," or "Pentecost")

Shavuot commemorates the wheat and barley harvest, and is therefore also called the Feast of First Fruits, as these foods are the first to arrive after winter. The name Shavuot comes from a Hebrew word meaning "weeks," because this holiday occurs seven weeks and a day after Passover, which is usually calculated as the sixth day of the Jewish month Sivan (falling within May and June; see the sidebar "Understanding Ancient Israel's Calendar" in this chapter). Thus, other names for this festival include the Feast of Weeks and Pentecost (from a Greek word meaning "50," and referring to the 50 days from the Passover to Shavuot).

Like Passover, Shavuot was a pilgrimage feast, where every Israelite adult male was required to go to the Jerusalem Temple and offer sacrifices in recognition of God's goodness and provision. In later Jewish tradition, Shavuot became associated with Moses' receiving the *Torah* (ancient Israel's law code) on Mount Sinai, and so it is also a time to give thanks to God for revealing the Law. In the New Testament, Shavuot (or Pentecost, as it is called there) is the day when the Holy Spirit descended upon Jesus' disciples, giving them the ability to speak in various languages. This event marks the "birth" of the church (celebrated as Pentecost Sunday in Christian liturgy).

Understanding ancient Israel's calendar

Ancient Israel's calendar was lunisolar — that is, based on the cycles of both the moon and the sun. Therefore, Jewish months don't correspond directly to the months of the present-day Julian calendar but rather "float" from year to year within a two-month period. Here's a breakdown of how the months compare:

Hebrew Name	Modern Months
1. Aviv (or Nisan)	March/April
2. Ziv (or Iyyar)	April/May
3. Sivan	May/June
4. Tammuz	June/July
5. Av	July/August
6. Elul	August/September
7. Tishri (or Ethnaim)	September/October
8. Bul (or Marcheshvan)	October/November
9. Kislev	November/December
10. Teveth	December/January
11. Shevat	January/February
12. Adar	February/March

Note: Numbers reflect the number of that month in the Jewish calendar.

Sukkot ("Booths" or "Tabernacles")

Sukkot is the third and final pilgrimage feast of the biblical calendar (see Passover and Shavuot earlier in this chapter for the other two), and it marks the start of the harvesting of grapes and olives. Thus, Sukkot is also referred to as the Feast of Ingathering. This week-long celebration begins on the 15th of the Jewish month of Tishri (which falls within September and October; see the sidebar "Understanding Ancient Israel's Calendar" in this chapter), five days after Yom Kippur (see the following section).

The word *sukkot* means "booths" and refers both to the temporary shelters used by those harvesting grapes and olives during this season and to the temporary structures used by the Israelites during their wilderness wanderings under Moses. Therefore, another name for this holiday is the Feast of Booths or even Tabernacles.

Like the pilgrimage feast of Passover, Sukkot involves offering sacrifices made at the Jerusalem Temple in recognition of God's provision both of food and of freedom. Today, this holiday is observed in several ways, including offering prayers of thanksgiving, feasting, dancing, and hanging out in temporary structures (booths) built for the occasion.

Yom Kippur ("Day of Atonement")

Yom Kippur is a Hebrew word meaning "Day of Atonement," and refers to the one day each year (the tenth day of the month Tishri; see the sidebar "Understanding Ancient Israel's Calendar" in this chapter) when the High Priest could enter the Most Holy Place (also known as the Holy of Holies) of the Jerusalem Temple and offer a sacrifice to atone for Israel's sins. In an elaborate ritual described in Leviticus 16, the High Priest would first make himself ritually pure through ceremonial washings, the putting on of special priestly garments, and the offering of a sacrifice for himself and his fellow priests. The High Priest then took two goats and, as the goats no doubt looked anxiously on, would cast lots to see which one would be sacrificed and which one would be released. After sacrificing the unlucky goat, the High Priest would place his hands on the head of the remaining goat and confess Israel's sins, thus symbolically transferring the nation's wrongdoings onto the animal. This *scapegoat* (as it is called) would then be released into the wilderness — in essence, taking away the sins of Israel. If the goat returned, this meant God hadn't accepted the sacrifice, and Israel remained in its sins for another year. If the goat didn't return, everyone breathed a collective sigh of relief because God did accept the sacrifice, and Israel's sins were forgiven.

Today, Yom Kippur is a day of fasting, reflection, confession, asking for forgiveness from others, and extending forgiveness to others.

Rosh Hashanah ("New Year" or "Trumpets")

Rosh Hashanah literally means "head of the year" in Hebrew, but is usually translated "New Year." Today, Rosh Hashanah is celebrated in the fall (on the first day of the Jewish month Tishri; see the sidebar "Understanding Ancient Israel's Calendar" in this chapter). However, in ancient Israel the New Year seems to have originally occurred in the spring (the first day of the Jewish month Nisan or Aviv), when God brought Israel out of its Egyptian slavery (Exodus 12:2), and when everything was literally "new" (new growth, new lambs, and so on). Yet, because the fall is also an important time in the agricultural cycle, it ultimately became identified with Israel's new year (though Tishri is still considered the seventh month). Modern Rosh Hashanah corresponds roughly to the biblical Feast of Trumpets, when Israel offered sacrifices and sounded a trumpet made of a ram's horn (called a *shofar*). Rosh Hashanah has also been connected with the final Day of Judgment, and, therefore, the modern observance, far from being a raucous affair like most New Year's celebrations, is a time of solemn reflection and repentance. Rosh Hashanah and Yom Kippur (ten days later) are called the "High Holidays," because they're among the most important days of the Jewish calendar.

Purim

Purim celebrates the deliverance of the Jews living in the Persian Empire during the fifth century B.C.E. from a plot to kill them. According to the Book of Esther (see Chapter 11), an official of the Persian royal court named Haman tricked the Persian king, Ahasuerus (or Xerxes), into signing a law that called for the execution of all the Jews living in his empire. Haman's reasons? He hated a Jew named Mordecai because Mordecai refused to bow to him (some people have such big egos). When Mordecai heard about the law, he told his cousin Esther, who just happened to be the Queen of Persia, but who had kept her Jewish identity a secret. Risking her life, Esther informed the king of Haman's plot. In response, the king became enraged and had Haman executed.

Although the king couldn't reverse one of his own edicts, he passed another edict giving the Jews the right to defend themselves and encouraging others to defend the Jews as well. The Jews are saved, there's great rejoicing, and the book of Esther ends by commending its readers to celebrate the deliverance of the Jews every year on the 15th day of the Jewish month of Adar (falling within the months of February and March; see the sidebar "Understanding Ancient Israel's Calendar" in this chapter).

The celebration is called Purim because Haman used *purim,* or "lots" (ancient dice), to determine the day on which the Jews would be executed. Beyond parties and gift-giving, the modern celebration of Purim includes children dressing up in costumes, the reading of the story of Esther (complete with boos and hisses every time Haman's name is read), and adults being encouraged to get so drunk that they cannot distinguish between someone saying "Blessed be Mordecai" or "Cursed be Haman." (Now that's drunk!)

Hanukkah ("Dedication" or "Lights")

Hanukkah means "dedication," and refers to the *re*dedication of the Jerusalem Temple (165–164 B.C.E.) after its desecration by a Greek king, Antiochus IV. According to the books of 1 and 2 Maccabees, Antiochus IV (who gave himself the name Epiphanes, meaning "god manifest") not only desecrated the Temple by erecting images of Greek gods in its precincts and offering pagan sacrifices on its altar, but he also prohibited the Jews from reading the Mosaic Law, keeping kosher (Jewish diet), and circumcising their sons. What's more, Antiochus required that all Jews sacrifice to the Greek gods. Now that was going too far, and, understandably, the Jews revolted. Under the leadership of a man named Judah Maccabee, the Jews regained control of Jerusalem and cleansed and rededicated the Temple on the 25th day of the Jewish month Kislev — the same day, ironically enough, that Antiochus had three years earlier desecrated the Temple. Later Jewish tradition recounts that when the Temple was rededicated the priests could only find enough oil to keep the sacred candelabra (called the Menorah) burning for one day. Miraculously, however, it lasted for eight days.

Today, Hanukkah is celebrated for eight days and involves, among other things, gift-giving, lighting candles, saying prayers, and playing games.

Christmas

Christmas commemorates the birth of Jesus — the word Christmas derives from the combination of *Christ* and *mass* (*mass* being the Catholic term for the celebration of the Eucharist; see Chapter 19). Although Christmas is celebrated on December 25 in most Christian traditions, the New Testament actually doesn't specify the day of Jesus' birth. The choice of December 25 as Jesus' birthday is the consequence of Christianity's interaction with other religious traditions. As Christianity spread, rather than put an end to longstanding pagan traditions, the Church merely transformed these traditions into Christian celebrations. Christmas, it seems, replaced the Roman festival of

Saturnalia, which celebrated the winter solstice, when days begin getting longer. That is, the birthday of the "Sun" was changed to the birthday of the "Son." Remnants of these pagan celebrations are still evident in current Christmas traditions, including decorating one's home with evergreen trees, mistletoe, and holly (all of which were thought to have a magical quality because they stayed green in the winter), candles (which symbolized the light of the sun), and gift-giving (common during most festivals).

Easter

Easter celebrates the resurrection of Jesus from the dead, which occurred on the first day of the week following the beginning of Passover (a holiday described earlier in this chapter). Although various Christian traditions celebrate Easter on different days, it is usually within a few weeks of each other in the spring. The name Easter is another example of how Christianity adopted alternate religious traditions as it spread into "pagan territory." Eastre is the name of a fertility goddess whose festival was celebrated in the spring, when new life was blooming all around. Her celebrations were replete with symbols of fertility, including eggs (symbols of new life) painted in bright colors (representing the bright colors of spring) and bunnies (prolific propagators and, thereby, symbols of fertility). In other words, in the spring you could still celebrate the "resurrection" of new life all around you, but the *ultimate* reason to celebrate was Jesus' resurrection from the dead.

Index

• *H* •

Notes

Notes

Notes

Notes